SOMETHING ABOUT THE AUTHOR®

Something about
the Author *was named
an "Outstanding
Reference Source,"*
*the highest honor given
by the American
Library Association
Reference and Adult
Services Division.*

ISSN 0276-816X

SOMETHING ABOUT THE AUTHOR®

**Facts and Pictures about Authors
and Illustrators of Books for Young People**

volume 206

GALE
CENGAGE Learning™

Detroit • New York • San Francisco • New Haven, Conn • Waterville, Maine • London

GALE
CENGAGE Learning

Something about the Author, Volume 206

Project Editor: Lisa Kumar

Editorial: Laura Avery, Pamela Bow, Jim Craddock, Amy Fuller, Andrea Henderson, Margaret Mazurkiewicz, Tracie Moy, Jeff Muhr, Kathy Nemeh, Mary Ruby, Mike Tyrkus

Permissions: Margaret Abendroth, Dean Dauphinais, Jackie Jones

Imaging and Multimedia: John Watkins, Dean Dauphinais

Composition and Electronic Capture: Amy Darga

Manufacturing: Drew Kalasky

Product Manager: Janet Witalec

Gale
27500 Drake Rd.
Farmington Hills, MI, 48331-3535

LIBRARY OF CONGRESS CATALOG CARD NUMBER 62-52046

ISBN-13: 978-1-4144-4219-8
ISBN-10: 1-4144-4219-X

ISSN 0276-816X

This title is also available as an e-book.
ISBN-13: 978-1-4144-6438-1
ISBN-10: 1-4144-6438-X
Contact your Gale sales representative for ordering information.

Printed in the United States of America
1 2 3 4 5 6 7 14 13 12 11 10

Contents

Authors in Forthcoming Volumes ix

Introduction xi

SATA Product Advisory Board xiii

A

Acer, David 1

Adams, Nicholas
   See Smith, Sherwood 151

Alter, Anna 1974- 3

Ayto, Russell 1960- 5

B

Baker, Roberta 10

Barneda, David 11

Begin, Mary Jane 1963- 12

Begin-Callanan, Mary Jane
   See Begin, Mary Jane 12

Benjamin, Floella 1949- 14

Bolam, Emily 1969- 16

Boos, Ben 1971- 20

Brighton, Catherine 1943- 20

C

Cashore, Kristin 1976(?)- 26

Catrow, David 1952- 27

Charles, Nicholas
   See Kuskin, Karla 91

Charles, Nicholas J.
   See Kuskin, Karla 91

Connell, Tom 32

Corwin, Oliver
   See Corwin, Oliver J. 32

Corwin, Oliver J. 32

Crowe, Chris 33

D

Dahme, Joanne 36

Davis, Rich 1958- 37

Dumbleton, Mike 1948- 38

Dungy, Anthony
   See Dungy, Tony 41

Dungy, Tony 1955- 41

E

Ebbeler, Jeff
   See Ebbeler, Jeffrey 44

Ebbeler, Jeffrey 1974- 44

Elliott, Zetta 45

F

Falkner, Brian 1962- 47

Farris, Christine King 1927- 49

Feiffer, Kate 1964- 50

Friesen, Jonathan 1967(?)- 52

G

Gallagher-Cole, Mernie 1958- 55

George, Lindsay Barrett 1952- 56

George, Sally
   See Orr, Wendy 129

Gist, E.M. 60

Gorman, Mike 61

Grambling, Lois G. 1927- 61

H

Hammill, Matt 1982- 65

Harper, Jessica 1949- 66

Henson, Heather 69

Heo, Yumi 1964- 71

Humphreys, Susan L.
   See Lowell, Susan 101

Hutchins, Carleen M.
  See Hutchins, Carleen Maley 77

Hutchins, Carleen Maley 1911-2009
  Obituary Notice 77

J

Jackson, Donna M. 1959- 78

John, Antony 1972- 80

K

Kennett, David 1959- 81

Kessler, Liz 1966- 83

Kilpatrick, Don 85

King, Willie Christine
  See Farris, Christine King 49

Kolar, Bob 1960(?)- 85

Koren, Edward 1935- 87

Kuskin, Karla 1932-2009
  Obituary Notice 91

Kuskin, Karla Seidman
  See Kuskin, Karla 91

L

Ladd, London 1972(?)- 93

Landström, Lena 1943- 94

Launder, Sally 97

Lester, Mike 1955- 97

Lowe, Helen 1961- 100

Lowell, Susan 1950- 101

M

MacEachern, Stephen 107

Maguire, Jesse
  See Smith, Sherwood 151

Maley, Carleen
  See Hutchins, Carleen Maley 77

McKenzie, Riford
  See Waite, Michael P. 186

Meldrum, Christina 108

Mortimer, Anne 1958- 110

Mourning, Tuesday 112

Mussi, Sarah 112

Muth, Jon J. 1960- 113

N

Newton, Vanessa
  See Newton, Vanessa Brantley 119

Newton, Vanessa Brantley 1962(?)- 119

Nichols, Travis 120

Numeroff, Laura 1953- 121

Numeroff, Laura Joffe
  See Numeroff, Laura 121

Nyeu, Tao 127

O

Orr, Wendy 1953- 129

P

Pang, YaWen Ariel 134

Pendleton, Thomas 1965- 134

Pinkney, Brian 1961- 136

Pinkney, J. Brian
  See Pinkney, Brian 136

Purmell, Ann 1953- 141

R

Rawlins, Donna 1956- 146

Reed, Dallas
  See Pendleton, Thomas 134

Rozen, Anna 1960- 148

Rugg, Jim 149

S

Sasaki, Ellen Joy 151

Seidman, Karla
  See Kuskin, Karla 91

Smith, Sherwood 1951- 151
  Autobiography Feature 156

Spanyol, Jessica 1965- 170

Spencer, Britt 172

Stanley, Elizabeth 1947- 174

Stockdale, Susan 1954- 175

Sullivan, Edward T. 1966- 177

T

Tallis, Robyn
  See Smith, Sherwood 151

Taylor, Eleanor 1969- 179

Thomas, Lee
  See Pendleton, Thomas 134

Torrecilla, Pablo 1967- 180

U

Ulrich, Maureen 1958- 183

Underwood, Deborah 1962- 183

W

Waite, Michael
  See Waite, Michael P. 186

Waite, Michael P. 1960- 186

Ward, Helen 1962- 188

Welch, Holly 192

Y

Yamasaki, Katie 194

Yee, Tammy 195

Young, Anne Mortimer
  See Mortimer, Anne 110

Z

Zepeda, Gwendolyn 1971- 196

Authors in Forthcoming Volumes

Below are some of the authors and illustrators that will be featured in upcoming volumes of *SATA*. These include new entries on the swiftly rising stars of the field, as well as completely revised and updated entries (indicated with *) on some of the most notable and best-loved creators of books for children.

Eva Eriksson ▌ Eriksson is an award-winning Swedish artist and illustrator whose work has been featured in children's books since the 1970s. In addition to creating original, self-illustrated books such as her "Victor and Rosalie" series, Eriksson has contributed engaging, soft-edged watercolor and colored-pencil illustrations to numerous books by Barbro Lindgren, Ulf Nilsson, and Bo R. Holmberg, three of Sweden's most popular writers for young children.

Musharraf Ali Farooqi ▌ Although he originally planned to become an engineer, Pakistani-born Canadian writer Farooqi has become known for his translations of classical works written in Persian and Urdu. Also a versatile author of fiction, he has written the novel *The Story of a Widow* and the children's picture book *The Cobbler's Holiday; or, Why Ants Don't Have Shoes*. In addition, Farooqi is the founder and publisher of the Urdu Project, through which he has undertaken the translation, printing, and marketing of the "Hoshruba," a twenty-four-volume fantasy work first written in Urdu.

Heather Vogel Frederick ▌ Although Frederick worked as a journalist for many years, she turned to books for younger readers while raising her own two children. Beloved by the young fans of her fanciful "Spy Mice" series, Frederick is also the author of the award-winning middle-grade historical novel *The Voyage of Patience Goodspeed*. Her popular "Mother-Daughter Book Club" novels, which include *The Mother-Daughter Book Club, Much Ado about Anne*, and *Dear Pen Pal*, have inspired modern 'tweens with an appreciation for the role good books can play in shaping one's own life.

*Kevin Henkes ▌ Henkes is consistently praised for the funny and realistic way he portrays the childlike characters in his picture books. Many of his award-winning titles feature unforgettable mouse characters such as Lilly, Sheila Rae, Chester, Julius, Wemberly, and Owen, while his novels for young readers vividly capture the ups and downs of growing up. The winner of numerous awards, Henkes was honored with both the Caldecott Medal and the Charlotte Zolotow Award for his original picture book *Kitten's First Full Moon*.

Peter Menzel ▌ A photojournalist, Menzel collaborates with his wife, writer Faith D'Aluisio, on nonfiction books such as *Hungry Planet: What the World Eats*, winner of the James Beard Foundation Award. The duo has traveled the globe in search of interesting stories; their works have introduced readers to a restaurant that serves live scorpions, depicted the development of anthropomorphic robots, and followed the daily activities of a Mongolian family.

*Margie Palatini ▌ Palatini is a highly regarded author of humorous picture books for young readers. Her stories, which include *Bad Boys, The Three Silly Billies, Bedhead*, and *Lousy, Rotten, Stinkin' Grapes*, have drawn praise from critics due to their offbeat humor, rhyme, and allusion. Palatini's joy in wordplay such as puns and allusion ensures that each of her stories will be a humorous treat, each topped with a surprising twist or unexpected ending.

Colleen Sydor ▌ A native of Manitoba, Canada, Sydor has written a variety of works for children, ranging from picture books to elementary-school chapter books to young-adult novels. Since her first picture book, 1999's *Ooo-cha!*, she has produced an entertaining series of titles featuring an impressionable preteen girl named Norah that include *Smarty Pants, Fashion Fandango*, and *Maxwell's Metamorphosis*.

*Wendelin Van Draanen ▌ While she has also written the highly praised middle-grade novels *Swear to Howdy* and *Runaway*, Van Draanen is best known as the author of the popular "Sammy Keyes," "Shredderman," and "Gecko and Sticky" series. In "Sammy Keyes" readers meet a tomboy with a penchant for finding trouble, while the "Shredderman" books finds a geeky preteen using a cyber-hero to right wrongs in his middle school. Salted with Aztec magic, the "Gecko and Sticky" chapter-book series follows a boy and his talking gecko as they undo the devilish deeds of a dastardly villain while engaging in humorous banter.

Leah Wilcox ▌ In her picture-book stories for young children, Wilcox takes well-known fairy tales and reworks them with an eye toward fun. In *Falling for Rapunzel*, for example, the Oregon-based writer finds inspiration in the classic story of the beautiful princess trapped in a tower, while the story of Sleeping Beauty receives a quirky make-over in *Waking Beauty*. In Wilcox's rhyming versions, practical matters interfere, however, and the humorous results are captured in the cartoon artwork of Lydia Monk.

Introduction

Something about the Author (*SATA*) is an ongoing reference series that examines the lives and works of authors and illustrators of books for children. *SATA* includes not only well-known writers and artists but also less prominent individuals whose works are just coming to be recognized. This series is often the only readily available information source on emerging authors and illustrators. You'll find *SATA* informative and entertaining, whether you are a student, a librarian, an English teacher, a parent, or simply an adult who enjoys children's literature.

What's Inside *SATA*

SATA provides detailed information about authors and illustrators who span the full time range of children's literature, from early figures like John Newbery and L. Frank Baum to contemporary figures like Judy Blume and Richard Peck. Authors in the series represent primarily English-speaking countries, particularly the United States, Canada, and the United Kingdom. Also included, however, are authors from around the world whose works are available in English translation. The writings represented in *SATA* include those created intentionally for children and young adults as well as those written for a general audience and known to interest younger readers. These writings cover the entire spectrum of children's literature, including picture books, humor, folk and fairy tales, animal stories, mystery and adventure, science fiction and fantasy, historical fiction, poetry and nonsense verse, drama, biography, and nonfiction. Obituaries are also included in many volumes of *SATA* and are intended not only as death notices but also as concise overviews of people's lives and work. Additionally, each edition features newly revised and updated entries for a selection of *SATA* listees who remain of interest to today's readers and who have been active enough to require extensive revisions of their earlier biographies.

Autobiography Feature

Beginning with Volume 103, many volumes of *SATA* feature one or more specially commissioned autobiographical essays. These unique essays, averaging about ten thousand words in length and illustrated with an abundance of personal photos, present an entertaining and informative first-person perspective on the lives and careers of prominent authors and illustrators profiled in *SATA*.

Two Convenient Indexes

In response to suggestions from librarians, *SATA* indexes no longer appear in every volume but are included in alternate (odd-numbered) volumes of the series, beginning with Volume 57.

SATA continues to include two indexes that cumulate with each alternate volume: the Illustrations Index, arranged by the name of the illustrator, gives the number of the volume and page where the illustrator's work appears in the current volume as well as all preceding volumes in the series; the Author Index gives the number of the volume in which a person's biographical sketch, autobiographical essay, or obituary appears in the current volume as well as all preceding volumes in the series.

These indexes also include references to authors and illustrators who appear in *Gale's Yesterday's Authors of Books for Children, Children's Literature Review,* and *Something about the Author Autobiography Series.*

Easy-to-Use Entry Format

Whether you're already familiar with the *SATA* series or just getting acquainted, you will want to be aware of the kind of information that an entry provides. In every *SATA* entry the editors attempt to give as complete a picture of the person's life and work as possible. A typical entry in *SATA* includes the following clearly labeled information sections:

PERSONAL: date and place of birth and death, parents' names and occupations, name of spouse, date of marriage, names of children, educational institutions attended, degrees received, religious and political affiliations, hobbies and other interests.

ADDRESSES: complete home, office, electronic mail, and agent addresses, whenever available.

CAREER: name of employer, position, and dates for each career post; art exhibitions; military service; memberships and offices held in professional and civic organizations.

MEMBER: professional, civic, and other association memberships and any official posts held.

AWARDS, HONORS: literary and professional awards received.

WRITINGS: title-by-title chronological bibliography of books written and/or illustrated, listed by genre when known; lists of other notable publications, such as plays, screenplays, and periodical contributions.

ADAPTATIONS: a list of films, television programs, plays, CD-ROMs, recordings, and other media presentations that have been adapted from the author's work.

WORK IN PROGRESS: description of projects in progress.

SIDELIGHTS: a biographical portrait of the author or illustrator's development, either directly from the biographee—and often written specifically for the *SATA* entry—or gathered from diaries, letters, interviews, or other published sources.

BIOGRAPHICAL AND CRITICAL SOURCES: cites sources quoted in "Sidelights" along with references for further reading.

EXTENSIVE ILLUSTRATIONS: photographs, movie stills, book illustrations, and other interesting visual materials supplement the text.

How a *SATA* Entry Is Compiled

SATA editors examine a wide variety of published sources to gather information for an entry. Biographical and bibliographic sources are consulted, as are book reviews, feature articles, published interviews, and material sometimes obtained from the biographee's family, publishers, agent, or other associates. Whenever possible, the author or illustrator is sent a copy of the entry to check for accuracy and completeness.

Entries that have not been verified by the biographees or their representatives are marked with an asterisk (*).

Contact the Editor

We encourage our readers to examine the entire *SATA* series. Please write and tell us if we can make *SATA* even more helpful to you. Give your comments and suggestions to the editor:

Editor
Something about the Author
Gale, Cengage Learning
27500 Drake Rd.
Farmington Hills MI 48331-3535

Toll-free: 800-877-GALE
Fax: 248-699-8070

Something about the Author Product Advisory Board

The editors of *Something about the Author* are dedicated to maintaining a high standard of excellence by publishing comprehensive, accurate, and highly readable entries on a wide array of writers for children and young adults. In addition to the quality of the content, the editors take pride in the graphic design of the series, which is intended to be orderly yet inviting, allowing readers to utilize the pages of *SATA* easily and with efficiency. Despite the longevity of the *SATA* print series, and the success of its format, we are mindful that the vitality of a literary reference product is dependent on its ability to serve its users over time. As literature, and attitudes about literature, constantly evolve, so do the reference needs of students, teachers, scholars, journalists, researchers, and book club members. To be certain that we continue to keep pace with the expectations of our customers, the editors of *SATA* listen carefully to their comments regarding the value, utility, and quality of the series. Librarians, who have firsthand knowledge of the needs of library users, are a valuable resource for us. The *Something about the Author* Product Advisory Board, made up of school, public, and academic librarians, is a forum to promote focused feedback about *SATA* on a regular basis. The nine-member advisory board includes the following individuals, whom the editors wish to thank for sharing their expertise:

Eva M. Davis
Director,
Canton Public Library,
Canton, Michigan

Joan B. Eisenberg
Lower School Librarian,
Milton Academy,
Milton, Massachusetts

Francisca Goldsmith
Teen Services Librarian,
Berkeley Public Library,
Berkeley, California

Susan Dove Lempke
Children's Services Supervisor,
Niles Public Library District,
Niles, Illinois

Robyn Lupa
Head of Children's Services,
Jefferson County Public Library,
Lakewood, Colorado

Victor L. Schill
Assistant Branch Librarian/Children's Librarian,
Harris County Public Library/Fairbanks Branch,
Houston, Texas

Caryn Sipos
Community Librarian,
Three Creeks Community Library,
Vancouver, Washington

Steven Weiner
Director,
Maynard Public Library,
Maynard, Massachusetts

something about the author

ACER, David

Personal

Born in Canada.

Addresses

Home—Canada.

Career

Writer, comedian, and magician. Appeared in film *Levity*. Appeared in television programs, including *America's Funniest People, The Hunger, Comedy Tonite, Comedy at Club 54, Grand Illusions: The Story of Magic, Stand-up Montreal, Just for Laughs, The Secret World of Magic,* and *Prank Patrol II.* Actor, writer, and story editor in television series, including *Mystery Hunters,* 2004-09. Guest on television programs in North America, England, and Japan; performer at comedy clubs and at Comedy Festivals.

Member

Academy of Canadian Cinema and Television, Writers Guild, Academy of Canadian Television and Radio Artists.

David Acer (Photograph by Matthew Cope. Reproduced by permission.)

Awards, Honors

Gemini Award nominations, including for Best Writer, 2005, 2007, for *Mystery Hunters;* named Magician of the Year, Canadian Association of Magicians, 2009; Hackmatack Children's Choice Book Award nomination, 2010, for *Gotcha!*

Writings

Gotcha!: Eighteen Amazing Ways to Freak out Your Friends, illustrated by Stephen MacEachern, Kids Can Press (Toronto, Ontario, Canada), 2008.

Also author of television scripts for *Little Lulu* (animated series), HBO Kids; *Animal Crackers* (animated series), Teletoon; *Crossing the Main* (one-hour special), Canadian Broadcasting Corporation, *Prank Patrol* (series), YTV; *Popular Mechanics for Kids* (syndicated series), SDA Productions; and *Mystery Hunters,* Discovery Kids/YTV. Author of books on magic tricks. Columnist for *Genii* magazine, 2002—.

Sidelights

Well known in his native Canada for his work as a comedian and magician, David Acer is also one of the creative talents behind the long-running television program *Mystery Hunters.* Nominated for ten Gemini awards (Canada's Emmy Award equivalent) and winner of more than a half-dozen international honors, including a Japan prize and a Platinum Best-of-Show Aurora award, *Mystery Hunters* is a program cohosted by Acer and two teenagers. In the program, Doubting Dave and his curious young reporters attempt to find the answers to some of the world's most-puzzling mysteries, from the location of mythic cities, the whereabouts of legendary beasts, and the truth behind UFO's to investigations of vampires, psychics, and escape artists. As a comedian, Acer has produced short films, performed at comedy clubs and comedy festivals, and appeared as a guest on television programs airing throughout the world. He has also performed as a magician for more than two decades, and has created and published original magic tricks used by professional magicians around the world.

Based on his scripts for *Mystery Hunters,* Acer is also the author of *Gotcha!: Eighteen Amazing Ways to Freak out Your Friends.* Geared for children aged eight through twelve and featuring cartoon art by Stephen MacEachern, *Gotcha!* shares the secrets to performing nineteen "paranormal" tricks, hoaxes, and experiments that readers can master with a minimum of materials. Acer shares "clear, step-by-step instructions" as well as explanations for each illusion, from bending spoons, hypnotism, and teleportation to testing your house for ghosts and testing yourself for ESP. The book also encourages critical thinking as it shares some fo the discoveries Doubting Dave and the Mystery Hunters have made about ghosts, aliens, sea monsters, psychics, hypnotists, Bigfoot, and more.

Canadian performer and comic David Acer leaks his trade secrets to budding magicians in **Gotcha!** (Illustration © 2008 by Apartment II Productions and Stephen MacEachern. Reproduced by permission.)

In *Resource Links* Claire Hazzard dubbed *Gotcha!* "a must-read for any student who loves practical jokes," and *Canadian Review of Materials* critic Linda Ludke noted the myth-busting aspect of the book, writing that "hoaxes are deconstructed and scientific explanations are offered" within its pages. Acer's television persona, Doubting Dave, salts the text with "funny quips," Ludke added, and "critical thinking and scientific reasoning underscores the fun."

Biographical and Critical Sources

PERIODICALS

Canadian Review of Materials, December 5, 2008, Linda Ludke, review of *Gotcha!: Eighteen Amazing Ways to Freak out Your Friends.*
Kirkus Reviews, August 15, 2008, review of *Gotcha!*
Resource Links, December, 2008, Claire Hazzard, review of *Gotcha!,* p. 22

ONLINE

David Acer Home Page, http://www.davidacer.com (October 25, 2009).

*　　*　　*

ADAMS, Nicholas
See SMITH, Sherwood

*　　*　　*

ALTER, Anna 1974-

Personal
Born October 10, 1974, in Charlottesville, VA; daughter of Gary (a businessman) and Lee (a massage therapist and painter) Alter. *Education:* Rhode Island School of Design, B.F.A., 1997. *Hobbies and other interests:* Traveling, reading, yoga.

Addresses
Home—Northampton, MA. *E-mail*—anna@annaalter. com.

Career
Freelance writer and illustrator. Houghton Mifflin (publisher), Boston, MA, design assistant, 1998-2000; Boston Children's School, Boston, preschool teacher, 2000—.

Writings

SELF-ILLUSTRATED

Estelle and Lucy, Greenwillow (New York, NY), 2001.

Anna Alter (Photograph by Gary Alter. Reproduced by permission.)

(Reteller) *The Three Little Kittens,* Henry Holt (New York, NY), 2001.
Francine's Day, Greenwillow Press (New York, NY), 2003.
Abigail Spells, Alfred A. Knopf (New York, NY), 2009.
What Can You Do with an Old Red Shoe?: A Green Activity Book about Re-Use, Henry Holt (New York, NY), 2009.

ILLUSTRATOR

Patrick Jennings, *The Bird Shadow* ("Ike and Mem" chapterbook series), Holiday House (New York, NY), 2001.
Patrick Jennings, *The Tornado Watches* ("Ike and Mem" chapterbook series), Holiday House (New York, NY), 2002.
Patrick Jennings, *The Weeping Willow* ("Ike and Mem" chapterbook series), Holiday House (New York, NY), 2002.
Sharelle Byars Moranville, *The Purple Ribbon,* Henry Holt (New York, NY), 2003.
Patrick Jennings, *The Ears of Corn* ("Ike and Mem" chapterbook series), Holiday House (New York, NY), 2003.
Patrick Jennings, *The Lightning Bugs* ("Ike and Mem" chapterbook series), Holiday House (New York, NY), 2003.
Anne Broyles, *Priscilla and the Hollyhocks,* Charlesbridge (Watertown, MA), 2008.

Sidelights

Anna Alter is the author of a number of self-illustrated picture books for young readers, and her gentle pen-and-ink, acrylic, and watercolor renderings also create soft, soothing accompaniments to the texts of other writers. Beginning with her 2001 picture-book debut, *Estelle and Lucy,* Alter has a number of projects in the works, both in the picture-book and chapter-book genres.

Born in 1974, Alter began drawing at an early age. "Both my parents are artists," she once explained to *SATA,* "and we were often working on creative projects together. As a child I didn't differentiate between the art on walls and in museums, and the art in children's books. I was always surrounded by wonderful books and have wanted to illustrate children's books as long as I can remember." Among Alter's favorite illustrators are Beatrix Potter, Maurice Sendak, Garth Williams, Arnold Lobel, and James Marshall.

By the time she was in high school, Alter was writing and illustrating her own stories. Enrolling in the prestigious Rhode Island School of Design's illustration program, she studied drawing and painting, which Alter found to be "a wonderful point of departure" in preparation for a career as a professional illustrator. "In addition to illustration courses (mainly figurative drawing),

Alter's illustration projects include creating art for Anne Broyles' **Priscilla and the Hollyhocks.** (Illustration copyright © 2008 by Ann Alter. Used with permission by Charlesbridge Publishing, Inc. All rights reserved.)

I also did a lot of printmaking, mainly etching and linocut," she explained. In school she also came to appreciate the works of artists such as Rembrandt, Leonardo da Vinci, Käthe Kollwitz, Edvard Munch, and Georges Seurat.

Alter's first published book, *Estelle and Lucy,* is a picture book that introduces an interesting set of siblings: Estelle is a growing kitten, while little sister Lucy is a mouse. As the story progresses, Estelle lists her many accomplishments, including baking biscuits and being able to wear her father's slippers, while little sister Lucy tags along, her efforts clearly in a smaller scale than those of her big sister. Calling Alter's debut "a charmer," *Booklist* contributor Ilene Cooper added that "Alter shows strong talent as both a storyteller and an artist." A *Publishers Weekly* reviewer had reservations about the future friendship between the cat and mouse, but praised the book's "buttery-toned, crosshatched watercolor and ink artwork that harks back to times past." Reviewing *Estelle and Lucy* for *School Library Journal,* Karen Scott called the illustrations "a joy to look at" and noted that they are "perfectly suited" to Alter's text.

Other picture books by Alter include *Francine's Day* and *Abigail Spells,* both of which feature anthropomorphized animal characters. In *Francine's Day* a young fox sets about the business of her day, getting out of bed, going to school, and settling down to bed even though she does not feel like it. The fox is nudged along by caring friends, parents, and teachers, and finally makes it to the end of the long day, her foot-dragging resolve brought to life by Alter in what *School Library Journal* contributor Kathleen Simonetta described as "uncluttered pen-and-ink and watercolor illustrations." In *Publishers Weekly* a critic noted that Alter's art "beautifully expresses" a young child's feelings during a bad day, and the final illustration "makes a poignant statement about how tough it is to shake a bad mood." *Francine's Day* "is balanced with equal measures of gravity and levity," wrote a *Kirkus Reviews* contributor.

Abigail the chicken and George the bear star in *Abigail Spells,* as Abigail uses everyday events to practice for an upcoming school spelling bee. Citing Alter's illustrations, which she praised for their ability to "neatly capture both actions and emotions," Cooper added that *Abigail Spells* is also notable for its theme that "defeat is part of life."

In *What Can You Do with an Old Red Shoe?: A Green Activity Book about Re-Use* Alter employs an energetic and creative approach to recycling and re-using material goods. The book contains over a dozen craft projects in which "useless things become transformed," according to Cooper. Worn flip-flops, old shower curtains, used wrapping paper, a partner-less shoe, and the like all find new uses with instructions that are illustrated with "Alter's adorable artwork," added Cooper.

Alter introduces young children to a young bear determined to read in her self-illustrated picture book **Abigail Spells.** (Illustration copyright © 2009 by Ann Alter. Used by permission of Alfred A. Knopf, an imprint of Random House Children's Books, a division of Random House, Inc.)

What Can You Do with an Old Red Shoe? is geared for children as young as four years old, and Alter's experiences as a preschool teacher have helped her create a text that is easy to follow and also teaches an important lesson. As she explained to Jeanette Der Bedrosian in *USA Today,* her book "is the perfect avenue for teachers to use to teach kids about recycling and do it in a fun way."

In addition to writing and illustrating her own books, Alter has contributed her artistic talents to books by other authors, including *Priscilla and the Hollyhocks* by Anne Broyles and the "Ike and Mem" series of chapterbooks by author Patrick Jennings. She has also adapted a traditional story in *The Three Little Kittens,* which reveals the true reason for the kittens' lost mittens: a family of mice who make off with the mittens despite the kittens' best efforts to snatch them back. "Humor injects vitality into Alter's entertaining take on the traditional nursery rhyme," noted Ellen Mandel in her *Booklist* review, while in *School Library Journal,* Jane Marino dubbed *The Three Little Kittens* a "worthy" adaptation. Alter's acrylic paintings for *Priscilla and the Hollyhocks* were praised as "engaging" by *School Library Journal* critic Julie R. Ranelli, and in *Kirkus Reviews* a writer concluded that these same "simple, bold colorful paintings enhance" Broyles' tale. The artist's work for another picture book, Sharelle Byars Moranville's *The Purple Ribbon,* was also praised, *Booklist* critic Shelle

Rosenfeld noting that "Alter's softly rendered [pen, watercolor, and colored pencil] illustrations . . . are as charming as the story itself."

"I have always enjoyed representative imagery and meticulous observation of life in drawing, something I try to imitate in my work," Alter explained in discussing her role as an illustrator. "I find books a unique and interesting medium due to their ability to absorb and transport the child reader."

Biographical and Critical Sources

PERIODICALS

Booklist, April 1, 2001, Ilene Cooper, review of *Estelle and Lucy,* p. 1470; Ellen Mandel, October 1, 2001, review of *The Three Little Kittens,* p. 320; March 15, 2003, Shelle Rosenfeld, review of *The Purple Ribbon,* p. 1327; February 15, 2009, Ilene Cooper, review of *What Can You Do with an Old Red Shoe?: A Green Activity Book about Re-Use,* p. 93; March 15, 2009, Ilene Cooper, review of *Abigail Spells,* p. 64.

Kirkus Reviews, January 1, 2002, review of *The Bird Shadow,* p. 47; April 1, 2003, review of *The Purple Ribbon,* p. 537; July 1, 2003, review of *Francine's Day,* p. 905; February 1, 2008, Kristen McKulski, review of *Priscilla and the Hollyhocks,* p. 60; February 15, 2008, review of *Priscilla nd the Hollyhocks.*

Publishers Weekly, April 16, 2001, review of *Estelle and Lucy,* p. 64; March 24, 2003, review of *The Purple Ribbon,* p. 76; August 25, 2003, review of *Francine's Day,* p. 63.

School Library Journal, July, 2001, Karen Scott, review of *Estelle and Lucy,* p. 72; November, 2001, Jane Marino, review of *The Three Little Kittens,* p. 110; December, 2002, Shawn Brommer, review of *The Tornado Watches,* p. 98; February, 2003, JoAnn Jonas, review of *The Weeping Willow,* p. 114; May, 2003, Jody McCoy, review of *The Purple Ribbon,* p. 126; September, 2003, Kathleen Simonetta, review of *Francine's Day,* p. 166; February, 2004, Jean Lowery, review of *The Ears of Corn,* p. 114; March, 2008, Julie R. Ranelli, review of *Priscilla and the Hollyhocks,* p. 155.

USA Today, April 22, 2009, Jeanette Der Bedrosian, "Help Kids Go Green with *Old Red Shoe,*" p. D7.

ONLINE

Anna Alter Home Page, http://www.annaalter.com (October 20, 2009).

*   *   *

AYTO, Russell 1960-

Personal

Born July 10, 1960, in Chichester, Sussex, England; son of Glyn Melvyn (a groundskeeper) and Christina Pearl (a postal clerk) Ayto; married Alyx Mary Louise Bennett (a secretary), March 3, 1990; children: Greta, Emilio, Loveday. *Education:* Attended Oxford Polytechnic; Exeter College of Art and Design, B.A. (graphic design; with honors). *Hobbies and other interests:* Collecting books on art and illustration.

Addresses

Home—Penzance, Cornwall, England.

Career

Illustrator. John Radcliffe II Hospital, medical laboratory scientific officer in department of histopathology, 1979-80; also worked as a postman.

Awards, Honors

Mother Goose Award shortlist and Nestlé Children's Book Prize shortlist, both for *Quacky Quack-Quack!* by Ian Whybrow; Kate Greenaway Medal shortlist, and Smartie's Book Prize Gold Medal in under-five category, 2003, both for *The Witch's Children and the Queen* by Ursula Jones; Kate Greenaway Medal shortlist, 2004, for *One More Sheep* by Mij Kelly;City of Discovery Picture Book Award shortlist, 2006, for *Mr. Beast* by James Sage; Roald Dahl Funny Prize, British Booktrust, 2008, for *The Witch's Children Go to School* by Jones.

Illustrator

Gene Zion, *Harry and the Lady Next Door,* BBC Books (London, England), 1990.

Ian Whybrow, *Quacky Quack-Quack!,* Four Winds (New York, NY), 1991.

Nicholas Fisk, *Broops! Down the Chimney,* Walker (London, England), 1991.

Effin Older, *Trouble at the North Pole,* Heinemann (London, England), 1992.

Ann Jungman, *Cinderella and the Hot Air Balloon,* Frances Lincoln (London, England), 1992.

Andrew Matthews, *Denzil the Dog-polisher,* Methuen (London, England), 1993.

Ann Jungman, *Little Luis and the Bad Bandit,* Walker (London, England), 1993.

Vivian French, reteller, *Lazy Jack,* Candlewick Press (Cambridge, MA), 1995.

Anne Cottringer, *Ella and the Naughty Lion,* Houghton (Boston, MA), 1996.

Phyllis Root, *Mrs. Potter's Pig,* Candlewick Press (Cambridge, MA), 1996.

Hazel Townson, *Tale of the Terrible Teeth,* Heinemann (London, England), 1996.

Karen Wallace, *Rollerblading Royals,* Hodder Children's Books (London, England), 1997.

Karen Wallace, *A Hiccup on the High Seas,* A. &C. Black (London, England), 1997.

Elizabeth Laird, *A Funny Sort of Dog,* Heinemann (London, England), 1997.

Ann Ibbotson, *The Worm and the Toffee-nosed Princess,* Hodder Children's Books (London, England), 1997.

Norman Silver, *Choose Your Superhero* (poems), Hodder Children's Books (London, England), 1998.

Joyce Dunbar, *The Baby Bird,* Candlewick Press (Cambridge, MA), 1998.

Ian Whybrow, *Whiff; or, How the Beautiful Big Fat Smelly Baby Found a Friend,* Barron's (Hauppauge, NY), 1999.

Anne Cottringer, *Gordon,* Orchard (London, England), 1999.

The Nursery Collection, Mammoth (London, England), 1999.

Ian Whybrow, *Where's Tim's Ted?,* HarperCollins (London, England), 1999, Barron's (Hauppauge, NY), 2000.

Andrea Shavick, *You'll Grow Soon, Alex,* Walker (New York, NY), 2000.

The Other Day I Met a Bear: A Traditional Tale, Walker (London, England), 2001.

June Crebbin, *My Dog,* Walker (London, England), 2001.

(With others) Adrian Mitchell, *A Poem a Day,* Orchard (London, England), 2001.

Martin Waddell, *Herbie Monkey,* Walker (London, England), 2001.

Ursula Jones, *The Witch's Children,* Orchard (London, England), 2001, Henry Holt (New York, NY), 2003.

James Sage, *Fat Cat,* HarperCollins (London, England), 2002, published as *Farmer Smart's Fat Cat,* Chronicle Books (San Francisco, CA), 2002.

Ursula Jones, *The Witch's Children and the Queen,* Orchard (London, England), 2003.

Martin Waddell, *Cup Run,* Walker (London, England), 2003.

Martin Waddell, *Going Up!,* Walker (London, England), 2003.

Martin Waddell, *Star Striker Titch,* Walker (London, England), 2003.

Mij Kelly, *One More Sheep,* Hodder Children's Books (London, England), 2004, Peachtree Publishers (Atlanta, GA), 2006.

James Sage, *Mr. Beast,* HarperCollins (London, England), 2004, Henry Holt (New York, NY), 2005.

Giles Andreae, *Captain Flinn and the Pirate Dinosaurs,* Margaret K. McElderry Books (New York, NY), 2005.

Sam McBratney, *One Voice, Please: Tales of Truth and Trickery,* Walker (London, England), 2005, published as *One Voice, Please: Favorite Read-aloud Stories,* Candlewick Press (Cambridge, MA), 2008.

Cressida Cowell, *Super Sue at Super School,* Candlewick Press (Cambridge, MA), 2005.

Andy Cutbill, *The Cow That Laid an Egg,* HarperCollins (London, England), 2006.

Rose Impey, *Monster and Frog Get Fit,* Orchard (London, England), 2006.

Rose Impey, *Monster and Frog and the Terrible Toothache,* Orchard (London, England), 2006.

Rose Impey, *Monster and Frog and the All-in-Together Cake,* Orchard (London, England), 2006.

Ian Whybrow, *Tim, Ted, and the Pirates,* HarperCollins (London, England), 2006.

Rose Impey, *Monster and Frog and the Big Adventure,* Orchard (London, England), 2007.

Giles Andreae, *Captain Flinn and the Pirate Dinosaurs: Missing Treasure!,* Puffin (London, England), 2007, Margaret K. McElderry Books (New York, NY), 2008.

Ursula Jones, *The Witch's Children Go to School,* Orchard (London, England), 2008.

Mark Burgess, *Where Teddy Bears Come From,* Puffin (London, England), 2008, Peachtree Publishers (Atlanta, GA), 2009.

Andy Cutbill, *The Cow That Was the Best Moo-ther,* HarperCollins (New York, NY), 2009.

Also contributor to periodicals, including *Time Out* and London *Sunday Observer.*

Adaptations

Portions of the book *Quacky Quack-Quack!* have been animated for a videotape featuring various children's books.

Sidelights

Russell Ayto is a popular British children's-book illustrator who has worked on such titles as *One More Sheep, Mr. Beast,* and *The Witch's Children Go to School,* the last a winner of the inaugural Roald Dahl Funny Prize. A graduate of the Exeter College of Art and Design, Ayto worked at a number of magazines and even held a position as a part-time postman prior to turning to the field of freelance illustration. As Ayto once told *SATA:* "I've always liked painting and drawing and have really just ended up illustrating children's books! I never had an idea where or what I might have ended up doing. I just love the process of bringing characters and stories to life visually, adding something extra to the books. The most important thing for me, when illustrating, is to try and bring visual surprises to a book, so that, when you turn a page, you never know quite what is coming."

Critics have praised Ayto's gentle watercolor-and-ink illustrations in books such as *Mrs. Potter's Pig* by Phyllis Root, *Ella and the Naughty Lion* by Anne Cottringer, and *The Witch's Children* by Ursula Jones. The first title concerns a fastidious mother and her extremely messy baby, Ermajean. Worried Mother admonishes Ermajean that if she is not tidier she may turn into an actual pig, and when Ermajean and a little piglet actually switch places, surprises abound. *Booklist* reviewer Susan Dove Lempke applauded the "ingenious interplay between text and pictures" in the book, calling Ayto "a master of framing and white space." A contributor to *Kirkus Reviews* also noted that the "illustrations are a perfect complement for the rollicking text, imbuing every character with lots of personality."

A jealous sibling protests the arrival of a new baby and welcomes the simultaneous appearance of a troublesome lion in *Ella and the Naughty Lion.* At first Ella does not care for her new brother, Jasper, and the lion shows his equal distaste for the infant by chewing up Jasper's teddy bear and pulling off his blanket. As Ella gradually warms to her new little brother, the lion magically fades away and disappears. A contributor to *Publishers Weekly* observed that Ayto's color-washed "imprecise squiggles of ink" lend a "stuffed-animal softness to the imagery," and *Booklist* critic Ilene Cooper stated that Ayto's illustrations propel "a rather pedestrian story to a book with so many amusing visual details that young listeners will take a second look."

In *The Witch's Children,* a work by Ursula Jones, animals and people alike attempt to steer clear of the three mischievous witch's children as they head out for a day of spells and shenanigans in their neighborhood park. After casting a variety of spells, they realize they do not know how to undo their own magic and must put their minds to the test to correct their mishaps. "Ayto's characters are wonderfully expressive," commented *Horn Book* critic Joanna Rudge Long. *School Library Journal* reviewer Maryann H. Owen also enjoyed *The Witch's Children,* noting that "small details in the drawings add to the humor." A *Publishers Weekly* reviewer believed that Ayto's artwork adds depth to the amusing storyline, writing that, "kinetic and creatively skewed, these illustrations make the most of the slender tale."

In a follow-up, *The Witch's Children and the Queen,* the youngsters' inability to harness their magic once again creates havoc. On a visit to the palace, the children transform their bus into a flying carpet and convert the soldiers into pastries, angering the queen so much that she places a call to the siblings' mother. "Ayto's funny and spiky illustrations capture the anarchic hu-

Russell Ayto's humorous cartoon art is a feature of several picture books, among them **Mrs. Potter's Pig** *by Phyllis Root.* (Illustration copyright © 1996 by Russell Ayto. Reproduced by permission of Walker Books, Ltd. Published in the U.S. by Candlewick Press, Inc., Cambridge, MA.)

Ayto teams up with Joyce Dunbar, providing his cartoon art to her story in **Baby Bird.** (Illustration copyright © 1998 by Russell Ayto. All rights reserved. Reproduced by permission of Walker Books, Ltd. Published in the U.S. by Candlewick Press, Inc., Cambridge, MA.)

mour," Julia Eccleshare noted in the London *Guardian*. The trio of spellcasters attempts to help an undersized classmate overcome her fears by turning her into an ogre in *The Witch's Children Go to School*. According to Eccleshare, the "results go from bad to worse" when the children convert their school building into a storybook world.

Ayto has also enjoyed successful collaborations with authors such as James Sage and Giles Andreae. In *Fat Cat,* a work by Sage, a pair of blustery farmers concocts ludicrous contraptions to rid their fields of mice while a third farmer employs a simpler and much more effective solution. Ayto's "flamboyant illustrations provide a theatrical partnership" for Sage's narrative, Lindsey Fraser commented in the London *Guardian*. Sage's *Mr. Beast* centers on Charlie, a youngster who possesses an undying love for both treats and monsters. When Charlie's mother needs a frying pan to bake doughnuts, she sends the boy to Mr. Beast, who reminds Charlie to return the pan along with a selection of doughnuts. Charlie cannot ignore his sweet tooth, however, and when he arrives with an empty pan, Mr.

Beast (in reality, Charlie's father) threatens to devour the youngster that very evening. Ayto's mixed-media, cartoon-style illustrations "add drama and suspense to the text," Teresa Pfeifer observed in *School Library Journal*. "Instead of being frightening, however, they are whimsical and funny, keeping the tone firmly tongue-in-cheek."

In Andreae's *Captain Flinn and the Pirate Dinosaurs,* a young boy discovers a stranded sea captain in his school's supply closet. Along with three classmates, Flinn helps Captain Stubble retake his ship, the *Acorn,* from a band of marauding dinosaurs led by a ferocious Tyrannosaurus rex. According to Linda Staskus in *School Library Journal,* "the pirate dinosaurs—complete with eye patches and pointy weapons—are a curious combination of ferocious and precious," and a *Kirkus Reviews* critic remarked that Ayto's "riotous art and the jagged-toothed, drooling dinosaurs will make this a sure hit" with readers. In *Captain Flinn and the Pirate Dinosaurs: Missing Treasure!* the youngster magically travels to Bag o' Bones Island to recover the treasure of Captain Rufus Rumblebelly that has been stolen from a museum. Flinn and his cohorts must also battle Giganotosaurus, a terrifying beast with a surprising weakness. In *School Library Journal,* Jayne Damron praised the "childlike yet masterful mixed-media paintings of spiky-haired Flinn, the rotund pirate, and a fanciful cast of dinosaurs," and a contributor in *Kirkus Reviews* noted that Ayto's "frenzied cartoon collages" feature a pirate vessel "that looks like a fugitive from a Monty Python animation."

One More Sheep, a tale by Mij Kelly that was shortlisted for the Kate Greenaway Medal, centers on a well-meaning shepherd with a short attention span. When Sam brings his ten sheep indoors on a stormy night, he falls asleep before he finishes counting them, and then inadvertently allows a wolf in sheep's clothing to join the flock. According to Kitty Flynn in *Horn Book,* "Ayto's pen-and-ink and watercolor illustrations, with their sharp angles and large, rotund figures, steal the show." *Booklist* reviewer Carolyn Phelan observed that "the stylized ink drawings and fine watercolor work give the art real pizzazz," and a *Publishers Weekly* contributor noted that his "saturated watercolor palette of charcoal gray, turquoise and fuchsia on snowy white . . . strongly recall Satoshi Kitamura's graphics and humor."

Ayto has also contributed illustrations to a pair of works by Andy Cutbill. *The Cow That Laid an Egg* focuses on Marjorie, a rather ordinary bovine who longs for a special talent to call her own. A group of helpful chickens hatch a secret plan to assist Marjorie that soon has the whole barnyard buzzing. "Ayto's goofy, mixed-media collages are a perfect match" for Cutbill's story, Lee Bock stated in *School Library Journal.* Marjorie makes a return appearance in *The Cow That Was the Best Moo-ther.* Here, the farmer's wife announces a beautiful baby contest, Marjorie is determined to enter her special offspring, a tiny chick with a penchant for mooing. "Ayto's busy cartoon illustrations match the off-kilter humor of the story," Kathleen Kelly MacMillan remarked in *School Library Journal.*

Biographical and Critical Sources

PERIODICALS

Booklist, September 1, 1995, Hazel Rochman, review of *Lazy Jack,* p. 73; August, 1996, Susan Dove Lempke, review of *Mrs. Potter's Pig,* p. 1905; September 1, 1996, Ilene Cooper, review of *Ella and the Naughty Lion,* p. 141; June 1, 1998, Helen Rosenberg, review of *Baby Bird,* p. 1778; October 15, 2000, Shelley Townsend-Hudson, review of *You'll Grow Soon, Alex,* p. 447; July, 2002, GraceAnne A. DeCandido, review of *Farmer Smart's Fat Cat,* p. 1860; November 15, 2006, Carolyn Phelan, review of *One More Sheep,* p. 53; February 15, 2008, Hazel Rochman, review of *The Cow That Laid an Egg,* p. 85.

Bookseller, December 5, 2003, "Smarties Success," p. 29.

Guardian (London, England), February 4, 2003, Lindsey Fraser, review of *Growing Up!,* p. 57; April 5, 2003, Julia Eccleshare, review of *The Witch's Children and the Queen,* p. 33; July 8, 2003, Lindsey Fraser, review of *Fat Cat,* p. 57; July 1, 2006, Julia Eccleshare, review of *Tim, Ted, and the Pirates,* p. 20; May 10, 2008, Julia Eccleshare, review of *The Witch's Children Go to School,* p. 20.

Horn Book, July-August, 2003, Joanna Rudge Long, review of *The Witch's Children,* p. 443; November-December, 2006, Kitty Flynn, review of *One More Sheep,* p. 700; May-June, 2008, Joanna Rudge Long, review of *One Voice, Please: Favorite Read-aloud Stories,* p. 334.

Kirkus Reviews, July 15, 1996, review of *Mrs. Potter's Pig,* p. 1046; April 1, 2003, review of *The Witch's Children,* p. 535; August 15, 2005, review of *Mr. Beast,* p. 921; October 1, 2005, review of *Captain Flinn and the Pirate Dinosaurs,* p. 1075; August 15, 2006, review of *One More Sheep,* p. 845; September 1, 2008, review of *Captain Flinn and the Pirate Dinosaurs: Missing Treasure!;* January 15, 2009, review of *The Cow That Was the Best Moo-ther.*

Publishers Weekly, July 10, 1995, review of *Lazy Jack,* p. 57; September 2, 1996, review of *Ella and the Naughty Lion,* p. 130; March 17, 2003, review of *The Witch's Children,* p. 75; September 4, 2006, review of *One More Sheep,* p. 66; February 4, 2008, review of *The Cow That Laid an Egg,* p. 56.

School Library Journal, July, 1996, Wendy Lukehart, review of *Mrs. Potter's Pig,* p. 71; July, 1998, Paula A. Kiely, review of *Baby Bird,* p. 73; October, 2000, Kathleen Whalin, review of *You'll Grow Soon, Alex,* p. 136; July, 2002, Marlene Gawron, review of *Farmer Smart's Fat Cat,* p. 98; July, 2003, Marann H. Owen, review of *The Witch's Children,* p. 99; September, 2005, Teresa Pfeifer, review of *Mr. Beast,* p. 186; December, 2005, Linda Staskus, review of *Captain Flinn and the Pirate Dinosaurs,* p. 100; October, 2006, Carolyn Janssen, review of *One More Sheep,* p. 114; February, 2008, Lee Bock, review of *The Cow That Laid an Egg,* p. 84; November, 2008, Jayne Damron, review of *Captain Flinn and the Pirate Dinosaurs: Missing Treasure!,* p. 84; January, 2009, Kathleen Kelly MacMillan, review of *The Cow That Was the Best Moo-ther,* p. 73.

ONLINE

Hodder Children's Books Web site, http://www.hodder childrens.co.uk/ (October 10, 2009), "Russell Ayto."

Walker Books Web site, http://www.walkerbooks.co.uk/ (October 10, 2009), "Russell Ayto."*

B

BAKER, Roberta

Personal

Born in New York, NY; married; husband's name Jim; children: one daughter. *Education:* Attended Middlebury College; graduated from Yale College and Columbia University. *Hobbies and other interests:* Skiing, snowshoeing, hiking, swimming, yoga.

Addresses

Home—Tilton, NH.

Career

Author and journalist. Worked variously as a disc jockey, tollbooth attendant, ski instructor, camp counselor, financial analyst, art teacher, set designer, and archaeological excavator.

Member

Society of Children's Book Writers and Illustrators, National Writers' Union, New Hampshire Writers Project.

Writings

No Ordinary Olive, illustrated by Debbie Tilley, Little, Brown (New York, NY), 2002.
Lizard Walinsky, illustrated by Debbie Tilley, Little, Brown (New York, NY), 2004.
Olive's Pirate Party, illustrated by Debbie Tilley, Little, Brown (New York, NY), 2005.
Olive's First Sleepover, illustrated by Debbie Tilley, Little, Brown (New York, NY), 2007.

Sidelights

Roberta Baker has written a number of highly regarded works for young readers, including *No Ordinary Olive* and *Lizard Walinsky.* A graduate of Yale College and Columbia University, she has also worked as a newspaper reporter, a tollbooth attendant, a camp counselor, and an assistant to a traveling veterinary pharmacist. "But my favorite occupation has been being a work-at-home mom," she noted on the *Friends of the Arts* Web site. Inspired by the birth of her daughter, Baker began writing children's books, and her debut title, *No Ordinary Olive,* was published in 2002. "It's a pint-sized celebration of using your talents, and a story about being yourself," the author remarked to a *Seacoast Online* contributor.

In *No Ordinary Olive* Baker introduces Olive Elizabeth Julia Jerome, an imaginative, exuberant youngster whose parents encourage her free-spirited ways, including her love of bubble gum-raisin pancakes. When Olive enters the structured environment of the classroom, however, she runs afoul of her strict kindergarten teacher, Ms. Fishbone. The girl is sent to the principal's office and proceeds to redecorate his desk in a jungle motif, creating a stir throughout the school. Olive's big plans for her seventh birthday hit a snag in *Olive's Pirate Party,* a "high-energy tale of intergenerational connection," according to a critic in *Kirkus Reviews.* As Olive looks forward to her pirate-themed bash, she learns that the event will have to be held at the home of her matronly Aunt Tiffany. Olive's worries that her party will be dull and forgettable disappear when she spies her elderly aunt dressed in full pirate regalia and uttering pirate lingo. Olive's guests are also treated to a treasure hunt and a galleon-shaped cake complete with cannons and flags. Writing in *Booklist,* Carolyn Phelan called *Olive's Pirate Party* "good fun for young buccaneer wannabes."

In *Olive's First Sleepover,* the rambunctious youngster agrees to spend the night at the home of her friend, Lizard. To get the evening started, the girls collect bugs, play pizza parlor, and construct a tent from blankets before settling down to listen to Lizard's older sister, Lulu, tell ghost stories. Once the lights are out, Olive becomes concerned about some strange noises, and she and Lizard decide to build a monster trap. "Elementary-age kids will easily recognize the giddy, exhausting play as well as the disorienting fears," *Booklist* reviewer Gillian Engberg commented, and a *Kirkus Reviews* contributor stated that Baker's "splendid tale is just the thing to share with readers approaching" their first night away from home.

Olive's friend Lizard is the focus of *Lizard Walinsky,* "a lively celebration of special friends," as a critic in *Kirkus Reviews* wrote. Elizabeth Ann "Lizard" Walinsky is somewhat of a loner: she has a tremendous interest in dinosaurs, while the other girls prefer playing with dolls. One summer, Lizard finds a kindred spirit in Spider, a boy who is fascinated by arachnids, and the two become fast friends. When the summer ends, however, Spider attends a different school, and Lizard is devastated, until she meets another girl with unusual tastes. "This amiable story provides readers with an effective model about friendships," according to a reviewer in *Publishers Weekly.*

Biographical and Critical Sources

PERIODICALS

Booklist, August, 2005, Carolyn Phelan, review of *Olive's Pirate Party,* p. 2033; July 1, 2007, Gillian Engberg, review of *Olive's First Sleepover,* p. 66.
Gifted Child Today, spring, 2006, review of *No Ordinary Olive,* p. 56.
Kirkus Reviews, February, 2002, review of *No Ordinary Olive,* p. 250; May 1, 2004, review of *Lizard Walinsky,* p. 438; July 1, 2005, review of *Olive's Pirate Party,* p. 730; June 15, 2007, review of *Olive's First Sleepover.*
Publishers Weekly, April 8, 2002, review of *No Ordinary Olive,* p. 226; June 7, 2004, review of *Lizard Walinsky,* p. 49.
School Library Journal, May, 2002, Kathleen Kelly MacMillan, review of *No Ordinary Olive,* p. 104; June, 2004, Kelley Rae, review of *Lizard Walinsky,* p. 96; November, 2005, Tracy Bell, review of *Olive's Pirate Party,* p. 82; July, 2007, Susan Moorhead, review of *Olive's First Sleepover,* p. 66.

ONLINE

Friends of the Arts Web site, http://www.friends-of-the-arts.org/ (March 1, 2008), "Roberta Baker."
Seacoast Online, http://archive.seacoastonline.com/ (April 18, 2006), Sheila Tanguay, "Children's Books Author Shares Tips with Students."*

*　　*　　*

BARNEDA, David

Personal

Male. *Education:* Bucknell University, B.A., 1996; Art Center College of Design, degree, 1999.

Addresses

Home—Los Angeles, CA. *E-mail*—contact@barneda. com.

Career

Illustrator and designer. *Exhibitions:* Work included in shows sponsored by Society of Illustrators of Los Angeles, 2004, and Society of Illustrators, New York, NY, 2005. Work exhibited at galleries, including; Compound Gallery, Portland, OR, 2005; Jose Drudis-Biada Art Gallery, Los Angeles, CA, 2005; Storyopolis, Studio City, CA, 2005; and Siren's Salon, Los Angeles, 2008.

Awards, Honors

Second-place award, Long Beach Arts, 1999; ECPA/ Dickinson Press Book-Cover Award finalist, 2007, for cover design of *The Fabulous Reinvention of Sunday School.*

Illustrator

James Otis Thach, *The Tickle Monster Is Coming!,* Bloomsbury Children's Books (New York, NY), 2008.

Contributor of illustrations to periodicals, including *Print Regional Design Annual.*

David Barneda creates engaging cartoons for James Otis Thach's picture book **The Tickle Monster Is Coming!** (Illustration copyright © 2008 by David Barneda. Reprinted by permission of Bloomsbury Publishing Inc. All rights reserved.)

Sidelights

David Barneda is an illustrator who creates colorful, whimsical art, and his work has been exhibited at galleries on both the east and west coast. In 2008 Barneda's artwork was introduced to new audiences in the pages of James Otis Thach's picture book *The Tickle Monster Is Coming!*

In *The Tickle Monster Is Coming!* Thach tells the story of a young monster who worries that the frightening Tickle Monster will creep his room in the dark of night and then will tickle him relentlessly. In bringing to life Thach's rhyming text, Barneda creates colored pencil-and-acrylic images that, with "somber" tones of brown and green, "create . . . a spooky atmosphere," according to *School Library Journal* contributor Linda Ludke. In *Kirkus Reviews* a critic dubbed *The Tickle Monster Is Coming!* "giggle-inducing," and added that the illustrator's artistic contributions "are rollicking and nonthreatening" to younger children.

Biographical and Critical Sources

PERIODICALS

Kirkus Reviews, August 1, 2008, review of *The Tickle Monster Is Coming!*
School Library Journal, October 2008, Linda Ludke, review of *The Tickle Monster Is Coming!,* p. 126.

ONLINE

ChildrensIllustrators.com, http://www.childrensillustrators. com/ (October 25, 2009), "David Barneda."
Dave Barneda Home Page, http://www.barneda.com (October 20, 2009).

*   *   *

BEGIN, Mary Jane 1963-
(Mary Jane Begin-Callanan)

Personal

Born January 28, 1963, in Pawtucket, RI; married Brian Callanan (an editorial and advertising illustrator), October 29, 1988; children: two children. *Education:* Rhode Island School of Design, B.F.A., 1985.

Addresses

Home and office—Barrington, RI. *E-mail*—mjbegin@ cox.net.

Career

Illustrator and graphic designer. Freelance illustrator for advertising and merchandise, including for Hasbro, See's Candies, Franklin Mint, and Disney. Rhode Island School of Design, part-time instructor beginning c. 1992. Former art editor. Presenter in conferences and workshops and at schools. *Exhibitions:* Work exhibited at Faber Biron Art Association, Stamford, CT, 1985; Springfield Art Association, Springfield, IL, 1989; Rhode Island School of Design Museum of Art, Providence, 1992; Books of Wonder Gallery, Beverly Hills, CA, 1992; Central Piedmont College, Charlotte, NC, 1993; Elizabeth Stone Gallery, Birmingham, MI, 1993; Mazza Collection Gallery, Finlay, OH; Society of Illustrators Gallery, New York, NY; Providence, RI, Art Club; Spring Bull Gallery, Newport, RI, 2007; and National Museum of American Illustration, Newport, RI, 2008.

Member

Society of Illustrators, Society of Book Writers and Illustrators.

Awards, Honors

Merit Award, Art Directors' Club, 1986; Certificates of Merit, Society of Illustrators, 1986, 1988, 1989, 1991, 1992, 1995, 2001; Awards of Excellence, *Communication Arts* magazine, 1986, 1988, 1989, 1991, 1995, 1996; Certificate of Excellence, American Institute of Graphic Arts Book Show, 1988; Irma Simonton Black Award, Bank Street College of Education, 1989, for *The Porcupine Mouse;* First Place award for juvenile trade book, New York Book Show, 1992, and Critici in Erba prize, Bologna Book Fair, 1993, both for *Little Mouse's Painting;* Steven Donahos Award, Society of Illustrators, 1995; Ruth W. Finley Award, Providence Art Club; Associated Press Best Books of the Year designation, 2002, for *The Wind in the Willows;* Citizen Citation, City of Providence, RI, 2005; Scenes of Rhode Island Award, Governor of Rhode Island, 2006.

Writings

SELF-ILLUSTRATED

(Adaptor) *The Sorcerer's Apprentice,* Little, Brown (New York, NY), 2005.
The Tale of Toad and Badger ("Willow Buds" series; based on *The Wind in the Willows* by Kenneth Grahame), Little, Brown (New York, NY), 2008.
When Toady Met Ratty ("Willow Buds" series; based on *The Wind in the Willows* by Kenneth Grahame), Little, Brown (New York, NY), 2008.

ILLUSTRATOR

Bonnie Pryor, *The Porcupine Mouse,* Morrow (New York, NY), 1988.
(As Maryjane Begin-Callanan) Thomas Hood, *Before I Go to Sleep,* Putnam (New York, NY), 1990.

Diane Wolkstein, *Little Mouse's Painting,* Morrow (New York, NY), 1992.

Kenneth Grahame, *The Wind in the Willows,* new edition, North-South (New York, NY), 2002.

Mark R. Allio, *R Is for Rhode Island Red: A Rhode Island Alphabet,* Sleeping Bear Press (Chelsea, MI), 2005.

Sidelights

Mary Jane Begin's early ambitions included becoming a teacher, an archeologist, and a veterinarian. However, drawing was her first love, and after high school she studied under children's book illustrator Chris Van Allsburg at the Rhode Island School of Design and received her first illustration assignment in 1985, the same year she graduated. Begin has won several awards for her book illustration, and she credits such early influences as Dr. Seuss and Garth Williams's illustrations for Laura Ingalls Wilder's "Little House" series. Discussing Van Allsburg, Begin told an interviewer for *Art and Design News:* "His work made me more aware of the potential for creating a reality that only exists on the page, but is so convincing that you believe it might really exist somewhere else."

Begin's illustrations are noted for their realistic detail and humorous, often whimsical, commentary on the text. Her first illustration assignment, *The Porcupine Mouse* by Bonnie Pryor, was praised for the warmth with which she depicts the book's main characters. In the story, Dan and Louie are two mouse brothers who discover all sorts of things about the world when they set off on their own. As Begin remarked to *Art and Design News,* "The Porcupine Mouse had very rich, believable characters who defined the story they were in, and in some ways dictated the atmosphere of the book." Reviewers praised Begin's dramatic illustration of the story's climax, a frightening confrontation between Dan and a cat whom Louie cleverly outwits. A *Booklist* critic characterized the art for *The Porcupine Mouse* as "so alive that the cat and mouse brothers seem ready to spring off the pages." "The snug, miniature world of the mice is created as much by an illusionist as by a skillful artist," a *Publishers Weekly* contributor commented. Begin's more-recent work, creating art for her original retelling of *The Sorcerer's Apprentice,* prompted *School Library Journal* contributor Margaret Bush to note that the artist's "attractive acrylic paintings add drama and bits of fun" through their "rich blue borders" and "beautifully costumed" characters.

The task of illustrating a modern edition of nineteenth-century poet Thomas Hood's *Before I Go to Sleep* provided different challenges for the artist. As Begin noted in her *Art and Design News* interview, "*Before I Go to Sleep* has no characters; it is a poem with 'scenes' of activity and no . . . 'players' of any kind. What I had to create from the poetry was a sense of 'the child,' any

Mary Jane Begin creates humorous, detailed images to pair with her child-centered story in **The Tale of Toad and Badger.** (Little, Brown, 2008. Illustration copyright © 2008 by Mary Jane Begin. Reproduced by permission.)

child, as the main character, choosing what his personality would be based on the type of scenes the author had written." The poem describes a child imagining ten animals he would like to be as he tries to fall asleep. Marianne Pilla, writing in *School Library Journal*, praised Begin's "exquisite illustrations" for *Before I Go to Sleep*, adding that "her interpretations [of Hood's verses], in full-color, are clever and creative."

The accolade "exquisite" was used by a *Kirkus Reviews* critic in describing Begin's illustrations for *Little Mouse's Painting*, a picture book by Diane Wolkstein. Critics praised the charm and unusual message of this story, which focuses on the various interpretations of an artist's work. Writing in *Booklist*, Ilene Cooper singled out Begin's "attention-grabbing art" in her review of the book. "With almost photographic clarity," Cooper continued, Begin "creates an animal world that is richly detailed." Lisa Dennis, writing in *School Library Journal*, concluded that "Wolkstein's expressive, straightforward narrative and Begin's beautiful, luminous watercolor and acrylic illustrations combine to produce an appealing, insightful look at friendship and creativity."

Among Begin's other picture-book projects has been illustrating a new edition of Kenneth Grahame's childhood classic *The Wind in the Willows*. This project inspired her to go further and adapt the book's character into short stories for younger readers. Her "Willow Buds" books include *The Tale of Toad and Badger*, which imagines the first meeting of Grahame's beloved characters when both creatures were young. Toad is the spoiled scion of an affluent toad family, while young Badger is the son of Toad's nanny, and their growing friendship is brought to life in Begin's "elaborately detailed, watercolor-and-pastel pictures," according to *Booklist* contributor Hazel Rochman. A second book, *When Toady Met Ratty*, focuses on Badger's decision to introduce Toad to his other friend, Ratty. Here Begin enhances her story with what *School Library Journal* critic Marilyn Ackerman described as "attractive old-fashioned . . . paintings and ornamental borders."

Biographical and Critical Sources

PERIODICALS

Art and Design News, November-December, 1991, interview with Begin, pp. 18-19.
Booklist, March 1, 1988, review of *The Porcupine Mouse*; April 1, 1992, Ilene Cooper, review of *Little Mouse's Painting*, p. 1450; December 1, 2002, Carolyn Phelan, review of *The Wind in the Willows*, p. 664; December 15, 2005, Jennifer Mattson, review of *The Sorcerer's Apprentice*, p. 49; March 15, 2008, Hazel Rochman, review of *The Tale of Toad and Badger*, p. 50.
Kirkus Reviews, May 1, 1992, review of *Little Mouse's Painting*; March 1, 2008, review of *The Tale of Toad and Badger*.
Publishers Weekly, March 18, 1988, review of *The Porcupine Mouse*; July 29, 2002, review of *The Wind in the Willows*, p. 74; April 14, 2008, review of *The Tale of Toad and Badger*, p. 53.
School Library Journal, March, 1990, Marianne Pilla, review of *Before I Go to Sleep*; June, 1992, Lisa Dennis, review of *Little Mouse's Painting*; January, 2003, review of *The Wind in the Willows*, p. 96; February, 2006, Margaret Bush, review of *The Sorcerer's Apprentice*, p. 114; June, 2008, Donna Cardon, review of *The Tale of Toad and Badger*, p. 95; January, 2009, Marilyn Ackerman, review of *When Toady Met Ratty*, p. 71.

ONLINE

Mary Jane Begin Home Page, http://www.maryjanebegin.com (October 26, 2009).*

*   *   *

BEGIN-CALLANAN, Mary Jane
See BEGIN, Mary Jane

*   *   *

BENJAMIN, Floella 1949-

Personal

Born September 23, 1949, in Pointe-à-Pierre, Trinidad; immigrated to England, 1960; daughter of Roy (a musician and policeman) and Veronica Benjamin; married Keith Taylor, September, 1980; children: Aston, Alvina. *Hobbies and other interests:* Marathon running, singing, gardening.

Addresses

Home—London, England. *Office*—Benjamin-Taylor Associates, 73 Palace Rd., London SW2 3LB, England. *E-mail*—website@floellabenjamin.com.

Career

Actress, author, advocate, and businessperson. Stage work includes *Hair*, c. 1969, *Black Mikado*, and *Jesus Christ, Superstar*. Film work includes *I Don't Want to Be Born*, 1975, and *Black Joy*, 1977. Television work includes (as shoplifter) *Within These Walls; Crown Court; Dixon of Dock Green; Bergerac*, 1981; and (as Professor Rivers) *The Sarah Jane Adventures*, 2007-08. Host of radio program *Black Londoners;* host of television programs, including *Play School, Play Away, Humpty and Little Ted*, and c. 1976-80s. Floella Benjamin Productions, founder, with husband Keith Taylor, and chief executive, 1987—; founder of Floella Benjamin's Caribbean Kitchen (food company). Dulwich College, former governor; Exeter University, chancellor; Elizabeth R. Commonwealth Broadcasting Fund, president; National Film and Television School, governor; appointed deputy lieutenant of Greater London, 2008. Founder of charities, including Touching Success (children's charity); cultural ambassador for 2012 London Olympics. Formerly worked as a bank accounts manager and stage manager.

Member

British Academy of Film and Television Arts (chairman, c. 2001).

Awards, Honors

Named to Order of the British Empire, 2001; Special Lifetime Achievement Award, British Academy of Film and Television Arts, 2004; Champion Award, IVCA Clarion Awards, 2005; honorary graduate and honorary D.Lit., University of Exeter, 2005.

Writings

FOR CHILDREN

Fall about with Flo: A Collection of Zany Jokes, Sparrow (London, England), 1984.

Floella's Fun Book, illustrated by Eileen Browne, Methuen (London, England), 1984.

Why the Agouti Has No Tail; and Other Stories, illustrated by Jennifer Northway, Hutchinson (London, England), 1984, reprinted, Macmillan Education (Basingstoke, Hampshire, England), 1998.

Floella's Fabulous Bright Ideas Book, Methuen Children's (London, England), 1985.

Floella's Funniest Jokes, illustrated by Susan George, Beaver (London, England), 1985.

Floella's Cardboard Box Book, Methuen Children's (London, England), 1987.

How Will We Go?, illustrated by Graham Philpot, Deutsch (London, England), 1987.

Snotty and the Rod of Power, Heinemann (London, England), 1987.

Where's the Giraffe?, illustrated by Graham Philpot, Deutsch (London, England), 1987.

How Do You Eat It?, illustrated by Graham Philpot, Deutsch (London, England), 1988.

For Goodness Sake!: A Guide to Choosing Right from Wrong, illustrated by Peter Doherty, HarperCollins (London, England), 1994.

Skip across the Ocean: Nursery Rhymes from around the World, illustrated by Sheila Moxley, Orchard Books (New York, NY), 1995.

Coming to England (autobiographical picture book), illustrated by Michael Frith, Puffin Books (London, England), 1997.

My Two Grannies, illustrated by Margaret Chamberlain, Frances Lincoln Children's (London, England), 2007.

OTHER

Caribbean Cookery, illustrated by Jennifer Northway, Rider (London, England), 1986.

Exploring Caribbean Food in Britain, Mantra, 1988.

Adaptations

Coming to England was adapted for film by British Broadcasting Corporation, 2004. Produced by Keith Taylor, it won a Royal Television Society award.

Sidelights

In her long career in television and advocacy, Floella Benjamin has lived the values she promotes on her home page: "I believe one should always give as much as possible to try and make a difference wherever or whenever you can." In the 1970s and 1980s, Benjamin was known throughout her native England as the beloved host of a sequence of children's programs that included *Play School.* A television producer and an author whose work includes books for children as well as cookbooks, Benjamin is also active in numerous civic and charitable organizations and has been an outspoken advocate for quality children's programming. "People think it's only children, so we don't have to put much money in it," she noted in discussing contemporary children's television programming in the United Kingdom with London *Guardian* contributor Sally Williams. "But TV is formulating their thoughts, ideas and values. If you don't give them core values of morality and integrity, thinking about other people, all the emotions children need to develop, then how can we expect them not to be antisocial and hyper and for feeling they are not part of anything."

One of six children, Benjamin grew up in Trinidad, in a close-knit family where books and music played important parts. In 1960, at age nineteen, she immigrated to England, following her parents who had moved there in search of work several years earlier. She captures this experience—the loss of her parents and her eventual reunion—in her book *Coming to England.* Along with a new climate and new culture came Benjamin's first experiences of racism. As she recalled to London *Sunday Times* interviewer Sally Day: "[My sister] Sandra and I had to help with the shopping. Sometimes we'd walk two miles to the grocer. We didn't know who would spit and call us names, or which grown man would lift up a dress and say: 'Where's your tail, monkey?' It wasn't easy being black. We'd be ignored in the shop for half an hour." Fortunately, Benjamin's mother instilled resilience and determination in her daughters, and these characteristics were key in shaping Benjamin's future as an actress and author.

Benjamin's books for young readers include *Floella's Fabulous Bright Ideas Book, Floella's Cardboard Box Book, My Two Grannies,* and *Skip across the Ocean: Nursery Rhymes from around the World,* the last a col-

Floella Benjamin's nursery-rhyme collection Skip across the Ocean *is brought to life in Sheila Moxley's stylized paintings.* (Frances Lincoln Children's Books, 2008. Illustration copyright © by Sheila Moxley, 1995. Reproduced by permission.)

lective of thirty-two poems that are enhanced by Sheila Moxley's ethnically inspired artwork. Featuring artwork by Margaret Chamberlain, *My Two Grannies* draws from Benjamin's own experience as it described a girl of mixed race who has a white British granny as well as a black granny from Trinidad. Alvina's time spent with Granny Vero is spent dancing to calypso music, while at Granny Rose's home dancing is done to brass bands. When both grannies stay with Alvina during the girl's parents absence, differences threaten to ruin the

visit until Alvina finds a way to make everyone happy. Calling *My Two Grannies* "a simple offering," *School Library Journal* reviewer Mary N. Oluonye praised Chamberlain's "bright, vivid" cartoon art and predicted that young readers will "empathize with Alvina's dilemma." Benjamin's young "heroine" is one "readers will enjoy and appreciate," according to a *Kirkus Reviews* writer, and *My Two Grannies* gains "a gently humorous touch" from Chamberlain's art.

Biographical and Critical Sources

PERIODICALS

Booklist, October 1, 1995, review of *Skip across the Ocean: Nursery Rhymes from around the World,* p. 322.
Guardian (London, England), November 15, 2008, Sally Williams, interview with Benjamin.
Kirkus Reviews, September 1, 2008, review of *My Two Grannies.*
New Yorker, November 27, 1995, review of *Skip across the Ocean,* p. 99.
School Library Journal, November, 1995 Sally R. Dow, review of *Skip across the Ocean,* p. 87; December, 2008, Mary N. Oluonye, review of *My Two Grannies,* p. 84.
Sunday Times (London, England), February 18, 2007, Sue Fox, interview with Benjamin.
Times Educational Supplement, February 5, 1988, review of *Snotty and the Rod of Power,* p. 54; July 8, 1988, review of *Why the Agouti Has No Tail, and Other Stories,* p. 27; November 11, 1988, review of *Exploring Caribbean Food in Britain,* p. 30.

ONLINE

Floella Benjamin Home Page, http://www.floellabenjamin. com (October 26, 2009).*

*   *   *

BOLAM, Emily 1969-

Personal

Born 1969, in Amersham, Buckinghamshire, England; father an art teacher. *Education:* Brighton Art College, degree, 1990.

Addresses

Home—Brighton, England. *E-mail*—emily.bolam@ virgin.net.

Career

Author and illustrator.

Writings

SELF-ILLUSTRATED

(Reteller) Rudyard Kipling, *The Elephant's Child,* Dutton (New York, NY), 1992.

(Reteller) *The House That Jack Built,* Dutton (New York, NY), 1992.

(Adaptor) *The Twelve Days of Christmas: A Song Rebus,* Atheneum (New York, NY), 1997.

Farm, Harcourt Brace (San Diego, CA), 1997.

Jungle, Harcourt Brace (San Diego, CA), 1997.

Cow, Barron's (Hauppauge, NY), 2000.

Horse, Barron's (Hauppauge, NY), 2000.

Pig, Barron's (Hauppauge, NY), 2000.

Sheep, Barron's (Hauppauge, NY), 2000.

Elephant, Barron's (Hauppauge, NY), 2001.

Lion, Barron's (Hauppauge, NY), 2001.

Rhino, Barron's (Hauppauge, NY), 2001.

Zebra, Barron's (Hauppauge, NY), 2001.

Kisses for Baby, Grosset & Dunlap (New York, NY), 2001.

Charlie Crocodile, Campbell Books (London, England), 2004.

Twelve Days of Christmas Presents, Sterling Publishing (New York, NY), 2004.

(Adaptor) *And the Spring Grass Grew All Around,* Sterling Publishing (New York, NY), 2008.

ILLUSTRATOR

Caroline Ness, *Star Signs,* Turner Publishing (Atlanta, GA), 1994.

Margaret Mayo, *How to Count Crocodiles,* Orion (London, England), 1994, published as *Tortoise's Flying Lesson,* Harcourt Brace (San Diego, CA), 1995.

Francesca Simon, *The Topsy-Turvies,* Orion (Oxford, England), 1995.

Harriet Ziefert, *The Gingerbread Boy,* Viking (New York, NY), 1995.

Harriet Ziefert, *The Little Red Hen,* Viking (New York, NY), 1995.

Harriet Ziefert, *Oh, What a Noisy Farm!,* Tambourine Books (New York, NY), 1995.

Kara May, *Creepy Crawly Caterpillar,* Doubleday (New York, NY), 1995.

Harriet Ziefert, *The Princess and the Pea,* Viking (New York, NY), 1995.

Vic Parker, *Bearobics: A Hip-Hop Counting Story,* Hodder (London, England), 1996, Viking (New York, NY), 1997.

Harriet Ziefert, *The Magic Porridge Pot,* Viking (New York, NY), 1997.

Harriet Ziefert, *Mother Goose Math,* Viking (New York, NY), 1997.

Harriet Ziefert, *No Bath Tonight!,* Dorling Kindersley (New York, NY), 1997.

Harriet Ziefert, *The Ugly Duckling,* Viking (New York, NY), 1997.

Harriet Ziefert, *The Cow in the House,* Viking (New York, NY), 1997.

Harriet Ziefert, *Henny Penny,* Viking (New York, NY), 1997.

Francesca Simon, *Moo Baa Baa Quack,* Orion (London, England), 1997.

Suzannah Olivier, *What Should I Feed My Baby?: The Complete Nutrition Guide from Birth to Two Years,* with recipes by Susan Herrmann Loomis, Weidenfeld & Nicolson (London, England), 1998.

Jill Hassall, *Along the Road,* Levinson (London, England), 1998.

Harriet Ziefert, *I Swapped My Dog,* Houghton Mifflin (Boston, MA), 1998.

Harriet Ziefert, *A Polar Bear Can Swim: What Animals Can and Cannot Do,* Puffin (New York, NY), 1998.

Harriet Ziefert, *Rabbit and Hare Divide an Apple,* Viking (New York, NY), 1998.

Harriet Ziefert, *Waiting for Baby,* Henry Holt (New York, NY), 1998.

Harriet Ziefert, *Clara Ann Cookie,* Houghton Mifflin (Boston, MA), 1999.

Harriet Ziefert, *Max's Potty,* Dorling Kindersley (New York, NY), 1999, published as *No Potty! Yes, Potty!,* Sterling Publishing (New York, NY), 2005.

Harriet Ziefert, *Sara's Potty,* Dorling Kindersley (New York, NY), 1999 published as *Go, Girl! Go Potty!,* Sterling Publishing (New York, NY), 2005.

Harriet Ziefert, *Talk, Baby!,* Henry Holt (New York, NY), 1999.

Ian Whybrow, *Little Wonder,* Hodder (London, England), 1999.

June Crebbin, *Snap-happy Annie,* Viking (London, England), 1999.

Harriet Ziefert, *Mother Goose Counting Rhymes,* Puffin (London, England), 1999.

Lucy Coats, *One Smiling Sister,* Dorling Kindersley (New York, NY), 2000.

H.M. Ehrlich, *Louie's Goose,* Houghton Mifflin (Boston, MA), 2000.

Harriet Ziefert, *Little Red Riding Hood,* Viking (New York, NY), 2000.

Harriet Ziefert, *Clara Ann Cookie, Go to Bed!,* Houghton Mifflin (Boston, MA), 2000.

Francesca Simon, *Miaow Miaow Bow Wow,* Orion (London, England), 2000.

Vivian French, *Big Bad Bug,* Walker (London, England), 2001.

Georgie Adams, *The Three Little Witches Storybook,* Hyperion (New York, NY), 2001.

Harriet Ziefert, *Murphy Meets the Treadmill,* Houghton Mifflin (Boston, MA), 2001.

Fred Ehrlich, *Does a Lion Brush?* ("Early Experiences" series), Blue Apple Books (Brooklyn, NY), 2002.

Fred Ehrlich, *Does a Pig Flush?* ("Early Experiences" series), Blue Apple Books (Brooklyn, NY), 2002.

H.M. Ehrlich, *Gotcha, Louie!,* Houghton Mifflin (Boston, MA), 2002.

H. Ellen Margolin, *Goin' to Boston: An Exuberant Journey in Song,* Handprint Books (New York, NY), 2002.

Vic Parker, *Bearum Scarum,* Hodder (London, England), 2002.

Lucy Coats, *Down in the Daisies: A Baby Animal Counting Book,* Orion (London, England), 2002.

Harriet Ziefert, *Cousins Are for Holiday Visits,* Puffin (New York, NY), 2002.

Harriet Ziefert, *Teachers Are for Reading Stories,* Puffin (New York, NY), 2002.

Harriet Ziefert, *My Funny Valentine,* Puffin (New York, NY), 2002.

Fred Ehrlich, *Does a Hippo Say Ahh?* ("Early Experiences" series), Blue Apple Books (Brooklyn, NY), 2003.

Fred Ehrlich, *Does a Panda Go to School?* ("Early Experiences" series), Blue Apple Books (Brooklyn, NY), 2003.

Fred Ehrlich, *Does a Tiger Open Wide?* ("Early Experiences" series), Blue Apple Books (Brooklyn, NY), 2003.

Fred Ehrlich, *Does a Yak Get a Haircut?* ("Early Experiences" series), Blue Apple Books (Brooklyn, NY), 2003.

Harriet Ziefert, *This Little Egg Went to Market,* Puffin (New York, NY), 2003.

Simon Puttock, *You're Too Big!,* Doubleday (London, England), 2003.

Tony Payne and Jan Payne, *Plummet,* Barron's (Hauppauge, NY), 2004.

David Bedford, *The Copy Crocs,* Peachtree Publishers (Atlanta, GA), 2004.

Harriet Ziefert, *Sometimes Buzzy Shares,* Blue Apple Books (Maplewood, NJ), 2004.

Fred Ehrlich, *Does a Duck Have a Daddy?* ("Early Experiences" series), Blue Apple Books (Maplewood, NJ), 2004.

Fred Ehrlich, *Does a Mouse Have a Mommy?* ("Early Experiences" series), Blue Apple Books (Maplewood, NJ), 2004.

Harriet Ziefert, *Buzzy's Big Bedtime Book,* Blue Apple Books (Maplewood, NJ), 2004.

Harriet Ziefert, *Buzzy's Birthday,* Blue Apple Books (Maplewood, NJ), 2004.

Harriet Ziefert, *Buzzy's Boo-boo,* Blue Apple Books (Maplewood, NJ), 2004.

Harriet Ziefert, *Murphy Meets Paris,* Blue Apple Books (Maplewood, NJ), 2004.

Fred Ehrlich, *Does a Chimp Wear Clothes?* ("Early Experiences" series), Blue Apple Books (Maplewood, NJ), 2005.

Fred Ehrlich, *Does an Elephant Take a Bath?* ("Early Experiences" series), Blue Apple Books (Maplewood, NJ), 2005.

Harriet Ziefert, *Buzzy Had a Little Lamb,* Blue Apple Books (Maplewood, NJ), 2005.

Harriet Ziefert, *Knick-Knack Paddywhack,* Sterling Publishing (New York, NY), 2005.

Harriet Ziefert, *Murphy Jumps a Hurdle,* Blue Apple Books (Maplewood, NJ), 2006.

Harriet Ziefert, *Time Out, Buzzy,* Blue Apple Books (Maplewood, NJ), 2006.

Fred Ehrlich, *Can a Seal Smile?* ("Early Experiences" series), Blue Apple Books (Maplewood, NJ), 2006.

Fred Ehrlich, *Does a Baboon Sleep in a Bed?* ("Early Experiences" series), Blue Apple Books (Maplewood, NJ), 2006.

Harriet Ziefert, *Buzzy's Big Beach Book,* Blue Apple Books (Maplewood, NJ), 2006.

Harriet Ziefert, *Fooba Wooba John,* Sterling Publishing (New York, NY), 2006.

Harriet Ziefert, *When Daddy Travels,* Sterling Publishing (New York, NY), 2007.

Harriet Ziefert, *When Mommy Travels,* Sterling Publishing (New York, NY), 2007.

Harriet Ziefert, *Buzzy's Balloon,* Blue Apple Books (Maplewood, NJ), 2007.

Georgie Adams, *The Three Little Pirates,* Orion (London, England), 2007.

Fred Ehrlich, *Does a Camel Cook?* ("Early Experiences" series), Blue Apple Books (Maplewood, NJ), 2007.

Fred Ehrlich, *Does a Giraffe Drive?* ("Early Experiences" series), Blue Apple Books (Maplewood, NJ), 2007.

Harriet Ziefert, *Buzzy: Lots and Lots,* Blue Apple Books (Maplewood, NJ), 2008.

Sidelights

A native of England, Emily Bolam is a highly regarded illustrator of children's books that include works by such celebrated authors as Francesca Simon and Georgie Adams. Bolam has also produced more than a dozen self-illustrated titles, among them *The Twelve Days of Christmas: A Song Rebus* and an adaptation of Rudyard Kipling's *The Elephant's Child.*

Bolam made her literary debut in 1992 with the publication of *The Elephant's Child,* a work she began while a student at the Brighton College of Art. The story concerns a curious young pachyderm that unwisely decides to investigate a crocodile's meal. A *Publishers Weekly* contributor praised Bolam's artwork, stating that "the jungle animals' childlike facial expressions are particularly engaging." Bolam later presented a new twist on an old favorite in *The Twelve Days of Christmas,* a songbook in rebus form. "The bright artwork has a comic feel," wrote Ilene Cooper in *Booklist.*

In 1994 Bolam began illustrating titles for other authors. One of her early efforts was Margaret Mayo's *How to Count Crocodiles,* a collection of animal stories that was published in the United States as *Tortoise's Flying Lesson.* Here, "Bolam's stylishly slapdash paintings exhibit a winning combination" of form and color, a *Publishers Weekly* critic observed. In *The Three Little Witches Storybook* Adams presents eight tales featuring Zara, Ziggy, and Zoe and their adventures in Magic Wood. "Watercolor pictures splash the pages with bright images of the girls and their friends," noted *School Library Journal* reviewer Maryann H. Owen in a review of the chapter book.

Inspired by an Appalachian folksong, *Goin' to Boston: An Exuberant Journey in Song,* a work by H. Ellen Margolin, concerns an impromptu parade that ends in Boston Common. In illustrating the story, Bolam "has chosen a spring palette of new greens, sunny yellows, and clear blues," remarked Blair Christolon in *School*

Library Journal, and a *Publishers Weekly* critic noted that the artist "evokes the ebullient atmosphere of a well-loved park on a sunny afternoon, with maypole dancing, fiddling and jump-roping." In David Bedford's *The Copy Croc,* a crocodile's efforts to find some peace and quiet are constantly disrupted by his friends. Bolam's "lush full-and double-page paintings colorfully convey the subtle humor of this comical story," wrote Shawn Brommer in *School Library Journal.*

Bolam has enjoyed an enduring partnership with Harriet Ziefert; since 1995 the pair has collaborated on more than thirty books. Ziefert's *Talk, Baby!* concerns a young boy's efforts to help his infant sister learn to speak. According to *New York Times Book Review* critic Cynthia Zarin, this "text gets a tremendous boost from Bolam's simple, appealing illustrations." In *Clara Ann Cookie,* a work told in verse, the title character tests her mother's patience while deciding what to wear for the day. Bolam's "pared-down style does full justice to Clara's expressions, and gives equal emphasis to Clara's surroundings," a critic in *Publishers Weekly* remarked. *Clara Ann Cookie, Go to Bed!,* a sequel, follows the youngster's attempts to stay up late one evening. The artist's pictures "seem to pop off the page like the bed-jumping little girl," Connie Fletcher wrote in *Booklist.*

A pudgy pooch is the focus of Ziefert's *Murphy Meets the Treadmill,* in which a yellow Lab named Murphy finds the perfect method to drop a few pounds. "Using the sparest of line work," observed Cooper, Bolam "coaxes all sorts of expressions from Murphy," and Louie Lahana, reviewing the work in *School Library Journal,* noted that "the pictures are humorous and include just the right amount of detail." In a follow-up, *Murphy Meets Paris,* the dog and his owner head to Paris, France, for a special vacation. "The illustrator's "pencil-and-watercolor scenes possess a certain joie de vivre," a *Publishers Weekly* contributor commented of this work.

Boland has also teamed with Fred Ehrlich on the "Early Experiences" series of books for young readers. In works like *Does a Lion Brush?, Does an Elephant Take a Bath?,* and *Does a Panda Go to School?* Ehrlich compares the behaviors and habits of creatures in the animal kingdom to those of humans. In a *Publishers Weekly* review of *Does a Pig Flush?,* a critic noted that her "vignettes and characterizations, set against bright, saturated backgrounds, strike a welcome balance between earnest sweetness and deadpan humor," and a *Kirkus Reviews* critic, reviewing *Does a Seal Smile?,* predicted that Bolam's "appealing and wry illustrations will charm."

Biographical and Critical Sources

PERIODICALS

Booklist, February 15, 1997, Shelley Townsend-Hudson, review of *Bearobics: A Hip-Hop Counting Story,* p. 1028; September 1, 1997, Ilene Cooper, review of *The Twelve Days of Christmas: A Song Rebus,* p. 141; December 15, 1998, Stephanie Zvirin, review of *Waiting for Baby,* p. 756; March 1, 2000, Kathy Broderick, review of *Louie's Goose,* p. 1250; September 1, 2000, Connie Fletcher, review of *Clara Ann Cookie, Go to Bed!,* p. 126; September 1, 2001, Ilene Cooper, review of *Murphy Meets the Treadmill,* p. 118; March 1, 2002, Kathy Broderick, review of *Bearum Scarum,* p. 1143; April 15, 2002, Ilene Cooper, review of *Gotcha, Louie!,* p. 1407; August, 2004, Jennifer Mattson, review of *Does a Duck Have a Daddy?,* p. 1938; July, 2005, Ilene Cooper, review of *Buzzy Had a Little Lamb,* p. 1931; October 15, 2005, Hazel Rochman, review of *Does an Elephant Take a Bath?,* p. 57; May 15, 2006, Hazel Rochman, review of *Does a Baboon Sleep in a Bed?,* p. 48; August 1, 2006, Hazel Rochman, review of *Does a Seal Smile?,* p. 80.

Kirkus Reviews, June 1, 2002, review of *Goin' to Boston: An Exuberant Journey in Song,* p. 807; July 15, 2003, review of *Down in the Daisies: A Baby Animal Counting Book,* p. 962; June 1, 2004, review of *Buzzy's Boo-boo,* p. 543; July 1, 2004, review of *You're Too Big!,* p. 635; July 15, 2006, review of *Does a Seal Smile?,* p. 721.

New York Times Book Review, November 21, 1999, Cynthia Zarin, "A Joyful Noise," review of *Talk, Baby!*

Publishers Weekly, November 22, 1991, review of *The Elephant's Child,* p. 55; May 1, 1995, review of *Tortoise's Flying Lesson,* p. 58; March 9, 1998, review of *I Swapped My Dog,* p. 67; April 5, 1999, review of *Clara Ann Cookie,* p. 239; May 6, 2002, review of *Goin' to Boston,* p. 56; December 9, 2002, reviews of *Does a Pig Flush?* and *Does a Lion Brush?,* p. 81; May 9, 2005, review of *Murphy Meets Paris,* p. 69.

School Library Journal, March, 2000, Sheilah Kosco, review of *Louie's Goose,* p. 196; October, 2000, Piper L. Nyman, review of *Clara Ann Cookie, Go to Bed!,* p. 144; October, 2001, Louie Lahana, review of *Murphy Meets the Treadmill,* p. 134; April, 2002, Genevieve Gallagher, review of *Gotcha, Louie!,* p. 109; July, 2002, Blair Christolon, review of *Goin' to Boston,* p. 108; December, 2002, Maryann H. Owen, review of *The Three Little Witches Storybook,* p. 84; March, 2003, Olga R. Kuharets, review of *Does a Lion Brush?,* p. 192; October, 2003, Jody McCoy, review of *Down in the Daisies,* p. 116; February, 2004, Julie Roach, review of *Does a Panda Go to School?,* p. 112; March, 2004, Shawn Brommer, review of *The Copy Crocs,* p. 152; August, 2004, Olga R. Kuharets, review of *Does a Duck Have a Daddy?,* p. 107; May, 2005, Catherine Threadgill, review of *Murphy Meets Paris,* p. 106; August, 2005, Rachel G. Payne, review of *Buzzy Had a Little Lamb,* p. 110; October, 2005, Bina Williams, review of *Knick-Knack Paddywhack,* p. 147.

ONLINE

Emily Bolam Home Page, http://www.emilybolam.com (March 1, 2008).*

BOOS, Ben 1971-

Personal

Born 1971, in San Jose, CA; married; children: three. *Education:* Attended San Jose State University.

Addresses

Home—CA. *E-mail*—swords@benboos.com.

Career

Artist and author. Blizzard North (computer gaming company), San Mateo, CA, senior artist, 1997-2004; also worked as a freelance illustrator and as an artist at Flagship Studios (computer gaming company), San Francisco, CA.

Awards, Honors

Cybils Awards shortlist, Children's Choice Book Award finalist, Parents' Choice Recommended designation, and Quick Picks for Reluctant Young-Adult Readers designation, American Library Association, all 2008, all for *Swords.*

Writings

(Self-illustrated) *Swords: An Artist's Devotion,* Candlewick Press (Cambridge, MA), 2008.

Sidelights

A former computer game developer, Ben Boos is the author and illustrator of *Swords: An Artist's Devotion,* a work of nonfiction. "I grew up obsessed with video games, computer games, movies, and books," Boos remarked in an online interview for *Diii.net.* "My father loved to travel, so I was taken here and there about the world, which filled my head with history and its crazy imagery and ideas. I knew early on that I wanted to pursue a creative career of making books, games and art, so I mentally steered in that direction."

Boos attended San Jose State University and worked as a freelance illustrator before entering the gaming world. During his eight-year stint with Blizzard North, a company based in California, he worked on the "Diablo" series of computer games. As he recalled to *WarCry* online interviewer John Funk, "I created quite a variety of work, and had the chance to go artistically wild. It was an absolute blast. I enjoyed sketching monsters; creating environments; designing weapons; painting user interface art or some box art." Boos left the industry after getting the urge to write a book. "I wanted to zoom-in and work in detail, and to spend longer with each painting than game development allowed . . . ," he noted in his *Diii.net* interview. "My head was so full of colorful visions, I just wanted to grab my pen and see what a few years of manic work could produce."

In *Swords* Boos offers historical information on sword craft through the ages, punctuating his work with paintings and sketches. According to Rebecca Donnelly in *School Library Journal,* Boos's "artwork is outstanding, combining meticulous attention to detail and a designer's sense for layout." A *Kirkus Reviews* contributor also praised the work, noting that the weaponry is presented "with every nick, notch, decorative motif and gleaming highlight rendered in lovingly realistic detail."

Boos keeps an open mind about his literary future. "I love making books and I also love game development," he remarked to *Diii.net.* "I'm happily working full-time making books, but there may eventually be game related news. I actually took special care to own the video game rights related to the book, I'll admit. So who knows what time will bring?"

Biographical and Critical Sources

PERIODICALS

Kirkus Reviews, August 1, 2008, review of *Swords: An Artist's Devotion.*
School Library Journal, October, 2008, Rebecca Donnelly, review of *Swords,* p. 165.

ONLINE

Ben Boos Web log, http://benjaminboos.blogspot.com/ (October 10, 2009).
Candlewick Press Web site, http://www.candlewick.com/ (October 10, 2009), "Ben Boos."
Diii.net, http://www.diii.net/ (August 15, 2008), interview with Boos.
WarCry Web site, http://www.warcry.com/ (September 16, 2008), John Funk, interview with Boos.

*   *   *

BRIGHTON, Catherine 1943-

Personal

Born May 20, 1943, in London, England; daughter of Stuart (an artist) and Vera (a writer) Boyle; married Andrew Brighton (an art critic), July 16, 1966; children: Shane, Henry. *Education:* St. Martin's School of Art, diploma (art and design), 1966; Royal College of Art, M.A., 1969.

Addresses

Home—London, England. *E-mail*—contact@catherinebrighton.com.

Career

Writer and illustrator of children's books. Freelance illustrator, c. 1970s.

Awards, Honors

Children's Book of the Year selection, Child Study Association of America, 1986, for *My Hands, My World;* premio Grafico, 1987, for *The Fantastic Book of Board Games; Observer/Cape/Comica* Graphic Short-Story Prize 2007, for "Away in a Manger."

Writings

SELF-ILLUSTRATED

Cathy's Story, Evans (London, England), 1980.
Maria, Faber (London, England), 1984, published as *My Hands, My World,* Macmillan (New York, NY), 1984.
The Picture, Faber (London, England), 1985.
(Editor) Walter de la Mare, *The Voice: A Sequence of Poems,* Faber (London, England), 1986, Delacorte, 1986.
Five Secrets in a Box, Dutton (New York, NY), 1987, published as *Galileo's Treasure Box,* introduction by Dava Sobel, Walker (New York, NY), 2001.
Hope's Gift, Doubleday (New York, NY), 1988.
Nijinsky, Methuen (London, England), 1989, published as *Nijinsky: Scenes from the Childhood of the Great Dancer,* Doubleday (New York, NY), 1989.
Mozart, Lincoln (London, England), 1990, published as *Mozart: Scenes from the Childhood of the Great Composer,* Doubleday (New York, NY), 1990.
Dearest Grandmama, Doubleday (New York, NY), 1991.
The Brontës: Scenes from the Childhood of Charlotte, Branwell, Emily and Anne, Chronicle Books (San Francisco, CA), 1994.
Rosalee and the Great Fire of London, Jonathan Cape (London, England), 1994.
My Napoleon, Millbrook Press (Brookfield, CT), 1997.
The Fossil Girl: Mary Anning's Dinosaur Discovery, Millbrook Press (Brookfield, CT), 1999.
Keep Your Eye on the Kid: The Early Years of Buster Keaton, Roaring Brook Press (New York, NY), 2008.

ILLUSTRATOR

J.J. Strong, *Emily's a Guzzleguts,* Evans (London, England), 1979.
Sian Victory, *Two Little Nurses,* Methuen (London, England), 1983.
J.J. Strong, *I Was Only Trying to Help,* Evans (London, England), 1984.
(With others) *The Fantastic Book of Board Games,* St. Martin's Press (New York, NY), 1988.
Ellen Jackson, editor, *My Tour of Europe: By Teddy Roosevelt, Age Ten,* Millbrook Press (Brookfield, CT), 2003.

ILLUSTRATOR; "BOOKS BEYOND WORDS" SERIES

Sheila Hollins and Valerie Sinason, *Susan's Growing Up,* Gaskell/St. George's Hospital Medical School (London, England), 2001.

Sheila Hollins, Margaret Flynn, and Philippa Russell, *George Gets Smart,* Gaskell/St. George's Hospital Medical School (London, England), 2001.
Sheila Hollins and Margaret Flynn, *Food . . . Fun, Healthy and Safe,* Gaskell/St. George's Hospital Medical School (London, England), 2003.
Sheila Hollins, Sandra Dowling, and Noelle Blackman, *When Somebody Dies,* Gaskell/St. George's Hospital Medical School (London, England), 2003.
Sheila Hollins, Kathryn Stone, and Valerie Sinason, *Supporting Victims,* Gaskell/St. George's Hospital Medical School (London, England), 2007.

Sidelights

Children's author and illustrator Catherine Brighton is the creator of picture books that portray, in rich and precise detail, the lives of both famous and obscure children. Many of her titles, including *Five Secrets in a Box, Rosalee and the Great Fire of London,* and *Keep Your Eye on the Kid: The Early Years of Buster Keaton,* focus on historical events or the accomplishments of famous figures, and her settings—ranging from Renaissance Italy to Hollywood to the Vienna of Mozart's time—offer a delicious opportunity for a devotee of the visual riches of the past. As Brighton noted on her home page, "I have tried in my own picture-books to evoke other places, times and lives."

Brighton was born in 1943 in London. Unlike her siblings, she was a bookish, introspective child. Along with the many books in the Boyles family home, relatives in America also sent children's titles, as Brighton later recalled in a *Publishers Weekly* interview with Kimberly Olson Fakih. "That sense of being different is at the core of my books," she added. "I pored over the tiniest details of everyday life in those books, looking for the differences."

After earning degrees from the prestigious St. Martin's School of Art and the Royal College of Art, Brighton worked as a freelance illustrator for several years before illustrating J.J. Strong's *Emily's a Guzzleguts* in 1979. The next year, she published *Cathy's Story,* the first of several books for which she created both text and illustrations. Cathy is a young girl who likes to pass the quiet afternoons before her mother returns from work by delivering the mail in her building. In this way she meets an elderly neighbor, Mrs. Slinger, who enjoys Cathy's visits; Cathy, in turn, enjoys the stories Mrs. Slinger tells about each of her framed photographs of family and friends. When Mrs. Slinger passes away, Cathy must come to terms with her first experience of loss, and she finds that her friend has left her a meaningful parting gift. In a *Growing Point* review, Margery Fisher asserted that the story "is conceived in large, well-composed pictures in which the child's environment, her relationships and her mood are forcefully and elegantly expressed."

In *Maria,* published in the United States as *My Hands, My World,* Brighton presents a collection of vignettes from a day in the life of a blind girl. Maria shows readers how she uses her other senses to learn about her environment, such as feeling the window glass to tell the weather. Maria also has a make-believe friend—Bumpers, a girl from the Elizabethan era—to keep her company. Fisher praised Brighton's "eloquent, richly coloured pictures" in a *Growing Point* review. The author/illustrator continues her Elizabethan theme in *The Picture,* in which a little girl, confined to her bed with a fever, is transported to another era through a piece of art on the wall. Brighton relates much of the protagonist's sense of wonder through her illustrations, which are framed in her characteristic style: either employing an actual frame designed onto the page, or endeavoring to capture a scene as viewed through a window.

In *Five Secrets in a Box*, a book that has also been published as *Gilileo's Treasure Box,* Virginia Galileo is the daughter of the famous scientist. Little Virginia wanders around her fifteenth-century Florentine home while her astronomer father sleeps during the day. The house, shown in Brighton's detailed illustrations, is elegant and full of beautiful objects, but the ones that Virginia loves best rest inside a box in her father's observatory. To Virginia they have magical, but also troublesome, properties. In the end, her preoccupied and politically persecuted father sends her to a convent, a place where the real-life Virginia died twenty-two years later. Brighton illustrated her scenes in hues of pink, brown, and turquoise, mimicking the Tuscan light and marbled decorative elements of the period. Fisher, reviewing the book for *Growing Point,* wrote that Brighton has "succeeded brilliantly" in her task, while a *Publishers Weekly* critic termed *Five Secrets in a Box* a "captivating and imaginative work."

Brighton again presents an unusual setting with unique visual characteristics in *Hope's Gift,* a portrayal of life in a traveling theater troupe in sixteenth-century Europe. The story's focus is Hope, considered the least intellectually blessed among three Van Missen actor-siblings. However, Hope possesses a magical power, which she discovers when she holds a parakeet in her hand and heals its broken wing. Her sister Mercy goads her into doing the same for a paralyzed girl. Although disturbed by her newfound power, Hope finally accepts her gift and also graciously accepts the parakeet as payment. A reviewer for *Junior Bookshelf* called *Hope's Gift* "a clever and original story" and praised Brighton's artistry, while Fisher termed the work "a remarkable marriage of words and illustrations."

As in *Five Secrets in a Box,* the protagonist of Brighton's *Dearest Grandmama* is the daughter of a scientist. The story is related through Maudie-Ann's letters to her grandmother while the girl is on board a ship with her naturalist father. Brighton's profusion of drawings detail the unusual plants, animals, and even bone specimens that Maudie-Ann's father is busy collecting. Maudie-Ann, however, is preoccupied with her new friend, a young boy who does not speak, nor cast a shadow. He also carries a letter saying that he is a passenger on a ship called the *Marie Celeste* in the year 1872, forty years into the future. An explanatory endnote from Brighton reveals a real-life mystery behind the story. Though some reviewers found the plot a bit complex for its age group, most lavished praise upon Brighton for her efforts. A *Junior Bookshelf* contributor lauded Brighton's illustrations, asserting that they demonstrated "her extravagantly brilliant technique and her feeling for atmosphere." Karen K. Radtke, writing for *School Library Journal,* called *Dearest Grandmama* a work "designed to capture readers' imagination and take them on a mysterious journey."

Two of Brighton's works take a biographical approach to the lives of famous personages from history, focusing in particular on their childhoods. In *Nijinsky,* about the famous Russian ballet dancer, Brighton was inspired by a vintage photograph of a Russian ballet master standing in the snow, holding a child. As Brighton noted in *Publishers Weekly,* after she saw the photograph, she tracked down a biography about the dancer's tragic life that was written by his wife. "And there was this amazing, powerful childhood," she recalled. "It was all there for the taking. Even the tragedy was built in at an early age." The 1989 publication of *Nijinsky* coincided with the one-hundredth anniversary of the dancer's birth. As Brighton recounts through words and images, Nijinsky grew up in Tsarist Russia after being abandoned by his father, who was also a dancer. Yet his own promise was evident soon after, when his mother took him to audition at the Imperial School of Ballet. Brighton's endnote explains that Nijinsky's fame and fortune did not save him from a tragic end. "Atmospheric illustrations—both rich and sombre . . . convey the feel of old Russia," noted Jennifer Taylor in a *School Librarian* review of *Nijinsky,* while in *Booklist* Denise Wilms dubbed the work "handsome and clearly a labor of love."

In *Mozart* Brighton tells the composer's life story through the eyes of his sister, Nannerl. She recounts the excitement of various occasions in the life of the eighteenth-century musical prodigy, including performing before emperors and kings and traveling all the way to England. The work is told in diary form, and its creamy pink, blue, and gold-toned illustrations, done in the style of the era, are framed in similarly appropriate baroque swirls.

Also set in England, *Rosalee and the Great Fire of London* presents a little girl and her adventures at the time of the 1663 fire that destroyed much of the city of London. Rosalee possesses an ancestral book of mystic recipes that the Cunning Man, an evil alchemist, would like to steal; he pursues her and her pet pig, Roger Bacon, as flames engulf the city. The pig is named after a thirteenth-century thinker, whose ideas about science were far ahead of his time and foreshadowed the Enlightenment. "This remarkable book offers a feast, in terms of literary appreciation and visual spectacle," as-

Cover of Catherine Brighton's self-illustrated, history-based picture book **My Napoleon.** (Millbrook Press, 1997. Illustration copyright © 1997 by Catherine Brighton. Reproduced by permission.)

serted Mandy Cheetham, the *Magpies* critic going on to term the book "a treasure that should not be missed." Julia Marriage, writing in *School Librarian,* deemed *Rosalee and the Great Fire of London* "a book to rival the best of the year."

The Brontës: Scenes from the Childhood of Charlotte, Branwell, Emily and Anne was inspired by the revival of interest in the lives and works of the nineteenth-century literary family. Told through the voice of Charlotte—author of *Jane Eyre*—Brighton's book follows the rural English lives of a very imaginative family. The girls release geese in the house of their parson father, make up elaborate fantasies, and eventually begin setting their ideas to paper. "The life of the young Brontës is recorded as if by the eye of a camera," noted *School Librarian* contributor Maggi Waite, "with [Brighton's] now familiar sense of detachment. Life at Haworth is depicted with great attention to detail, interspersed with visual references to the children's imaginary world."

In *My Napoleon,* Brighton once again creates a fictional situation from an actual event. The French emperor was

exiled to the island of St. Helena, and years later the daughter of Napoleon's prison-keeper wrote in her journal about her friendship with the diminutive but formidable former dictator. *My Napoleon* presents in words and pictures the story of Betsy Balcombe and her unusual older friend. At first, Betsy admits to being intimidated by Napoleon's impending visit, until she discovers he is not that much greater in height than herself. It pleases him that she can speak French—Betsy is English—and at one point he allows her to have so much candy that she becomes ill all over his imported rug. "A delicious little corner of history is brought to life in Brighton's sparkling pictures, at once graceful and vigorous in their soft, bright colours," Sarah Johnson remarked in the London *Times. School Library Journal* contributor Amelia Kalin maintained that Brighton's illustrations for *My Napoleon* are "truly descriptive" and incorporate a format that "contributes to the sense that readers are unfolding a rediscovered time and place."

In *Keep Your Eye on the Kid,* a critically acclaimed self-illustrated title, Brighton looks at the childhood of

Buster Keaton, one of American film's earliest pioneers. Keaton was an actor, director, producer, film editor, and screenwriter whose silent movies of the 1920s, including *Steamboat Bill, Jr.* and *The General,* rank among the best films ever done. Keaton was the son of vaudeville performers Joe and Myra Keaton, and he soon became a part of their act. He first appeared on stage when he crawled between his father's legs and the elder Keaton played along with the audience's laughter. Thereafter, his parents included him as part of their act, which they renamed "The Three Keatons," and Buster quickly became a star. In the physical comedy routines performed with his father, Keaton gained experience at pratfalls and also developed an impassive facial expression that delighted audiences. He continued to work in vaudeville until 1917, when he appeared in his first film, *The Butcher Boy.* Keaton was known throughout his career as "The Great Stone Face" for the way his character faced any catastrophe perfectly unperturbed.

Keep Your Eye on the Kid earned strong reviews, a *Publishers Weekly* critic remarking that Brighton "has created many picture biographies, and this may be her best effort yet." The book's "engaging look back at the silver screen's silent era captures the heady excitement" of the times, a contributor in *Kirkus Reviews* noted, and Betty Carter, writing in *Horn Book,* explained that "art imitates life through a deadpan text that outlines Buster's life from birth to his early days in Hollywood."

Brighton's illustrations for *Keep Your Eye on the Kid,* which employ cartoon-style panels and clean lines, earned comparisons to the artwork of David Wiesner and Winsor McKay. According to Margaret Bush in *School Library Journal,* the "drawings shaded in umber and gray tones have a graphic look quite appropriate to the comic subject." As *Fuse #8 Production* online critic Elizabeth Bird stated, "The art complements the action so completely that it's hard for me to know how to begin to describe it." Bird added that Brighton "loves her angles and dimensions. The perspective in this book is impressive as well. Sometimes you'll be looking down on the action and at other times you're on the level. Brighton borrows some comic book techniques as well, incorporating them seamlessly into the whole." Carolyn Phelan, reviewing *Keep Your Eye on the Kid* in *Booklist,* called the work "a fitting tribute to a movie legend."

As an illustrator, Brighton created the images for *My Tour of Europe: By Teddy Roosevelt, Age Ten,* a collection of journal entries edited by Ellen Jackson. In 1869 Roosevelt, who would become the twenty-sixth president of the United States, ventured to Europe for a year-long stay with his family, traveling in England, France, and Italy. Jackson includes excerpts from Roosevelt's log, including his accounts of injuring his leg while riding a donkey in Liverpool, England; playing with siblings in the botanic gardens in Antwerp, Belgium; standing astride the border of Italy and Switzerland; viewing the Leaning Tower of Pisa; and being scolded by chambermaids in Chamonix, France.

"Youngsters will enjoy the pictures filled with 19th-century details," Susan Lissim predicted in *School Library Journal.* Other reviewers offered further praise for Brighton's contributions to the volume. The "detailed but airy illustrations greatly enhance the volume's charm and accessibility," a critic in *Publishers Weekly* stated, and GraceAnne A. DeCandido, writing in *Booklist,* observed that the "meticulous and historically researched illustrations make a fascinating study."

Although Brighton has occasionally been criticized for limiting readers' view of a time and place by not including explanatory detail, the author/artist views her work in a different light. "When you're walking down a dark street, and someone has the curtains open, you have a glimpse of their lives," she told Kimberly Olson Fakih in *Publishers Weekly.* "Someone else's life is going on and you get that and then move on."

Biographical and Critical Sources

PERIODICALS

Booklist, November 15, 1989, Denise Wilms, review of *Nijinsky: Scenes from the Childhood of the Great Dancer,* p. 660; April 15, 2003, GraceAnne A. DeCandido, review of *My Tour of Europe: By Teddy Roosevelt, Age Ten,* p. 1473; April 15, 2008, Carolyn Phelan, review of *Keep Your Eye on the Kid: The Early Years of Buster Keaton,* p. 43.

Growing Point, November, 1987, Margery Fisher, review of *Five Secrets in a Box,* p. 4892; September, 1988, Margery Fisher, review of *Hope's Gift,* pp. 5044-5045; January, 1985, Margery Fisher, review of *Maria,* p. 4375; November, 1980, Margery Fisher, review of *Cathy's Story,* p. 3793.

Horn Book, May-June, 2008, Betty Carter, review of *Keep Your Eye on the Kid,* p. 336.

Junior Bookshelf, August, 1988, review of *Hope's Gift,* pp. 179-80; August, 1991, review of *Dearest Grandmama,* p. 143.

Kirkus Reviews, March 1, 2008, review of *Keep Your Eye on the Kid.*

Magpies, May, 1995, Mandy Cheetham, review of *Rosalee and the Great Fire of London,* p. 31.

Publishers Weekly, July 10, 1987, review of *Five Secrets in a Box,* p. 67; July 28, 1989, Kimberly Olson Fakih, interview with Brighton, pp. 132-134; January 6, 1997, review of *My Napoleon,* p. 73; October 27, 2003, review of *My Tour of Europe,* p. 69; April 14, 2008, review of *Keep Your Eye on the Kid,* p. 53.

School Librarian, November, 1989, Jennifer Taylor, review of *Nijinsky,* p. 142; November, 1993, Maggi Waite, "Children Waiting in the Wings," pp. 136-137; February, 1995, Julia Marriage, review of *Rosalee and the Great Fire of London,* p. 21.

School Library Journal, November, 1991, Karen K. Radtke, review of *Dearest Grandmama,* p. 90; June, 1997, Amelia Kalin, review of *My Napoleon,* p. 79; June, 2003, Susan Lissim, review of *My Tour of Europe,* p. 129; April, 2008, Margaret Bush, review of *Keep Your Eye on the Kid,* p. 128.

Times (London, England), March 1, 1997, Sarah Johnson, review of *My Napoleon,* p. 14.

ONLINE

Catherine Brighton Home Page, http://www.catherine brighton.com (October 10, 2009).

Fuse #8 Production Web log, http://www.schoollibrary journal.com/ (February 18, 2008), Elizabeth Bird, review of *Keep Your Eye on the Kid.**

C

CASHORE, Kristin 1976(?)-

Personal

Born 1976, in PA; father a professor of religion, mother a middle-school science teacher. *Education:* Williams College, B.A. (English literature); Simmons College Center for the Study of Children's Literature, M.A.

Addresses

Home—Cambridge, MA. *Agent*—Faye Bender Literary Agency, 337 W. 76th St., Ste. E1, New York, NY 10023.

Career

Writer. Worked as a legal assistant in New York, NY; former freelance educational writer for K-6 market.

Awards, Honors

Mythopoeic Fantasy Award for Children's Literature, SIBA Book Award for Young-Adult Literature, Best Book for Young Adults designation, American Library Association, Andre Norton Award finalist, and Indies Choice Book Award finalist, all 2009, all for *Graceling*.

Writings

YOUNG-ADULT NOVELS

Graceling, Harcourt (Orlando, FL), 2008.
Fire, Dial Books (New York, NY), 2009.

Author's work has been translated into more than twenty languages, including Spanish, German, French, Vietnamese, and Turkish.

OTHER

A Time of Change: Women in the Early Twentieth Century,
Pearson/Scott Foresman (Glenview, IL), 2005.

Also author of educational materials for elementary-grade readers.

Adaptations

Graceling was adapted as an audiobook, narrated by David Baker, Full Cast Audio, 2009. *Fire* was adapted as an audiobook, read by Xanthe Elbrick, Penguin Audio, 2009.

Sidelights

"I remembered when I was 11—oh, how miserable I was when I was 11—and how I escaped into books, and books got me through," Kristin Cashore recalled in an interview with *School Library Journal* interviewer Rick Margolis. "And I thought, 'Oh, I would love to be able to do that for young people.'" As the author of the young-adult novels *Graceling* and *Fire,* Cashore has accomplished her dream; when *Graceling* was released in 2008, *Kliatt* reviewer Deirdre Root hailed it as a "stunning" fantasy fiction debut and *New York Times Book Review* critic Katie Roiphe dubbed it "eccentric and absorbing," with a heroine who "comes from the tradition of . . . Pippi Longstocking."

An avid reader since childhood, Cashore eventually attended Williams College and obtained a degree in English literature. After a short stint as a legal assistant, she returned to school, earning an M.A. in children's literature at Boston's Simmons College. At Simmons Cashore started her first middle-grade novel—yet unpublished—and realized that the writing life was worth the risk.

In *Graceling* readers are transported to a medievalesque world of seven kingdoms where they meet Lady Katsa, an eighteen-year-old warrior who works for her uncle, the brutal and unjust King Randa. Possessing one green eye and one blue eye, Katsa is "graced" with a unique skill, and in her case it is the ability to kill. While serving as Randa's mercenary, Katsa also hopes to turn her talent to good by forming a secret society dedicated to right the kingdom's wrongs. Together with other graced individuals, such as Prince Po, Katsa soon finds herself facing a king with a skill more powerful than her own in a tale that "treats readers to compelling and eminently likable characters," according to *School Library Journal* critic Sue Giffard. The novel "grapples with questions of identity, authenticity, and autonomy," wrote a *Kirkus Reviews* contributor, and Katsa "is an ideal adolescent heroine" due to her combination of self-confidence and introspection. Praising Cashore's "gorgeous storytelling," Giffard also deemed *Graceling* "exciting, stirring, and accessible," while in *Booklist* Carolyn Phelan predicted that the "well-crafted and rewarding fantasy will leave readers hoping for more."

Taking place thirty or forty years before the action in *Graceling*, *Fire* is set in the rocky, barren Dells, across the mountains from the seven kingdoms. A land of monsters, the Dells is also the home of Fire, a teen monster in human form who has the ability to read minds and shares a human's sense of right and wrong. Living in relative isolation at the start of the novel, the seventeen year old is drawn back into the political machinations of the Dells. In *School Library Journal* Giffard de-

Cover of Kristin Cashore's award-winning fantasy novel Graceling, *which transports readers to a medievalesque world.* (Harcourt, 2008. Jacket photograph (face) copyright © by Steve Gardner/PixelWorks Studio. Reproduced by permission.)

scribed *Fire* as "shot through with romance and suspense" and featuring "a larger cast and . . . more complex canvas than *Graceling*." A *Publishers Weekly* critic described Cashore's theme in her second fantasy novel as "embracing your talents and moving out of your parents' shadow," while in *Kirkus Reviews* a contributor observed that *Fire* "inverts the trope of the exotic, gifted, irresistible fantasy heroine" with the monstrous Fire. The resulting novel is "fresh, hopeful, tragic and glorious," concluded the *Kirkus Reviews* writer, while in *Horn Book* Claire E. Gross praised the author's "inventive world-building" and asserted that *Fire* "surpasses Cashore's debut and paves the way for further exploration of a world in which readers will happily immerse themselves."

Biographical and Critical Sources

PERIODICALS

Booklist, October 1, 2008, Carolyn Phelan, review of *Graceling,* p. 42.
Horn Book, November-December, 2008, Claire E. Gross, review of *Graceling,* p. 697; September-October, 2009, Claire E. Gross, review of *Fire,* p. 554.
Kirkus Reviews, September 1, 2009, review of *Fire.*
Kliatt, November, 2008, Deirdre Root, review of *Graceling,* p. 8.
New York Times Book Review, November 9, 2008, Katie Roiphe, review of *Graceling,* p. 33.
Publishers Weekly, July 21, 2008, review of *Graceling,* p. 697; December 22, 2008, interview with Cashore, p. 24; July 20, 2009, review of *Fire,* p. 141.
School Library Journal, October, 2008, Rick Margolis, interview with Cashore, p. 34, and Sue Giffard, review of *Graceling,* p. 140; August, 2009, Sue Giffard, review of *Fire,* p. 99.

ONLINE

Kristin Cashore Web log, http://kristincashore.blogspot.com (October 30, 2009).

*   *   *

CATROW, David 1952-

Personal

Born 1952, in Richmond, VA; married; wife's name Deborah; children: Hillary, David IV. *Education:* Attended Kent State University. *Hobbies and other interests:* Bicycling, birdwatching, painting.

Addresses

Home—Springfield, OH. *Office*—Springfield News-Sun, 202 North Limestone St., Springfield, OH 45503.

David Catrow (Photograph by Deborah Catrow. Reproduced by permission.)

Career

Cartoonist, painter, animator, and commercial illustrator. *Springfield News-Sun,* Springfield, OH, editorial cartoonist, 1984—; Copley News Service, syndicated cartoonist, 1988—; freelance illustrator. Worked as a paramedic for ten years. *Exhibitions:* Work held in permanent collections of the National Archives, Ronald Reagan Presidential Library, U.S. Department of Health and Human Services, and Museum of Cartoon Art, San Francisco, CA, and in private holdings.

Awards, Honors

New York Times Best Illustrated Book of the Year designation, 1995, for *She's Wearing a Dead Bird on Her Head!* by Kathryn Lasky; awards for political cartooning.

Writings

SELF-ILLUSTRATED

We the Kids: The Preamble to the Constitution of the United States, Dial (New York, NY), 2002.
Max Spaniel: Dinosaur Hunt, Orchard Books (New York, NY), 2009.
Max Spaniel: Funny Lunch, Orchard Books (New York, NY), 2010.

ILLUSTRATOR

Ethel Pochocki, *Attic Mice,* Holt (New York, NY), 1990.
Margery Cuyler, *That's Good! That's Bad!,* Holt (New York, NY), 1991.

Charles Ghigna, *Good Dogs,* Hyperion Books (New York, NY), 1992.
Robert Southey, *The Cataract of Lodore,* Holt (New York, NY), 1992.
Harriet Berg Schwartz, *Backstage with Clawdio,* Knopf (New York, NY), 1993.
John Walker, *Ridiculous Rhymes from A to Z,* Holt (New York, NY), 1994.
Kathryn Lasky, *She's Wearing a Dead Bird on Her Head!,* Hyperion Books (New York, NY), 1995.
William Kotzwinkle, *The Million-Dollar Bear,* Knopf (New York, NY), 1995.
Lydia Maria Child, *Over the River and through the Wood,* Holt (New York, NY), 1996.
Elizabeth Spurr, *The Long, Long Letter,* Hyperion Books (New York, NY), 1996.
Robert Burleigh, *Who Said That?: Famous Americans Speak,* Holt (New York, NY), 1997.
Sharon Arms Doucet, *Why Lapin's Ears Are Long, and Other Tales from the Louisiana Bayou,* Orchard Books (New York, NY), 1997.
Candace Fleming, *Westward Ho, Carlotta!,* Atheneum (New York, NY), 1998.
Howard W. Reeves, *There Was an Old Witch,* Hyperion Books (New York, NY), 1998.
Laura Simms, *Rotten Teeth,* Houghton Mifflin (Boston, MA), 1998.
Stephen Phillip Policoff, *Cesar's Amazing Journey,* Viking (New York, NY), 1999.
Kathryn Lasky, *The Emperor's Old Clothes,* Harcourt (New York, NY), 1999.
Arthur Dorros, *The Fungus That Ate My School,* Scholastic (New York, NY), 2000.
Mike Reiss, *How Murray Saved Christmas,* Price Stern Sloan (New York, NY), 2000.
Robert D. San Souci, *Cinderella Skeleton: A Fractured Fairy Tale in Rhyme,* Silver Whistle/Harcourt (New York, NY), 2000.
Patty Lovell, *Stand Tall, Molly Lou Melon,* Putnam (New York, NY), 2001.
Alan Katz, *Take Me out of the Bathtub, and Other Silly Dilly Songs,* Margaret K. McElderry Books (New York, NY), 2001.
Mike Reiss, *Santa Claustrophobia,* Price Stern Sloan (New York, NY), 2002.
Jerdine Nolen, *Plantzilla,* Harcourt (New York, NY), 2002.
Margery Cuyler, *That's Good! That's Bad! in the Grand Canyon,* Holt (New York, NY), 2002.
Alan Katz, *I'm Still Here in the Bathtub: Brand New Silly Dilly Songs,* Margaret K. McElderry Books (New York, NY), 2003.
Robert D. San Souci, *Little Pierre: A Cajun Story from Louisiana,* Harcourt (New York, NY), 2003.
Karin Ireland, *Don't Take Your Snake for a Stroll,* Harcourt (New York, NY), 2003.
Mike Reiss, *The Boy Who Looked like Lincoln,* Price Stern Sloan (New York, NY), 2003.
Alan Katz, *Where Did They Hide My Presents?: Silly Dilly Christmas Songs,* Margaret K. McElderry Books (New York, NY), 2004.
James Carville and Patricia C. McKissack, *Lu and the Swamp Ghost,* Atheneum (New York, NY), 2004.

Karen Beaumont, *I Like Myself!,* Harcourt (New York, NY), 2004.

Karen Kaufman Orloff, *I Wanna Iguana,* Putnam (New York, NY), 2004.

Karent Beaumont, *I Ain't Gonna Paint No More!,* Harcourt (Orlando, FL), 2005.

Elise Broach, *Wet Dog!,* Dial Books for Young Readers (New York, NY), 2005.

Alan Zweibel, *Our Tree Named Steve,* Putnam's (New York, NY), 2005.

Alan Katz, *Are You Quite Polite?: Silly Dilly Manners Songs,* Margaret K. McElderry Books (New York, NY), 2006.

Jerdine Nolen, *Plantzilla Goes to Camp,* Simon & Schuster (New York, NY), 2006.

Mike Reiss, *Merry Un-Christmas,* HarperCollins (New York, NY), 2006.

Alan Katz, *Don't Say That Word!,* Margaret K. McElderry Books (New York, NY), 2007.

Karen Beaumont, *Doggone Dogs!,* Dial Books for Young Readers (New York, NY), 2008.

Alan Katz, *On Top of the Potty, and Other Get-up-and-Go Songs,* Margaret K. McElderry Books (New York, NY), 2008.

Alan Katz, *Smelly Locker: Silly Dilly School Songs,* Margaret K. McElderry Books (New York, NY), 2008.

Mike Reiss, *The Boy Who Wouldn't Share,* HarperCollins (New York, NY), 2008.

Kristyn Crow, *The Middle-Child Blues,* Putnam's (New York, NY), 2009.

Alan Katz, *Going, Going, Gone!; and Other Silly Dilly Sports Songs,* Margaret K. McElderry Books (New York, NY), 2009.

Alan Katz, *Too Much Kissing!; and Other Silly Dilly Songs about Parents,* Margaret K. McElderry Books (New York, NY), 2009.

Freelance illustrator for *Cleveland Plain Dealer* and *Akron Beacon-Journal;* illustrator of *Wild Things* (weekly pet column).

ILLUSTRATOR; "CORNERSTONES OF FREEDOM" SERIES

R. Conrad Stein, *The Story of the Little Bighorn,* Children's Press (Chicago, IL), 1983.

R. Conrad Stein, *The Story of Wounded Knee,* Children's Press (Chicago, IL), 1983.

R. Conrad Stein, *The Story of the Johnstown Flood,* Children's Press (Chicago, IL), 1984.

R. Conrad Stein, *The Story of the Oregon Trail,* Children's Press (Chicago, IL), 1984.

R. Conrad Stein, *The Story of Apollo 11,* Children's Press (Chicago, IL), 1985.

R. Conrad Stein, *The Story of the Trail of Tears,* Children's Press (Chicago, IL), 1985.

Zachary Kent, *The Story of the Battle of Bull Run,* Children's Press (Chicago, IL), 1986.

Adaptations

Plantzilla was adapted for television by National Geographic Kids, 2003. *We the Kids* was adapted for film, 2003.

Sidelights

David Catrow is an award-winning political cartoonist for the *Springfield News-Sun.* His work is syndicated to more than 900 newspapers in the United States and Canada, and it has also appeared on the editorial pages of the *New York Times, USA Today,* and the *Washington Post.* Catrow is also the illustrator of several critically acclaimed children's books. His work is often cited for its dark, biting humor and for employing unusual, squiggly lines that remind critics of Dr. Seuss.

Catrow's *We the Kids: The Preamble to the Constitution of the United States* is a self-illustrated work that explains the opening lines of that famous document. With the actual words of the preamble serving as his text, Catrow "uses his marvelous, witty style to create a visual delight, encouraging kids to giggle and then claim ownership of the words and the basic concepts they ensure," according to Pamela K. Bomboy in *School Library Journal.* A *Publishers Weekly* critic stated that the author's "zany, patriotic paean offers kids lighthearted but meaningful incentive to reflect further on the relevance" of the preamble, while a *Kirkus Reviews* critic praised *We the Kids* as "an engaging way of removing barriers to understanding raised by the Constitution's stylized language." Other original picture books by Catrow include the easy-readers *Max Spaniel: Dinosaur Hunt* and *Max Spaniel: Funny Lunch.*

Catrow introduces young children to the tenets of a free nation in his illustrated picture book **We the Kids.** (Copyright © 2002 by David Catrow. Used by permission of Dial Books for Young Readers, a division of Penguin Young Readers Group. A Member of Penguin Group (USA), Inc., 345 Hudson St., New York, NY 10014. All rights reserved.)

While Catrow has written two self-illustrated picture books, he is best known for his collaborations with other children's authors, such as Kathryn Lasky, Robert D. San Souci, Alan Katz, and Arthur Dorros. Set in 1896, Lasky's *She's Wearing a Dead Bird on Her Head!* tells the story of Harriet Hemenway and Minna Hall, founders of the Massachusetts Audubon Society. Angered by the latest fashion statement—ladies' hats decorated with the preserved corpses of dead birds—the two women are roused to action. In *School Library Journal* Steven Engelfried remarked of *She's Wearing a Dead Bird on Her Head!* that "the exaggerated expressions and postures of Catrow's figures bring humor to every page, but the serious business of political action comes through just the same." Carolyn Phelan, reviewing the work in *Booklist,* noted that "the colorful ink-and-watercolor artwork pokes fun at the extremes of fashion and the haughty pretensions of society." A *Publishers Weekly* contributor stated that Catrow "contributes flamboyant caricatures of the behatted Bostonians in convincing period costume, and his watercolors of birds mimic John James Audubon's own naturalistic paintings."

San Souci's *Cinderella Skeleton: A Fractured Fairy Tale in Rhyme* is a somewhat ghoulish take on the "Cinderella" motif. In this retelling, Cinderella dashes away from the Halloween Ball at midnight, leaving behind a glass slipper that still contains her bony foot. Susan Hepler, writing in *School Library Journal,* commented on the book's quirky story and described the accompanying artwork as "wonderfully weird pencil-and-watercolor illustrations [that] feature wiggly lines, lurid pink and bilious green accents." In *Horn Book* Anita L. Burkam stated that Catrow's drawings "employ the long lines and angles of the skeletons to create particularly dynamic compositions." *The Fungus That Ate My School,* a book by Dorros, follows the exploits of three schoolchildren who return from spring vacation to find a class experiment gone horribly wrong. With the help of Professor Macademia and the Fungus Unit, the slimy, multi-tentacled creature is eventually brought under control. A critic in *Publishers Weekly* stated that "Dr. Seuss's influence can be seen in Catrow's squiggly line drawings, which feature mushroom-like trees and eccentric characters." GraceAnne A. DeCandido, reviewing *The Fungus That Ate My School* in *Booklist,* added that "words can scarcely do justice to the whorls and splotches of vertiginous color."

Ten dogs and their myriad ways of frustrating their ten human owners are the subject of *Doggone Dogs!* a humorous picture by Karen Beaumont, while in *Wet Dog!* Elise Broach creates a humorous vignette about a beloved household pet that provides the perfect vehicle for what *School Library Journal* critic Linda M. Kenton dubbed Catrow's "exuberant pencil-and-watercolor" art. In bringing to life *Doggone Dogs!* the illustrator produces pencil-and-watercolor cartoon images in which "frenetic, goofy-looking dogs . . . are sure to bring

smiles to young faces," according to *School Library Journal* critic Linda Staskus. In *Kirkus Reviews* a critic cited "Catrow's signature watercolor-and-pencil illustrations" as "bouncy as spirited." Another book teaming up the talents of Beaumont and Catrow, *I Ain't Gonna Paint No More!* finds a young boy creating murals on his bedroom walls that his mother does not appreciate. Beamont's rhyming text follows the boy as he discovers an alternative canvas, and Catrow's "elongated figures and exaggerated expressions match the silly tone of the story," according to *School Library Journal* contributor Steven Engelfried.

One of Catrow's frequent collaborators has been comedy writer Alan Katz, with whom he has produced *Take Me out of the Bathtub, and Other Silly Dilly Songs, Smelly Locker: Silly Dilly School Songs, Going, Going, Gone!; and Other Silly Dilly Sports Songs,* and *Where Did They Hide My Presents?: Silly Dilly Christmas Songs.* In his texts Katz provides humorous new lyrics to well-known children's songs: "I've Been Working on the Railroad" is remade as "I've Been Cleaning up My Bedroom," "Deck the Halls" becomse "At the Malls," and "Row Row Row Your Boat" becomes "Clean Clean Clean Your Room." Jane Marino, reviewing *Take Me out of the Bathtub, and Other Silly Dilly Songs* for *School Library Journal,* lauded Katz's tunes and noted that Catrow's "watercolor illustrations are equally entertaining, with exaggerated features and situations giving them a cartoon look." Lauren Peterson commented in a review of the same book for *Booklist* that Catrow's "animated double-spread pictures are at least as silly as the song lyrics." *Smelly Locker* features fourteen "gleefully illustrated" poems "on the tamer side of subversive," according to *Horn Book* critic Roger Sutton, and in *Booklist* Phelan noted of *Going, Going, Gone!* that Catrow's "droll, large-scale illustrations amplify the humor of [Katz's] . . . verse tenfold."

While Catrow has provided artwork for R. Conrad Stein's "Cornerstones of Freedom" series of nonfiction books on serious themes—titles include such sobering works as *The Story of the Little Bighorn* and *The Story of the Johnstown Flood*—the illustrator otherwise continues to specialize in the humorously offbeat and quirky. His artwork for Jerdine Nolen's *Plantzilla* was praised by a *Kirkus* reviewer for its "characteristic comic extravagance," and the book also sparked a spinoff as well as an animated television program inspired by Catrow's art. Karin Ireland's *Don't Take Your Snake for a Stroll,* a work that discusses the pitfalls that await people who dare to take their exotic pets outside the home, is subjected to a similar treatment. A critic in *Kirkus Reviews* observed that Catrow's "bright, typically bizarre watercolors" are "an excellent match" for Ireland's rhyming text. According to a contributor for *Publishers Weekly,* Catrow's illustrations "plunge readers in a funhouse-mirror world."

Biographical and Critical Sources

PERIODICALS

Booklist, June 1, 1992, Karen Hutt, review of *The Cataract of Lodore,* p. 1764; March 1, 1993, Ilene Cooper, review of *Backstage with Clawdio,* p. 1237; October 15, 1995, Carolyn Phelan, review of *She's Wearing a Dead Bird on Her Head!,* p. 404; January 1, 1996, Hazel Rochman, review of *Ridiculous Rhymes from A to Z,* pp. 841-842; March 1, 1997, Stephanie Zvirin, review of *Who Said That?: Famous Americans Speak,* p. 1166; August, 1997, Karen Morgan, review of *Why Lapin's Ears Are Long, and Other Tales from the Louisiana Bayou,* p. 1894; May 1, 1998, Helen Rosenberg, review of *Westward Ho, Carlotta!,* p. 1520; September 1, 1998, Stephanie Zvirin, review of *Rotten Teeth,* pp. 128-129; December 15, 1998, Karen Morgan, review of *There Was an Old Witch,* p. 755; March 1, 1999, Susan Dove Lempke, review of *The Emperor's Old Clothes,* p. 1221; June 1, 2000, GraceAnne A. DeCandido, review of *The Fungus That Ate My School,* p. 1907; July, 2001, Lauren Peterson, review of *Take Me out of the Bathtub, and Other Silly Dilly Songs,* p. 2016; October 15, 2002, Lauren Peterson, review of *Plantzilla,* p. 413; May 15, 2003, Diane Foote, review of *Don't Take Your Snake for a Stroll,* pp. 1670-1671; April 15, 2006, Randall Enos, review of *Plantzilla Goes to Camp,* p. 54; June 1, 2008, Hazel Rochman, review of *On Top of the Potty, and Other Get-up-and-go Songs,* p. 84; January 1, 2009, Carolyn Phelan, review of *Going, Going, Gone!; and Other Silly Dilly Sports Songs,* p. 78.

Horn Book, September-October, 1997, Nancy Vasilakis, review of *Why Lapin's Ears Are Long, and Other Tales from the Louisiana Bayou,* p. 586; March, 2000, Kitty Flynn, review of *The Fungus That Ate My School,* p. 183; September, 2000, Anita L. Burkam, review of *Cinderella Skeleton: A Fractured Fairy Tale in Rhyme,* p. 589; January-February, 2004, Betty Carter, review of *Little Pierre: A Cajun Story from Louisiana,* p. 95; November-December, 2005, Bridget T. McCaffrey, review of *Where Did They Hide My Presents?: Silly Dilly Christmas Songs,* p. 695; November-December, 2006, Kitty Flynn, review of *Merry Un-Christmas,* p. 692; September-October, 2008, Roger Sutton, review of *Smelly Locker: Silly Dilly School Songs,* p. 604.

Kirkus Reviews, March 15, 2002, review of *That's Good! That's Bad! in the Grand Canyon,* p. 408; April 15, 2002, review of *We the Kids: The Preamble to the Constitution of the United States,* p. 564; July 15, 2002, review of *Plantzilla,* p. 1040; November 1, 2002, review of *Santa Claustrophobia,* pp. 1624-1625; March 1, 2003, review of *I'm Still Here in the Bathtub: Brand New Silly Dilly Songs,* p. 389; May 15, 2003, review of *Don't Take Your Snake for a Stroll,* p. 752; June 15, 2004, review of *My School's a Zoo!,* p. 581; August 15, 2004, review of *I Wanna Iguana,* p. 811; April 15, 2005, review of *Wet Dog!;* November 1, 2005, review of *Where Did They Hide My Presents,* p. 1194; September 15, 2006, review of *Are You Quite Polite?;* July, 15, 2008, review of *Smelly Locker;* September 15, 2008, review of *Doggone Dogs!*

Language Arts, September, 1992, Miriam Martinez and Marcia F. Nash, review of *That's Good, That's Bad,* p. 374.

New York Times Book Review, November 12, 1995, Karen Leggett, review of *She's Wearing a Dead Bird on Her Head!,* p. 36; November 19, 2000, Kathryn Harrison, "If the Shoe Fits . . . the Evil Stepsisters, the Fairy Godmother, the Handsome Prince—Yes, It's 'Cinderella,' Retold in Six New Books," p. 24.

Parenting, February, 1992, Leonard S. Marcus, review of *That's Good, That's Bad,* p. 26.

Publishers Weekly, October 18, 1991, review of *That's Good, That's Bad,* p. 60; June 8, 1992, review of *The Cataract of Lodore,* p. 63; August 24, 1992, review of *Good Cats, Bad Cats* and *Good Dogs, Bad Dogs,* p. 78; October 16, 1995, review of *The Million-Dollar Bear,* p. 60; November 20, 1995, review of *She's Wearing a Dead Bird on Her Head!,* p. 77, and *Ridiculous Rhymes from A to Z,* p. 78; April 8, 1996, review of *The Long, Long Letter,* p. 68; September 30, 1996, review of *Over the River and through the Wood,* pp. 86-87; October 20, 1997, review of *Why Lapin's Ears Are Long and Other Tales from the Louisiana Bayou,* p. 76; May 25, 1998, review of *Westward Ho, Carlotta!,* p. 88; August 24, 1998, review of *Rotten Teeth,* p. 56; March 8, 1999, review of *The Emperor's Old Clothes,* p. 67; May 15, 2000, review of *The Fungus That Ate My School,* p. 117; September 25, 2000, review of *How Murray Saved Christmas,* p. 69; April 16, 2001, review of *Take Me out of the Bathtub, and Other Silly Dilly Songs,* p. 63; March 18, 2002, "Encore Performances," pp. 105-106; March 25, 2002, review of *We the Kids,* p. 62; August 12, 2002, review of *Plantzilla,* p. 300; May 5, 2003, review of *Don't Take Your Snake for a Stroll,* pp. 219-220; October 13, 2003, review of *Little Pierre,* p. 79: June 28, 2004, review of *My School's a Zoo!,* p. 50; August 23, 2004, review of *Lu and the Swamp Ghost,* p. 53; April 18, 2005, review of *I Ain't Gonna Paint No More!,* p. 61, and *Our Tree Named Steve,* p. 62; June 25, 2007, review of *Don't Say That Word!,* p. 59.

Reading Teacher, February, 2003, "Paired Books," p. 508.

School Library Journal, April, 1985, Dana Whitney Pinizzoto, review of *The Story of the Oregon Trail,* pp. 93-94; March, 1987, Sylvia S. Marantz, review of *The Story of the Battle of Bull Run,* pp. 153-154; October, 1990, Virginia Golodetz, review of *The Attic Mice,* p. 118; November, 1991, Mary Lou Budd, review of *That's Good, That's Bad,* p. 92; May, 1992, Helen Gregory, review of *The Cataract of Lodore,* p. 110; April, 1993, George Delalis, reviews of *Good Cats, Bad Cats* and *Good Dogs, Bad Dogs,* p. 96; June, 1993, Marianne Saccardi, review of *Backstage with Clawdio,* p. 89; December, 1995, Steven Engelfried, review of *She's Wearing a Dead Bird on Her Head!,* p. 84; February, 1996, Sally R. Dow, review of *Ridiculous Rhymes from A to Z,* p. 99; July, 1998, Steven Engelfried, review of *Westward Ho, Carlotta!,* p. 74; September, 1998, Jackie Hechtkopf, review of *Rotten Teeth,* p. 182; March, 1999, Lucinda Snyder Whitehurst, review of *There Was an Old Witch,* p. 184; May, 1999, Donna L. Scanlon, review of *The Emperor's*

Old Clothes, p. 92; September, 2000, Susan Hepler, review of *Cinderella Skeleton,* p. 256; April, 2001, Jane Marino, review of *Take Me out of the Bathtub, and Other Silly Dilly Songs,* p. 132; May, 2002, Pamela K. Bomboy, review of *We the Kids,* p. 135; June, 2002, Marian Drabkin, review of *That's Good! That's Bad! in the Grand Canyon,* p. 92; September, 2002, Judith Constantinides, review of *Plantzilla,* p. 202; July, 2003, Nina Lindsay, review of *I'm Still Here in the Bathtub,* p. 114; July, 2004, Elaine Lesh Morgan, review of *I Like Myself!,* p. 68; October, 2004, Judith Constantinides, review of *Lu and the Swamp Ghost,* p. 110, and Lee Bock, review of *I Wanna Iguana,* p. 126; April, 2005, Marianne Saccardi, review of *Our Tree Named Steve,* p. 117; May, 2005, Steven Engelfried, review of *I Ain't Gonna Paint No More!,* p. 76; June, 2005, Steven Engelfried, review of *Take Me out of the Bathtub, and Other Silly Dilly Songs,* p. 56; July, 2005, Linda M. Kenton, review of *Wet Dog!,* p. 65; March, 2006, Blair Christolon, review of *Plantzilla Goes to Camp,* p. 200; October, 2006, Grace Oliff, review of *Are You Quite Polite?: Silly Dilly Manners Songs,* p. 136; July, 2007, Mary Hazelton, review of *Don't Say That Word!,* p. 78; March, 2008, Martha Simpson, review of *On Top of the Potty, and Other Get-up-and-go Songs,* p. 185; October, 2008, Linda Staskus, review of *Doggone Dogs!,* p. 100, and Mary Elam, review of *Smelly Locker,* p. 132; February, 2009, Martha Simpson, review of *Going, Going, Gone!,* p. 92.

Time, December 21, 1992, Stefan Kanfer, review of *The Cataract of Lodore,* p. 69.

ONLINE

BookPage.com, http://www.bookpage.com/ (March 10, 2004), "Meet the Illustrator: David Catrow."

Copley News Service Web site, http://www.copleynews.com/ (March 10, 2004), "David Catrow."

Dave Catrow Home Page, http://www.catrow.com (October 30, 2009).

Dave Catrow Web log, http://www.davecatrow.blogspot.com (October 30, 2009).*

* * *

CHARLES, Nicholas
See KUSKIN, Karla

* * *

CHARLES, Nicholas J.
See KUSKIN, Karla

* * *

CONNELL, Tom

Personal

Born in England.

Addresses

Home—England. *E-mail*—tommconnell@btinternet.com.

Career

Illustrator.

Illustrator

Sarah Angliss, *Movers and Shapers,* New Discovery Books (New York, NY), 1989.

Ian Graham, *Aircraft,* Raintree Steck-Vaughn (Austin, TX), 1999.

Ian Graham, *Boats,* Raintree Steck-Vaughn (Austin, TX), 1999.

Ian Graham, *Cars,* Raintree Steck-Vaughn (Austin, TX), 1999.

Ian Graham, *Motorcycles,* Raintree Steck-Vaughn (Austin, TX), 1999.

Claire Llewellyn, *Arthritis,* Thameside Press (North Mankato, MN), 2001.

Claire Llewellyn, *Asthma,* Thameside Press (North Mankato, MN), 2001.

Claire Llewellyn, *Diabetes,* Thameside Press (North Mankato, MN), 2001.

(With Sally Launder and Michael Woods) Charlie Samuels, *America: The Making of a Nation,* Little, Brown (New York, NY), 2008.

Biographical and Critical Sources

PERIODICALS

School Library Journal, February, 2009, Sarah Provence, review of *America: The Making of a Nation,* p. 126.*

* * *

CORWIN, Oliver
See CORWIN, Oliver J.

* * *

CORWIN, Oliver J.
(Oliver Corwin)

Personal

Male. *Education:* Pratt Institute, B.F.A.

Addresses

Home—New York, NY. *Office*—The Arsenal, Central Park, 830 5th Ave., New York, NY 10065.

Career

New York City Department of Parks and Recreation, New York, NY, graphic designer. Has designed stamps for United Nations and decorative elements for a New York City park.

Writings

SELF-ILLUSTRATED

(Reteller) *Hare and Tortoise Race to the Moon: An Aesop's Fable,* Abrams Books (New York, NY), 2002.

ILLUSTRATOR

Tina Louise, *When I Grow Up,* Abrams Books (New York, NY), 2007.

Sidelights

Oliver J. Corwin, a graphic designer for the New York City Department of Parks and Recreation, published his debut picture book, *Hare and Tortoise Race to the Moon: An Aesop's Fable,* in 2002. In Corwin's self-illustrated work, Tortoise responds to Hare's taunts about his lack of speed by challenging his antagonist to race to the lunar surface. Though Hare purchases a state-of-the-art spaceship and takes a commanding early lead, Tortoise eventually guides his manmade contraption to victory. Corwin's "text is direct and includes satisfying rocket noises and spiffy vocabulary," remarked *School Library Journal* critic Carol Ann Wilson, and Diane Foote, writing in *Booklist,* noted the "flat, slightly retro look to the pictures that recalls visions of early space exploration."

In 2007 Corwin provided the illustrations for *When I Grow Up,* a children's book by actress Tina Louise. Louise—who played Ginger Grant on the popular 1960s sitcom *Gilligan's Island*—offers career advice for young readers by using role models from the animal kingdom. In one example, Louise shows how a spider's web-building achievements may inspire a child to become an architect. A contributor in *Kirkus Reviews* praised Corwin's "kaleidoscopic, super-bright illustrations," and a critic in *Publishers Weekly* noted that his artwork "should strike the fancy of preschoolers who enjoy imaginative play."

Biographical and Critical Sources

PERIODICALS

Booklist, October 15, 2002, Diane Foote, review of *Hare and Tortoise Race to the Moon: An Aesop's Fable,* p. 410.
Kirkus Reviews, July 1, 2002, review of *Hare and Tortoise Race to the Moon,* p. 951; January 15, 2007, review of *When I Grow Up,* p. 76.
Publishers Weekly, February 12, 2007, review of *When I Grow Up,* p. 85.
School Library Journal, November, 2002, Carol Ann Wilson, review of *Hare and Tortoise Race to the Moon,* p. 120; April, 2007, Julie Roach, review of *When I Grow Up,* p. 112.*

CROWE, Chris

Personal

Son of Richard and Ruth Anne Crowe; married; wife's name Elizabeth; children: Christy, Jonathan, Carrie, Joanne. *Education:* Brigham Young University, B.A., 1976; Arizona State University, M.Ed., 1980, Ed.D., 1986.

Addresses

Office—4121 JFSB, Brigham Young University, Provo, UT 84602. *E-mail*—chrisecrowe@gmail.com.

Career

Author and professor of young-adult literature. McClintock High School, Tempe, AZ, English teacher, 1977-83, 1984-87; Mesa Community College, Mesa, AZ, visiting instructor in English, 1980-84; Himeji City Schools, Himeji, Japan, assistant supervisor of English education, 1983-84. Himeji Dokkyo University, assistant professor of English, 1987-89; Brigham Young University, Laie, HI, assistant professor, 1989-92, associate professor of English, 1992-93; Brigham Young University, Provo, UT, associate professor, 1993-98, professor of English, 1988—.

Member

International Reading Association, National Council of Teachers of English, Society of Children's Book Writers and Illustrators, National Association for the Advancement of Colored People.

Awards, Honors

Children's Book Award for Young-Adult Fiction, International Reading Association, Notable Social Studies Trade Book for Young People selection, Children's Book Council/National Council for the Social Studies, and Book for the Teen Age selection, New York Public Library, all 2003, all for *Mississippi Trial, 1955;* Jane Addams Honor Book Award, Jane Addams Peace Association, Book for the Teen Age selection, New York Public Library, and Best Book for Young Adults selection, American Library Association, all 2004, all for *Getting away with Murder.*

Writings

What Americans Don't Understand about Japanese Life, Kinseido (Toyko, Japan), 1990.
(With Takeo Hikichi) *How to Write Heading Abstracts,* Medical View (Toyko, Japan), Volume 1, 1994, Volume 2, 1995.
Two Roads, Bookcraft (Salt Lake City, UT), 1994.
Fatherhood, Football, and Turning Forty, Bookcraft (Salt Lake City, UT), 1995.

For the Strength of You, Bookcraft (Salt Lake City, UT), 1997.

(Editor) *From the Outside Looking In: Short Stories from LDS Teenagers,* Bookcraft (Salt Lake City, UT), 1998.

Presenting Mildred D. Taylor, Twayne (New York, NY), 1999.

Mississippi Trial, 1955, Phyllis Fogelman Books (New York, NY), 2002.

Getting away with Murder: The True Story of the Emmett Till Case, Phyllis Fogelman Books (New York, NY), 2003.

More than a Game: Sports Literature for Young Adults, Scarecrow Press (Lanham, MD), 2004.

Teaching the Selected Works of Mildred D. Taylor, Heinemann (Portsmouth, NH), 2007.

Thurgood Marshall: A Twentieth-Century Life, Viking (New York, NY), 2008.

Columnist for *Latter Day Sentinel,* 1981-88, and *Chandler Arizonan,* 1983. Author of numerous articles, book reviews, and chapters of books. Contributing editor, *Medical English,* 1988-90.

Sidelights

As a university professor of young-adult literature and the author of hundreds of articles, newspaper columns, and book reviews, Chris Crowe nonetheless found himself surprised at the critical response to his first work of children's fiction, *Mississippi Trial, 1955.* Notified by the International Reading Association that his book had earned the organization's top prize for children's books, Crowe told *Teacher Librarian* interviewer Teri Lesesne that he could not initially comprehend the contents of the award letter. "My mind wouldn't accept that this novel could have won an award. . . . Then I re-read [the letter] and re-read it again. I couldn't believe it!"

Published in 2002, *Mississippi Trial, 1955* offers a fictional story narrated by a young boy named Hiram Hillburn who spends his summer vacation with his grandfather in Greenwood, Mississippi. In the book, Crowe blends Hiram's story with the true story of Emmett Till, the young black teenager from Chicago who was murdered for allegedly whistling at an attractive white woman. Over the summer, Hiram becomes aware of the racism present not only in the American South but also among his own family members. Upon hearing of Emmett's fate, the boy initially believes that a cruel and bigoted acquaintance known as R.C. Rydell likely was involved in the lynching. However, when Hiram realizes that he knows the actual perpetrators of the crime, he must summon the courage to join the fight against racism. Writing in *School Library Journal,* Bruce Ann Shook wrote that "Southern racial attitudes from the period are accurately portrayed" in *Mississippi Trial, 1955,* while *Booklist* reviewer Hazel Rochman predicted that Crowe's "edgy whodunit mystery element . . . will hold readers to the end."

Crowe followed *Mississippi Trial, 1955* with a nonfiction book about the Till murder titled *Getting away with Murder: The True Story of the Emmett Till Case.*

Using contemporary articles, interviews, and photographs, the author gives teen readers a more complete picture of the crime, from the chain of events culminating in the fourteen year old's death to the trial of the men suspected of the crime and the near-confessions of those same men that were released to the public several months later. At Till's viewing in Chicago, his mother opted to keep his casket open, allowing all to see the possible fate of African Americans who violate the social mores of the Deep South. In *Getting away with Murder,* Crowe suggests that Till's fate—and the eventual freeing of the men accused of his death despite overwhelming evidence against them—pushed the entire country into a reexamination of the racist "Jim Crow" laws that were then on the books in both the North and South during the 1950s. "Crowe's powerful, terrifying account does justice to its subject in bold, direct telling, supported by numerous archival photos and quotes from those who remember," claimed Gillian Engberg in her *Booklist* review of *Getting away with Murder.* Writing in *Publishers Weekly,* a critic noted that Crowe's work offers a "searing impact" and "pays powerful tribute to a boy whose untimely death spurred a national chain of events."

Crowe again turns to nonfiction in producing *Thurgood Marshall: A Twentieth-Century Life.* Here he details the

Cover of Chris Crowe's **Thurgood Marshall: A Twentieth-Century Life,** *a biography of the first African-American Supreme Court justice.*
(Viking, 2008. Front Cover photograph copyright © Keystone/Getty Images. Reproduced by permission.)

story of the noted jurist, following Marshall's life from his childhood to his twenty-four years spent as the first African-American justice seated on the U.S. Supreme Court. Much of *Thurgood Marshall* focuses on the efforts of Marshall as a young lawyer for the National Association for the Advancement of Colored People (NAACP). While working for the NAACP, he participated in some of the landmark court cases challenging and eventually dismantling segregation laws that deprived African Americans of their rights as full citizens of the United States. Offering highlights of the twenty-nine cases Marshall argued successfully before the U.S. Supreme Court, Crowe gives "an engaging, insightful portrait" of Marshall, as well as "great insight into the most pivotal moments of the Civil Rights Movement," observed a *Kirkus Reviews* contributor.

In his interview with Lesesne, Crow shared his advice to those wishing to become an author. "Read a lot," Crowe suggested. "Write a lot. Revise what you write. Solicit advice from trusted readers, and then revise some more. Keep reading. Keep writing. Keep rewriting. Persevere until your work is good enough to be published. Don't give up hope even when countless rejections make writing seem hopeless."

Biographical and Critical Sources

PERIODICALS

Booklist, February 15, 2000, Hazel Rochman, review of *Presenting Mildred D. Taylor,* p. 1093; February 15, 2002, Hazel Rochman, review of *Mississippi Trial, 1955,* p. 1024; February 15, 2003, Gillian Engberg, review of *Getting away with Murder: The True Story of the Emmett Till Case,* p. 1079; June 1, 2008, Hazel Rochman, review of *Thurgood Marshall: A Twentieth-Century Life,* p. 94.

Horn Book, July-August, 2003, Christine M. Heppermann, review of *Getting away with Murder,* p. 476.

Journal of Adolescent and Adult Literacy, September, 2002, Alleen Pace Nilsen, review of *Mississippi Trial, 1955,* p. 80; September, 2003, Alleen Pace Nilsen, review of *Getting away with Murder,* p. 94.

Kirkus Reviews, April 1, 2002, review of *Mississippi Trial, 1955,* p. 489; May 15, 2003, review of *Getting away with Murder,* p. 748; June 15, 2008, review of *Thurgood Marshall.*

Kliatt, May, 2002, Claire Rosser, review of *Mississippi Trial, 1955,* p. 8.

Publishers Weekly, June 17, 2002, review of *Mississippi Trial, 1955,* p. 66; April 21, 2003, review of *Getting away with Murder,* p. 64.

School Library Journal, May, 2002, Bruce Ann Shook, review of *Mississippi Trial, 1955,* p. 147; May, 2003, Lynn Evarts, review of *Getting away with Murder,* p. 164; October, 2008, Mary Mueller, review of *Thurgood Marshall,* p. 167.

Teacher Librarian, April, 2004, Teri Lesesne, interview with Crowe, p. 58.

ONLINE

Chris Crowe Home Page, http://www.chriscrowe.com (October 24, 2009).*

D

DAHME, Joanne

Personal

Married; children: one son. *Education:* Villanova University, B.S. (civil engineering), 1980; Temple University, M.J. (journalism) and M.A. (creative writing).

Addresses

Home—Philadelphia, PA.

Career

City administrator and author. Philadelphia Water Department, Philadelphia, PA, Watersheds programs manager.

Writings

NOVELS

Creepers, Running Press (Philadelphia, PA), 2008.
The Plague, Running Press (Philadelphia, PA), 2009.
Tombstone Tea, Running Press (Philadelphia, PA), 2009.

Sidelights

Working by day as a program manager with the Philadelphia Water Department, Joanne Dahme uses her free time to write young-adult thrillers, among them *Creepers* and *The Plague. Creepers* centers on thirteen-year-old Courtney, who moves with her parents into an eighteenth-century home in Murmur, Massachusetts. The stone house, which is covered in ivy, sits next to the town's Puritan cemetery, a site that draws the interest of Christian and Margaret Geyer. The father-and-daughter team draws Courtney into a mystery involving their ancestors. Courtney and Margaret soon join forces to search for the missing remains of Prudence, a girl

who died in 1712, in the hopes that they can release Courtney's home from a evil spell. A critic in *Kirkus Reviews* praised Dahme's portrayal of her protagonist, stating that Courtney "retains just enough disbelief to

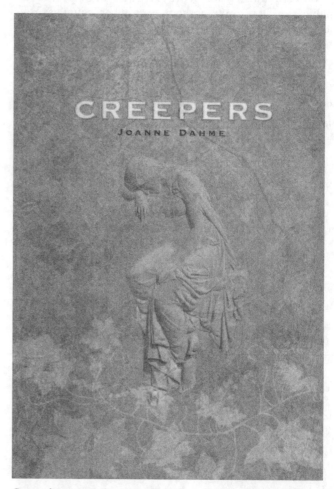

Cover of Joanne Dahme's young-adult novel Creepers, *featuring artwork by Frances J. Soo Ping Chow.* (Running Press, 2008. Illustration by Frances J. Soo Ping Chow. Reproduced by permission.)

prove credible amid the graveyard gloom and irrational ivy." In *Publishers Weekly,* a contributor described the novel's setting as "more atmospheric than scary" and noted that readers "can enjoy Dahme's New England-style hauntings without risking their sleep."

Set in fourteenth-century England, *The Plague* concerns Nell, an orphaned fifteen year old who is summoned to the palace to serve as a double for the king's daughter. When Princess Joan dies, however, the Black Prince makes plans for Nell to enter an arranged marriage, and in response she flees across plague-infested Europe. "Dahme's strengths are in the moods she creates," observed *New York Times* reviewer Sophie Pollitt-Cohen. "Everything feels dark, wet and scary. She conveys the panic of being chased by terrible things—Black Prince and black plague—one is helpless to stop."

Biographical and Critical Sources

PERIODICALS

Kirkus Reviews, July 1, 2008, review of *Creepers.*
New York Times, August 13, 2009, Sophie Pollitt-Cohen, review of *The Plague,* p. 75.
Publishers Weekly, August 25, 2008, review of *Creepers,* p. 75.

ONLINE

Perseus Books Group Web site, http://www.perseusbooks group.com/ (October 10, 2009), "Joanne Dahme."*

*　　*　　*

DAVIS, Rich 1958-

Personal

Born 1958; married; wife's name, Angie.

Addresses

Home—Siloam Springs, AR. *E-mail*—frontporch creations@gmail.com.

Career

Illustrator and graphic-design artist. Dayspring Greeting Cards, Siloam Springs, AR, creator of greeting card artwork for twenty-one years; creator of "Pick and Draw" children's drawing game. Presenter at schools.

Awards, Honors

Two national greeting card award nominations; Beginning Readers list inclusion, Arkansas Bureau of Education and Research, 2009, for *Tiny on the Farm.*

Illustrator

Cari Meister, *Tiny's Bath,* Viking (New York, NY), 1998.
Cari Meister, *When Tiny Was Tiny,* Viking (New York, NY), 1999.
Cari Meister, *Tiny Goes to the Library,* Viking (New York, NY), 2000.
Cari Meister, *Tiny the Snow Dog,* Viking (New York, NY), 2001.
Joan Holub, *Scat Cats!,* Viking (New York, NY), 2001.
K.R. Hamilton, *Firefighters to the Rescue!,* Viking (New York, NY), 2005.
Cari Meister, *Tiny Goes Camping,* Viking (New York, NY), 2006.
Cari Meister, *Tiny on the Farm,* Viking (New York, NY), 2008.

Also illustrator of coloring books.

Sidelights

In addition to producing artwork for greeting cards and the "Pick and Draw" children's game, which encourages imaginative drawing, Rich Davis has also joined with several authors to create picture books and beginning readers for youngsters. Together with writer Cari Meister, Davis brings to life the larger-than-life character of Tiny, an oversized dog that is featured in seven books geared to help strengthen the skills of newly independent readers. In addition, his popular "Pick and Draw" game is used in occupational therapy, creative-writing classes, children's grief counseling, art education, and home-school curricula.

The first book in Meister's series, *Tiny's Bath,* introduces the large canine and his nameless owner, a young boy who is considerably smaller than his beloved pet. Noticing that Tiny needs a wash, the boy tries to find an adequately sized tub and finally settles on a backyard swimming pool. After a bit of a struggle, the boy scrubs Tiny clean, only to have the dog run off for a roll in the nearest mud puddle. In her *Horn Book* review of *Tiny's Bath,* Betty Carter wrote that Meister and Davis succeed at developing a book suitable for emergent readers because the "illustrations mirror text, providing clues that support readers as they decipher both words and events." In *Booklist* John Peters also offered favorable comments about *Tiny's Bath,* remarking that the loving "bond between the two is evident in the simple illustrations."

Other adventures featuring Tiny and his owner have followed, including *Tiny Goes to the Library, Tiny Goes Camping,* and *Tiny on the Farm.* Tiny accompanies the young boy to check out books in *Tiny Goes to the Library,* only to discover that dogs cannot enter the building. When the boy returns with a wagon-load of books, Tiny quickly steps into service, pulling the large load home. The large canine also becomes useful in *Tiny Goes Camping.* After creating a mess in the kitchen while preparing for their backyard camping trip, Tiny offers a simple solution when the boy discovers that his pet cannot fit inside the small tent. The gigantic dog again provides a valuable service in *Tiny on the Farm.* During a visit at Uncle John's farm a new batch of kittens are lost, but with the help of Tiny and his young owner, the furry creatures are soon found to be safe and sound in the barnyard. Reviewing *Tiny Goes to the Library* in *School Library Journal,* DeAnn Tabuchi predicted that Meister's narrative and Davis's "expressive, cartoonlike, brightly colored illustrations will have beginning readers clamoring for more." Writing in the same periodical, Mary Hazelton suggested that the book's "illustrations make a significant contribution to the story" in *Tiny Goes Camping,* and described Davis's artwork for *Tiny on the Farm* as "cartoon-like and cheery, providing visual clues for the more difficult vocabulary."

In addition to his books with Meister, Davis has also worked with Joan Holub to produce *Scat Cats!* and with K.R. Hamilton to create *Firefighters to the Rescue!* In *Scat Cats!* two young children find their home overrun by a large number of cats, some of them calmly napping on the furniture and others involved in mischievous activities. Tired of the chaos, the boy and girl chase away all of the creatures, only to find the newly quiet house to be far too dull and boring. In the end, the pair invites the assorted felines back inside, reaffirming their loving attachment to the furry pets. Writing in *Booklist,* Stephanie Zvirin applauded the "loosely sketched, double-spread cartoon illustrations" in *Scat Cats!,* which Zvirin praised as "loaded with entertaining kitty antics."

Rich Davis creates amusing art that draws readers into Carl Meister's rural-themed picture book Tiny on the Farm. (Illustration copyright © 2008 by Rich Davis. Reproduced by permission.)

Set in small-town America, *Firefighters to the Rescue!* offers young readers an energetic story about first responders. Featuring the excitement of rushing to an emergency and rescuing a young boy's puppy from a burning house, *Firefighters to the Rescue!* also covers more mundane, day-to-day tasks such as cleaning the fire station and preparing communal meals. "Hamilton and Davis have created a sure fire hit," claimed a *Kirkus Reviews* critic, the reviewer adding that the cars featured in the illustrations for *Firefighters to the Rescue!* are "glorious in their retro colors and designs."

Biographical and Critical Sources

PERIODICALS

Booklist, March 15, 1999, John Peters, review of *Tiny's Bath,* p. 1338; October 1, 1999, Hazel Rochman, review of *When Tiny Was Tiny,* p. 336; April 15, 2000, Ilene Cooper, review of *Tiny Goes to the Library,* p. 1555; April 15, 2001, Stephanie Zvirin, review of *Scat Cats!,* p. 1568; November 1, 2001, Gillian Engberg, review of *Tiny the Snow Dog,* p. 487; May 15, 2005, John Peters, review of *Firefighters to the Rescue!,* p. 1665; May 1, 2006, Hazel Rochman, review of *Tiny Goes Camping,* p. 93.

Horn Book, May, 1999, Betty Carter, review of *Tiny's Bath,* p. 335.

Kirkus Reviews, May 15, 2005, review of *Firefighters to the Rescue!,* p. 589; April 15, 2008, review of *Tiny on the Farm.*

School Library Journal, July, 2000, DeAnn Tabuchi, review of *Tiny Goes to the Library,* p. 83; August, 2001, Louie Lahana, review of *Scat Cats!,* p. 153; October, 2001, Olga R. Kuharets, review of *Tiny the Snow Dog,* p. 126; July, 2005, Kathleen Meulen, review of *Firefighters to the Rescue!,* p. 74; June, 2006, Mary Hazelton, review of *Tiny Goes Camping,* p. 123; May, 2008, Mary Hazelton, review of *Tiny on the Farm,* p. 103.

ONLINE

Rich Davis Home Page, http://www.richdavis.freeweb space.com (October 26, 2009).

Rich Davis Web Log, http://richdavis1.wordpress.com (October 26, 2009).

*   *   *

DUMBLETON, Mike 1948-

Personal

Born January 6, 1948, in Chipping Norton, England; immigrated to Australia, 1972; son of Ernest George (an industrial planner) and Susie Dumbleton; married Linda Jean Collard (a teacher), June 28, 1969; children:

Jay, Luke, Nathan. *Education:* Nottingham University, B.Ed., 1970, teaching certificate, 1970. *Religion:* Christian. *Hobbies and other interests:* Jazz, basketball, soccer, tennis.

Addresses

Home—New York, NY; and Australia. *Agent*—Jenny Darling & Associates, P.O. Box 413, Toorak, Victoria 3142, Australia.

Career

Author and literacy consultant. South Australian Education Department, Adelaide, South Australia, Australia, English teacher, 1973-74, faculty coordinator, 1975-87, deputy principal, 1988, literacy project coordinator, beginning 1989; currently serves as an English and literacy coordinator at an Adelaide high school.

Member

South Australian Writers' Centre.

Awards, Honors

"Children's Books Mean Business" listee, American Booksellers Association/Children's Book Council, and Notable Book selection, Australian Children's Book Council (ACBC), both 1992, both for *Dial-a-Croc;* literature grant, South Australian Department for the Arts and Cultural Heritage, 1993; Writers' Performance and Presentation Course grant, Literature Board of the Australia Council, 1994; Notable Book selection, ACBC, 1994, for *Mr. Knuckles* and *Granny O'Brien and the Diamonds of Selmore,* 2000, for *Downsized,* 2002, for *Passing On;* South Australian Government literature grant, 2001; Notable Book selection, ACBC, 2002, Speech Pathology Australia Book of the Year, 2003, and National Simultaneous Storytime Book, 2004, all for *Muddled-up Farm;* Arts South Australia Festival Awards for Literature shortlist, 2004, for *Watch out for Jamie Joel;* Minister's Award 2005, for outstanding contribution to improving literacy; Picture Book to Performance winner, 2007, and Notable Book selection, ACBC, 2008, both for *Cat.*

Writings

Dial-a-Croc, illustrated by Ann James, Orchard (New York, NY), 1991.

Granny O'Brien and the Diamonds of Selmore, illustrated by David Cox, Omnibus (Norwood, South Australia, Australia), 1993.

Mrs Watson's Goat ("Connections" series, Volume 7), illustrated by Marina McAllan, Macmillan (South Melbourne, Melbourne, Australia), 1993.

Mr Knuckles, Allen & Unwin (St. Leonards, New South Wales, Australia), 1993.

Ms MacDonald's Farm, illustrated by Ann Whitehead, Macmillan (South Melbourne, Victoria, Australia), 1994.

I Hate Brussels Sprouts, illustrated by Rebecca Pannell, Macmillan (South Melbourne, Victoria, Australia), 1994.

Pumped Up! (short stories), illustrated by Shane Nagle, Allen & Unwin (St. Leonards, New South Wales, Australia), 1995.

Let's Escape, illustrated by Kim Gamble, Scholastic Australia (Gosford, New South Wales, Australia), 1997.

Downsized, illustrated by Tom Jellet, Random House (Milsons Point, New South Wales, Australia), 1999.

Muddled-up Farm, illustrated by Jobi Murphy, Random House (Milsons Point, New South Wales, Australia), 2001.

Passing On, illustrated by Terry Denton, Red Fox (Milsons Point, New South Wales, Australia), 2001.

Watch out for Jamie Joel (young-adult novel), Allen & Unwin (Crows Nest, New South Wales, Australia), 2003.

Giraffe in a Scarf, illustrated by Donna Gynell, Era Publications (Brooklyn Park, South Australia, Australia), 2007.

Hippopotamouse, illustrated by Nina Rycroft, Era Publications (Brooklyn Park, South Australia, Australia), 2007.

You Must Be Joking!, illustrated by Greg Holfeld, Working Title Press (Kingswood, South Australia, Australia), 2007.

Cat, illustrated by Craig Smith, Working Title Press (Kingswood, South Australia, Australia), 2007, Kane/Miller (La Jolla, CA), 2008.

Jet-ball, illustrated by Roger Roberts, Era Publications (Brooklyn Park, South Australia, Australia), 2008.

One Cool Kangaroo, illustrated by Richard Dall, Era Publications (Brooklyn Park, South Australia, Australia), 2008.

What Will Baby Do?, illustrated by Craig Smith, Working Title Press (Kingswood, South Australia, Australia), 2009.

OTHER

Can Cards, Hawker Brownlow Education, 1989.

(With Jeff Guess) Hands on Poetry—A Practical Anthology, Twilight Publishers, 1991, Educational Supplies, 1993.

Real Writing across the Curriculum: A Practical Guide to Improving and Publishing Student Work, South Australian Education Department, 1993.

(With Ken Loutain) *Addressing Literacy in Society and Environment,* Curriculum (Carlton South, Victoria, Australia), 1999.

(With Ken Loutain) *Addressing Literacy in Science,* Curriculum (Carlton South, Victoria, Australia), 1999.

(With Ken Loutain) *Addressing Literacy in the Arts,* Curriculum (Carlton South, Victoria, Australia), 1999.

Also author of *Online Literacy* (Web site for South Australia Department of Education, Training, and Employment), 1999.

Adaptations

Mr Knuckles was adapted for the stage by South Australian Children's Theatre Company, 1994; *Pumped Up!* was adapted for television by Australian Broadcasting Corporation (ABC), 1996; *Dial-a-Croc* and three other stories were read by Mark Mitchell on audiocassette for ABC, 1995; *Muddled-up Farm* was adapted for television by ABC, 2003; *Watch out for Jamie Joel* was adapted as an audio book, Louis Braille Audio, 2004; *Cat* was adapted for the stage by Windmill Performing Arts, 2007.

Sidelights

Australian writer and literacy consultant Mike Dumbleton is the author of several well-received books for children and teens, including *Mr Knuckles, Cat,* and *Watch out for Jamie Joel.* "I started writing when I decided I wasn't getting any better at basketball, and my three children were old enough to allow me some uninterrupted time," he once told *SATA.* "I began devising educational texts for teachers at the same time that I started writing picture book manuscripts, and it was a proposal for an educational text which was first accepted and published in Australia. *Dial-a-Croc* was accepted soon afterwards.

Dumbleton became an international success with his first book for children, *Dial-a-Croc,* in which a girl captures a crocodile in the Australian outback and puts him to work earning her fame and fortune. "This is a great romp of a book," avowed Judith Sharman in *Books for Keeps,* praising Dumbleton's spunky heroine and the book's silly antics. "The initial idea for *Dial-a-Croc* came from a play on words whereby you can reverse the syllables in the word crocodile to make the name Dial-a-Croc," the author once told *SATA.* "The early sequences in which Vanessa heads off into the Outback are based on a real Vanessa who is mentioned in the dedication, along with my sons. She is a friend of the family and was my eldest son's girlfriend at the time. She is a self-assured, purposeful young lady, and visited us wearing fashionable safari shorts when I was planning the book. It gave me just the image I needed for the Vanessa in the story with her 'jungle jeans' and 'hunting jacket,' to which I added her 'bull whip, camping knife' and other suitable accessories before letting her venture into the 'Outback, beyond the Back of Beyond.'"

Silliness is again the point in Dumbleton's picture book *Mr Knuckles,* in which Tracey arrives at school on the first day of term to find that her teacher is a gorilla. The author spins this premise to its logical—and absurd—limits, including having the class take a field trip to Africa. He leaves behind the silliness in *Downsized,* in which a girl narrates what happens to her family after her father loses his job. First, everything begins to get smaller, as the family moves to a smaller house, gets a smaller car, and gives away their two large dogs. Even her father begins to seem smaller as his interest in what

is going on around him shrinks. When the narrator finally goads her dad into helping her redesign the back garden in their shabby new house, the family is starting to get back on its feet emotionally. *Downsized* "conveys with sensitivity and gentle humour the difficulties faced by a family when Dad has lost his job and is not coping well with that situation," observed Anne Hanzl in *Magpies.* Hanzl also noted that the author and illustrator work well together, each augmenting what the other reveals.

Dumbleton's picture book *Cat,* illustrated by Craig Smith, depicts a day in the life of a lively, orange-striped feline. The work opens as Cat escapes the clutches of an angry dog by climbing a tree and then unsuccessfully attempts to catch a tasty meal by pursuing a bird and a mouse. Things do not get much better as the day wears on: Cat gets doused by a sprinkler and barely avoids getting hit by a youngster on a bicycle. Despite the chaos and near misses, the night ends well as Cat finds a warm, welcome spot in the house. Dumbleton tells his tale using few words, a fact noted by critics. "An appealing feature of this book is that early readers can easily read the text," stated a contributor in *Kirkus Reviews,* and Ieva Bates, writing in *School Library Journal,* noted that the story "is told mainly through the pictures." Discussing the origins of the work on his home page, Dumbleton remarked: "The idea for *Cat* came from reversing the words cat and dog then seeing the potential for a mixture of dramatic tension and comedy which could be developed in the visual text. I remember 'holding my breath' and wondering if a series of similar reversals could be sustained for the length of a picture book."

Watch out for Jamie Joel, Dumbleton's first young-adult novel, centers on the title character, a bright but

Mike Dumbleton follows the active life of a typical feline in the aptly titled Cat, *featuring artwork by Craig Smith.* (Illustration copyright © 2007 by Craig Smith. Reproduced by permission.)

troubled high school student, and her relationship with Craig Eliot, the deputy principal at her school. Although Eliot recognizes Jamie's potential and tries to form a personal connection with her, the temperamental teen gets suspended and runs away from home, where she lives with her abusive aunt. When another truant is involved in a horrible accident, Jamie realizes that she must regain control of her life. In *School Library Journal*, Susan M. Hunter complimented the novel, which is told in the alternating voices of the two main characters. Eliot's "harried moments and humorous self-reflections are portrayed in a first-person narrative that alternates sharply with Jamie's detached third-person portrayal," Hunter wrote. Reviewing *Watch out for Jamie Joel* in *Kliatt*, Nancy Chrismer described the work as "a realistic picture of life in today's high schools, and [it] draws the reader into caring about both characters."

Biographical and Critical Sources

PERIODICALS

Books for Keeps, May, 1993, Judith Sharman, review of *Dial-a-Croc,* p. 8; November, 1996, Pam Harwood, review of *Mr Knuckles,* p. 9.

Kirkus Reviews, February 15, 2008, review of *Cat.*

Kliatt, November, 2004, Nancy Chrismer, review of *Watch out for Jamie Joel,* p. 16.

Magpies, September, 1999, Anne Hanzl, review of *Downsized,* p. 30.

School Library Journal, June, 2004, Susan W. Hunter, review of *Watch out for Jamie Joel,* p. 138; April, 2008, Ieva Bates, review of *Cat,* p. 106.

ONLINE

Mike Dumbleton Home Page, http://www.mikedumbleton. cjb.net (October 10, 2009).

South Australian Writers' Centre Web site, http://www. sawc.org.au/ (October 10, 2009), "Mike Dumbleton."*

*   *   *

DUNGY, Anthony
See DUNGY, Tony

*   *   *

DUNGY, Tony 1955-
(Anthony Dungy)

Personal

Born October 6, 1955, in Jackson, MI; son of Wilbur (a physiology professor) and Cleomae (an English teacher) Dungy; married Lauren Harris, c. 1982; children: Tiara,

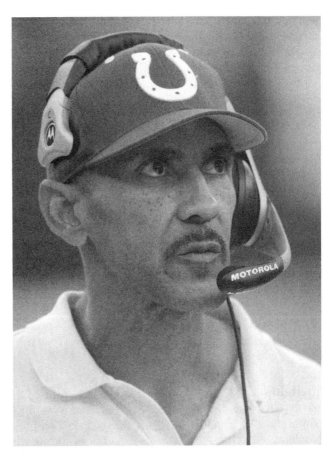

Tony Dungy (Photograph by Tom Strattman, AP/Wide World Photos.)

Jade, James (died 2005), Eric, Jordan, Justin. *Education:* University of Minnesota, BA, 1977. *Religion:* Evangelical Christian.

Addresses
Home—FL.

Career
Football coach. Pittsburgh Steelers, defensive back, 1977-78, defensive assistant, 1981, defensive backs coach, 1982-83, defensive coordinator, 1984-88; San Francisco 49ers, defensive back, 1979; University of Minnesota, defensive backs coach, 1980; Kansas City Chiefs, defensive backs coach, 1989-91; Minnesota Vikings, defensive coordinator, 1992-95; Tampa Bay Buccaneers, head coach, 1996-2001; Indianapolis Colts, head coach, 2002-09. Football analyst for television program *Football Night in America,* NBC, beginning 2009. Active in community service organizations, including (and founder) Mentors for Life, All Pro Dad, and Abe Brown Ministries. American Diabetes Association, national spokesman for African-American Program and School Walk for Diabetes campaign, 2003. Member, President's Council on Service and Civic Participation, 2007.

Awards, Honors
Member of 1979 Super Bowl Champion Pittsburgh Steelers; National Fatherhood Initiative, Fatherhood

Award, 2002; coach of 2007 Super Bowl Champion Indianapolis Colts; inducted into Society of World Changers, Indiana Wesleyan University, 2008.

Writings

(With Nathan Whitaker) *Quiet Strength: The Principles, Practices, and Priorities of a Winning Life,* Tyndale House (Carol Stream, IL), 2007.

Quiet Strength: Men's Bible Study, Group Pub. (Loveland, CO), 2007.

(Author of foreword) Warrick Dunn, *Running for My Life,* HarperEntertainment (New York, NY), 2008.

You Can Do It!, illustrated by Amy June Bates, Little Simon Inspirations (New York, NY), 2008.

(With Nathan Whitaker) *Uncommon: Finding Your Path to Significance,* Tyndale House (Carol Stream, IL), 2009.

Adaptations

Quiet Strength was adapted for audiobook by Tyndale Audio (Carol Stream, IL), 2007.

Sidelights

The first African-American coach to head a winning team in the NFL Super Bowl, Tony Dungy is known for his talents as a coach as well as his ability to inspire a winning attitude in less-than-winning teams. In 2007, when Dungy led the Indianapolis Colts to their first Super Bowl victory in over twenty years, he also earned another "first" when he became the first African-American coach ever to win the championship.

In addition to his triumphs on the football field, Dungy's personal life has also been inspirational. Active in community service organizations that mentor and otherwise minister to young people, he wrote the bestselling books *Quiet Strength: The Principles, Practices, and Priorities of a Winning Life* and *Uncommon: Finding Your Path to Significance* as a way to share his views on personal responsibility, the importance of family, and his faith in God. Hoping to inspire younger readers, Dungy shares his memories of his younger brother, Linden, in the picture book *You Can Do It!*

Growing up in Jackson, Michigan, Dungy benefited from a family that valued intellectual as well as athletic success. Despite the influence of his father, a college professor, and his mother, a high-school English teacher, the young Dungy was drawn to sports, and enjoyed attending Detroit Lions football games with his father. He played basketball and football in high school, and his talents on the football field were noted by a University of Minnesota head coach who encouraged Dungy to join his team. Dungy was part of the starting lineup on his freshman year at the University of Minnesota, and by his senior year he ranked fourth in total offense among all players in the history of the Big Ten conference.

After graduation, Dungy coached briefly at the University of Minnesota, then moved to Pennsylvania to serve as assistant coach to the Pittsburgh Steelers. In 1989 he signed on as defensive backs coach for the Kansas City Chiefs, and in 1992 he became defensive coordinator of the Minnesota Vikings. In 1996 Dungy became head coach of the Tampa Bay Buccaneers, the least-successful team in the history of the league. Within his first year, the team advanced in the standings, abandoning the last-place status it had held for several years. Five years later he was offered the head coaching spot with the Indianapolis Colts, leading to the team's historic 2007 NFL win.

In *You Can Do It!* Dungy shares an inspiring message about perseverance and loyalty by telling the story of Linden, a boy who discovers his unique gifts and decides on his mission in life during a trip to the dentist. "Dungy is a natural storyteller," asserted *School Library Journal* contributor Lisa Egly Lehmuller, and in *You Can Do It!* the author shares his Christian faith and the support of his "warm family." Dubbing the book an "earnest effort" from the noted football coach, a *Kirkus Reviews* writer also praised Amy June Bates' "attractive" artwork, noting that it "depict[s] the close-knit, loving African-American family with warmth."

Discussing his role as a coach and mentor with *Black Enterprise* interviewer Tennille M. Robinson, Dungy noted: "I tell our guys all the time to be very positive role models, because there are so many people watching everything they do. And you do have those who say, 'Hey my private life should be private. As long as I do my job on the field, that's what everybody should be concerned about.' That is true, that's what we get paid for. But when we're held up as icons in society, then I think we have a responsibility to do more than that. We owe our community; we owe our country a little bit more than just being a good player. And African American boys, in particular, need to see guys doing well not only on the field with their athletic ability, but with what they are doing off the field as well."

Biographical and Critical Sources

BOOKS

Dungy, Tony, with Nathan Whitaker, *Quiet Strength: The Principles, Practices, and Priorities of a Winning Life,* Tyndale House Publishers (Carol Stream, IL), 2007.

PERIODICALS

Black Enterprise, November, 2007, Tennille M. Robinson, "Backtalk with Tony Dungy," p. 132.

Ebony, December, 2007, Lynette Holloway, review of *Quiet Strength: The Principles, Practices, and Priorities of a Winning Life,* p. 37; May, 2009, review of *Uncommon: Finding Your Path to Significance,* p. 49; September, 2008, review of *You Can Do It!,* p. 55.

Essence, July, 2008, review of *You Can Do It!,* p. 66.

Kirkus Reviews, June 15, 2008, review of *You Can Do It!*

Newsweek, July 16, 2007, "Coach, Teacher, Believer; For Tony Dungy, There's a Lot More to Life than Winning the Super Bowl," p. 52.

School Library Journal, August, 2008, Lisa Egly Lehmuller, review of *You Can Do It!,* p. 88.

Sports Illustrated, February 12, 2007, Peter King, "A Father's Wish," p. 47.*

E-F

EBBELER, Jeff
See EBBELER, Jeffrey

*   *   *

EBBELER, Jeffrey 1974-
(Jeff Ebbeler)

Personal

Born 1974; married; wife's name Eileen (an artist). *Education:* Art Academy of Cincinnati.

Addresses

Home—Chicago, IL. *Agent*—Portfolio Solutions LLC., 136 Jameson Hill Rd., Clinton Corners, NY 12514. *E-mail*—jeff@jeffillustration.com.

Career

Illustrator, muralist, paper engineer, and graphic artist. Publications International, Ltd., Lincolnwood, IL, former art director. Musician, performing drums with Chicago bands; puppet-maker and puppeteer. Presenter at schools and museums.

Member

Society of Children's Book Writers and Illustrators, Picture Book Artists Association.

Illustrator

Learn and Grow!: Four Lift-a-flap Books, Publications International (Lincolnwood, IL), 2005.

Susanna Leonard Hill, *Punxsutawney Phyllis,* Holiday House (New York, NY), 2005.

Ellen Olson-Brown and Brian Claflin, *Bake You a Pie* (with CD), Tricycle Press (Berkeley, CA), 2006.

Jeffery L. Schatzer, *The Runaway Garden: A Delicious Story That's Good for You, Too!,* Mitten Press (Ann Arbor, MI), 2007.

Judy Cox, *One Is a Feast for Mouse: A Thanksgiving Tale,* Holiday House (New York, NY), 2008.

(With Steve Smallman) Gwen Ellis, *Our Together-Time Bible,* Thomas Nelson (Nashville, TN), 2008.

Charity Nebbe, *Our Walk in the Woods,* Mitten Press (Ann Arbor, MI), 2008.

Lori Sunshine, *I'm Really Not Tired,* Flashlight Press, 2008.

David Michael Slater, *Battle of the Books,* Magic Wagon (Edina, MN), 2009.

Jingle Bells (board books), CandyCane Press, 2009.

David Michael Slater, *Milo and the Monster,* Magic Wagon (Edina, MN), 2009.

Judy Cox, *Cinco de Mouse-O!,* Holiday House (New York, NY), 2010.

(As Jeff Ebbeler) Kelly Chapman, *A Warrior Prince for God,* Harvest House, 2010.

ILLUSTRATOR, UNDER NAME JEFF EBBELER; "MAIN STREET SCHOOL" SERIES

Anastasia Suen, *Cutting in Line Isn't Fair!,* Magic Wagon (Edina, MN), 2008.

Anastasia Suen, *Helping Sophia,* Magic Wagon (Edina, MN), 2008.

Anastasia Suen, *Raising the Flag,* Magic Wagon (Edina, MN), 2008.

Anastasia Suen, *Scissors, Paper, and Sharing,* Magic Wagon (Edina, MN), 2008.

Anastasia Suen, *Show Some Respect,* Magic Wagon (Edina, MN), 2008.

Anastasia Suen, *Times Tables Cheat,* Magic Wagon (Edina, MN), 2008.

Anastasia Suen, *Don't Forget!: A Responsibility Story,* Magic Wagon (Edina, MN), 2009.

Anastasia Suen, *Game Over: Dealing with Bullies,* Magic Wagon (Edina, MN), 2009.

Anastasia Suen, *Girls Can, Too!: A Tolerance Story,* Magic Wagon (Edina, MN), 2009.

Anastasia Suen, *A Good Team: A Cooperation Story,* Magic Wagon (Edina, MN), 2009.

Anastasia Suen, *Trust Me: A Loyalty Story,* Magic Wagon (Edina, MN), 2009.

Anastasia Suen, *Vote for Isaiah!: A Citizenship Story,* Magic Wagon (Edina, MN), 2009.

Sidelights

After working for several years as an art director for a Midwestern publisher, Jeffrey Ebbeler made the transition to becoming an illustrator and artist while still retaining his ties to children's literature. In addition to working as a muralist and magazine illustrator, Ebbeler creates artwork for book covers as well as illustrations for picture books such as *Our Walk in the Woods* by Charity Nebbe, *One Is a Feast for Mouse: A Thanksgiving Tale* by Judy Cox, and *Bake You a Pie* by Ellen Olson-Brown. Reviewing Ebbeler's art for *Bake You a Pie*, a *Kirkus Reviews* writer noted that the artist contributes "vibrant pictures . . . in acrylic paint and black pencil, and full of cheeky humor."

In *One Is a Feast for Mouse* Ebbeler brings to life Cox's story about a tiny mouse that plans to feast on a human family's Thanksgiving leftovers until the family cat surprises him in his foraging efforts. Praising Cox's tale as "lively," *Booklist* contributor Shelle Rosenfeld added that Ebbeler's "colorful, animated, mixed-media illustrations" feature "dramatic" perspectives. The artist's "bright acrylic paintings" mirror a text that "gets funnier" with every page, noted *Horn Book* Chelsey Philpot, and in *Kirkus Reviews* a contributor cited the

Jeffrey Ebbeler creates the engaging artwork that captivates readers of Judy Cox's **One Is a Feast for Mouse.** (Illustration copyright © 2008 by Jeffrey Ebbeler. Reproduced by permission of Holiday House, Inc.)

book's colorful double-page images as "mak[ing] . . . the most of the humor made available by situation and scale." Ebbeler's "whimsical . . . illustrations. . . . are a perfect complement to the story," concluded *School Library Journal* reviewer Sally R. Dow, the critic dubbing *One Is a Feast for Mouse* "a wonderful holiday read-aloud."

Punxsutawney Phyllis is Susanna Leonard Hill's feminist take on a whimsical American tradition: Groundhog Day. Phyllis is a young groundhog who aspires to follow in the footsteps of her revered uncle, Punxsutawney Phil. Uncle Phil is the resident groundhog of Punxsutawney, Pennsylvania, as well as the most-referenced groundhog of all time. Although Phyllis is discouraged from her dream because Phil is a boy groundhog, the young rodent is not to be dissuaded. In *Children's Bookwatch* a critic concluded that "Ebbeler's whimsical color drawings lend to an inviting story," while in *School Library Journal* Linda Staskus cited the artist's depiction of "bright and lush" forest scenes and "rustic, cozy" groundhog burrows.

Biographical and Critical Sources

PERIODICALS

Booklist, October 1, 2008, Shelle Rosenfeld, review of *One Is a Feast for Mouse: A Thanksgiving Tale,* p. 47.
Children's Bookwatch, November, 2005, review of *Punxsutawney Phyllis.*
Horn Book, November-December, 2008, Chelsey Philpot, review of *One Is a Feast for Mouse,* p. 648.
Kirkus Reviews, October 1, 2006, review of *Bake You a Pie,* p. 1021; August 15, 2008, review of *One Is a Feast for Mouse.*
School Library Journal, October, 2005, Linda Staskus, review of *Punxsutawney Phyllis,* p. 116; November, 2006, Linda Staskus, review of *Bake You a Pie,* p. 108; September, 2008, Sally R., review of *One Is a Feast for Mouse,* p. 144; December, 2008, Susan E. Murray, review of *I'm Really Not Tired,* p. 104.

ONLINE

Jeffrey Ebbeler Home Page, http://www.jeffillustration.com (October 28, 2009).*

*   *   *

ELLIOTT, Zetta

Personal

Born in Ajax, Ontario, Canada; daughter of George (a teacher) and Frances (a teacher) Hood. *Education:* Bishop's University (Lennoxville, PQ), B.A. (humanities;

Zetta Elliot (Reproduced by permission.)

with distinction), 1993; New York University, M.A. (American studies), 1997, Ph.D. (American studies), 2003. *Hobbies and other interests:* Bird watching, African-American history, gardens, reading.

Addresses

Home—Brooklyn, NY. *E-mail*—zettaelliott@yahoo.com.

Career

Playwright, poet, novelist, and educator. Visiting assistant professor at Ohio University, 2002-03, Louisiana State University, 2005-06, and Mt. Holyoke College, 2006-09; University of Massachusetts, Amherst, lecturer in Women's Studies Program, 2008. Frederick Douglass Creative Arts Center, New York, NY, instructor in after-school program. Presenter at conferences. Gibraltar Point International Artists' Residency, fellow, 2006.

Awards, Honors

New Voices Award Honor designation, 2005, for short story "Bird"; Chicago Dramatists' Many Voices Project award finalist, 2006, for *Nothing but a Woman;* Best Children's Books of the Year designation, Bank Street College of Education, Notable Children's Book selection, American Library Association, Paterson Prize for Books for Young People, and Ezra Jack Keats Book Award, all 2009, all for *Bird.*

Writings

Bird, illustrated by Shadra Strickland, Lee & Low Books (New York, NY), 2008.

A Wish after Midnight (young-adult novel), Rosetta Press, 2009.

PLAYS

Noting but a Woman, staged in Chicago, IL, 2006.
Quality (short play), staged in New York, NY, 2007.
girl/power, staged at New Perspectives Theater, New York, NY, 2008.
Connor's Boy, staged at Karamu House, Cleveland, OH, 2008.
Ten-minute Plays (contains "Stash," "Quality," "Innocents," "Self/Preservation," and "Her Vow"), Rosetta Press, 2009.
Ten-minute Plays (contains "girl/power," "Brotherhood," "Deluged," and "Men of All Work"), Rosetta Press, 2009.
Three Plays (contains "Connor's Boy," "Mother Load," and "Beast"), Rosetta Press, 2009.

OTHER

Stranger in the Family (memoir), Rosetta Press, 2009.

Contributor to anthologies, including *Coloring Book: An Eclectic Anthology of Fiction and Poetry by Multicultural Writers,* edited by Boice-Terrel Allen, Rattlecat Press, 2003; *T-dot Griots: An Anthology of Toronto's Black Storytellers,* edited by Karen Richardson and Steven Green, Trafford Publishing, 2006; *Check the Rhyme: An Anthology of Female Poets and Emcees,* edited by DuEwa M. Frazier, Lit Noire Publishing, 2006; and *The Ringing Ear: Black Poets Lean South,* edited by Nikky Finney, University of Georgia Press (Athens, GA), 2007. Contributor to periodicals, including *Black Arts Quarterly, Black Arts Quarterly, thirdspace, Horn Book, WarpLand,* and *Rain and Thunder.*

Sidelights

Zetta Elliott, a writer and cultural critic with a black feminist perspective, is the author of *Bird,* an award-winning picture book about a child's attempts to cope with loss. Elliott is also an accomplished poet and playwright, and many of her works examine the importance of family and tradition, the inevitability of change, and the power of art. "Ultimately, I try to tell stories that give voice to the diverse realities of children," Elliott remarked on her home page. "I write as much for parents as I do for their children, because sometimes adults need the simple instruction a picture book can provide. I write books my parents never had the chance to read to me. I write the books I wish I had had as a child."

A native of Canada, Elliott developed an early interest in literature. As she told a *Color Online* interviewer, "I read constantly as a child. My parents were divorced, things at home weren't great, and my mother basically was either at work or immersed in a book. So I followed her lead." As a teen, Elliott read a great deal of British literature, including the works of Charles Dickens, the Brontë sisters, Jane Austen, George Eliot, and Frances Hodgson Burnett. As a child, she was drawn to stories featuring children of color, although very few of these were available in Canada at that time. As she recalled in an interview on the *Embracing the Child* Web site, "I loved the books of Ezra Jack Keats—when I look back at those books now, I'm grateful for the way Keats both normalized urban children, and revealed the beauty of their lives." Elliott credits her mother, a kindergarten teacher, with introducing her to Keats's work.

At age fifteen, encouraged by her English teacher, Elliott decided to become a writer. She found her calling during her senior year of college, when she was introduced to the works of Toni Morrison and Jamaica Kincaid. "Their writing changed the course of my life," Elliot recalled in her *Color Online* interview. "Once I discovered the tradition of black women writers, I knew where I belonged." She was also impressed by a keynote address given by Morrison in 2003 at the College of St. Catherine in Minnesota. Morrison noted the important distinction between being a writer and being an author: one needs permission to be the latter, but not the former. Undeterred by years of rejection by traditional publishers, Elliott continued to write and ultimately started her own imprint, Rosetta Press. She encourages all marginalized writers to make their voices heard, quoting the words of black feminist poet June Jordan: "We are the ones we have been waiting for."

In *Bird*, illustrated by Shadra Strickland, Elliott introduces Mehkai, a young African-American boy with a love of drawing who idolizes his older brother, Marcus, a graffiti artist. After Marcus becomes addicted to drugs, is expelled from their home, and dies, Mehkai—nicknamed Bird—turns to his late grandfather's friend for wisdom and guidance. "To me, [*Bird* is] about a child's love of art, and the process by which he learns to use his creativity to make sense of the world around him," the author told a *Brown Bookshelf* interviewer. "The book deals with some difficult, serious issues that children unfortunately have to confront: death, addiction, grief. But I don't think of *Bird* as a book about those things—it's the child's response that matters, and the help he receives from those who love him."

Bird received a Paterson prize, among other honors, and garnered strong reviews. "The simplicity of the narrative belies the complexity of the themes," a *Publishers Weekly* critic noted, and Kate McClelland, writing in *School Library Journal,* called the work "a sad truth of contemporary life successfully leavened with hopeful optimism." "With unusual depth and raw conviction," stated a contributor in *Kirkus Reviews,* "Elliott's child-centered narrative excels in this debut."

Biographical and Critical Sources

PERIODICALS

Booklist, November 1, 2008, Hazel Rochman, review of *Bird,* p. 54.

Kirkus Reviews, September 1, 2008, review of *Bird.*
Publishers Weekly, October 20, 2008, review of *Bird,* p. 50.
School Library Journal, October, 2008, Kate McClelland, review of *Bird,* p. 106.

ONLINE

Brown Bookshelf Web site, http://thebrownbookshelf.com/ (February 7, 2009), interview with Elliott."
Color Online Web log, http://coloronline.blogspot.com/ (March 20, 2009), interview with Elliott.
Embracing the Child Web site, http://www.embracingthe child.org/ (January, 2009), interview with Elliott.
Lee & Low Books Web site, http://www.leeandlow.com/ (October 10, 2009), "Zetta Elliott."
Zetta Elliott Home Page, http://www.zettaelliott.com (October 10, 2009).
Zetta Elliott Web log, http://zettaelliott.wordpress.com (October 10, 2009).

                               *   *   *

FALKNER, Brian 1962-

Personal

Born 1962, in New Zealand; married; children: two daughters. *Education:* Attended college. *Hobbies and other interests:* Community theatre, photography, rugby, bicycling, travel.

Addresses

Home—Auckland, New Zealand. *E-mail*—brian@ brianfalkner.co.nz.

Career

Author. Worked variously as a journalist, advertising copywriter, radio announcer, and Internet developer.

Awards, Honors

New Zealand Post Children and Young Adult's Book Awards shortlist in Junior-Fiction category, 2006, for *The Super Freak.*

Writings

Henry and the Flea, Mallinson Rendel (Wellington, New Zealand), 2003, published as *The Flea Thing,* Walker Books (Newtown, New South Wales, Australia), 2007.
The Real Thing, Mallinson Rendel (Wellington, New Zealand), 2004.
The Super Freak, Mallinson Rendel (Wellington, New Zealand), 2005.
The Tomorrow Code, Random House Children's Books (New York, NY), 2008.

Brian Falkner (Reproduced by permission.)

Brainjack, Walker Books (Newtown, New South Wales, Australia), 2009, Random House Children's Books (New York, NY), 2010.

Sidelights

Brian Falkner, a novelist living in New Zealand, began his career writing for preteens. Drawing from his own experiences, Falkner has produced the humorous middle-grade novels *The Flea Thing, The Real Thing,* and *The Super Freak,* as well as turning to science fiction in *The Tomorrow Code* and *Brainjack*

Falkner began college intending to study computers, but along the way he decided to change his focus to something more creative. Studying journalism, he worked as a reporter and copywriter before turning to longer fiction. Published in New Zealand in 2003 as *Henry and the Flea,* Falkner's first novel *The Flea Thing* finds a twelve year old able to play on a professional rugby team due to a surprising talent. In *The Real Thing* a boy's talent for identifying soft-drink brands through taste alone comes in handy when the formula for the world's most popular soft drink goes missing and soda-pop addicts start to panic A young trouble maker is the star of *The Super Freak,* as Jacob channels his recently revealed superpower into being a criminal but finds that causing trouble as an evil-doer actually generates positive results.

With *The Tomorrow Code,* Falkner's fiction was introduced to North American readers. In the story, set in the author's native Auckland, fourteen-year-old Rebecca Richards and her friends, brothers Tane and Fatboy Williams, crack the code of a series of messages written in 1's and O's. They soon realize that the messages are

their own, and are being written by their future selves as warnings to the present about a looming threat to humanity. While noting that the scientific basis of Falkner's story is somewhat "sketchy," *School Library Journal* contributor Jane Henriksen Baird added that *The Tomorrow Code* boasts a "dramatic" story line, an "intriguing" theme, and a "timely" "pro-ecology message." In *Kirkus Reviews* a contributor cited the book's "tautly constructed plot" and concluded that in *The Tomorrow Code* Falkner shares an "exciting and thought-provoking" sci-fi tale that "will raise awareness of serious issues as it entertains." Hinting at the possibility of a sequel, John Peters wrote in *Booklist* that the author's novel "features an open ending that will leave readers waiting with fingers crossed."

Biographical and Critical Sources

PERIODICALS

Booklist, September 15, 2008, John Peters, review of *The Tomorrow Code,* p. 49.
Kirkus Reviews, September 1, 2008, review of *The Tomorrow Code.*

Cover of Brian Falkner's **The Tomorrow Code,** *featuring artwork by* ***Dominic Harman.*** (Jacket illustration copyright © 2008 by Dominic Harman. Used by permission of Random House Children's Books, a division of Random House, Inc.)

School Library Journal, February, 2009, Jane Henriksen, review of *The Tomorrow Code,* p. 98.

ONLINE

Brian Falkner Home Page, http://www.brianfalkner.com (October 30, 2009).*

*   *   *

FARRIS, Christine King 1927-
(Willie Christine King)

Personal

Born September 11, 1927; daughter of Martin Luther King, Sr. (a minister) and Alberta Christine Williams King (a musician); married Isaac Farris, Sr.; children: Angela Christine; Isaac, Jr. *Education:* Spelman College, B.A., 1948; Columbia University, M.A.

Addresses

Office—Spelman College, 350 Spelman Ln. SW, Box 229, Atlanta, GA 30314-4399. *E-mail*—cfarris@spelman.edu.

Career

Author and professor. Spelman College, Atlanta, GA, member of staff, beginning c. 1950s, including as associate professor of education and director of Learning Resources Center. Vice chair and treasurer, King Center.

Awards, Honors

D.H.L., Bennett College.

Writings

My Brother Martin: A Sister Remembers Growing up with the Rev. Martin Luther King, Jr., illustrated by Chris Soentpiet, Simon & Schuster (New York, NY), 2003.

March On!: The Day My Brother Martin Changed the World, illustrated by London Ladd, Scholastic (New York, NY), 2008.

Through It All: Reflections on My Life, My Family, and My Faith, Atria (New York, NY), 2009.

Sidelights

The older sister of the late Reverend Martin Luther King, Jr., Christine King Farris began telling her experiences with the civil rights leader to children in her book *My Brother Martin: A Sister Remembers Growing up with the Rev. Martin Luther King, Jr.* A teacher at Spelman College for over fifty years, Farris offers readers a unique portrait of her younger sibling as she shares stories about their childhood, including time spent play-ing pranks, visiting grandparents, and learning the piano. For a *Kirkus Reviews* critic, the perspective in *My Brother Martin* provides children with an approachable view of King and contrasts with biographers who have made him "more of an idealized heroic icon than a real person." Raised in the shadow of Atlanta's Ebenezer Baptist Church, Farris and her siblings were shielded by their parents from the demeaning aspects of racial segregation in the South and provided a positive, uplifting environment. As the King children matured and began to understand the unfair conditions to which American blacks were subject, notes Farris, the education their parents instilled allowed them the freedom to dream of and eventually fight for the day all individuals would be treated as equals. "Many of the [children's] books about King . . . tend to place him on a pedestal," observed *Horn Book* reviewer Mary M. Burns, but *My Brother Martin* reveals "why and how that pedestal was built." Writing in *School Library Journal,* Susan Scheps suggested that the work will prove useful in "help[ing] young children understand the concept of segregation and the importance of Dr. King's message."

Continuing to explain to young readers the importance of her late brother's leadership in the civil rights movement, Farris penned *March On!: The Day My Brother Martin Changed the World.* Considered by a *Kirkus Reviews* critic as "more oral history than a strictly fact-based narrative," *March On!* details the events surrounding King's historic 1963 March on Washington. Leading several hundred-thousand men and women in a peaceful protest on the National Mall, King delivered his "I Have a Dream" speech on the steps of the Lincoln Memorial, raising national awareness for the growing civil rights movement. Through her first-hand perspective, Farris offers readers more information about the event, including the painstaking process King used to craft his memorable speech. According to a *Publishers Weekly* reviewer, Farris humanizes her subject by "effectively us[ing] plain language and well-chosen facts to explain her brother's extraordinary achievements." In her second book about her brother, as Lucinda Snyder Whitehurst noted in a *School Library Journal* review, "Farris's unique perspective on her subject continues to be compelling," while *Booklist* contributor Hazel Rochman called *March On!* "a stirring, intimate view of a watershed moment."

In an interview with *Time for Kids* reporter Elizabeth Winchester, Farris remarked that her purpose for writing about King began with her desire for children to see that her late brother "was a typical boy." "If I can get young people to understand that," she explained, "then they too can make a difference in the world."

Biographical and Critical Sources

PERIODICALS

Black Issues Book Review, January-February, 2003, Lynda Jones, review of *My Brother Martin: A Sister Remembers Growing up with the Rev. Martin Luther King, Jr.,* p. 65.

Christine King Farris describes the life of her famous sibling in **March On!: The Day My Brother Martin Changed the World,** *featuring artwork by* **London Ladd.** (Illustration copyright © 2008 by London Ladd. Reproduced by permission of Scholastic, Inc.)

Booklist, February 15, 2003, Julie Cummins, review of *My Brother Martin,* p. 1088; August 1, 2008, Hazel Rochman, review of *March On!: The Day My Brother Martin Changed the World,* p. 66.

Horn Book, March-April, 2003, Mary M. Burns, review of *My Brother Martin,* p. 224.

Jet, January 28, 2008, Marti Parham, "King Sister's Tenacity Inspires Family of Leaders," p. 14.

Journal-Constitution (Atlanta, GA), Ernie Suggs, "King Matriarch at 80: MLK's Big Sister a Living Legend," p. F7.

Kirkus Reviews, December 15, 2002, review of *My Brother Martin,* p. 1849; August 15, 2008, review of *March On!*

Publishers Weekly, November 18, 2002, review of *My Brother Martin,* p. 58; August 11, 2008, review of *March On!,* p. 47.

School Library Journal, February, 2003, Susan Scheps, review of *My Brother Martin,* p. 129; October, 2008, Lucinda Snyder Whitehurst, review of *March On!,* p. 130.

Time for Kids, January 17, 2003, Elizabeth Winchester, "A Sister Remembers," interview with Farris, p. 2.*

*   *   *

FEIFFER, Kate 1964-

Personal

Born 1964, in New York, NY; daughter of Jules (a writer and cartoonist) and Judy (a writer) Feiffer; married Chris Alley (a civil engineer), September, 1996; children: Madeline. *Education:* Sarah Lawrence College, B.A.

Addresses

Home—Oak Bluffs, Martha's Vineyard, MA. *E-mail*—kfeiffer@comcast.net.

Career

Television producer and author. J.B. Pictures, New York, NY, former picture researcher and editor; television work in Boston, MA, beginning 1991, including researcher and associate producer for nationally syndicated talk show and associate producer of films for *Frontline;* WHDH-TV, Boston, political producer and producer of news program *Reallife.* Freelance writer and publicist, 1998—. Artist-in-residence for elementary schools, producing news programs with children.

Member

Authors Guild, Society of Children's Book Writers and Illustrators.

Writings

Double Pink, illustrated by Bruce Ingman, Simon & Schuster Books for Young Readers (New York, NY), 2005.

Henry, the Dog with No Tail, illustrated by father, Jules Feiffer, Simon & Schuster Books for Young Readers (New York, NY), 2007.

President Pennybaker, illustrated by Diane Goode, Simon & Schuster Books for Young Readers (New York, NY), 2008.

My Mom Is Trying to Ruin My Life, illustrated by Diane Goode, Simon & Schuster Books for Young Readers (New York, NY), 2009.

The Problem with the Puddles, illustrated by Tricia Tusa, Simon & Schuster Books for Young Readers (New York, NY), 2009.

Which Puppy?, illustrated by Jules Feiffer, Simon & Schuster Books for Young Readers (New York, NY), 2009.

The Wild Wild Inside: A View from Mommy's Tummy, illustrated by Laura Huliska-Beith, Simon & Schuster Books for Young Readers (New York, NY), 2010.

But I Wanted a Baby Brother!, illustrated by Diane Goode, Simon & Schuster Books for Young Readers (New York, NY), 2010.

Producer and writer of documentary films, including *Matzo and Mistletoe,* 2008. Columnist for *Martha's Vineyard* magazine.

Sidelights

Starting her career as a Boston-based television producer, Kate Feiffer eventually exchanged her fast-paced city lifestyle for the slower pace of life on Martha's Vineyard. Her career as a freelance writer and full-time mom allowed Feiffer to find an outlet for her quirky humor in children's books that are inspired by her home and family. Her first picture book, *Double Pink,* was published in 2005, and her fictionalized family chronicle has continued in books such as *My Mom Is Trying to Ruin My Life, The Wild, Wild Inside: A View from Mommy's Tummy,* and *But I Wanted a Baby Brother!* On occasion, Feiffer has collaborated with her father, noted cartoonist and writer Jules Feiffer, producing on the dog-centered *Henry the Dog with No Tail* and *Which Puppy?,* a story about the U.S. president's search for a "First Dog" that a *Publishers Weekly* critic dubbed a "whimsical imagining by the father-daughter team."

Double Pink was inspired by Feiffer's own daughter, Madeline; in the book a girl named Madison is absolutely obsessed with the color pink. Even as a toddler, pink was a priority, and toys, clothes, and Madison's room all had to be pink. From preference, Madison's craving for pink has since moved to obsession, but when the girl takes things too far and colors even her self bright pink, she is swallowed up in the pink world she has created and even her mother cannot find her amid all the pinkness. Illustrator Bruce Ingman captures the humor in Feiffer's story; according to *New York Times Book Review* contributor Penelope Green, he "careens happily over the edge when the story does, painting a raucous fuchsia delirium." Green went on to praise Feiffer for her "economy of style and understated wit," adding that the author's prose recalls the work of her award-winning father. Catherine Threadgill, writing in *School Library Journal,* joked that "young readers are likely to identify with Madison, and a few might even be tickled—well, you know . . . ," and a *Kirkus Reviews* predicted that "little girls . . . will enjoy Madison's over-the-top exploration of this favorite shade."

As they did in *Which Puppy?,* Feiffer and Feiffer once again go to the dogs in *Henry, the Dog with No Tail.* Full of "droll humor, wonderfully outlandish plot twists, and a satisfying journey of self-discovery," according to *School Library Journal* critic Joy Fleishhacker, the story was inspired by Feiffer's own dog and follows the canine's wish for a tail. Unfortunately, Australian shepherds do not come with a tail for wagging, so Henry decides to acquire one. Although a visit to a tailor earns him a button-on tail, getting the tail to wag requires a much longer hunt that takes Henry on a surprising voyage. Noting Feiffer's pun-filled text, a *Publishers Weekly* contributor also cited Jules Feiffer's characteristic "insouciant, loose-lined" drawings.

Feiffer captures a young girl's efforts to distance herself from her annoying parents in *My Mom Is Trying to Ruin My Life,* a picture book featuring artwork by Diane Goode. In a text praised by a *Kirkus Reviews* writer for its "sly humor," the imperious young narrator lists the many ways her parents are troublesome, from being mushy and affectionate in front of her friends to insisting on a clean room and a way-too-early bed time. However, imagining what would result if her loving parents were jailed for crimes against their offspring causes the girl to rethink her attitude. "Goode's watercolor illustrations adeptly convey [Feiffer's] . . . wry tone," wrote the *Kirkus Reviews* critic, while a *Publishers Weekly* critic described them as "gems of wry intelligence and comic understatement." In *Booklist* Courtney Jones predicted that children "will enjoy the fantasy of freedom" captured in Feiffer's "fable about independence."

Feiffer and Goode also team up in several more picture books, including *President Pennybaker* and *But I Wanted a Baby Brother!* Imagining what might happen if a child ran for U.S. president is the conceit behind *President Pennybaker,* as young Luke Pennybaker campaigns for president on the promise of making things fair. However, when he wins the election, he realizes an important truth: his promise of fairness has been interpreted differently by each of his constituents. Deciding that living at home with his parents was not so unfair after all, Luke resigns, leaving the highest office in the land to his four-legged running mate: the Pennybaker family dog. Paired with Goode's cartoon art, Feiffer's "deadpan narration allows the absurdity of the premise to carry the day," according to *School Library Journal* critic Steven Engelfried. In *Publishers Weekly* a critic dubbed *President Pennybaker* a "spirited picture book" in which "the line between fantasy and real-world politics stays clear."

Featuring artwork by Tricia Tusa, Feiffer's chapter book *The Problem with the Puddles* once again invites readers into a loving family. While driving home to the city after a vacation in the country, the eccentric Puddles family—Mom, Dad, and their two children—realizes that the family's two dogs are not in the car. The family encounters all manner of confusion in attempting to reunite with their pets; meanwhile, the clear-thinking dogs undertake a trek in the tradition of Canadian author Sheila Burnford's *The Incredible Journey,* their adventures captured in what a *Publishers Weekly* critic described as Tusa's "lively . . . spot art." *School Library Journal* reviewer Laura Stanfield dubbed the parental Puddles "enjoyably frustrating," and in *Booklist* Carolyn Phelan described *The Problem with the Puddles* as "an offbeat but rewarding chapter book."

Biographical and Critical Sources

PERIODICALS

Booklist, August 1, 2008, Ilene Cooper, review of *President Pennybaker,* p. 82; February 15, 2009, Carolyn Phelan, review of *The Problem with the Puddles,* p. 83; March 15, 2009, Courtney Jones, review of *My Mom Is Trying to Ruin My Life,* p. 66.

Cape Cod Times, January 20, 2006, C.K. Wolfson, "Vineyard Author's Children's Book Wins Raves."

Kirkus Reviews, October 15, 2005, review of *Double Pink,* p. 1136; September 15, 2007, review of *Henry, the Dog with No Tail;* January 15, 2009, reveiw of *The Problem with the Puddles;* February 15, 2009, review of *My Mom Is Trying to Ruin My Life;* April 15, 2009, review of *Which Puppy?*

New York Times Book Review, December 4, 2005, Penelope Green, review of *Double Pink,* p. 60; November 11, 2007, Emily Jenkins, review of *Henry, the Dog with No Tail,* p. 43; October 12, 2008, review of *President Pennybacker,* p. 23.

Publishers Weekly, November 7, 2005, review of *Double Pink,* p. 72; October 8, 2007, review of *Henry, the Dog with No Tail,* p. 51; July 21, 2008, review of *President Pennybaker,* p. 158; December 1, 2008, review of *My Mom Is Trying to Ruin My Life,* p. 45; March 15, 2009, review of *The Problem with the Puddles,* p. 62; April 6, 2009, review of *Which Puppy?,* p. 46.

Martha's Vineyard Times, December 1, 2005, Perry Garfinkel, "Feiffers in the Pink."

School Library Journal, November, 2005, Catherine Threadgill, review of *Double Pink,* p. 90; October, 2007, Joy Fleishhacker, review of *Henry, the Dog with No Tail,* p. 114; August, 2008, Steven Engelfried, review of *President Pennybaker,* p. 88; April, 2009, Laura Stanfield, review of *The Problem with the Puddles,* p. 104; June, 2009, Barbara Elleman, review of *Which Puppy?,* p. 84.

Vineyard Gazette, October 25, 2005, Julia Rappaport, "Colored in Shades of Pink."

ONLINE

Kate Feiffer Home Page, http://katefeiffer.com (October 30, 2009).

New England Film Online, http://newenglandfilm.com/ (April 1, 2008), Deborah J. Hahn, interview with Feiffer.

*   *   *

FRIESEN, Jonathan 1967(?)-

Personal

Born c. 1967; married; children: three. *Education:* Attended college.

Addresses

Office—P.O. Box 59, Mora, MN 55051.

Career

Author and teacher. Fifth-grade teacher in Minnesota for fifteen years.

Awards, Honors

Schneider Family Book Award, American Library Association, 2009, for *Jerk, California.*

Writings

Jerk, California, Speak (New York, NY), 2008.

Sidelights

After working as a fifth-grade teacher for fifteen years, Jonathan Friesen recognized his interest in becoming an author and made a career change. "I found I was scribbling more notes for stories than I was correcting papers," he told Minneapolis *Star Tribune* interviewer Tony Gonzalez. Making a decision to become a full-time writer, Friesen found success in his first attempt at publication but "102 rejections after that," as he shared with Gonzales. However, drawing on his experiences with Tourette's syndrome as a teen, the author found a new purpose to his writing efforts: he produced the awarding-winning young-adult novel *Jerk, California.*

Jerk, California follows the painful life of Sam Carrier, an older teen afflicted with Tourette's syndrome and hounded by an abusive stepfather who torments the boy for his inability to control his twitches. Feeling like an outcast in school due to the disease's manifestation as constant movement, Sam finds little relief at home,

Cover of Jonathan Friesen's young-adult novel Jerk, California, *which focuses on a teen combating a serious mental illness.* (Speak/Penguin, 2008. Reproduced by permission.)

where his stepfather enjoys demeaning the boy by describing Sam's father as a worthless deadbeat. Curious to discover the truth about his biological father, Sam makes the acquaintance of Old Bill, one of his father's friends, marking the start of a long journey to discover the life of a man he never knew. Together with a beautiful girl named Naomi, Sam sets out on a road trip to California, visiting friends of his father's along the way and learning the facts behind his father's real character. Much to his surprise, the teen uncovers information about his parents' association with a Mennonite religious community as well as his father's unusual work constructing windmills.

With *Jerk, California* Friesen earned the attention not only of reviewers but also of the American Library Association which gave the author the Schneider Family Book Award, an honor presented to books dealing with children confronting physical, mental, or emotional disabilities. Other critics also found much to like about *Jerk, California,* with *School Library Journal* contributor Nora G. Murphy writing that "the excitement of [Sam's] journey will keep most readers turning the pages to see what's around the bend." Describing the main character as "a good-hearted dreamer," *Booklist* reviewer Heather Booth noted that the author "brings complexity and nuance to Sam's struggle for understanding and self-acceptance." In *Voice of Youth Advocates* Kevin Beach maintained that Friesen "conveys Sam's utter sense of frustration with his condition and his accompanying low self-esteem and self-loathing," going on to call the novel's storyline "emotionally rewarding and effective."

Although *Jerk, California* is not an autobiography, Friesen explained to Gonzales that "the emotions behind [Sam] are everything I experienced as a kid" and putting his thoughts down on paper became "a real healing thing for me." When asked by the interviewer to reflect on his feelings about *Jerk, California,* the author explained: "I wanted to show a young man's heart—the heart of a rather tormented young man, at the beginning—and show that there is hope in the areas of love, self-acceptance, forgiveness." Additionally, the author concluded, "I wanted people to close it and feel hope."

Biographical and Critical Sources

PERIODICALS

Booklist, September 1, 2008, Heather Booth, review of *Jerk, California,* p. 91.

Horn Book, March-April, 2009, "Schneider Family Book Award," p. 221.

Kirkus Reviews, August 15, 2008, review of *Jerk, California.*

School Library Journal, December, 2008, Nora G. Murphy, review of *Jerk, California,* p. 124.
Star Tribune (Minneapolis, MN), August 12, 2008, Tony Gonzalez, "Minnesota Writer Channels 'Lost Years' for Novel" (interview), p/ 1E.
Voice of Youth Advocates, August, 2008, Kevin Beach, review of *Jerk, California,* p. 240.

ONLINE

Jonathan Friesen Home Page, http://www.jonathanfriesen. com (October 25, 2009).
Jonathan Friesen Web Log, http://jonathanfriesen.typepad. com/ (October 25, 2009).*

G

GALLAGHER-COLE, Mernie 1958-

Personal
Born 1958.

Addresses
Agent—Bernadette Szost, Portfolio Solutions, Inc., 136 Jameson Hill Rd., Clinton Corners, NY 12514.

Career
Illustrator of children's books.

Illustrator
Bonnie Bader, *Graphs,* Grosset & Dunlap (New York, NY), 2003.

Susan Blackaby, *Wes Gets a Pet,* Picture Window Books (Minneapolis, MN), 2005.

Susan Blackaby, *Jen Plays,* Picture Window Books (Minneapolis, MN), 2005.

Susan Blackaby, *A Place for Mike,* Picture Window Books (Minneapolis, MN), 2005.

Ann Heinrichs, *Dia de los muertos,* Child's World (Chanhassen, MN), 2006.

Adria F. Klein, *Max Goes to the Dentist,* Picture Window Books (Minneapolis, MN), 2006.

Adria F. Klein, *Max Goes to the Library,* Picture Window Books (Minneapolis, MN), 2006.

Adria F. Klein, *Max Goes Shopping,* Picture Window Books (Minneapolis, MN), 2006.

Adria F. Klein, *Max Goes on the Bus,* Picture Window Books (Minneapolis, MN), 2006.

Adria F. Klein, *Max Goes to School,* Picture Window Books (Minneapolis, MN), 2006.

Adria F. Klein, *Max Goes to the Barber,* Picture Window Books (Minneapolis, MN), 2006.

Charnan Simon, *Messy Molly,* Child's World (Chanhassen, MN), 2007.

Cynthia Klingel, *You Let the Cat out of the Bag,* Child's World (Chanhassen, MN), 2007.

Adria F. Klein, *Max's Fun Day,* Picture Window Books (Minneapolis, MN), 2007.

Adria F. Klein, *Max Stays Overnight,* Picture Window Books (Minneapolis, MN), 2007.

Adria F. Klein, *Max Learns Sign Language,* Picture Window Books (Minneapolis, MN), 2007.

Adria F. Klein, *Max and the Adoption Day Party,* Picture Window Books (Minneapolis, MN), 2007.

Adria F. Klein, *Max Goes to a Cookout,* Picture Window Books (Minneapolis, MN), 2007.

Charnan Simon, *To Grandmother's House We Go,* Children's Press (New York, NY), 2007.

Adria F. Klein, *Max Celebrates Chinese New Year,* Picture Window Books (Minneapolis, MN), 2007.

Jessica Gunderson, *A Stormy Surprise,* Picture Window Books (Minneapolis, MN), 2008.

Joan Holub, *Bed, Bats, and Beyond,* Darby Creek Publishing (Plain City, OH), 2008.

Adria F. Klein, *Max and Buddy Go to the Vet,* Picture Window Books (Minneapolis, MN), 2008.

Adria F. Klein, *Max Goes to the Doctor,* Picture Window Books (Minneapolis, MN), 2008.

Adria F. Klein, *Max Goes to the Farm,* Picture Window Books (Minneapolis, MN), 2008.

Adria F. Klein, *Max Goes to the Grocery Store,* Picture Window Books (Minneapolis, MN), 2008.

Adria F. Klein, *Max Goes to the Playground,* Picture Window Books (Minneapolis, MN), 2008.

Adria F. Klein, *Max Goes to the Zoo,* Picture Window Books (Minneapolis, MN), 2008.

Adria F. Worsham, *Max Celebrates Cinco de Mayo,* Picture Window Books (Minneapolis, MN), 2008.

Adria F. Worsham, *Max Celebrates Groundhog Day,* Picture Window Books (Minneapolis, MN), 2008.

Adria F. Worsham, *Max Celebrates Martin Luther King, Jr., Day,* Picture Window Books (Minneapolis, MN), 2008.

Adria F. Worsham, *Max Celebrates Ramadan,* Picture Window Books (Minneapolis, MN), 2008.

Adria F. Klein, *Max Goes to the Recycling Center,* Picture Window Books (Minneapolis, MN), 2009.

Adria F. Klein, *Max Goes to the Nature Center,* Picture Window Books (Minneapolis, MN), 2009.

Adria F. Klein, *Max Goes to the Fire Station,* Picture Window Books (Minneapolis, MN), 2009.

Adria F. Klein, *Max Goes to the Farmers' Market,* Picture Window Books (Minneapolis, MN), 2009.

Sidelights

In her work as a picture-book illustrator, Mernie Gallagher-Cole has contributed art to dozens of stories for young children, including a book series written by Adria F. Klein about a young boy named Max. After introducing the young African-American character in *Max Goes to the Dentist,* Gallagher-Cole and Klein take the youngster through a variety of common childhood experiences, like visiting the zoo, enjoying different holidays, and seeing a doctor. Reviewing the beginning-to-read trio of *Max Goes to School, Max Goes to the Barber,* and *Max Goes to the Dentist, School Library Journal* critic Melinda Piehler described Gallagher-Cole's pictures for these books as "appealing and helpful to readers trying to decode the texts."

Gallagher-Cole has also worked with writer Joan Holub, creating the artwork for Holub's *Bed, Bats, and Beyond,* a short chapter book for early-elementary-grade readers. With the sun nearly ready to rise, a young bat named Fink finds falling asleep difficult. After his brother Fang volunteers to tell him a scary story about a swamp monster, Fink becomes even more upset, leading third brother Batrick to share an adventure tale about pirates. Sister Batsy offers her own romantic story

Mernie Gallagher-Cole's illustration projects include creating art for Joan Holub's Bed, Bats, and Beyond. (Illustration copyright © 2008 by Mernie Gallaher-Cole. Reproduced by permission.)

featuring a prince and princess, but none of the sibling's efforts help the young creature fall asleep. Not until his mother returns home and shares with him a bedtime story does Fink relax into his comfortable routine and finally take some rest. Writing that Gallagher-Cole's illustrations add a dose of comedy to Holub's text, Jackie Partch also highlighted the art's "humorous details" in her *School Library Journal* review of *Bed, Bats, and Beyond.* A *Kirkus Reviews* contributor, who also found Gallagher-Cole's drawings entertaining, cited in particular an image of the frightened Fink "clutching his stuffed bat doll while swamp bats, pirates and an eye-shadowed Cleobatra keep him awake."

Biographical and Critical Sources

PERIODICALS

Booklist, November 15, 2007, Hazel Rochman, review of *You Let the Cat out of the Bag,* p. 47.

Kirkus Reviews, September 1, 2008, review of *Bed, Bats, and Beyond.*

School Library Journal, January, 2006, Melinda Piehler, reviews of *Max Goes to School, Max Goes to the Barber,* and *Max Goes to the Dentist,* p. 104; May, 2006, Sandra Welzenbach, review of *Dia de los muertos,* p. 111; April, 2007, Colleen D. Bocka, review of *Messy Molly,* p. 116; July, 2007, Erika Qualls, reviews of *Max and the Adoption Day Party, Max Celebrates Chinese New Year,* and *Max Learns Sign Language,* p. 79; December, 2008, Jackie Partch, review of *Bed, Bats, and Beyond,* p. 92.*

*   *   *

GEORGE, Lindsay Barrett 1952-

Personal

Born July 22, 1952, in Dominican Republic; daughter of Hugh Campbell (a brewmaster) and Beryl (a homemaker) Barrett; married William T. George (a writer), November 22, 1984; children: William, Campbell. *Education:* Attended Boston Museum School of Fine Arts, 1972-73; Manhattanville College, B.F.A., 1974; University of Wisconsin, M.A., 1976, M.F.A., 1977. *Politics:* Democrat. *Religion:* Roman Catholic. *Hobbies and other interests:* Canoeing, hiking, travel.

Addresses

Home and office—White Mills, PA.

Career

Fine art printer in Englewood, NJ, and New York, NY, 1978-81; mechanical artist for New York, NY, publishers, 1981-84; children's book author and illustrator, 1985—. Lecturer and artist-in-residence at elementary schools, beginning 1989.

Lindsay Barrett George (Photograph by Mickey Kaufman. Reproduced by permission.)

Awards, Honors

Caroline Field Award, Pennsylvania Library Association, 1990; National Science Teachers Association/ Children's Book Council Outstanding Science Trade Books for Children designation, for *Beaver at Long Pond, Box Turtle at Long Pond,* and *Fishing at Long Pond;* Library of Congress Children's Book of the Year designation, for *Box Turtle at Long Pond*; American Booksellers Association Pick of the Lists designation, 1991, for *Fishing at Long Pond;* Baker's Dozen Best Book for Family Literacy, Pennsylvania Center for the Book, 2004, and Pennsylvania One Book, Every Young Child selection, 2006, both for *Inside Mouse, Outside Mouse.*

Writings

FOR CHILDREN; SELF-ILLUSTRATED

William and Boomer, Greenwillow Books (New York, NY), 1987.
(With William T. George), *Beaver at Long Pond,* Greenwillow Books (New York, NY), 1988.
In the Snow: Who's Been Here?, Greenwillow Books (New York, NY), 1995.
In the Woods: Who's Been Here?, Greenwillow Books (New York, NY), 1995.

Around the Pond: Who's Been Here?, Greenwillow Books (New York, NY), 1996.
Around the World: Who's Been Here?, Greenwillow Books (New York, NY), 1999.
My Bunny and Me, Greenwillow Books (New York, NY), 2001.
Inside Mouse, Outside Mouse, Greenwillow Books (New York, NY), 2004.
The Secret, Greenwillow Books (New York, NY), 2005.
In the Garden: Who's Been Here?, Greenwillow Books (New York, NY), 2006.
Alfred Digs, Greenwillow Books (New York, NY), 2008.
Maggie's Ball, Greenwillow Books (New York, NY), 2010.

Several of George's books have been published in French.

ILLUSTRATOR

William T. George, *Box Turtle at Long Pond,* Greenwillow Books (New York, NY), 1989.
William T. George, *Fishing at Long Pond,* Greenwillow Books (New York, NY), 1991.
William T. George, *Christmas at Long Pond,* Greenwillow Books (New York, NY), 1992.
Charlotte Huck, compiler, *Secret Places* (poetry collection), Greenwillow Books (New York, NY), 1993.
Lola M. Schaefer, *Pick, Pull, Snap!: Where Once a Flower Bloomed,* Greenwillow Books (New York, NY), 2003.

Sidelights

Lindsay Barrett George is an award-winning artist and children's book author who creates works that often feature countryside landscapes as their settings, including her critically acclaimed titles in the "Long Pond" and "Who's Been Here?" series. Inspired by the work of naturalist painter James Audubon, fifteenth-century engraver Albrecht Dürer, and Wisconsin painter John Wilde, her gouache paintings are notable for their realism and controlled composition. In a review of George's illustrations for Lola M. Schaefer's picture book *Pick, Pull, Snap!: Where Once a Flower Bloomed,* Gillian Engberg in *Booklist* praised George's "inviting, realistic color art," and a *Kirkus Reviews* contributor cited the "detailed, scientific-quality drawings" as "perfect for budding greenthumbs."

Born in the Dominican Republic, George first began to paint as a young girl when her grandfather presented her with a gift of paints and brushes. Speaking only Spanish when her parents brought her to the United States, the eight-year-old George learned to make friends by drawing pictures of her former West Indies home. As George recalled on the HarperCollins Web site, "As a child, all I knew was that I wanted to draw, that I needed to make marks on paper. And if paper was not available, any blank surface would do, especially the brown paper bags from the grocery store. Pastel pencil marks looked especially beautiful on that soft, brown background."

After attending college in the Midwest and majoring in fine arts, George moved to New York City, where she found a job with a publisher working as a mechanical artist in the children's book division. "In all of my free time, I was in my studio making little handmade books, telling stories with only pictures and no words," she added in her HarperCollins Web site interview. Despite her illustrator tendencies, George did not think seriously about creating children's books herself, however, until after she was married, living in a log cabin in Pennsylvania, and raising a family. Enjoying the out-of-doors, she spent a great deal of time sketching the plants and animals she discovered in the woods near her new home. The idea then came to her to share these drawings and describe the sights and sounds of nature in picture books for children.

George's first book, *William and Boomer,* is a quiet tale about a boy who raises a gosling that has been separated from its parents. The boy, William, wants to learn how to swim; when he finally masters the water, he and his pet can enjoy swims together. While a *Bulletin of the Center for Children's Books* critic felt the tale is lacking in excitement, the reviewer praised George for her "simple and effective" illustrations.

For her next project, George began work on the "Long Pond" series. She coauthored the first of these, *Beaver at Long Pond,* with her husband; the three other books in the series are written by William T. George and feature Lindsay Barrett George's illustrations. The main purpose of these books is to introduce children to the native plants and animals typically found in parts of North America. Dialogue, narrative, and illustrations work together to tell about the wonders of nature. As *Booklist* contributor Deborah Abbott pointed out in a review of *Christmas at Long Pond,* these books clearly convey an "appreciation of the balance of nature, and respect for the environment."

Inside Mouse, Outside Mouse was inspired by an elementary-school assignment. As George recalled in her HarperCollins Web site essay, her daughter was asked to write a story about a mouse roaming around in a house; George, who had several drawings of mice on her studio wall, decided to tackle the project as well. In *Inside Mouse, Outside Mouse,* George opens up a world in miniature, as young readers are introduced to a house mouse who makes her home inside a wind-up clock case, and a tree stump-dwelling field mouse. The simple story follows each mouse as both rodents wake up and make the journey to a window in the house, where they greet each other every morning. "On every page, George couples her eye for particulars . . . with brilliant colors and a masterful sense of light," observed a critic in *Publishers Weekly,* and *Booklist* contributor Ilene Cooper similarly noted the author's "precisely rendered paintings." Praising the work for its easy-to-understand text and "pictures packed with interesting details just waiting to be explored," *School Library Journal* reviewer Wanda Meyers-Hines dubbed *Inside Mouse, Out-*side Mouse useful for "teaching the concept of compare/contrast." Noting that the book possesses a "large format, clear illustrations, and the most appealing mice readers have ever seen," a *Kirkus Reviews* contributor added that George's picture-book concept is "cleverly engaging."

In addition to her other work for children, George has also received considerable recognition for her "Who's Been Here?" books, which include *In the Snow: Who's Been Here?, Around the World: Who's Been Here?,* and *In the Garden: Who's Been Here?* In most of the series she uses the same formula: siblings William and Cammy take a walk through a natural setting and discover evidence of animal activity, such as plants that have had their flowers eaten, molted feathers, or paw prints visible across the trail. Each clue is accompanied by a two-page spread that shows the animal that was there and how it left the clue.

In *Around the World,* the focus shifts due to the book's broader scope, as globetrotting teacher Miss Lewis sends her class letters that incorporate the same type of wildlife clues. *Booklist* reviewer Carolyn Phelan complimented George's "large, detailed, brilliantly colored" illustrations, and Elizabeth S. Watson, writing in *Horn Book,* similarly noted that her pictures of such creatures as the giant panda and African elephant "are superbly rendered to provide sufficient detail and maximum appeal." George introduces two new protagonists, Christina and Jeremy, in *In the Garden* As the children gather vegetables for their family's evening meal, they discover that their garden has been visited by a host of animals, including a crow that has nibbled on kernels of corn and a slug that has left a slimy trail. *Booklist* contributor Gillian Engberg complimented George's "detailed, realistic watercolor-and-ink illustrations" as well as her "smooth text and its rhythmic refrain." A critic in *Kirkus Reviews* remarked of *In the Garden* that "children working on sharpening their powers of observation won't want to miss this outing."

The "Who's Been Here?" books have been praised for the quality and accuracy of their illustrations, as well as for their use of a simple, instructive format which adapts well to teaching nature classes. Joanne Schott, writing in *Quill and Quire,* asserted that *In the Woods,* for example, "could be the first step to a deeper interest in natural history" for a young reader. *Booklist* contributor Lauren Peterson described the series as "superb" and "unique," while Watson wrote that the "connection between scientific observation and resulting discoveries is well made" through both illustrations and text.

Romance is at the heart of *The Secret,* another of George's self-illustrated titles. After Mr. Snail confides in his gossipy mouse friend, his sweet message is quickly and playfully transmitted along a chain of creatures, including a beetle, a caterpillar, and a chickadee, before it reaches the ears of Miss Snail, the object of Mr. Snail's affections. Her warmhearted response makes it clear that his original message was not lost in translation. *The Secret* "is simple but sweet," Roxanne Burg commented in *School Library Journal,* and a *Kirkus Reviews* critic remarked that the story "offers unusual measures of verbal and visual delights." A *Publishers Weekly* critic noted that the "main attraction" of the work is George's mixed-media collages, "which combine 3-D naturalistic elements (flowers, tree bark, rocks) with cutouts of lissome and brilliantly colored animal portraits."

A young, one-dimensional aardvark searches for its missing pet in George's *Alfred Digs.* When Itty Bitty, the pet ant of Alfred the aardvark, disappears one day, Alfred leaves the cozy confines of his home on the first page of the dictionary and burrows through the rest of the volume to find his companion. Upon reaching the letter "W," the aardvark locates his errant pet, but before they can return home Alfred and Itty Bitty are both threatened by a hungry woodpecker. Fortunately, Alfred's mother arrives in the nick of time, and after a trip to the letter "Z," she takes the frightened duo to a special venue. "Even younger children will have no trouble accepting the unusual shape of Alfred's universe," a contributor in *Kirkus Reviews* stated, and Randall Enos, reviewing *Alfred Digs* for *Booklist,* wrote that George's "cartoon-style watercolor-and-ink pictures . . . perfectly fit the fantasy element of the adventure."

George once told *SATA:* "I've always been a serious 'looker' of things. Although my work has been referred to as photographic, I don't draw exactly what I see—I draw things the way that I need them to be, for me. The inclination for some artists is sometimes to go far for inspiration. I tend to look no further than the earth beneath my feet or the tree in front of my nose for subjects that matter.

"To show a child some familiar bark, as if for the first time, [or] to have a child feel as though he/she is holding a chipmunk or a squirrel, that's why I make paintings. And the reason I make books [is that] I love what makes a book 'work'—the turning of pages and of images. I enjoy making pictures that will fill a child with a curiosity about the next page or picture.

"The motivation behind the books that I've written and illustrated was to create a place for children to 'go' and be shown thing about animals that either they would never see or could never see on their own. When I left New York City in 1984, I moved into a log cabin on a lake in Pennsylvania with my husband, Bill. We spent four years in our rustic home, with the animals in the woods as our neighbors. The question was obvious—why not write about this for children? So we did."

Apart from the joy she finds in artistic expression, George views each of her children's books as a mystery to be solved. "Writing the story and designing the book is my way of finding the solution," she noted in her HarperCollins Web site essay. "There is magic for me in creating children's books. I also love the 'aha' moments, when ideas come together and pop."

Proud of being part of the group of writers and artists creating books for young readers, George passes along advice for others who would like to be part of the profession: "Write the story that only you can write, and make the pictures that show your originality of vision. Drawing has always been a way for me to communicate the pleasure of looking, daydreaming, and simply being here. So, to everyone, DRAW ON!"

Biographical and Critical Sources

PERIODICALS

Booklist, October 1, 1992, Deborah Abbott, review of *Christmas at Long Pond,* p. 335; April 15, 1995, Kay Weisman, review of *In the Woods: Who's Been Here?,* p. 1501; September 15, 1996, Lauren Peterson, review of *Around the Pond: Who's Been Here?,* p. 247; August, 1999, Carolyn Phelan, review of *Around the World: Who's Been Here?,* p. 2063; January 1, 2001, Gillian Engberg, review of *My Bunny and Me,* p. 967; May 1, 2003, Gillian Engberg, review of *Pick, Pull, Snap!: Where Once a Flower Bloomed,* p. 1603; August, 2004, Ilene Cooper, review of *Inside Mouse, Outside Mouse,* p. 1942; April 15, 2006, Gillian Engberg, review of *In the Garden: Who's Been Here?,* p. 51; April 1, 2008, Randall Enos, review of *Alfred Digs,* p. 53.

Bulletin of the Center for Children's Books, April, 1987, review of *William and Boomer.*

Horn Book, March, 1999, Elizabeth S. Watson, review of *Around the World,* p. 222.

Kirkus Reviews, April 15, 2003, review of *Pick, Pull, Snap!,* p. 612; February 15, 2004, review of *Inside Mouse, Outside Mouse,* p. 178; January 15, 2005, review of *The Secret,* p. 120; April 1, 2006, review of *In The Garden,* p. 347; February 15, 2008, review of *Alfred Digs.*

Publishers Weekly, October 11, 1993, review of *Secret Places,* p. 88; May 1, 1995, review of *In the Woods,* p. 57; March 31, 2003, review of *Pick, Pull, Snap!,* p. 70; April 5, 2004, review of *Inside Mouse, Outside Mouse,* p. 60; March 21, 2005, review of *The Secret,* p. 50.

Quill and Quire, July, 1995, Joanne Schott, review of *In the Woods,* p. 64.

School Library Journal, December, 1991, p. 90; April, 2001, Rosalyn Pierini, review of *My Bunny and Me,* p. 108; April, 2004, Wanda Meyers-Hines, review of *Inside Mouse, Outside Mouse,* p. 111; May, 2005, Roxanne Burg, review of *The Secret,* p. 83; May, 2006, Lauralyn Persson, review of *In the Garden,* p. 88; June, 2008, review of *Alfred Digs,* p. 102.

ONLINE

Harper Collins Web site, http://www.harpercollins.com/ (October 10, 2009), "Lindsay Barrett George."*

GEORGE, Sally
See ORR, Wendy

* * *

GIST, E.M.

Personal

Born Erik M. Gist; married. *Education:* Studied art with Jeff Watts, beginning 1996; San Diego State University, B.A., 1998.

Addresses

Home—Carlsbad, CA. *Office*—Watts Atelier of the Arts, 171 Calle Magdalena, Ste. 103, Encinitas, CA 92024. *Agent*—Shannon Associates, 630 9th Ave., Ste. 707, New York, NY 10036. *E-mail*—emgist@erikgist.com.

Career

Artist and illustrator, 1998—. Illustrator of book covers and games. Watts Atelier of the Arts, Encinitas, CA, instructor in art. Also worked as concept designer and three-dimensional artist for Gratuitous Games (video-game designer).

Illustrator

Arielle North Olson and Howard Schwartz, retellers, *More Bones: Scary Stories from around the World,* Viking (New York, NY), 2008.

Contributor to anthologies, including *Spectrum 11: The Best in Contemporary Fantastic Art,* edited by Cathy Fenner and Arnie Fenner, Underwood Books (Nevada City, CA), 2004; *Spectrum 12: The Best in Contemporary Fantastic Art,* edited by Fenner and Fenner, Underwood Books 2005; *Aphrodisia: Art of the Female Form,* edited by Craig Elliott, Aristata Publishing (Santa Clarita, CA), 2005; *Spectrum 13: The Best in Contemporary Fantastic Art,* edited by Fenner and Fenner, Underwood Books, 2006; and *Spectrum 14: The Best in Contemporary Fantastic Art,* edited by Fenner and Fenner, Underwood Books, 2007.

Sidelights

A former video games designer, E.M. Gist works as a professional artist and educator. A graduate of San Diego State University, Gist began his formal art training in 1996 with Jeff Watts; he now serves as an instructor at Watts Atelier of the Arts, a California studio founded by his mentor. Gist also worked in the video-game industry as a concept designer and three-dimensional artist before turning to a career as a freelance illustrator. His clients include Wizards of the Coast, Upperdeck Entertainment, and Boom! Studios, and he has illustrated numerous book covers and games.

Gist provided the illustrations for *More Bones: Scary Stories from around the World,* a collection of twenty-two tales selected by Arielle North Olson and Howard

Schwartz. Olson and Schwartz include such thrillers as "Wishes Gone Awry," an Irish tale; "The Shaggy Gray Arm," a story from Iceland; "The Gruesome Test," a work of Japanese fiction; "The Evil Sea Ghost," a yarn from Norway; and "The Peasants' Revenge," a German folktale. Gist's "atmospheric illustrations, while not intricately detailed, are somewhat startling in their imagery," Abby Nolan remarked in her review of the anthology for *Booklist,* and Laurie Slagenwhite, writing in *School Library Journal,* stated that the illustrator's "dark, smudgy illustrations may prove more frightening" than the stories in *More Bones.*

Biographical and Critical Sources

PERIODICALS

Booklist, October 1, 2008, Abby Nolan, review of *More Bones: Scary Stories from around the World,* p. 46.
Kirkus Reviews, July 15, 2008, review of *More Bones.*
School Library Journal, September, 2008, Laurie Slagenwhite, review of *More Bones,* p. 209.

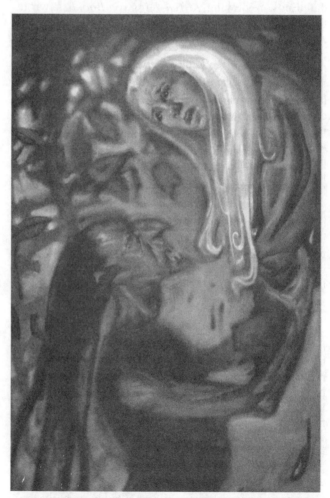

E.M. Gist adds a creepy element to Arielle North Olson's story anthology **More Bones: Scary Stories from around the World.** (Illustration copyright © 2008 by E.M. Gist. Reproduced by permission.)

ONLINE

E.M. Gist Home Page, http://www.erikgist.com (October 10, 2009).

E.M. Gist Web log, http://deadoftheday.blogspot.com/ (October 10, 2009).*

*   *   *

GORMAN, Mike

Personal

Male. *Education:* Parsons School of Design, B.F.A., 1992.

Addresses

Home—ME. *E-mail*—mg@mikegorman.com.

Career

Illustrator, graphic designer, and animator.

Awards, Honors

AltWeekly Award, Association of Alternative News-weeklies, 2007, for illustration work; two awards from New England Press Association.

Illustrator

Pamela F. Service, *My Cousin, the Alien,* Carolrhoda Books (Minneapolis, MN), 2008.

Pamela F. Service, *Camp Alien,* Carolrhoda Books (Minneapolis, MN), 2009.

Pamela F. Service, *Alien Expedition,* Carolrhoda Books (Minneapolis, MN), 2009.

Contributor to periodicals, including *New Yorker, Time for Kids, Entertainment Weekly, New York Times, Details, Conde Nast Traveler,* and *Village Voice.*

Biographical and Critical Sources

PERIODICALS

Kirkus Reviews, August 1, 2008, review of *My Cousin, the Alien;* March 1, 2009, review of *Camp Alien.*

ONLINE

Mike Gorman Home Page, http://www.mikegorman.com (October 10, 2009).*

*   *   *

GRAMBLING, Lois G. 1927-

Personal

Born August 20, 1927, in Elizabeth, NJ; daughter of Arthur and Ethel Goodwin; married F. Arthur Grambling, January 21, 1949; children: Jeffrey, Mark. *Education:* Drew University, B.A., 1949; Central State College, M.A., 1966.

Addresses

Home—Binghamton, NY.

Career

Writer and educator. Elementary school teacher in Denver, CO, 1950-52, Milwaukee, WI, 1953-56, and Oklahoma City, OK, 1963-65; school social worker in Oklahoma City, 1965-67, and Binghamton, NY, 1967-89. Leader of workshops for professional education groups and at schools and libraries in New York, Pennsylvania, and New Jersey.

Writings

A Hundred Million Reasons for Owning an Elephant: (Or at Least a Dozen I Can Think of Right Now), illustrated by Vickie M. Learner, Barron's (New York, NY), 1990.

Elephant and Mouse Get Ready for Christmas, illustrated by Deborah Maze, Barron's (New York, NY), 1990.

Elephant and Mouse Get Ready for Easter, illustrated by Deborah Maze, Barron's (New York, NY), 1991.

Elephant and Mouse Celebrate Halloween, illustrated by Deborah Maze, Barron's (New York, NY), 1991.

An Alligator Named . . . Alligator, illustrated by Doug Cushman, Barron's (New York, NY), 1991.

Mrs. Tittle's Turkey Farm, illustrated by Ellen Joy Sasaki, Thomasson-Grant (Charlottesville, VA), 1994.

Can I Have a Stegosaurus, Mom? Can I? Please!?, illustrated by H.B. Lewis, BridgeWater Books (Mahwah, NJ), 1995.

Night Sounds, illustrated by Randall F. Ray, Rayve Productions (Windsor, CA), 1996.

Daddy Will Be There, illustrated by Walter Gaffney-Kessell, Greenwillow Books (New York, NY), 1998.

Happy Valentine's Day, Miss Hildy!, illustrated by Bridget Starr Taylor, Random House (New York, NY), 1998.

Can I Have a Tyrannosaurus Rex, Dad? Can I? Please!?, illustrated by Penny L.C. Hauffe, BridgeWater Books (Mahwah, NJ), 2000.

Miss Hildy's Missing Cape Caper, illustrated by Bridget Starr Taylor, Random House (New York, NY), 2000.

Big Dog, illustrated by Andrew L. San Diego, Marshall Cavendish (New York, NY), 2001.

Grandma Tells a Story, illustrated by Fred Willingham, Whispering Coyote (Watertown, MA), 2001.

Nicky Jones and the Roaring Rhinos, illustrated by William Geer, Rayve Productions (Windsor, CA), 2002.

This Whole Tooth Fairy Thing's Nothing but a Big Rip-Off!, illustrated by Thomas Payne, Marshall Cavendish (New York, NY), 2002.

The Witch Who Wanted to Be a Princess, illustrated by Judy Love, Whispering Coyote (Watertown, MA), 2002.

Abigail Muchmore: An Original Tale, illustrated by Susan Havice, Marshall Cavendish (New York, NY), 2003.

Shoo! Scat!, illustrated by Barbara Johansen Newman, Marshall Cavendish (New York, NY), 2004.

Nicky Jones and the Roaring Rhinos, illustrated by William Geer, Rayve Productions (Windsor, CA), 2004.

T. Rex Trick-or-Treats, illustrated by Jack E. Davis, Katherine Tegen Books (New York, NY), 2004.

Can I Bring My Pterodactyl to School, Miss Johnson?, illustrated by Judy Love, Charlesbridge (Watertown, MA), 2006.

My Mom Is a Firefighter, illustrated by Jane Manning, HarperCollins (New York, NY), 2007.

Here Comes T. Rex Cottontail, illustrated by Jack E. Davis, Katherine Tegen Books (New York, NY), 2007.

T. Rex and the Mother's Day Hug, illustrated by Jack E. Davis, Katherine Tegen Books (New York, NY), 2008.

Contributor of stories to periodicals, including *Cricket, Hopscotch,* and *Jack and Jill.*

Sidelights

A former teacher and social worker, Lois G. Grambling turned her hand to children's literature after the birth of her first grandchild. Grambling has since published more than twenty works for children, including picture books and easy readers such as *Daddy Will Be There* and *T. Rex Trick-or-Treats.* "Watching your words being transformed into a book is an exhilarating and magical experience," she commented on the Charlesbridge Web site.

Grambling developed her love for literature at a young age. "My first really vivid childhood memory is that of getting my very own library card—no easy feat for a not quite five-year-old who was definitely not into printing or writing or spelling, yet," she once told *SATA.* "With card in hand my enthusiasm was boundless. Suddenly all those books on the library shelves were *mine,* too! I could take them home and read them. And I did—by the dozens. I've been taking them home and reading them by the dozens ever since. Grambling did not begin writing, however, until much later in life. As she once told *SATA,* "I was a late bloomer. I never gave much thought to putting pen to paper to express my feelings or to share my experiences until our first grandchild . . . was born in 1984. Then I had someone very important to write to and for."

Grambling's first published book, *A Hundred Million Reasons for Owning an Elephant: (Or at Least a Dozen I Can Think of Right Now),* appeared in 1990. "*A Hundred Million Reasons . . .* is great fun for reading aloud to groups of kids," the author once remarked to *SATA.* "It seems to get their imaginative juices flowing." That same year *Elephant and Mouse Get Ready for Christmas* was published. "I fell in love with Elephant and Mouse and their special relationship," Grambling recalled. "So I wrote *Elephant and Mouse Get Ready for Easter* and then *Elephant and Mouse Celebrate Halloween,* both in 1991. Holidays tend to bring out the best in all of us, and Elephant and Mouse in this series, I hope, prove it."

After completing her holiday tales, Grambling told *SATA,* "I felt I wanted to write something absolutely wacky. So I did. And that's when *An Alligator Named*

. . . *Alligator* was born. Published in 1991, it is an easy reader. I had such fun writing about Alligator that I missed him terribly when the book was completed. So I went out and got myself two alligator eggs. I don't miss Alligator so much now."

In *Mrs. Tittle's Turkey Farm* a kindly old lady loves her turkeys and takes good care of them. Each turkey has its own name and comfortable sleeping quarters. One bird is simply called Turkey, and as Thanksgiving approaches and his fellow creatures begin disappearing one by one, Turkey worries about his future. A quick-witted bird, he begins to frantically work out ways to keep himself from ending up on someone's dinner table. He saves himself by bravely foiling the plans of a would-be thief and earns the special name Some Tough Turkey. This keeps Turkey from the usual Thanksgiving Day fate: nobody wants to buy—or eat—the toughest turkey on the farm.

Grambling creates a tale of paternal protection and love for a child in *Daddy Will Be There.* Throughout her day's activities, a little girl knows that her father will always be there to protect and watch over her. She plays with her blocks, rides her bike, goes to a birthday party, spends time alone in the backyard, and does all the other things that five-year-old girls do. No matter what, Daddy remains close by or available to provide love, protection, and reassurance. Young readers "will find some level of comfort in this slight but reassuring story" highlighting the loving relationship between father and daughter, observed April Judge in *Booklist.* While finding "the atmosphere . . . profoundly melancholic," a *Kirkus Reviews* critic commented that Grambling "conjures a world of intimacy" between parent and child, and Scott Veale noted in the *New York Times Book Review* "the book's sweet, pragmatic message about the joys and benefits of having a dad close at hand."

Grambling offers an unusual look at gender roles and firehouse culture in *My Mom Is a Firefighter.* The work concerns young Billy and his two families: his mother and father as well as his "uncles" at the fire station. A contributor in *Publishers Weekly* complimented the book's "accessible text," and a *Kirkus Reviews* critic remarked that Grambling's story "is especially notable for the fact that no fuss is made about Billy's mom's 'nontraditional' career choice."

This Whole Tooth Fairy Thing's Nothing but a Big Rip-Off! is a more humorous offering from Grambling. Annoyed by the tooth fairy's tardiness in picking up his lost tooth, Little Hippo utters the exclamation of the book's title. Just then, the tooth fairy shows up, cold, wet, and cranky after being caught in a rainstorm. Indignant at Hippo's outburst, she enlists him to take care of her final job for the night while she rests. With the tooth fairy's wings glued to his back, Little Hippo successfully makes the tooth-for-coin exchange with Cub Bear, finding out in the process that he likes helping out the busy tooth fairy. Linda M. Kenton, writing in *School*

Library Journal, remarked of *This Whole Tooth Fairy Thing's Nothing but a Big Rip-Off!* that "there are some humorous moments that older children will appreciate."

In *The Witch Who Wanted to Be a Princess,* feisty modern witch Bella yearns to leave behind her small grubby cottage and witchy wardrobe to become a princess and live in a glorious castle with fine jewels and luxurious clothes. Since she was the top graduate in her witch class, turning one thing into another is usually a snap for Bella. After a changing spell proves unsuccessful, Bella reasons that the only way to become a princess is to marry a prince. Through the personal ads, she meets and falls in love with Franklyn of Styne (who bears a remarkable resemblance to the monster created by Dr. Frankenstein himself). In a story combining messages of self-esteem, self-acceptance, and inner beauty, Bella gets her wish. Grambling "swoops down on a broomstick of her own and pulls readers aboard for some full-throttle storytelling," remarked a *Publishers Weekly* critic, while Sally R. Dow, reviewing the book in *School Library Journal,* called *The Witch Who Wanted to Be a Princess* an "engaging story."

Grambling offers a story in the classic mode of the tall tale in *Abigail Muchmore: An Original Tale.* Spirited and active Abigail Muchmore tends to her farm from morning to night, fixing the damage from the constantly blowing West Wind. Not satisfied with what he has already done, West Wind decides to play some tricks on Abigail, blowing her fancy, store-bought underwear right off the clothesline and onto a neighbor's farm. Next, the wind blows the pears off Abigail's fruit trees. When West Wind tosses Abigail's beloved dog into the next county, she vows revenge. The old woman lassoes her impish adversary and confines him to the storm cellar under her house. Only when West Wind agrees to return her dog and stop his mischief does Abigail let him go, and the two live peacefully together from then on. Rosalyn Pierini, reviewing the book in *School Library Journal,* called *Abigail Muchmore* a "lively, humorous tall tale."

Grambling collaborates with illustrator Jack E. Davis on a number of humorous works about a lovable Tyrannosaurus. In *T. Rex Trick-or-Treats,* the title character determines that his Halloween costume will be the most frightening one of all. Though T. Rex is disappointed to learn that his friends Diplodocus, Stegosaurus, and Iguanodon have already taken the best costume ideas, he soon realizes that his mouthful of sharp teeth makes him scary enough. "Grambling's pared-down language, mouth-tickling adjectives, and repeating words and story patterns are right on target" for young readers, noted Jennifer Mattson in *Booklist.* When the Easter Bunny falls ill, the toothy dinosaur comes to the rescue in *Here Comes T. Rex Cottontail.* Donning fake whiskers and a false tail, Tyrannosaurus manages to deliver his Easter baskets, although their eggs contain a few surprises. According to a *Kirkus Reviews* contributor, "T. Rex displays an admirable generosity of spirit that nearly matches his great size." In *T. Rex and the*

Mother's Day Hug, the dinosaur's well-intentioned efforts to redecorate his mom's house end in disaster. "Gentle good humor and kindliness rolls through these pages," remarked a critic in *Kirkus Reviews.*

Biographical and Critical Sources

PERIODICALS

Booklist, January 15, 1995, Key Weisman, review of *Can I Have a Stegosaurus, Mom? Can I? Please!?,* p. 935; February 1, 1998, Ilene Cooper, review of *Happy Valentine's Day, Miss Hildy!,* p. 926; May 15, 1998, April Judge, review of *Daddy Will Be There,* pp. 1631-1632; May 15, 2003, Connie Fletcher, review of *Abigail Muchmore: An Original Tale,* p. 1670; September 1, 2005, Jennifer Mattson, review of *T. Rex Trick-or-Treats,* p. 144; December 15, 2005, Hazel Rochman, review of *Can I Bring My Pterodactyl to School, Ms. Johnson?,* p. 50; October 1, 2007, Shelle Rosenfeld, review of *My Mom Is a Firefighter,* p. 65.

Bulletin of the Center for Children's Books, February, 1995, Susan Dove Lempke, review of *Can I Have a Stegosaurus, Mom?,* p. 198.

Christian Science Monitor, March 30, 1995, Karen Williams, review of *Can I Have a Stegosaurus, Mom?,* p. 83.

Humpty Dumpty, October-November, 1995, review of *Mrs. Tittle's Turkey Farm,* p. 18.

Kirkus Reviews, May 1, 1998, review of *Daddy Will Be There,* p. 658; June 15, 2002, review of *The Witch Who Wanted to Be a Princess,* p. 881; February 15, 2003, review of *Abigail Muchmore,* pp. 305-306; August 15, 2005, review of *T. Rex Trick-or-Treats,* p. 914; December 15, 2006, review of *Here Comes T. Rex Cottontail,* p. 1268; August 1, 2007, review of *My Mom Is a Firefighter;* January 1, 2008, review of *T. Rex and the Mother's Day Hug.*

New York Times Book Review, May 17, 1998, Scott Veale, review of *Daddy Will Be There,* p. 31.

Publishers Weekly, September 19, 1994, review of *Mrs. Tittle's Turkey Farm,* pp. 26-27; January 23, 1995, review of *Can I Have a Stegosaurus, Mom?,* p. 69; June 1, 1998, review of *Daddy Will Be There,* p. 48C; June 3, 2002, review of *The Witch Who Wanted to Be a Princess,* p. 87; August 1, 2005, review of *T. Rex Trick-or-Treats,* p. 63; September 17, 2007, review of *My Mom Is a Firefighter,* p. 57.

School Library Journal, December, 1994, Martha Topol, review of *Mrs. Tittle's Turkey Farm,* p. 75; June, 1995, Judy Constantinides, review of *Can I Have a Stegosaurus, Mom?,* p. 81; August, 1996, Ruth K. McDonald, review of *Night Sounds,* p. 122; June, 1998, Joan Zaleski, review of *Daddy Will Be There,* p. 106; July, 2001, Linda M. Kenton, review of *Grandma Tells a Story,* p. 81; December, 2001, Kathleen Simonetta, review of *Big Dog,* p. 103; July, 2002, Linda M. Kenton, review of *This Whole Tooth Fairy Thing's Nothing but a Big Rip-Off!,* pp. 90-91; August, 2002, Sally R. Dow, review of *The Witch Who Wanted to Be a Princess,* p. 156; May, 2003, Rosalyn Pierini, review of *Abigail Muchmore: An Original Tale,* p. 119; November, 2004, John Sigwald, review of *Shoo! Scat!,* p. 104; August, 2005, Angela J. Reynolds, review of *T. Rex Trick-or-Treats,* p. 95; March, 2006, Marge Loch-Wouters, review of *Can I Bring My Pterodactyl to School, Ms. Johnson?,* p. 187; May, 2007, Piper L. Nyman, review of *Here Comes T. Rex Cottontail,* p. 97.

ONLINE

Charlesbridge Web site, http://www.charlesbridge.com/ (March 1, 2008), "Lois G. Grambling."*

H

HAMMILL, Matt 1982-

Personal

Born 1982, in Mississauga, Ontario, Canada. *Education:* Sheridan Institute, degree (illustration and computer animation). *Hobbies and other interests:* Watching *Star Trek.*

Addresses

Home—Mississauga, Ontario, Canada. *E-mail*—matt@matthammill.com.

Career

Author, illustrator, animator, and graphic artist. Short films include *Psychedelish, Comic Dice, Toys, How Plants Grow,* 2008, and *Hazed,* 2009.

Writings

(Self-illustrated) *Sir Reginald's Logbook,* Kids Can Press (Toronto, Ontario, Canada), 2008.

Contributor to periodicals, including *Ryerson Review of Journalism, Cottage Live, Naked Eye, Phoenix Metropolitan,* and *Institutional Investor.*

Sidelights

Although he did not realize it at the time, Matt Hammill started working on what would become his first published book for children while earning his illustration degree at Canada's Sheridan College. "For one of my projects I decided to make a zine (that is, a small print run of photocopied, stapled books)," Hammill explained on his home page. "I wrote and drew the first version of *Sir Reginald's Logbook,* and printed about fifty copies to take to our program's graduation show." At this student show, several editors saw the work, and

they sought the young artist out. Months later, after Hammill had expanded his story and added full-color art, *Sir Reginald's Logbook* became a reality.

Geared for the early elementary grades and designed to mimic an actual adventurer's log book, *Sir Reginald's Logbook* tells an amusing story about Sir Reginald's adventure to find an object known only as the Lost Tablet of Illusion. While the language of Hammill's story is lofty and archaic, the accompanying black-and-white artwork tells a quite different story: while colorful wa-

Matt Hammill's self-illustrated picture book Sir Reginald's Logbook *features an intriguing format.* (Illustration copyright © 2008 by Matt Hammill. Reproduced by permission.)

tercolors feature the hero in dramatic situations, the pen-and-ink drawings reveal Sir Reginald to be a pajama-clad fellow hunting around the house for the television remote control, hoping that the misplaced technological marvel can be found in time to watch his favorite program. "Hammill's keen sense of humor abounds," wrote *School Library Journal* contributor Maura Bresnahan in a review of *Sir Reginald's Logbook,* the critic adding that the language of the story's Quixotic hero "introduces readers to . . . old-fashioned phrasing and adds to the silliness." Noting that the images are not "overly frightening for young kids," Huai-Yang Lim explained that Hammill's "cartoon-like" rendering "convey the immensity of the creatures that Sir Reginald encounters, but their fearfulness is diffused by the comical juxtapositions" of the hero's "other reality in which the monsters he fights are actually a pair of pants, a pair of socks, a lamp cord, a girl scout, and his pet dog." *Sir Reginald's Logbook* "celebrates the pleasures of a freewheeling imagination," maintained a *Kirkus Reviews* writer, and in *Quill & Quire* Nathan Whitlock concluded that "Hammill's drawings are as fun and energetic as his story."

Biographical and Critical Sources

PERIODICALS

Booklist, November 15, 2008, Ian Chipman, review of *Sir Reginald's Logbook,* p. 52.
Canadian Review of Materials, October 24, 2008, Huai-Yang Lim, review of *Sir Reginald's Logbook.*
Kirkus Reviews, August 1, 2008, review of *Sir Reginald's Logbook.*
Quill & Quire, September, 2008, Nathan Whitlock, review of *Sir Reginald's Logbook.*
School Library Journal, November, 2008, Maura Bresnahan, review of *Sir Reginald's Logbook,* p. 90.

ONLINE

Matt Hammill Home Page, http://www.matthammill.com (October 30, 2009).*

*   *   *

HARPER, Jessica 1949-

Personal

Born October 3, 1949, in Chicago, IL; daughter of Paul (a painter) and Emery (a writer) Harper; married Tom Rothman (a film production executive), March 11, 1989; children: Elizabeth, Nora. *Education:* Attended Sarah Lawrence College. *Hobbies and other interests:* Reading, photography.

Addresses

Home—Los Angeles, CA. *E-mail*—jessica@jessicaharper.com.

Career

Actress, author, and songwriter. Actress in films, including *Stardust Memories, Pennies from Heaven, My Favorite Year,* and *Minority Report;* actress in television programs, including *The Garry Shandling Show;* actress in stage productions. Writer, singer, and producer of compact discs for children.

Member

Society of Children's Book Writers and Illustrators, American Society of Composers, Authors, and Publishers, Actors Equity Association, Screen Actors Guild, American Federation of Television and Radio Artists.

Awards, Honors

Gold Award, Parent's Choice, 1994, for *A Wonderful Life,* 1996, for *Not a Traditional Christmas,* 1998, for *Forty Winks,* 2000, for *Rhythm in My Shoes,* and 2001, for *Inside Out;* Silver Award, National Parenting Publications Awards (NAPPA), 1994, for *A Wonderful Life,* and 1995, for *Not a Traditional Christmas;* Gold Award, NAPPA, 1996, for *Nora's Room,* 1998, for *Forty Winks,* 2000, for *Rhythm in My Shoes,* and 2006, for *A Place Called Kindergarten;* Indie Award, Association for Independent Music/National Association of Independent Record Distributors and Manufacturers, 1997, for *Nora's Room;* Oppenheim Platinum Audio Award, 1999, for *Forty Winks,* and 2000, for *Rhythm in My Shoes;* Notable Children's Recording selection, American Library Association, 2001, for *Rhythm in My Shoes;* CableAce Award for Best Actress in a Comedy Series, for role in *The Garry Shandling Show.*

Writings

I Forgot My Shoes, illustrated by Kathy Osborn, Putnam (New York, NY), 1999.
I'm Not Going to Chase the Cat Today, illustrated by sister, Lindsay Harper duPont, HarperCollins (New York, NY), 2000.
Nora's Room, illustrated by Lindsay Harper duPont, HarperCollins (New York, NY), 2001.
Lizzy's Do's and Don'ts, illustrated by Lindsay Harper duPont, HarperCollins (New York, NY), 2002.
Lizzy's Ups and Downs: Not an Ordinary School Day, illustrated by Lindsay Harper duPont, HarperCollins (New York, NY), 2004.
I Like Where I Am, illustrated by G. Brian Karas, Putnam (New York, NY), 2004.
Four Boys Named Jordan, illustrated by Tara Calahan King, Putnam (New York, NY), 2004.
A Place Called Kindergarten, illustrated by G. Brian Karas, Putnam (New York, NY), 2006.

"UH-OH, CLEO" SERIES

Uh-oh, Cleo, illustrated by Jon Berkeley, Putnam (New York, NY), 2008.

Underpants on My Head, illustrated by Jon Berkeley, Putnam (New York, NY), 2009.

I Barfed on Mrs. Kenly, illustrated by Jon Berkeley, Putnam (New York, NY), 2010.

LYRICIST; COMPACT DISCS; AND PERFORMER

A Wonderful Life, Alacazar (Waterbury, VT), 1994.

Not a Traditional Christmas, Alacazar (Waterbury, VT), 1995.

Nora's Room, Alacazar (Waterbury, VT), 1996.

Forty Winks, Alacazar (Waterbury, VT), 1998.

Rhythm in My Shoes, Rounder (Cambridge, MA), 2000.

Inside Out, Rounder (Cambridge, MA), 2001.

Hey, Picasso, Rounder (Cambridge, MA), 2004.

Sidelights

Jessica Harper has used her creative talents in a variety of ways. As an actress, she has performed in more than a dozen films, including *Stardust Memories, Pennies from Heaven, My Favorite Year,* and *Minority Report,* and she has numerous television and New York stage appearances to her credit. In 1994, Harper produced the first of several award-winning music recordings for children, and in 1999, she released her first children's book. "I think your passions change with your life," Harper stated in a *Celebrity Parents* interview with Teri Brown. "Writing satisfies my need for creativity and my need for peace and solitude," she added.

In *I Forgot My Shoes,* Harper's picture-book debut, each character has left something behind—an overcoat, purse, paper route, or backpack—including the narrator, who has forgotten her shoes. In *I'm Not Going to Chase the Cat Today,* illustrated by Harper's sister Lindsay Harper duPont, a dog wakes up from a nap and decides that it will not trouble the cat sharing its home. When the cat realizes that it is not going to get chased by the dog, it makes a surprising decision: since it really does not care for chasing mice, it will not chase them anymore. In *School Library Journal* Linda Ludke commented of *I Forgot My Shoes* that "the engaging repetition and rhyme of the text begs to be read aloud."

In *Nora's Room,* also illustrated by duPont, Mom and the other children can only imagine what is gong on behind Nora's closed door, as all kinds of strange, loud noises emanate. Written in verse, they decide that it "sounds like hippos at a hippo hop, or when you pick up a piano and let it drop." *Nora's Room* was also recorded by Harper on compact disc.

Lizzie's Do's and Don'ts is another work that teams Harper and duPont. This picture book concerns a mother and her young daughter who feel that they reprimand each other far too offer and make the decision to emphasize the positive. As Laurie von Mehren wrote in *School Library Journal,* Harper's "simple, engaging pictures focus attention on the characters' relationship

Jessica Harper captures a young child's feelings during an off-kilter day in I Forgot My Shoes, *featuring artwork by Kathy Osborn.* (Illustration copyright © 1999 by Kathy Osborn. Used by permission of G.P. Putnam's Sons, a Division of Penguin Young Readers Group, a Member of Penguin Group (USA) Inc., 345 Hudson St., New York, NY 10014.)

and match the fun-loving mood of the story," and a *Kirkus Reviews* critic dubbed *Lizzie's Do's and Don'ts* "a spunky tale about the woes and challenges of growing up." The spunky protagonist makes a return appearance in *Lizzy's Ups and Downs: Not an Ordinary School Day.* At the end of the youngster's frustrating day— during she wore mismatched socks, performed poorly on a spelling test, and learned that her best friend is moving—Lizzie's mom helps her remember some happy memories from the day, which included a game of Twister. "Rather than extraordinary," noted a critic in *Kirkus Reviews,* "Lizzy's tale is comfortingly familiar, reminding readers that everyone has their ups and downs." In *School Library Journal,* Linda L. Walkins praised Harper and duPont's collaborative effort, remarking that "the warm and loving relationship between mother and daughter is apparent in both the text and pictures."

Harper looks at a familiar childhood experience in *I Like Where I Am,* illustrated by G. Brian Karas. In the work, which is told in verse, a six-year-old boy dreads his family's impending move. As the movers pack their truck with the boy's belongings, he voices his concerns about leaving a place he clearly loves and his fears of the unknown. Once the youngster arrives at his new home, however, a new neighbor offers a welcoming presence. "Kids facing a move will find Harper's story a reassuring choice," Todd Morning noted in *Booklist*, and Linda Staskus concluded in *School Library Journal* that the author "presents an honest, comforting depiction of what can often be a traumatic event." Harper and Karas have also joined forces for *A Place Called Kindergarten,* a humorous tale about a group of befuddled farm animals. When young Tommy fails to visit the barnyard one morning, a cow, sheep, horse, and hen wonder about his absence. When the family dog informs them that the youngster has journeyed to "a place called kindergarten," the animals become alarmed until Tommy reappears, eager to tell them about his day. The boy's enthusiasm for school, "wrapped within this story of friendship, will send a reassuring message to would-be kindergartners," a *Publishers Weekly* reviewer stated.

In *Four Boys Named Jordan,* a tale based on one of Harper's musical efforts, an elementary-school student named Elizabeth has trouble distinguishing between a quartet of classmates who share the same first name. The story "boasts some jaunty rhythms (befitting the tune from which it was adapted)," a contributor in *Publishers Weekly* wrote. Noting Harper's sly poke at baby-naming fads, a *Kirkus Reviews* critic deemed *Four Boys Named Jordan* "required reading for prospective parents."

In *Uh-oh, Cleo,* a chapter book illustrated by Jon Berkeley, Harper introduces plucky eight-year-old Cleo

Harper's picture book Lizzy's Do's and Don'ts *is brought to life in artwork by her sister,* Lindsay Harper duPont. (Illustration copyright © 2002 by Lindsay Harper duPont. Reproduced by permission.)

Small, one of six children in a rambunctious but loving family. Cleo recounts the tale of "Stitches Saturday," a particularly calamitous episode involving an overturned toy shelf, a trip to the hospital, and a raucous party. According to *Booklist* reviewer Carolyn Phelan, *Uh-oh, Cleo* "is studded with observations, incidents, and conversations that reflect true-to-life sibling relationships and realistic individual foibles." In *Underpants on My Head,* a sequel, Cleo describes her family's unforgettable vacation to Colorado. While hiking on Mount Baldy, Cleo, two of her siblings, and her parents finds themselves stranded by a freak snowstorm and must resort to wearing spare undergarments on their heads in order to stay warm. *Underpants on My Head* "shares the first book's gentle humor and familiar family dynamics," remarked Kathleen Isaacs in *Booklist* and Jennifer M. Brabander, writing in *Horn Book,* described the volume as "a family story that's got adventure, humor, and just a touch of suspense."

Biographical and Critical Sources

BOOKS

Harper, Jessica, *Nora's Room,* illustrated by Lindsay Harper duPont, HarperCollins (New York, NY), 2001.

PERIODICALS

Booklist, November 1, 1998, Cindy Lombardo, review of *Forty Winks,* p. 515; November 1, 1999, Ilene Cooper, review of *I Forgot My Shoes,* p. 538; April 15, 2000, Ilene Cooper, review of *I'm Not Going to Chase the Cat Today,* p. 1550; July, 2001, Connie Fletcher, review of *Nora's Room,* p. 2019; February 15, 2004, Todd Morning, review of *I Like Where I Am,* p. 1062; September 1, 2004, Stephanie Zvirin, review of *Lizzy's Ups and Downs: Not an Ordinary School Day,* p. 131; August 1, 2006, Hazel Rochman, review of *A Place Called Kindergarten,* p. 95; April 1, 2008, Carolyn Phelan, review of *Uh-oh, Cleo,* p. 49; February 1, 2009, Kathleen Isaacs, review of *Underpants on My Head,* p. 44.
Good Housekeeping, May, 2000, Beth Johnson, "A Mom and Her Songs," p. 28.
Horn Book, March-April, 2009, Jennifer M. Brabander, review of *Underpants on My Head,* p. 196.
Kirkus Reviews, August 1, 1999, review of *I Forgot My Shoes,* p. 1226; May 15, 2001, review of *Nora's Room,* p. 740; March 1, 2002, review of *Lizzy's Do's and Don'ts,* p. 335; January 15, 2004, review of *I Like Where I Am,* p. 83; June 15, 2004, review of *Four Boys Named Jordan,* p. 577; May 15, 2004, review of *Lizzy's Ups and Downs,* p. 492; December 15, 2008, review of *Uh-oh, Cleo.*
Publishers Weekly, March 9, 1998, review of *Forty Winks,* p. 29; January 10, 2000, review of *Rhythm in My Shoes,* p. 24; May 29, 2000, review of *I'm Not Going to Chase the Cat Today,* p. 82; July 2, 2001, review of *Nora's Room,* p. 74; September 10, 2001, review of

Harper teams with artist Jon Berkeley to produce the amusing chapter book Uh-oh, Cleo. *(Illustration copyright © 2008 by Jon Berkeley. Reproduced by permission.)*

Inside Out, p. 28; March 25, 2002, review of *Lizzy's Do's and Don'ts,* p. 64; July 26, 2004, review of *Four Boys Named Jordan,* p. 54; June 12, 2006, review of *A Place Called Kindergarten,* p. 51.

School Library Journal, August, 1998, Kirsten Martindale, review of *Forty Winks,* p. 80; October, 1999, John Sigwald, review of *I Forgot My Shoes,* p. 114; May, 2000, Linda Ludke, review of *I'm Not Going to Chase the Cat Today,* p. 142, and Beverly Bixler, review of *Rhythm in My Shoes,* p. 74; July, 2001, Debbie Stewart, review of *Nora's Room,* p. 82; July, 2002, Laurie von Mehren, review of *Lizzy's Do's and Don'ts,* p. 92; March, 2004, Linda Staskus, review of *I Like Where I Am,* p. 169; June, 2004, Linda L. Walker, review of *Lizzy's Ups and Downs,* p. 110; September, 2004, Roxanne Burg, review of *Four Boys Named Jordan,* p. 161; August, 2006, Suzanne Myers Harold, review of *A Place Called Kindergarten,* p. 88; August, 2008, Jennifer Cogan, review of *Uh-oh, Cleo,* p. 92; March, 2009, Jackie Partch, review of *Underpants on My Head,* p. 114.

Tribune Books (Chicago, IL), July 21, 2002, review of *Lizzy's Do's and Don'ts,* p. 5.

ONLINE

Barnes & Noble Web site, http://music.barnesandnoble.com/ (October 10, 2009), Moira McCormick, "She's Got the Beat: Jessica Harper Puts Rhythm into Kid's Music."

Celebrity Parents Web site, http://www.celebrityparents.com/ (October 10, 2009), Teri Brown, "Jessica Harper: A Mom Who's Passing on the Gift of Creativity."
Jessica Harper Home Page, http://www.jessicaharper.com (October 10, 2009).
Jessica Harper Web log, http://blog.jessicaharper.com/ (October 10, 2009).*

*   *   *

HENSON, Heather

Personal

Born in Danville, KY; daughter of Eben (a theater owner) and Charlotte Henson; married Tim Ungs; children: Daniel, Lila and Theo (twins). *Education:* New School for Social Research (now New School University), B.A.; City College of New York, M.A.

Addresses

Home—KY. *E-mail*—hensonbooks@yahoo.com.

Career

Writer. Worked as a children's book editor at Harper-Collins, New York, NY, and as a freelance editor.

Awards, Honors

Books for the Teen Age selection, New York Public Library, for *Making the Run;* Christopher Award, and Great Lakes Book Award, Great Lakes Booksellers Association, and Bluegrass Awards masterlist inclusion, all 2009, all for *That Book Woman.*

Writings

NOVELS

Making the Run, Joanna Cotler Books (New York, NY), 2002.
Here's How I See It—Here's How It Is, Atheneum Books for Young Readers (New York, NY), 2009.

PICTURE BOOKS

Angel Coming, illustrated by Susan Gaber, Atheneum Books for Young Readers (New York, NY), 2005.
That Book Woman, illustrated by David Small, Atheneum Books for Young Readers (New York, NY), 2008.
Grumpy Grandpa, illustrated by Ross MacDonald, Atheneum Books for Young Readers (New York, NY), 2009.

ADAPTOR

Laura Ingalls Wilder, *Little House Friends* (based on *Little House in the Big Woods*), illustrated by Renée Graef, HarperCollins (New York, NY), 1998.

Heather Henson (Photograph by Tim Ungs. Reproduced by permission.)

Laura Ingalls Wilder, *Christmas Stories* (based on *Little House in the Big Woods*), illustrated by Renée Graef, HarperCollins (New York, NY), 1998.

Laura Ingalls Wilder, *Laura and Mr. Edwards* (based on *Little House in the Big Woods*), illustrated by Renée Graef, HarperCollins (New York, NY), 1999.

Laura Ingalls Wilder, *Little House Parties* (based on *Little House in the Big Woods*), illustrated by Renée Graef, HarperCollins (New York, NY), 1999.

James Howe, *The Vampire Bunny,* illustrated by Jeff Mack, Atheneum Books for Young Readers (New York, NY), 2004.

Sidelights

A former children's book editor and the author of *Making the Run* and *That Book Woman,* Heather Henson sets her books for young readers in her native state of Kentucky. "Place is very important to me, almost as important as the story," Henson remarked in a *Publishers Weekly* interview with Diane Roback. "I'm so familiar with Kentucky and that culture." Although she lived and worked in New York City for many years, Henson returned to her home state to focus on her writing, and now lives in the home her mother grew up in on a farm near Danville.

Making the Run, Henson's debut young-adult novel, focuses on Lu McClellan, a troubled eighteen year old who is about to finish her senior year of high school in small-town Kentucky. A talented photographer, Lu often acts self-destructively, spending her nights getting stoned and speeding along the highway with her wild best friend, Ginny. Although Lu's much-older brother, Danny, worries about his sibling, he cannot prevent her from entering a sexual relationship with one of his former band members. Ultimately, Lu and Ginny's reckless lifestyle results in tragedy, and Lu is forced to re-examine her life. "Written in blunt and contemporarily savvy prose, this portrait of a girl on the brink of emerging from her past" will appeal to teen readers, wrote Francisca Goldsmith in a *School Library Journal* re-

view of *Making the Run.* Lu's "compelling narrative voice will keep readers rooting for her to make it out of her hometown and into the larger world," a *Publishers Weekly* contributor observed, and Claire Rosser, writing in *Kliatt,* stated that Henson's "skill at creating Lu's authentic voice during this catalytic 18th summer is enormous."

A thirteen year old who dreams of starring on Broadway comes face to face with reality in *Here's How I See It—Here's How It Is,* a semi-autobiographical novel. June Cantrell, nicknamed Junebug, loves nothing better than helping her parents at the Blue Moon Playhouse, their summer stock theater, and she has great expectations for their production of Shakespeare's *The Tempest.* Junebug's world is turned upside-down, however, after her mother moves out of their house, her father takes a romantic interest in the play's leading lady, and her older sister lands an important role, all of which force the young teen into the background. According to a contributor in *Kirkus Reviews,* "Henson's work possesses a gutsy authenticity," and *Booklist* critic Heather Booth wrote that the wealth of "theatrical details provide a unique frame for this gentle story about family and personal growth."

Angel Coming, Henson's debut picture book, was inspired by the Frontier Nursing Service, which provided nurses and midwives to families living in rural areas during the early twentieth century. The work centers on a young girl who lives in a mountainous region of Eastern Kentucky with her father and mother. The parents bring an old cradle out of storage and host a quilting bee in anticipation of their new baby. One morning the girl returns from a walk to find that her mother has given birth to a son, the delivery assisted by a woman who arrived on horseback. Writing in *Booklist* Carolyn Phelan complimented the lyricism of the narrative, commenting that Henson's "text is unrhymed, but its cadence has the grace of speech and the meter of song." *School Library Journal* reviewer Maryann H. Owen described *Angel Coming* as "an engaging piece of historical fiction."

Another picture book, *That Book Woman* pays homage to the Pack Horse Librarians, a group of women hired by the Works Progress Administration to deliver books throughout Appalachia during the Great Depression of the early twentieth century. The story focuses on Cal, a hard-working but distrustful youngster who slowly comes to admire the stranger on horseback who braves a snowstorm to visit his home, an event that inspires him to learn to read. Cal's "journey to reading is gentle and believable," Janice Del Negro stated in *Booklist,* and Angela J. Reynolds, reviewing *That Book Woman* for *School Library Journal,* remarked that Henson's narrative "is peppered with colloquialisms and authentic-sounding language that might be tricky for some readers, but lend immediacy and atmosphere to the story."

Biographical and Critical Sources

PERIODICALS

Booklist, July, 2005, Carolyn Phelan, review of *Angel Coming,* p. 1922; September 15, 2008, Janice Del Negro, review of *That Book Woman,* p. 51; April 1, 2009, Heather Booth, review of *Here's How I See It—Here's How It Is,* p. 40.
Horn Book, November-December 2008, Joanna Rudge Long, review of *That Book Woman,* p. 691.
Kirkus Reviews, April 15, 2002, review of *Making the Run,* p. 569; May 15, 2005, review of *Angel Coming,* p. 590; September 1, 2008, review of *That Book Woman;* March 1, 2009, review of *Here's How I See It—Here's How It Is.*
Kliatt, May, 2002, Claire Rosser, review of *Making the Run,* p. 10.
Lexington Herald-Leader (Lexington, KY), May 24, 2009, Rich Copley, "Children's Writer Owes It All to Mom."
New York Times Book Review, February 15, 2009, Julie Just, review of *That Book Woman,* p. 15.
Publishers Weekly, April 29, 2002, review of *Making the Run,* p. 72; June 24, 2002, Diane Roback, Flying Starts," p. 27; May 2, 2005, review of *Angel Coming,* p. 198.
School Library Journal, May, 2002, Francisca Goldsmith, review of *Making the Run,* p. 154; July, 2005, Mary-ann H. Owen, review of *Angel Coming,* p. 75; October, 2008, Angela J. Reynolds, review of *That Book Woman,* p. 110.

ONLINE

Cynsations Web log, http://cynthialeitichsmith.blogspot. com/ (March 16, 2009), Cynthia Leitich Smith, interview with Henson.
Heather Henson Home Page, http://www.heatherhenson books.com (October 10, 2009).

* * *

HEO, Yumi 1964-

Personal

Born 1964, in Korea; married; children: Auden, Sara Jane. *Education:* Sang Ji University (Korea), B.A.; New York School of Visual Arts, M.F.A., c. 1991. *Hobbies and other interests:* Gardening, antique hunting.

Addresses

Home—White Plains, NY.

Career

Author and illustrator of children's books, beginning 1994. Metropolitan Transit Authority, New York, NY, creator of "Q Is for Queens" glass art installation, 1997-2000. *Exhibitions:* Works exhibited at Storyopolis, Los Angeles, CA, Bologna Illustration Exhibit, Bologna, Italy, Itabashi Art Museum, Japan, and Art Institute of Chicago, Chicago, IL.

Awards, Honors

New York Times Best Illustrated Book of the Year designation, 1996, for *The Lonely Lioness and the Ostrich Chicks* written by Verna Aardema; Notable Books for Children selection, *Smithsonian* magazine, 2001, for *Henry's First-Moon Birthday* written by Lenore Look.

Writings

SELF-ILLUSTRATED

One Afternoon, Orchard (New York, NY), 1994.
Father's Rubber Shoes, Orchard (New York, NY), 1995.
(Reteller) *The Green Frogs: A Korean Folktale,* Houghton Mifflin (Boston, MA), 1996.
One Sunday Morning, Orchard (New York, NY), 1999.
Ten Days and Nine Nights: An Adoption Story, Schwartz & Wade (New York, NY), 2009.

ILLUSTRATOR

Suzanne Crowder Han, reteller, *The Rabbit's Judgment,* Holt (New York, NY), 1994.
Suzanne Crowder Han, reteller, *The Rabbit's Escape,* Holt (New York, NY), 1995.
Verna Aardema, reteller, *The Lonely Lioness and the Ostrich Chicks: A Masai Tale,* Knopf (New York, NY), 1996.
Cynthia Chin-Lee, *A Is for Asia,* Orchard (New York, NY), 1997.
Melrose Cooper, *Pets!,* Holt (New York, NY), 1998.
Nancy Van Laan, *So Say the Little Monkeys,* Atheneum (New York, NY), 1998.
The Not So Itsy-Bitsy Spider: A Pop-Up Book, Piggy Toes Press (Santa Monica, CA), 1999.
Kimiko Kamikawa, *Yoshi's Feast,* DK Ink (New York, NY), 2000.
Lenore Look, *Henry's First-Moon Birthday,* Atheneum (New York, NY), 2001.
Rachel Vail, *Sometimes I'm Bombaloo,* Scholastic (New York, NY), 2001.
Marguerite W. Davol, *The Snake's Tales,* Orchard (New York, NY), 2002.
Hugh Lupton, reteller, *Pirican Pic and Pirican Mor,* Barefoot Books (Cambridge, MA), 2003.
Candace Fleming, *Smile, Lily!,* Simon & Schuster (New York, NY), 2004.
Alice Hoffman and Wolfe Martin, *Moondog,* Scholastic (New York, NY), 2004.
Lenore Look, *Uncle Peter's Amazing Chinese Wedding,* Atheneum (New York, NY), 2004.
Ona Gritz, *Tangerines and Tea, My Grandparents and Me,* Harry N. Abrams (New York, NY), 2005.

Rachel Vail, *Jibberwillies at Night,* Scholastic (New York, NY), 2008.

Susan Wickberg, *Hey Mr. Choo-choo, Where Are You Going?,* Putnam's (New York, NY), 2008.

Contributor to anthologies, including *This Place I Know: Poems of Comfort,* compiled by Georgia Heard, Candlewick Press (Cambridge, MA), 2002; and *Knock, Knock!,* Dial (New York, NY), 2007. Contributor to periodicals, including *New Yorker, New York Times Sunday Magazine, Condé Nast Traveler,* and *Glamour.*

Books featuring Heo's illustrations have been translated into French.

Sidelights

Yumi Heo's distinctive artwork, which appears in her own picture books as well as those written by other au-

thors, is characterized by her eccentric use of perspective, energetic use of color, and unique blend of primitive and sophisticated styles.

Heo described her excitement at getting the assignment for her first book, Suzanne Crowder Han's retelling of a Korean folktale in *The Rabbit's Judgment,* by telling *Publishers Weekly* interviewer Sally Lodge: "This was a tale I had known since I was a child in Korea, and I felt a real connection with it." *The Rabbit's Judgment* tells of a man lured into rescuing a tiger from a pit; although the tiger promises not to attack, once the man is freed from the pit the animal changes its mind. The man looks first to a pine tree, then to an ox, and finally to a rabbit for a judgment that will rescue him; the first two are unsympathetic, but the rabbit slyly tricks the tiger back into the pit and the man goes on his way. Han's text "highlights amusingly eloquent interchanges" between the characters, noted a *Publishers Weekly* contributor,

Yumi Heo creates the colorful stylized illustrations for Vera Aardema's **The Lonely Lioness and the Ostrich Chicks.** (Illustration © 1996 by Yumi Heo. Reproduced by permission.)

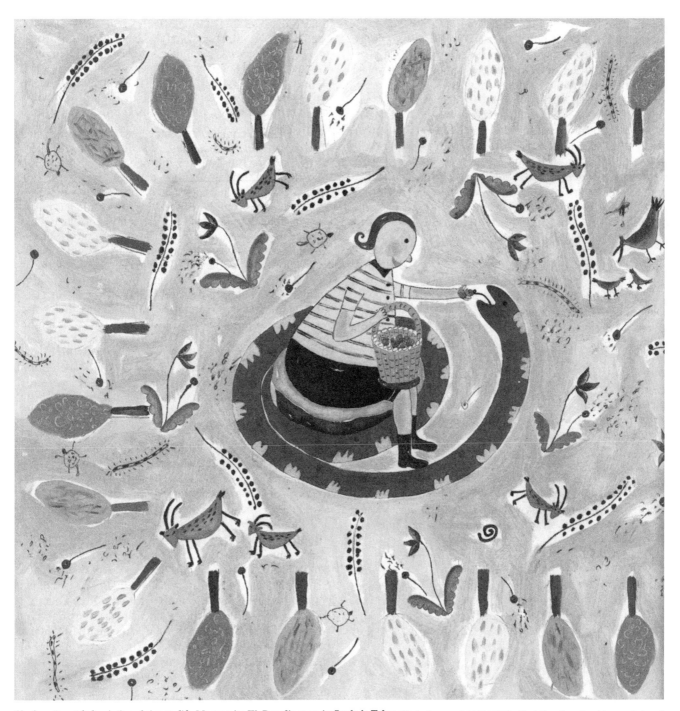

***Heo's naïve-styled paintings bring to life Marguerite W. Davol's story in* Snake's Tales.** (Illustration copyright © 2002 by Yumi Heo. Reproduced by permission of Orchard Books, an imprint of Scholastic, Inc.)

"while [Heo's] arrestingly skewed illustrations in a rich, natural palette illuminate the story's childlike wisdom." Other reviewers similarly highlighted the artwork accompanying Han's well-told story, a *Kirkus Reviews* critic describing the artist's style as "a pleasing blend of sophisticated design, ethnic reference, and visual storytelling."

Heo and Han again team up in *The Rabbit's Escape,* another adaptation of a Korean folk tale. This time a rabbit is tricked into visiting the Dragon King of the East Sea, who wants to eat the rabbit's liver in order to cure

his own illness. The fast-talking rabbit assures the king that he keeps his liver in a safe place and manages to escape when given permission to return to land to retrieve it. "Heo's original, quirky illustrations, with their Klee-like seas of floating figures, contribute significantly to the book's appeal," averred Nancy Vasilakis in *Horn Book.* Lisa S. Murphy, a contributor to *School Library Journal,* concluded of *The Rabbit's Escape* that "whimsical details reveal themselves with each new look, and this folktale is engaging enough to warrant many such readings!"

Heo's artwork for Cynthia Chin-Lee's *A Is for Asia* experiments in both traditional and tradition-breaking styles, a *Publishers Weekly* reviewer writing that the book's "illustrations make turning every page an adventure into contemporary and historical Asia." She creates a totally different mood in another alphabet book, Ona Gritz's *Tangerines and Tea, My Grandparents and Me*, in which two toddlers visit their grandparents' country home and make a different discovery with every turn of the book's pages. Praising *Tangerines and Tea, My Grandparents and Me* as "a book for sharing and teaching," *Booklist* critic Hazel Rochman also cited Heo's "bright, playful illustrations" while Kristine M. Casper remarked in *School Library Journal* on the "layers of delightful patterns" the artist uses "to engage the eye."

Heo's "stylishly drawn illustrations" for Nancy van Laan's *So Say the Little Monkeys* keep pace with the animated rainforest tale about a group of devil-may-care monkeys and "maintain . . . a sense of animated glee," in the opinion of *School Library Journal* contributor Alicia Eames. In *Pirican Pic and Pirican Mor*, Hugh Lupton's humorous retelling of a Scottish folktale, Heo complements Lupton's text with "stylized" paintings that employ what *School Library Journal* contributor Miriam Lang Budin dubbed a "wildly out-of-kilter perspective," resulting in a "jaunty, humorous" picture-book offering.

In *Pets!* a rhyming text by Melrose Cooper tracks a young boy's search for the perfect pet in a circus tent. Commenting on Heo's illustrations for this book, *School Library Journal* contributor Judith Constantinides wrote that they "reflect the rhymes with whimsy and humor,

Heo has collaborated with author Rachel Vail on several picture books that capture a child's emotions, among them Sometimes I'm Bombaloo.
(Illustration copyright © 2002 by Yumi Heo. Reproduced by permission of Scholastic, Inc.)

totally disregarding normal size relationships and perspective." The illustrator's stylized art is also a feature of *The Snake's Tales*, Marguerite W. Davol's retelling of a Seneca tale. Davol's story, about a greedy snake that trades stories for food, benefits from "cheerfully cluttered pencil-and-oil compositions [that] burn with activity," according to a *Publishers Weekly* reviewer.

Among Heo's collaborations are two stories by Rachel Vail. In the wacky *Sometimes I'm Bombaloo*, the artist brings to life the tantrum protocol of Vail's diminutive—and highly excitable—narrator, Katie Honors, whose temper sometimes takes control. Heo employs "vibrant backgrounds, blocks of color, and carefully chosen images to depict Katie's emotional tornado," explained a *Publishers Weekly* contributor, and a *Kirkus Reviews* critic dubbed the book's highly textural renderings "gloriously outlandish." Katie returns in *Jibberwillies at Night*, in which Vail addresses an imaginative child's fear of what might be hiding in the dark. Here Heo again creates "distinctive" illustrations that boast "bold colors and simple, expressive lines," according to *Booklist* reviewer Kristen McKulski, and a *Publishers Weekly* contributor made note of the artist's "bright and kicky mixed-media compositions." "In Heo's delightful artwork, the Jibberwillies are not frightening," assured *School Library Journal* critic Joan Kindig, the critic recommending *Jibberwillies at Night* as "well written and artfully designed."

Heo's self-authored picture books combine her signature illustrations with original stories. The story of a little boy named Minho who spends his day running errands with his mother, *One Afternoon* emphasizes the loud noises the pair encounters everywhere they go, and these noises appear as words within the art. In addition, Heo depicts each destination from the child's viewpoint; "perspective, comparative size, and realistic details are forgotten" in the process, explained Nancy Seiner in *School Library Journal*. In *Booklist*, Nancy Vasilakis reveled in the author-artist's "freewheeling style," concluding that the "vibrant look at bustling city life . . . offers ample opportunity for creative applications in group story sessions." "The kinetic energy of life in the big city motors this zippy picture book right along," concluded a *Publishers Weekly* critic in reviewing *One Afternoon*.

Minho returns in *One Sunday Morning*, which follows the boy during a treasured day with his father as he rides the subway, is entertained by street clowns, visits the zoo, and rides the carousel. It seems like a perfect day . . . until Minho wakes up in his bed and realizes that it has all been a dream. Author/illustrator Heo supplements her simple story with kinetic illustrations, according to a *Kirkus Reviews* critic; Minho's busy day "is depicted in exuberant paintings filled with the artist's signature shapes and forms." Several contributors praised the book's onomatopoeic text, which combines with Heo's illustrations to create a story that "hums with energy and offers plenty to hear and behold," according to *Booklist* contributor Shelley Townsend-Hudson.

The picture book* Hey, Mr. Choo-Choo, Where Are You Going? *pairs Heo's art with a story by Susan Wickberg. (Illustration copyright © by 2008 by Yumi Heo. Reproduced by permission.)

In *Father's Rubber Shoes* Heo tells the story of a young boy whose family has just moved to the United States from Korea. When Yungsu is understandably lonely at his new school, his father describes the poverty he once endured as a child in Korea—carrying his precious rubber shoes instead of wearing them—and explains that the family came to America so that Yungsu could have an easier childhood. "Heo's innovative compositions— flat, kinetic paintings incorporating many patterns and details—reflect Yungsu's changing feelings," observed Martha V. Parravano in a review of the story for *Horn Book*. While Rochman found "the understated story too elusive for young children," *School Library Journal* critic John Philbrook praised the artwork for *Father's Rubber Shoes* as "primitive and appealing in [its] simplicity."

Heo's retelling, *The Green Frogs: A Korean Folktale*, shares a *pourquoi* tale that explains why green frogs sing when it rains. The story of two naughty little frogs who love to disobey their mother concludes with a "gleefully fatalistic" ending, according to a *Kirkus Reviews* critic: granting their mother's dying wish, the frogs bury her near a stream, and every time it rains, they perch near her grave and cry out with worry that the rising water will wash her grave away. *The Green Frogs* "is a quirkier pourquoi tale than most," *Horn Book* critic Nancy Vasilakis observed, "but it's too mischievous to be morbid." A critic for *Kirkus Reviews* cited Heo's "magnificently eccentric illustrations" as the most successful element in the book, while a *Publishers Weekly* critic concluded that *The Green Frogs* "is so beguilingly retold and visualized with such individuality that it deserves a wide audience."

Heo's friendship with parents who have adopted children into their loving families inspired the picture book *Ten Days and Nine Nights: An Adoption Story*. The story is narrated by an Asian child who waits for her mother to return home with her new baby sister. While the girl marks off each day on her calendar, she also describes the preparations made by other members of her family: Daddy brings home baby furniture and takes a vacation from work, while Grandma sews a tiny pink dress. Calling *Ten Days and Nine Nights* "a welcome and endearing addition to adoption books," Julie Cummins cited Heo's "stylized artwork" in her review of the story for *Booklist,* and in *Publishers Weekly* a critic wrote that a "simple, graceful text and images of contentment distinguish" Heo's picture book.

Biographical and Critical Sources

PERIODICALS

Booklist, June 1, 1994, Deborah Abbott, review of *The Rabbit's Judgment,* p. 1825; August, 1994, Mary Harris Veeder, review of *One Afternoon,* p. 2048; September 15, 1995, Hazel Rochman, review of *Father's Rubber Shoes,* p. 175; July, 1996, Stephanie Zvirin, review of *The Green Frogs: A Korean Folktale,* p. 1827; March 1, 1997, Hazel Rochman, review of *A Is for Asia,* p. 1165; April 1, 1999, Shelley Townsend-Hudson, review of *One Sunday Morning,* p. 1420; March 1, 2000, Gillian Engberg, review of *Yoshi's Feast,* p. 1242; April 1, 2003, John Peters, review of *Pirican Pic and Pirican Mor,* p. 1394; June 1, 2004, Ilene Cooper, review of *Moondog,* p. 1742; May 15, 2005, Hazel Rochman, review of *Tangerines and Tea, My Grandparents and Me,* p. 1664; December 15, 2005, Jennifer Mattson, review of *Uncle Peter's Amazing Chinese Wedding,* p. 47; November 1, 2008, Kristen McKulski, review of *Jibberwillies at Night,* p. 43; April 1, 2009, Julie Cummins, review of *Ten Days and Nine Nights: An Adoption Story,* p. 45.

Bulletin of the Center for Children's Books, November, 1997, Deborah Stevenson, "Yumi Heo."

Horn Book, November, 1994, Nancy Vasilakis, review of *One Afternoon,* pp. 719-720; September, 1995, Nancy Vasilakis, review of *The Rabbit's Escape,* p. 613; November-December, 1995, Martha V. Parravano, review of *Father's Rubber Shoes,* p. 733; November, 1996, Nancy Vasilakis, review of *The Green Frogs,* pp. 748-749; March, 1999, Nancy Vasilakis, review of *One Sunday Morning,* p. 190; May, 2000, review of *Yoshi's Feast,* p. 325; July-August, 2003, Susan Dove Lempke, review of *Pirican Pic and Pirican Mor,* p. 471; March-April 2004, Kitty Flynn, review of *Smile, Lily!,* p. 170.

Kirkus Reviews, March 1, 1994, review of *The Rabbit's Judgment,* p. 305; June 1, 1996, review of *The Green Frogs,* p. 823; September 1, 1996, review of *The Lonely Lioness and the Ostrich Chicks,* p. 1318; February, 1999, review of *One Sunday Morning,* p. 300; January 1, 2002, review of *Sometimes I'm Bombaloo,* p. 53; August 15, 2002, review of *The Snake's Tales,* p. 1221; June 1, 2005, review of *Tangerines and Tea, My Grandparents and Me,* p. 636; December 1, 2005,

review of *Uncle Peter's Amazing Chinese Wedding,* p. 1277; March 1, 2008, Susan Wickberg, review of *Hey Mr. Choo-choo, Where Are You Going?*

Publishers Weekly, March 7, 1994, review of *The Rabbit's Judgment,* pp. 70-71; July 4, 1994, Sally Lodge, "Flying Starts," pp. 36-41; July 11, 1994, review of *One Afternoon,* p. 77; April 3, 1995, review of *The Rabbit's Escape,* p. 62; October 2, 1995, review of *Father's Rubber Shoes,* p. 72; August 26, 1996, review of *The Green Frogs,* pp. 96-97; February 3, 1997, review of *A Is for Asia,* p. 106; January 19, 1998, review of *Pets!,* p. 377; August 17, 1998, review of *So Say the Little Monkeys,* p. 70; February 8, 1999, review of *One Sunday Morning,* p. 212; February 28, 2000, review of *Yoshi's Feast,* p. 80; April 9, 2001, review of *Henry's First-Moon Birthday,* p. 73; December 24, 2001, review of *Sometimes I'm Bombaloo,* p. 63; July 22, 2002, review of *The Snake's Tales,* p. 177; February 17, 2003, review of *Pirican Pic and Pirican Mor,* p. 75; August 9, 2004, review of *Moondog,* p. 248; March 15, 2004, review of *Smile, Lily!,* p. 73; December 5, 2005, review of *Uncle Peter's Amazing Chinese Wedding,* p. 54; April 7, 2008, review of *Hey Mr. Choo-choo, Where Are You Going?,* p. 59; September 1, 2008, review of *Jibberwillies at Night,* p. 52; April 13, 2009, review of *Ten Days and Nine Nights,* p. 47.

School Library Journal, November, 1994, Nancy Seiner, review of *One Afternoon,* pp. 81-82; June, 1995, Lisa S. Murphy, review of *The Rabbit's Escape,* pp. 101-102; November, 1995, John Philbrook, review of *Father's Rubber Shoes,* p. 74; April, 1998, Judith Constantinides, review of *Pets!,* p. 97; September, 1998, Alicia Eames, review of *So Say the Little Monkeys,* pp. 198-199; April, 1999, Carol Schene, review of *One Sunday Morning,* p. 97; June, 2001, Alice Casey Smith, review of *Henry's First-Moon Birthday,* p. 126; September, 2002, Susan Pine, review of *The Snake's Tales,* p. 183; May, 2003, Miriam Lang Budin, review of *Pirican Pic and Pirican Mor,* p. 138; March, 2004, Marge Loch-Wouters, review of *Smile, Lily!,* p. 158; October, 2004, Maria B. Salvadore, review of *Moondog,* p. 118; September, 2005, Kristine M. Casper, review of *Tangerines and Tea, My Grandparents and Me,* p. 171; January, 2006, Maura Bresnahan, review of *Uncle Peter's Amazing Chinese Wedding,* p. 106; April, 2008, Gay Lynn Van Vleck, review of *Hey Mr. Choo-choo, Where Are You?,* p. 126; October, 2008, Joan Kindig, review of *Jibberwillies at Night,* p. 128.

ONLINE

Cooperative Children's Book Center Web site, http://www.soemadison.wisc.edu/ccbc/ (June 26, 2003), "Yumi Heo."

New York City Subway Web site, http://www.nycsubway.org/ (October 30, 2009), "Q Is for Queens: Yumi Heo."

School of Visual Arts Web site, http://www.schoolofvisualarts.edu/ (October 30, 2009), "Yumi Heo."*

*   *   *

HUMPHREYS, Susan L.
See LOWELL, Susan

HUTCHINS, Carleen M.
See HUTCHINS, Carleen Maley

*   *   *

HUTCHINS, Carleen Maley 1911-2009
(Carleen M. Hutchins, Carleen Maley)

OBITUARY NOTICE—

See index for *SATA* sketch: Born May 24, 1911, in Springfield, MA; died of congestive heart disease, August 7, 2009, in Wolfeboro, NH. Violin maker, educator, and author. Hutchins created some of the finest stringed instruments in the world, of a quality that reportedly rivaled even the violin masterpieces of Stradivarius. Her admirers described her as an artist, an artisan of the highest order, but she thought of herself as a scientist. Hutchins brushed aside the time-honored theories about mysterious woods, miraculous varnishes, and artistic genius that resulted in the highly prized instruments of seventeenth-and eighteenth-century Italy. Instead she studied the science of acoustics, and she experimented ceaselessly in her own basement workshop. Hutchins worked as a science and woodworking teacher at schools in and around New York City in the 1930s and 1940s, and in her free time she constructed violins of every possible size and style. Eventually Hutchins created a family of proportionally sized and pitched instruments called the violin octet. The instruments included the tiny treble violin, the soprano violin, the mezzo violin (similar to a conventional violin), the alto violin (a vertical viola), the tenor violin, the baritone violin (similar to a cello), the small bass violin, and the largest of the set, the contrabass violin. According to her supporters, she extended the conventional violin family range to more than seven octaves and corrected various long-standing acoustical issues of the conventional violin quartet. Hutchins's work was not universally celebrated; some traditional violin makers and musicians maintain cherished convictions regarding genius and art. Her most enthusiastic supporters may have been the scientists and musicians who joined her fledgling Catgut Acoustical Society to explore the relationships among physics, engineering, and mathematics that can lead to the perfect musical sound. Hutchins constructed hundreds of stringed instruments and published many scientific papers that enabled followers to learn her methods and preserve her legacy through their own creations. She was named an honorary fellow of the Acoustical Society of America and awarded Guggenheim fellowships and grants from learned organizations. The honor she appreciated most may have been the birth of the string octet that called itself the Hutchins Consort when it made its concert debut in 2000. Hutchins's writings include the children's books *Moon Moth* (1965) and *Who Will Drown the Sound* (1972). She edited the two-volume collections *Musical Acoustics* (1975-76) and *Research Papers in Violin Acoustics, 1975-1993: With an Introductory Essay, 350 Years of Violin Research* (1997).

OBITUARIES AND OTHER SOURCES:

PERIODICALS

Los Angeles Times, August 18, 2009, p. A20.
New York Times, August 9, 2009, p. A20.
Washington Post, August 16, 2009, p. C8.

J-K

JACKSON, Donna M. 1959-

Personal

Born 1959, in MA; married; husband's name Charlie; children: Christopher. *Education:* B.A.; University of Colorado, M.A. (journalism). *Hobbies and other interests:* Running, gardening, dogs, listening to music, hiking, traveling.

Addresses

Home—CO.

Career

Writer. Former journalist.

Awards, Honors

National Science Teachers Association/Children's Book Council Outstanding Science Trade Book designation, 2000, for *Twin Tales,* 2001, for *The Wildlife Detectives,* 2003, for *The Bug Scientists,* 2007, for *The Bone Detectives;* ASPCA Henry Bergh Children's Book Honor designation, 2005, Orbis Pictus Honor Book designation, 2006, and AAAS/Subaru SB&F Prize finalist, 2007, all for *ER Vets;* Best Book designation, American Library Association, and International Reading Association Teacher's Choice designation, both 2007, both for *The Bone Detectives.*

Writings

The Bone Detectives: How Forensic Anthropologists Solve Crimes and Uncover Mysteries of the Dead, photographs by Charlie Fellenbaum, Little, Brown (New York, NY), 1996.
The Wildlife Detectives: How Forensic Scientists Fight Crimes against Nature, photographs by Wendy Shattil and Bob Rozinski, Houghton Mifflin Harcourt (Boston, MA), 2000.

Twin Tales: The Magic and Mystery of Multiple Birth, Little, Brown (New York, NY), 2001.
The Bug Scientists ("Scientists in the Field" series), Houghton Mifflin Harcourt (Boston, MA), 2002.
Hero Dogs: Courageous Canines in Action, Little, Brown (New York, NY), 2003.
In Your Face: The Facts about Your Features, Viking (New York, NY), 2004.
ER Vets: Life in an Animal Emergency Room, Houghton Mifflin Harcourt (Boston, MA), 2005.
Phenomena: Secrets of the Senses, Little, Brown (New York, NY), 2008.
Extreme Scientists: Exploring Nature's Mysteries from Perilous Places, Houghton Mifflin Harcourt (Boston, MA), 2009.
The Name Game: A Look behind the Labels, Viking Children's (New York, NY), 2009.

Contributor to periodicals, including *Boston Globe.*

Sidelights

With her focus on nonfiction, former journalist Donna M. Jackson is the author of a number of nonfiction books for young readers that combine timely topics with up-to-date science. Explaining how she decides the subject she will explore in a book, Jackson wrote on her home page: "If an idea sparks my imagination quickly, I know I'm onto something. It's also important that I feel passionate about the topic. As I research a subject, the stories associated with it need to evoke strong feelings, such as joy, sorrow, curiosity, or inspiration."

Jackson's first book, *The Bone Detectives: How Forensic Anthropologists Solve Crimes and Uncover Mysteries of the Dead,* was inspired by research she did on an article for a major newspaper. Featuring photographs by Charlie Fellenbaum, the book focuses on forensic anthropologist Michael Charney as he assists in criminal and other investigations by deducing race, age, height, weight, and gender from teeth or bones. In *School Library Journal* Patricia Manning made special note of

Jackson's "clear text" and the book's compelling topic, while in *Horn Book* Margaret A. Bush concluded that the author's "well-organized" text "thoughtfully explains characteristics of human bones and scientific tasks" while also following the investigation into a skull that was actually unearthed at a Boy Scout camp in Missouri. In *The Bone Detectives* Jackson produces "a useful, enthralling work," concluded *Booklist* contributor Ilene Cooper, and the photo illustrations for the work "are crisp, clear, and always intriguing."

Several of Jackson's books focus on the natural world. In *The Bug Scientists* she follows three scientists whose work involves insects in three very different ways, producing a book that "may inspire many young readers to seek careers in etymology," according to *School Library Journal* contributor Louise L. Sherman. *The Wildlife Detectives: How Forensic Scientists Fight Crimes against Nature* reveals the way that scientists are helping to curtail the needless killing of elephants, bears, sea turtles, and other animals, some of which are endangered. In the same way that police investigate a crime scene, forensic scientists use advanced technology to track down those who hurt or fatally wound the earth's wild creatures. *The Wildlife Detectives* "will be welcomed by mystery fans and anyone who cares about animals," noted *Booklist* critic Kay Weisman, while in *School Library Journal* Arwen Mashall characterized Jackson's book as a welcome "foray into an intriguing and little-known area of wildlife conservation."

In *Hero Dogs: Courageous Canines in Action* Jackson shows the ways that humans and animals sometimes work together. From bomb-and drug-sniffing dogs and the rescue dogs that helped extract survivors from the rubble of the Twin Towers following the September 11, 2001 terrorist attacks to the guide dogs that serve as eyes for the blind, *Hero Dogs* combines stories of doggy heroism with interviews of the people who train and use helper dogs. Jackson's text in *Hero Dogs* is "notably restrained," observed a *Kirkus Reviews* writer, "eschewing the maudlin and letting the stories tell themselves." In *Booklist* Kathleen Odean described *Hero Dogs* as a "timely photo essay," and in *School Library Journal* John Sigwald predicted that Jackson's "profiles of exceptional canines and their appreciative owners" will likely "appeal to pet lovers."

Jackson's love of dogs comes through in her book *Hero Dogs,* and readers can detect the same sentiment in *ER Vets: Life in an Animal Emergency Room.* Based on interviews and illustrated with photographs, *ER Vets* shares with children the high-pressure work of emergency-care veterinarians. While noting that the work allows animal lovers to care for and learn about a diverse list of creatures, *Booklist* critic Stephanie Zvirin added that "Jackson doesn't sidestep the emotional and physical demands of working in an emergency clinic." In *School Library Journal* Anne Chapman Callaghan cited the "plentiful, excellent-quality photographs" in *ER Vets*, dubbing the work "an engaging book on a hot topic."

Science writer Donna M. Jackson explores the more intriguing possibilities in human sensory perception in her nonfiction book Phenomena: Secrets of the Senses. (Little, Brown, 2008. Reproduced by permission.)

More science is served up by Jackson in *Twin Tales: The Magic and Mystery of Multiple Birth, The Name Game: A Look behind Labels,* and *Phenomena: Secrets of the Senses.* Senses create a road map with which to navigate life, asserts Jackson in *Phenomena,* and here she "moves beyond the basics of sensory perception to explore its alluring edges," according to *Horn Book* contributor Danielle J. Ford. Intuition, psychic experiences, feelings of deja vu, and other sensory experiences are explored from a scientific basis, and the author draws on studies of the brain and the nervous system in exploring these experience. Another "eye-opening book on an unusual subject," according to *Booklist* critic Carolyn Phelan, *In Your Face: The Facts about Your Features* focuses on the many subtle differences caused by environment and ancestry that make each human face unique. In addition to Nature's handiwork, the book also describes cultural enhancements to faces, such as tattooing and piercing, styles of head and facial hair, and the use of cosmetics and paints. With its "well-captioned and colorful photos, logical organization, interesting topics, and profusion of ideas and information," *In Your Face* treats readers to "an unusual array of scientific and cultural concepts," concluded Linda Ritterman in her *School Library Journal* review of Jackson's work.

In *Twin Tales* Jackson shares her exploration of what life is like for two or more people who share a birthing experience. In this book she mixes "scientific facts with interesting personal anecdotes to create an informative and intriguing" work of nonfiction, according to *School Library Journal* critic Joy Fleishhacker. In what the critic called a "clearly written" and "lively" text, *Twin Tales* describes the different type of twins, the chain of events that produces twins, and stories of actual twins who have faced and surmounted challenges. Throughout all, Jackson "peppers the text with easy-to-understand explanations" and up-to-date research, Fleishhacker added, while in *Booklist* Kathy Broderick noted that the author's "emphasis on twin science is a welcome change from the focus of most children's books" on the subject.

Biographical and Critical Sources

PERIODICALS

Booklist, April 1, 1996, Ilene Cooper, review of *The Bone Detectives: How Forensic Anthropologists Solve Crimes and Uncover Mysteries of the Dead,* p. 1358; April 1, 2000, Kay Weisman, review of *The Wildlife Detectives: How Forensic Scientists Fight Crimes against Nature,* p. 1458; May 15, 2001, Kathy Broderick, review of *Twin Tales: The Magic and Mystery of Multiple Birth,* p. 1747; July, 2003, Kathleen Odean, review of *Hero Dogs: Courageous Canines in Action,* p. 1882; October 15, 2004, Carolyn Phelan, review of *In Your Face: The Facts about Your Features,* p. 401; November 1, 2005, Stephanie Zvirin, review of *ER Vets: Life in an Animal Emergency Room,* p. 43; October 1, 2008, Carolyn Phelan, review of *Phenomena: Secrets of the Senses,* p. 35.

Horn Book, May-June 1996, Margaret A Bush, review of *The Bone Detectives,* p. 348; March, 2001, review of *Twin Tales,* p. 230; May-June, 2002, Danielle J. Ford, review of *The Bug Scientists,* p. 347; September-October, 2004, Betty Carter, review of *In Your Face,* p. 606; November-December, 2008, Danielle J. Ford, review of *Phenomena,* p. 723.

Kirkus Reviews, February 15, 2002, review of *The Bug Scientists,* p. 259; July 1, 2003, review of *Hero Dogs,* p. 911; August 15, 2008, review of *Phenomena.*

New York Times Book Review, June 17, 2001, review of *Twin Tales,* p. 24.

School Library Journal, July, 2000, Arwen Marshall, review of *The Wildlife Detectives,* p. 118; May, 2001, Joy Fleishhacker, review of *Twin Tales,* p. 166; April, 2002, Louise L. Sherman, review of *The Bug Scientists,* p. 174; September, 2003, John Sigwald, review of *Hero Dogs,* p. 200; November, 2004, Lynda Ritterman, review of *In Your Face,* p. 166; October, 2005, Patricia Manning, review of *The Bone Detectives,* p. 63; January, 2006, Anne Chapman Callaghan, review of *ER Vets,* p. 153.

ONLINE

Donna M. Jackson Home Page, http://www.donnamjackson.net (October 30, 2009).*

JOHN, Antony 1972-

Personal

Born 1972, in England; married; children: two. *Education:* Oxford University, B.A., 1994; attended Washington and Lee University, 1994-95; Duke University, Ph.D., 2002.

Addresses

Home—St. Louis, MO. *Agent*—Ted Malawer, tedupstart crowliterary.com. *E-mail*—antony@antonyjohn.net.

Career

Writer and educator. Instructor at Duke University and University of South Carolina. Worked variously as an ice cream seller, tour guide, chauffeur, and barista.

Writings

Busted: Confessions of an Accidental Player, Flux (Woodbury, MN), 2008.
Five Flavors of Dumb, Dial (New York, NY), 2010.

Sidelights

Antony John is the author of several young-adult novels that are written with a male readership in mind. His fiction debut, *Busted: Confessions of an Accidental Player,*

Antony John (Photograph by Audrey John. Reproduced by permission.)

Cover of John's middle-grade novel **Busted: Confessions of an Accidental Player.** (Cover image copyright © 2008 by Onoky/SuperStock and Llewellyn Art Department. Reproduced by permission.)

is a humorous look at peer pressure and interpersonal relations, while the novel *Five Flavors of Dumb* chronicles the mayhem that ensues when a deaf high-school senior becomes manager of a rock band.

Born in England, John displayed a talent for music at a young age and decided to become a composer of classical music. After earning a bachelor's degree from Oxford University and a doctorate from Duke University, he taught at the University of South Carolina and Duke until his first child was born. As a stay-at-home dad, John took a break from music and turned to writing novels; *Busted,* his literary debut, was released in 2008.

Busted centers on Kevin Mopsely, a nerdy high-school senior who earns plaudits for his flute solos but fails miserably when it comes to romance. Unexpectedly, Brandon Trent, Kevin's wildly popular alpha-male classmate, assigns him a momentous task as part of the school's time-honored graduation rituals: Kevin must compile the Book of Busts, a secret notebook containing the bust, waist, and hip measurements of every senior girl, including Kevin's best friend and neighbor, Abby. Kevin soon finds himself caught in a moral dilemma: although he enjoys being a part of his school's upper echelon, he also knows that compiling a record

of the physical characteristics of female classmates is degrading. "The message about feminism and respect between the sexes is certainly a valuable one," Meredith Robbins commented in her review of *Busted* for *School Library Journal.*

Biographical and Critical Sources

PERIODICALS

Kirkus Reviews, September 1, 2008, review of *Busted: Confessions of an Accidental Player.*
School Library Journal, January, 2009, Meredith Robbins, review of *Busted,* p. 106.

ONLINE

Antony John Home Page, http://antonyjohn.net (October 10, 2009).
Antony John Web log, http://antonyjohn.net/blog/ (October 10, 2009).

*   *   *

KENNETT, David 1959-

Personal

Born October 5, 1959, in Adelaide, South Australia, Australia; son of Dean Daniel (a building contractor) and Peggy Lenore (a nurse) Kennett. *Education:* Underdale College of Advanced Education, B.A. (design and illustration), 1985.

Addresses

Home—Glenside, South Australia, Australia. *E-mail*—davidckennett@hotmail.com.

Career

Author and illustrator.

Writings

SELF-ILLUSTRATED

Polar Bear, Omnibus (Norwood, South Australia, Australia), 2000.
Wolf, Omnibus (Norwood, South Australia, Australia), 2000.
Elephant, Omnibus (Norwood, South Australia, Australia), 2001.
Lion, Omnibus (Norwood, South Australia, Australia), 2001.

Chimpanzee, Omnibus (Norwood, South Australia, Australia), 2002.

Killer Whale, Omnibus (Norwood, South Australia, Australia), 2002.

Pharaoh: Life and Afterlife of a God, Walker (New York, NY), 2008.

ILLUSTRATOR

Gwen Pascoe, *Two Feet,* Era (Flinders Park, South Australia, Australia), 1986.

Glen Pascoe, *Huggly, Snuggly Pets,* Era (Flinders Park, South Australia, Australia), 1987.

Harry Breidahl, *Ecology: The Story of Life, the Earth, and Everything,* Macmillan Australia (South Melbourne, Victoria, Australia), 1987.

Kath Lock, *Jennifer and Nicholas,* Keystone (Flinders Park, South Australia, Australia), 1989.

Yvonne Winer, *Herbertia the Vile,* Era (Flinders Park, South Australia, Australia), 1990.

Edel Wignell, *Voices,* Era (Flinders Park, South Australia, Australia), 1990.

Jane O'Loughlin, reteller, *Folk Tales: A Short Anthology,* Era (Flinders Park, South Australia, Australia), 1991.

Beryl Ayers, *Lucky I Have My Umbrella,* Martin International, 1992.

Josephine Croser, *Baleen,* Era (Flinders Park, South Australia, Australia), 1992.

Josephine Croser, *Patrick,* Era (Flinders Park, South Australia, Australia), 1992.

Kath Lock, reteller, *Little Burnt-Face,* Keystone (Flinders Park, South Australia, Australia), 1994.

Kath Lock, reteller, *The Tiger, the Brahmin, and the Jackal,* Keystone (Flinders Park, South Australia, Australia), 1994.

Kath Lock, reteller, *The Sea of Gold,* Keystone (Flinders Park, South Australia, Australia), 1994.

Nigel Croser, *Changing Shape,* Era (Flinders Park, South Australia, Australia), 1994.

June Loves, *One Week with My Grandmother,* Era (Flinders Park, South Australia, Australia), 1995.

Kath Lock, reteller, *Anansi and the Rubber Man,* Era (Flinders Park, South Australia, Australia), 1995.

Kath Lock, reteller, *The King's Gift,* Era (Flinders Park, South Australia, Australia), 1995.

Nigel Croser, *Cats,* Era (Flinders Park, South Australia, Australia), 1996.

Telene Clarke-Giles, *Molly McClog,* Era (Flinders Park, South Australia, Australia), 1996.

Dave Luckett, *The Best Batsman in the World,* Omnibus (Norwood, South Australia, Australia), 1996.

Josephine Croser, *Grandpa's Breakfast,* Era (Flinders Park, South Australia, Australia), 1997.

June Loves, *One Wild Weekend with My Grandmother,* Era (Flinders Park, South Australia, Australia), 1997.

Dave Luckett, *The Last Eleven,* Omnibus (Norwood, South Australia, Australia), 1997.

June Loves, *One Slow Saturday with My Grandmother,* Era (Flinders Park, South Australia, Australia), 1998.

Jonathan Harlen, *The Crescent Moon,* Lothian (Port Melbourne, Victoria, Australia), 1998.

Dyan Blacklock, *Olympia: Warrior Athletes of Ancient Greece,* Omnibus (Norwood, South Australia, Australia), 2000, Walker (New York, NY), 2001.

Dyan Blacklock, *The Roman Army: The Legendary Soldiers Who Created an Empire,* Walker (New York, NY), 2004.

Josephine Croser, reteller, *The Story of Atlas,* Era (Flinders Park, South Australia, Australia), 2004.

Michael Steer, reteller, *The Sun Chariot,* Era (Flinders Park, South Australia, Australia), 2004.

Max Fatchen and Dave Luckett, *Howzat!: A Celebration of Cricket,* Omnibus (Norwood, South Australia, Australia), 2005.

Sidelights

David Kennett is an artist and author who has contributed illustrations to a number of picture books published in his native Australia. Reviewing his work for Dyan Blalock's *The Roman Army: The Legendary Soldiers Who Created an Empire, Booklist* contributor Carolyn Phelan cited the "dignity and originality" of Kennett's "impressive illustrations," which include depictions of the activities, clothing and equipment, weaponry, and battle stance of the army that once conquered much of the world. The comic-book format employed in *The Roman Army,* which pairs Blalock's "clear and

David Kennett's interest in Ancient Egypt inspired his self-illustrated picture book **Pharaoh: Life and Afterlife of a God.** (Illustration copyright © 2008 by David Kennett. Reprinted by permission of Walker Books for Young Readers, an imprint of Bloomsbury Publishing Inc. All rights reserved.)

lively" text and Kennett's "dramatic cartoon illustrations," in the words of *School Library Journal* critic Anne Chapman Callaghan, is also used in *Olympia: Warrior Athletes of Ancient Greece. Olympia* features "sophisticated, spectacular artwork" depicting races, wrestling, and several now-forgotten athletic challenges that challenged young competitors. The book "will grab readers," according to Roger Leslie in *Booklist,* and Callaghan dubbed *Olympia* "an enticing look at the ancient Olympics."

In addition to Kennett's work as an illustrator, he has also produced a series of books on animals as well as the self-illustrated *Pharaoh: Life and Afterlife of a God.* In the book, Kennett centers on the reign of Rameses II, and focuses on the culture prevalent in the kingdom of Egypt over 3,000 years ago. His text is augmented with paintings of various sizes that capture the rich details of many Egyptian artifacts. "Each page presents a richly colored visual melange that will draw viewers in," wrote John Peters in his *School Library Journal* review of *Pharaoh,* and in *Kirkus Reviews* a critic characterized the book as "a beautiful encapsulation of a pharaoh's duties, from life to death and beyond." In *Booklist* Ilene Cooper praised Kennett's "masterful artwork" and wrote that his detailed "narrative" takes readers from topic to topic "simply and logically."

Kennett once told *SATA:* "My maternal grandfather had a wonderful library—many books on mythology, ancient history, and natural history. I particularly remember some illustrations that I now suppose were Gustav Doré's Bible illustrations.

"My childhood and a lot of my adolescence were spent in a perpetual daydream of Vikings, Native Americans, and Greek myths. In the later 1960s and 1970s the work of Frank Frazetta overwhelmed me and I tried unsuccessfully to draw and paint just like him. I still regard him as my most important and lasting influence.

"Rosemary Sutcliffe and Henry Treece are the two authors whose books have meant most to me. Sutcliffe was particularly helpful to me as I was a very shy boy and she wrote very well of outsiders and I felt that at least one person understood how I felt. She also wrote me two very nice letters telling me about her latest projects and research. I did feel like her special friend. As an adult I realise it was also a very kind and generous amount of time to spend on a complete stranger on the other side of the world. The work of Victor Ambrus, Charles Keeping, N.C. Wyeth, and Howard Pyle have also had a lasting and continuing influence on my work.

"I hope that some of the pictures I draw will leave some kind of lasting impression on some child in much the same way that pictures of my childhood have stayed with me."

Biographical and Critical Sources

PERIODICALS

Arithmetic Teacher, October, 1993, David J. Whittin, review of *Two Feet,* p. 123.
Booklist, September 15, 2001, Roger Leslie, review of *Olympia: Warrior Athletes of Ancient Greece,* p. 217; March 1, 2004, Carolyn Phelan, review of *The Roman Army: The Legendary Soldiers Who Created an Empire,* p. 1189; May 1, 2008, Ilene Cooper, review of *Pharaoh: Life and Afterlife of a God,* p. 89.
School Library Journal, October, 2001, Anne Chapman Callaghan, review of *Olympia,* p. 178; April, 2004, Anne Chapman Callaghan, review of *The Roman Army,* p. 165; February, 2008, John Peters, review of *Pharaoh,* p. 136.

ONLINE

David Kennett Web log, http://bce-kennettdraws.blogspot. com (October 30, 2009).*

*   *   *

KESSLER, Liz 1966-

Personal

Born 1966, in Southport, England. *Education:* Attended Loughborough University; Keele University, teaching qualification; Manchester Metropolitan University, M.A. *Hobbies and other interests:* Sailing, playing the guitar, surfing, poi.

Addresses

Home—Cornwall, England. *Agent*—Catherine Clarke, Felicity Bryan Agency, 2A N. Parade Ave., Oxford OX2 6LX, England. *E-mail*—lizkesslerweb@hotmail.co.uk.

Career

Author, educator, and journalist. Has taught English, media studies, and creative writing; journalist for local and regional newspapers in Manchester, England, and York, England; Cornerstones (advisory and editorial service), managing editor for children's division.

Writings

"EMILY WINDSNAP" MIDDLE-GRADE NOVEL SERIES

The Tail of Emily Windsnap, illustrated by Sarah Gibb, Orion (London, England), 2003, Candlewick Press (Cambridge, MA), 2004.
Emily Windsnap and the Monster from the Deep, illustrated by Sarah Gibb, Orion (London, England), 2004, Candlewick Press (Cambridge, MA), 2006.

Emily Windsnap and the Castle in the Mist, illustrated by Natacha Ledwidge, Orion (London, England), 2006, Candlewick Press (Cambridge, MA), 2007.

Emily Windsnap's Friendship Book, Orion (London, England), 2008, Candlewick Press (Cambridge, MA), 2009.

Emily Windsnap and the Siren's Secret, Orion (London, England), 2009, Candlewick Press (Cambridge, MA), 2010.

"PHILIPPA FISHER" MIDDLE-GRADE NOVEL SERIES

Philippa Fisher's Fairy Godsister, illustrated by Katie May, Orion (London, England), 2007, Candlewick Press (Cambridge, MA), 2008.

Philippa Fisher and the Dream-maker's Daughter, illustrated by Katie May, Candlewick Press (Cambridge, MA), 2009.

Adaptations

The Tail of Emily Windsnap, Emily Windsnap and the Monster from the Deep, and *Emily Windsnap and the Castle in the Mist* were adapted as audiobooks.

Sidelights

A former teacher and journalist, Liz Kessler is the author of the popular "Emily Windsnap" middle-grade novels. The series features the adventures of the title character, a seventh grader who is half human and half mermaid. "I am fascinated by the sea and all the mysteries of the ocean," Kessler stated on her home page. "It's so huge and there is so much of it that we haven't discovered and know nothing about. To me, mermaids represent the possibilities of what might just exist, on the edges of our imaginations and our world. In real life, the only mermaids I know are the ones in my books, but I like to believe that they might, just might, exist out there somewhere."

In *The Tail of Emily Windsnap,* the first work in the fantasy series, Kessler introduces her unusual protagonist, who lives on a houseboat with her mother. When Emily takes a swim class at school, she immediately notices her body undergoing a bizarre transformation: her legs begin melding into a fishtail once she enters the water and return to their normal state as soon as she returns to dry land. Fascinated, Emily begins exploring the undersea world at night, and she soon discovers a "mer-city" where she meets a new friend, the mermaid Shona. With Shona's help, Emily learns about the history of illegal marriages between mer-people and humans, a history that helps shed light on the secret identity of her father. According to *School Library Journal* critic Beth Tegart, *The Tail of Emily Windsnap* "has some delightful moments," and Jennifer Mattson noted in *Booklist* that Kessler's "premise of someone slipping easily into a shimmery underwater world has considerable allure."

Emily Windsnap and the Monster from the Deep continues the adventures of the young mer-creature, who now lives with her human mother and merman father on Al-

lpoints Island, a safe haven in the center of the Bermuda Triangle. While investigating a hidden lagoon, Emily inadvertently awakens a kraken, a ferocious monster that threatens the island. She also outrages Neptune, the god of the sea, who has placed her family under his protection. Emily must take responsibility for her actions and stop the kraken before it destroys a cruise ship carrying a rival from Emily's old school. "High-action adventure, a plucky protagonist, and whimsical illustrations enliven this sea fantasy," Anne O'Malley remarked in a review of *Emily Windsnap and the Monster from the Deep* for *Booklist.* In *School Library Journal* Elizabeth Bird predicted that "mermaid lovers everywhere will undoubtedly enjoy this story."

In the third series entry, *Emily Windsnap and the Castle in the Mist,* the young protagonist once again upsets Neptune after she finds a diamond ring that the god discarded long ago. An angry Neptune now places a curse on the girl that will force her to become fully human or fully mermaid and thus lose contact with one of her parents forever. Along with Shona and a mysterious mer-boy who lives in a secret castle, Emily attempts to undo Neptune's curse. Kessler "keeps the story moving, with each chapter posing a new problem," Adrienne Furness remarked in *School Library Journal,* and a *Kirkus Reviews* contributor described *Emily Windsnap and the Castle in the Mist* as "a friendship story with more than a touch of make believe."

In addition to her "Emily Windsnap" series, Kessler is also the creator of the "Philippa Fisher" series of middle-grade novels, including *Philippa Fisher's Fairy Godsister,* called "a realistic school story with a magical twist" by *Horn Book* contributor Susan Dove Lempke. The work centers on a lonely eleven-year-old girl whose best friend has recently moved and whose free-spirited parents are a constant source of embarrassment to her. Philippa receives help in the form of Daisy, a surly fairy who will grant the youngster three wishes, although not without complications. Kessler's "gentle storytelling and theme of finding oneself will resonate with girls going through their own emotional awakenings," predicted Robyn Gioia in her *School Library Journal* review of *Philippa Fisher's Fairy Godsister.* As Kay Weisman wrote of the same novel in *Booklist,* Kessler's "message of being careful what you wish for is delivered with a light touch."

Biographical and Critical Sources

PERIODICALS

Booklist, May 1, 2004, Jennifer Mattson, review of *The Tail of Emily Windsnap,* p. 1559; June 1, 2006, Anne O'Malley, review of *Emily Windsnap and the Monster from the Deep,* p. 72; September 15, 2007, Jennifer Mattson, review of *Emily Windsnap and the Castle in the Mist,* p. 61; October 15, 2008, Kay Weisman, review of *Philippa Fisher's Fairy Godsister,* p. 42.

Horn Book, November-December, 2008, Susan Dove Lempke, review of *Philippa Fisher's Fairy Godsister,* p. 707.

Kirkus Reviews, April 1, 2006, review of *Emily Windsnap and the Monster from the Deep,* p. 350; April 1, 2007, review of *Emily Windsnap and the Castle in the Mist;* August 1, 2008, review of *Philippa Fisher's Fairy Godsister.*

Publishers Weekly, May 31, 2004, review of *The Tail of Emily Windsnap,* p. 74.

School Library Journal, June, 2004, Beth Tegart, review of *The Tail of Emily Windsnap,* p. 144; July, 2006, Elizabeth Bird, review of *Emily Windsnap and the Monster from the Deep,* p. 106; June, 2007, Adrienne Furness, review of *Emily Windsnap and the Castle in the Mist,* p. 150; November, 2008, Robyn Gioia, review of *Philippa Fisher's Fairy Godsister,* p. 124.

ONLINE

Bookwitch Web log, http://bookwitch.wordpress.com/ (October 10, 2009), "Liz Kessler—'Straightforward and Simple, That's Me.'"

Library of Congress Web site, http://www.loc.gov/bookfest/2009/toolkit/ (October 10, 2009), "Meet the Authors: Liz Kessler."

Liz Kessler Home Page, http://www.lizkessler.co.uk (October 10, 2009).

Liz Kessler Web log, http://lizkessler.blogspot.com/ (October 10, 2009).

*   *   *

KILPATRICK, Don

Personal

Born in UT; married; children. *Education:* Utah State University, B.A. (illustration); Syracuse University, M.F.A.

Addresses

Home—MI. *Agent*—Morgan Gaynin, Inc., 194 3rd Ave., Ste. 3, New York, NY 10003; infomorgangaynin.com.

Career

Illustrator, educator, and graphic artist. College of Creative Studies, Detroit, MI, instructor; illustration work includes designing medal for 2002 Winter Olympics. ICON 5 (illustration conference), member of board.

Member

San Francisco Society of Illustrators (former president).

Awards, Honors

Honors from AIGA and Society of Illustrators.

Illustrator

Dianne Billstrom, *You Can't Go to School Naked!,* G.P. Putnam's Sons (New York, NY), 2008.

Contributor to periodicals, including *American Illustration, 3x3, Bicycling, Fortune, Business Week, PC, Los Angeles Times Book Review,* and *Communication Arts.*

Biographical and Critical Sources

PERIODICALS

Kirkus Reviews, June 15, 2008, review of *You Can't Go to School Naked!*

School Library Journal, July, 2008, Catherine Callegari, review of *You Can't Go to School Naked!,* p. 66.

ONLINE

Don Kilpatrick Home Page, http://www.donkilpatrick.com (October 20, 2009).

Don Kilpatrick Web log, http://www.drawger.com/donkilpatrick (October 20, 2009).*

*   *   *

KING, Willie Christine
See FARRIS, Christine King

*   *   *

KOLAR, Bob 1960(?)-

Personal

Born c. 1960; children: Jonathan.

Addresses

Home—Kansas City, MO.

Career

Author and illustrator.

Writings

SELF-ILLUSTRATED

Stomp, Stomp!, North-South Books (New York, NY), 1997.

Do You Want to Play?: A Book about Being Friends, Dutton (New York, NY), 1999.

Racer Dogs, Dutton (New York, NY), 2003.

Big Kicks, Candlewick Press (Cambridge, MA), 2008.

Code Blue, Cartwheel Books (New York, NY), 2010.

ILLUSTRATOR

Claire Masurel, *A Cat and a Dog,* North-South Books (New York, NY), 2001.

Marjorie Blain Parker, *Hello School Bus!*, Cartwheel Books (New York, NY), 2004.

Marjorie Blain Parker, *Hello Fire Truck!*, Scholastic (New York, NY), 2004.

Marjorie Blain Parker, *Hello Freight Train!*, Scholastic (New York, NY), 2005.

Alethea Kontis, *Alpha Oops!: The Day the Z Went First,* Candlewick Press (Cambridge, MA), 2006.

Margery Cuyler, *The Little Dump Truck,* Holt (New York, NY), 2009.

Alethea Kontis, *Alpha Oops!: H Is for Halloween,* Candlewick Press (Somerville, MA), 2010.

Adaptations

Racer Dogs was adapted as the animated film *Turbo Dogs* and produced for National Broadcasting Company (NBC) television, 2008.

Sidelights

After publishing his first self-illustrated picture book, *Stomp, Stomp!,* in 1997, Bob Kolar produced *Do You Want to Play?: A Book about Being Friends* two years later. In a story aimed at young readers, Kolar helps children identify and develop qualities that foster good relationships with others. Featuring a board game in the center pages of the book, *Do You Want to Play?* helps friends learn ways to resolve differences in a positive manner and provides ideas for making new friends by telling silly jokes. Writing in *School Arts,* Ken Marantz described *Do You Want to Play?* as "a frenetic, wildly imaginative exposition on a child's perspective about friendship," while *Booklist* contributor Michael Cart wrote that Kolar offers readers "a veritable paean to 'palship'" in his picture book. A *Publishers Weekly* critic suggested that *Do You Want to Play?* invites repeated readings, calling the book "ideal when shared among two or more readers at a time."

Enthusiastic animals take center stage in two other books by Kolar. In *Racer Dogs* eight canines set out on a competition to discover who can race his or her car the fastest. Following the story's action, readers can absorb the several layers of detail the author/illustration includes on each page, from information on the varied vehicles driven by the pups to material explaining each animal's unique personality. "Young motor-heads will enjoy the giddy humor and multiple subplots of this speedfest," wrote a *Publishers Weekly* contributor. In *Booklist* Tim Arnold also predicted that children would

Bob Kolar's illustration projects include creating whimsical art for Claire Masurel's picture-book story **A Cat and a Dog.** (Illustration copyright © 2001 by Bob Kolar. Reproduced by permission.)

enjoy reading about the characters, finding *Racer Dogs* "a handsome, enjoyable book, especially for children willing to spend time deconstructing the pictures."

Big Kicks features a large, but unathletic bear recruited to fill an empty spot on the soccer team. Happy to help his friends, Biggie Bear nonetheless struggles to keep up with the other animals, finding the game a challenge. However, when the stamp-collecting bear reaches down to pick up an errant specimen he inadvertently heads the ball into the net, winning the game for his team. Several reviewers offered enthusiastic comments about Kolar's text and artwork, *School Library Journal* critic Gay Lynn Van Vleck predicting that "this simple tale that encourages trying things out of one's comfort zone will capture prospective players." In *Booklist* Ilene Cooper described Kolar's "delightful digital artwork" as "vibrant without being garish and simple without being simplistic."

In addition to his own books, Kolar has also illustrated the works of other authors, including Claire Masurel's *A Cat and a Dog* and Alethea Kontis's *Alpha Oops!: The Day the Z Went First*. Eternal enemies, Cat and Dog engage in perpetual hostilities, either actively quarreling or ignoring each other in Masurel's story. However, after Cat's favorite toy mouse falls into a pond and Dog's ball becomes stuck high in a tree, the enemies decide to help one another retrieve their respective belongings and come to be friends. In *Alpha Oops!* mutiny breaks out among the letters of the alphabet when letter Z challenges the first-place position of leading letter A. Inspired by the rebellious Z, other letters begin questioning their position in the alphabet, too. Only at story's end does A take charge, restoring order among the out-of-control characters. A *Publishers Weekly* contributor wrote that the artist's "highly stylized watercolor-and-ink characterizations . . . distill the drama down to its comic essence" in *A Cat and a Dog*, while a *Kirkus Reviews* critic wrote of *Alpha Oops!* that the "hysterical" images "suit the zaniness of the text perfectly."

Kolar's original self-illustrated picture books include the energetic **Big Kicks.** (Illustration copyright © 2008 by Bob Kolar. Reproduced by permission of Candlewick Press, Inc., Somerville, MA.)

Biographical and Critical Sources

PERIODICALS

Booklist, July, 1999, Michael Cart, review of *Do You Want to Play?: A Book about Being Friends,* p. 1952; June 1, 2001, Lauren Peterson, review of *A Cat and a Dog,* p. 1894; February 1, 2003, Tim Arnold, review of *Racer Dogs,* p. 1001; May 15, 2005, Gillian Engberg, review of *Hello Freight Train!,* p. 1666; September 1, 2006, Carolyn Phelan, review of *Alpha Oops!: The Day the Z Went First,* p. 137; September 1, 2008, Ilene Cooper, review of *Big Kicks,* p. 115.

Kirkus Reviews, February 15, 2003, review of *Racer Dogs,* p. 309; August 1, 2006, review of *Alpha Oops!,* p. 789; July 15, 2008, review of *Big Kicks.*

Publishers Weekly, May 31, 1999, review of *Do You Want to Play?,* p. 93; March 26, 2001, review of *A Cat and a Dog,* p. 91; December 23, 2002, review of *Racer Dogs,* p. 69; August 21, 2006, review of *Alpha Oops!,* p. 67.

School Arts, February, 2000, Ken Marantz, review of *Do You Want to Play?,* p. 60.

School Library Journal, July, 2001, Sheilah Kosco, review of *A Cat and a Dog,* p. 85; September, 2008, Gay Lynn Van Vleck, review of *Big Kicks,* p. 152.

ONLINE

Bob Kolar Web Log, http://whoop-dee-do.blogspot.com (October 30, 2009).*

*   *   *

KOREN, Edward 1935-

Personal

Born December 13, 1935, in New York, NY; son of Harry L. (a dentist) and Elizabeth (a teacher) Koren; married Curtis Ingham (a school administrator); children: Nathaniel, Alexandra, Ben. *Education:* Columbia University, B.A., 1957; studied at Atelier 17 (Paris, France); Pratt Institute, M.F.A., 1964.

Addresses

Home and office—Brookfield, VT. *Agent*—Pippin Properties, 155 E. 38th St., Ste. 2H, New York, NY 10016.

Career

Artist, illustrator, and educator. Cartoonist for *New Yorker* magazine, 1962—. Brown University, Providence, RI, faculty member, 1964, associate professor of art, 1969-77, adjunct associate professor, 1977. Editor-in-chief, *Columbia Jester,* 1957. Fellow, American Academy, Berlin, Germany, 2003. Captain of Brookfield (VT) Volunteer Fire Department. *Exhibitions:* One-man traveling exhibition staged at Art Gallery, State University of New York, Albany, 1982. Work exhibited in group shows, including Exposition Dessins d'Humeur, Society Protectrice d'Humeur, Avignon, France, 1973, Biennale Illustration, Bratislav, Czechoslovakia, 1973, Society of Illustrators, New York, NY, 1973, Grolier Club, 1975, Terry Dintinfass Gallery, New York, NY, 1975-77, 1979, 1991, and Virginia Lynch Gallery, 1992, 1994, 2000, 2002. Work held in permanent collections at Fogg Museum, Princeton University Museum, Rhode Island School of Design Museum, Fitzwilliam Museum, Swann Collection of Cartoon and Caricature, and Library of Congress.

Member

Authors League, Society of American Graphic Artists.

Awards, Honors

Guggenheim fellowship, 1970-71; *New York Times* Best Illustrated Children's Book of the Year designation, 1972, for *Behind the Wheel;* D.H.L., Union College, 1984; Vermont Governor's Award for Excellence in the Arts, 2007.

Writings

SELF-ILLUSTRATED

Don't Talk to Strange Bears, Simon & Schuster (New York, NY), 1969.

Behind the Wheel, Holt, Rinehart & Winston (New York, NY), 1972.

Do You Want to Talk about It?, Pantheon (New York, NY), 1976.

Are You Happy?, and Other Questions Lovers Ask, Pantheon (New York, NY), 1978.

"Well, There's Your Problem," Penguin (New York, NY), 1980.

The Penguin Edward Koren, Penguin (New York, NY), 1982.

Caution: Small Ensembles, Pantheon (New York, NY), 1983.

What about Me?: Cartoons from the New Yorker, Pantheon Books (New York, NY), 1989.

Quality Time: Parenting, Progeny, and Pets, Villard Books (New York, NY), 1995.

The Hard Work of Simple Living: A Somewhat Blank Book for the Sustainable Hedonist, Chelsea Green (White River Junction, VT), 1998.

Very Hairy Harry, Joanna Cotler Books (New York, NY), 2003.

ILLUSTRATOR

Delia Ephron, *How to Eat like a Child, and Other Lessons in Not Being a Grown-up,* Viking (New York, NY), 1978.

Winifred Rosen, *Dragons Hate to Be Discreet,* Knopf (New York, NY), 1978.

Delia Ephron, *Teenage Romance; or, How to Die of Embarrassment,* Viking (New York, NY), 1981.

Burton Bernstein, *Plane Crazy: A Celebration of Flying,* Houghton Mifflin (New York, NY), 1985.

Bay Judson, *Art Ventures: A Guide for Families to Ten Works of Art in the Carnegie Museum of Art,* Carnegie Museum of Art (Pittsburgh, PA), 1987.

Delia Ephron, *Do I Have to Say Hello?,* Viking (New York, NY), 1989.

Peter Mayle, *A Dog's Life,* Knopf (New York, NY), 1995.

Alice Trillin, *Dear Bruno,* New Press (New York, NY), 1996.

Lewis Carroll, *Feeding the Mind,* Levenger Press (Delray Beach, FL), 1999.

Lewis Carroll, *Eight or Nine Wise Words about Letter-writing,* Levenger Press (Delray Beach, FL), 1999.

George Plimpton, *Pet Peeves; or, Whatever Happened to Doctor Rawff?,* Atlantic Monthly Press (New York, NY), 2000.

Mary-Lou Weisman, *Traveling while Married,* Algonquin Books (Chapel Hill, NC), 2003.

Judy Sierra, *Thelonius Monster's Sky-high Fly Pie,* Knopf (New York, NY), 2005.

Alan Katz, *Oops!* (poems), Margaret K. McElderry Books (New York, NY), 2008.

Jennifer Huget, *How to Clean Your Room in Ten Easy Steps,* Schwartz & Wade Books (New York, NY), 2009.

Alan Katz, *Uh-oh!* (poems), Margaret K. McElderry Books (New York, NY), 2010.

Contributor to books, including *The Gordon of Sesame Street Storybook,* 1972, and *Last Laughs: Cartoons about Aging, Retirement . . . and the Great Beyond,* edited by Mort Gerberg, Scribner (New York, NY), 2007. Contributor of drawings, caricatures, and illustrations to periodicals and magazines such as *New York Times, Newsweek, Time, Gentleman's Quarterly, Esquire, Sports Illustrated, Vogue, Fortune, Vanity Fair, Nation,* and *Boston Globe.*

Sidelights

Edward Koren's cartoons and magazine illustrations are populated by characters that are identifiably human, whether drawn as people or as sly but earnest human-animal hybrids. Koren is known for work infused with clever wordplay, insightful commentary, and ironic observations. Alongside his hapless men and women are his familiar furry, spike-toothed creatures, jovial anthropomorphic monsters with keen wits, bizarre lifestyles, and all-too-human reactions to everyday problems. Koren is a member of a "small, magic group of artists whose work generates instant recognition," wrote a critic writing in the *Washington Post Book World.*

Koren's drawings have appeared in top-flight magazines and newspapers such as *Vanity Fair, Time, Newsweek,* and the *New York Times.* Many of his works have appeared in the *New Yorker* magazine, and his collected works include these illustrations. "He is a brand—that's the best way to put it," Mark Singer remarked of Koren in a *Vermont Quarterly* interview with Joyce Marcel. "His style of drawings is fundamentally distinctive. A Koren drawing looks like a Koren drawing whether it's in the *New Yorker* or the *New York Times* or a Vermont publication. Or in the books Ed illustrates and writes. The other essential with a Koren drawing . . . is that the drawing itself is so wonderfully drawn."

In the title cartoon of *"Well, There's Your Problem,"* a car mechanic diagnoses the customer's problems when he finds one of Koren's trademark hairy, grinning monsters under the hood. In another cartoon, houses, trees, and other surroundings droop sadly as a woman is told her depression is contagious. William Bradley Hooper, writing in *Booklist,* called *"Well, There's Your Problem"* "wonderfully witty," and a *New York Times Book Review* critic observed that Koren's characters are "wonderful, vulnerable ugly ducklings" who "remain resilient, appearing to draw strength and vitality from the company of their peers."

What about Me?: Cartoons from the New Yorker offers cartoons with social commentary as well as the usual antics from Koren's furry, wooly semi-humans. There remains "something loveable" about Koren's characters, remarked a reviewer in the *Washington Post Book World.* "Maybe that's because their concerns are recognizably ours." Hooper, in another *Booklist* review, characterized *The Penguin Edward Koren* as "superior humor." Howard Kaplan, in a *Village Voice* review of *Caution: Small Ensembles,* concluded that Koren's work is "self-deprecating humor on a grand scale; for most of us, describing a Koren cartoon is like telling a joke on ourselves."

Outside of his humorous cartoons, Koren is an accomplished artist with numerous national and international exhibitions to his credit. He also lends his artistic skills to illustrating the works of others. *Teenage Romance; or, How to Die of Embarrassment,* written by Delia Ephron, is a lighthearted how-to manual for adolescents that covers the agonizing details of teenage relationships. Koren's illustrations for this book "capture the more unforgettable moments," such as awk-

Edward Koren contributes his unique scribbly pen-and-ink art to Peter Mayles's whimsical picture book **A Dog's Life.** (Vintage Books, 1995. Reproduced by permission of Edward Koren, www.rileyillustration.com.)

ward moments on dates, observed a critic in *New York Times Book Review.* Ephron and Koren have also produced *Do I Have to Say Hello?,* a book of manners that looks at the proper social behavior for children. "Everyone involved with children will recognize and enjoy (if ruefully) the trials so humorously presented by writer and artist," observed a critic in *Publishers Weekly. Plane Crazy: A Celebration of Flying,* by *New Yorker* writer Burton Bernstein, shares Bernstein's "personal joy, exuberance, and love of flight and the process of learning how to fly," wrote William A. McIntyre in *Library Journal.* Koren's "benignly squiggly drawings gracefully complement the book," commented Paul Sonnenburg in the *Los Angeles Times Book Review.*

Dear Bruno, written by Alice Trillin, is a "gently reassuring book, illustrated with whimsical drawings" that are intended to provide encouragement to children with cancer and to their parents and caregivers, wrote a *Publishers Weekly* reviewer. The text of the book is Trillin's letter to Bruno Navasky, a friend's twelve-year-old son who suffered from cancer. Trillin also relates her own experience with cancer. She offers Bruno encouragement through humor and urges him to develop personal resolve—even irreverence—in the face of his condition. Both Trillin and Bruno overcame their illnesses to lead successful lives.

In *The Hard Work of Simple Living: A Somewhat Blank Book for the Sustainable Hedonist,* Koren contributes cartoons that encourage the ideas of simple, sustainable living and of existing in harmony with nature. The "somewhat blank" format makes the book in reality a journal, with Koren's cartoons, commentary from other authors who support simple living, and plenty of empty space for readers to jot down their own ideas. Susan Dawson, writing in *Workbook,* called *The Hard Work of Simple Living* "a delightful collection" and a "light-hearted book" that seeks to help people "make fundamental shifts in their behavior to save the planet" by perceiving it to be fun—in other words, sustainable hedonism. Dawson quotes Bill McKibben, author of the book's foreword, as saying "The only genuinely subversive thing you can do in America is have more fun than other people. Which is not so hard. So get to it."

In Koren's children's book *Very Hairy Harry,* the "cartoonist employs his trademark line drawings for a barber's tall tale," Gay Lynn Van Vleck remarked in *School Library Journal.* Harry, a furry blue monster directly descended from Koren's well-known hairy half-humans, is considering the advantages and disadvantages of a haircut. Ben the Barber offers suggestions to Harry, noting that a lush long coat is good for such things as keeping warm in winter, hiding friends and pets, and for creating shade. But, Ben admits, being hairy can also mean being itchy—wildly, uncomfortably itchy. Harry chooses to have the haircut, but the trim leaves him looking little changed from the book's opening pages. "Koren allows readers to laugh with the fuzzy protagonist, and to recognize themselves in this all-too-familiar and often dreaded situation," observed a *Publishers Weekly* reviewer.

Koren has also provided the artwork for such children's works as *Thelonius Monster's Sky-high Fly Pie* by Judy Sierra and *Oops!* by Alan Katz. According to *Booklist* contributor Jennifer Mattson, Sierra's humorous story "provides . . . Koren with a vehicle for his signature snaggletoothed creatures." After swallowing a delicious fly, Thelonius Monster decides to throw an elaborate dinner party for his ravenous friends, with a culinary masterpiece—a pie filled with thousands of flies—planned for dessert. After e-mailing a friendly spider, who offers Thelonious helpful hints about trapping flies, the monster prepares a sticky crust that both lures and traps the insects. Once his monstrous guests have arrived, however, Theolonius realizes that he has forgotten to bake his creation, and the partygoers watch in horror as the pastry begins to soar through the air, powered by the flies' frantically beating wings. In the words of a *Publishers Weekly* reviewer, Koren's "endearing shaggy monsters leaven the half-baked tale with just the right amount of deadpan humor." In *School Library Journal,* Susan Weitz noted that the illustrator's "scruffy style gives all the characters a cheerful, easygoing beatnik look that is enormously appealing," and a critic in *Kirkus Reviews* praised the "irresistible and irrepressible monsters," garishly drawn in black and white with touches of green.

Oops!, a collection of nonsense poems by Katz, offers raucous takes on an eclectic set of kid-friendly topics, including annoying siblings, television viewing, passing gas, failing grades, and belly buttons. In "Whoosh!" a youngster realizes he has forgotten to dress properly when a breeze tickles him in surprising places, and "The Rear Wiper" concerns a misunderstanding about a car's back window. Koren's illustrations, remarked a critic in the *New York Times Book Review,* "give *Oops!* much of its scruffy charm," and a *Publishers Weekly* contributor noted that the illustrator "amplifies the humor with droll [black and white] drawings in his distinctive, antically cross-hatched style." Comparing Koren's work to that of Shel Silverstein, Donna Cardon wrote in *School Library Journal* that the "illustrations match the tone of the book and sometimes add extra interpretations of the poems."

Discussing his literary efforts, Koren noted on the Levenger Press Web site that his drawings maintain "the tradition of the frozen moment, the overarching sense of what the author is conveying." Recalling his decision to become a freelance artist, he told Marcel: "I made a choice, a decision that I was an artist and I'd just take my chances. So I left a steady job for the vicissitudes of the freelance life, and it's been up and down ever since. It hasn't changed. Sometimes I feel I'm a beginner all over again, and sometimes not. Art and illustrating—there's never anything certain. There's no steadiness to it at all. That's part of its charm, and that's part of its anxiety."

Koren once told *SATA:* "I write and draw for my own delight, for my children's amusement, and because I would be unhappy if I didn't. For example, I came to do *Behind the Wheel* because my son and I once explored construction equipment on a nearby highway construction site, and I was unable to satisfy his curiosity about the controls and instruments of the machines he was pretending to drive. The idea expanded to include a variety of machines that did different things. Of course, if I were not fascinated myself with them, I would not have done the book, nor would I have been interested in populating the pictures with the furry beasts who operate the machines, and which I love to draw. In all, most of my projects are labors of affection and humor."

Biographical and Critical Sources

BOOKS

Koren, Edward, *Do You Want to Talk about It?,* Pantheon Books (New York, NY), 1976.
Koren, Edward, *"Well, There's Your Problem,"* Penguin (New York, NY), 1980.
Koren, Edward, *The Hard Work of Simple Living: A Somewhat Blank Book for the Sustainable Hedonist,* Chelsea Green (White River Junction, VT), 1998.

PERIODICALS

Booklist, December 15, 1978, review of *Are You Happy?, and Other Questions Lovers Ask,* p. 652; November 15, 1980, William Bradley Hooper, review of *"Well, There's Your Problem,"* p. 431; January 1, 1983, William Bradley Hooper, review of *The Penguin Edward Koren,* p. 595; January 1, 1990, review of *What about Me? Cartoons from the New Yorker,* p. 878; May 1, 2006, Jennifer Mattson, review of *Thelonius Monster's Sky-high Fly Pie,* p. 94; March 1, 2008, Hazel Rochman, review of *Oops!,* p. 64.

Christian Science Monitor, December 4, 1978, review of *Are You Happy?, and Other Questions Lovers Ask.*

Cosmopolitan, December, 1981, Jane Clapperton, review of *Teenage Romance,* p. 22.

Horn Book, April, 1973, review of *Behind the Wheel,* p. 132.

Kirkus Reviews, July 1, 2003, review of *Very Hairy Harry,* p. 911; April 15, 2006, review of *Thelonius Monster's Sky-high Fly Pie,* p. 416; February 15, 2008, review of *Oops!*

Library Journal, December 1, 1980, A.J. Anderson, review of *"Well, There's Your Problem,"* p. 2498; September 1, 1985, William A. McIntyre, review of *Plane Crazy: A Celebration of Flying,* p. 206.

Los Angeles Times, October 27, 1985, review of *Plane Crazy,* p. B10.

Los Angeles Times Book Review, December 4, 1983, review of *Caution: Small Ensembles,* p. 9; October 20, 1985, Paul Sonnenburg, review of *Plane Crazy,* p. B2.

Modern Maturity, October-November, 1991, Charles Solomon, "Drawing from Experience: Four Grandmasters of Cartooning Look at the State of the Art," pp. 48-52.

Mother Jones, July, 1983, "Moods for Moderns," pp. 28-35.

New Yorker, December 13, 1976, review of *Do You Want to Talk about It?,* p. 162; December 21, 1998, review of *The Hard Work of Simple Living: A Somewhat Blank Book for the Sustainable Hedonist,* p. 99.

New York Times Book Review, April 9, 1972; September 4, 1977, review of *Do You Want to Talk about It?,* p. 23; November 13, 1977, review of *Behind the Wheel,* p. 40; December 14, 1980, review of *"Well, There's Your Problem,"* p. 18; September 5, 1982, review of *Teenage Romance,* p. 19; October 31, 1982, review of *The Penguin Edward Koren,* p. 35; April 9, 1995, review of *A Dog's Life,* p. 11; July 13, 2008, review of *Oops!,* p. 15.

Publishers Weekly, September 11, 1978, review of *Are You Happy?, and Other Questions Lovers Ask,* p. 84; September 29, 1989, review of *Do I Have to Say Hello?,* p. 53; February 13, 1995, review of *A Dog's Life,* pp. 63-64; March 11, 1996, review of *Dear Bruno,* p. 48; July 14, 2003, review of *Very Hairy Harry,* p. 76; May 15, 2006, review of *Thelonius Monster's Sky-high Fly Pie,* p. 71; March 17, 2008, review of *Oops!,* p. 70.

Rolling Stone, December 11, 1980, review of *"Well, There's Your Problem,"* p. 30.

School Library Journal, November, 2003, Gay Lynn Van Vleck, review of *Very Hairy Harry,* p. 104; May, 2006, Susan Weitz, review of *Thelonius Monster's Sky-high Fly Pie,* p. 104; April, 2008, Donna Cardon, review of *Oops!,* p. 164.

Scientific American, December, 1986, Philip Morrison, review of *Plane Crazy,* pp. 31-32.

Time, December 8, 1980, review of *"Well, There's Your Problem,"* p. 94.

Times Argus (Barre, VT), October 27, 2007, Daniel Barlow, "Cartoon Character: Ed Koren Honored."

Tribune Books (Chicago, IL), December 17, 1989, Clarence Petersen, review of *What about Me? Cartoons from the New Yorker,* p. 8.

Vermont Business, May 1, 2004, Joyce Marcel, "Profiles in Business: Edward Koren and the Economics of Cartooning."

Village Voice, December 6, 1983, Howard Kaplan, review of *Caution,* p. 54.

Washington Post Book World, October 23, 1977, review of *Do You Want to Talk about It?,* p. E7; November 5, 1989, review of *What about Me? Cartoons from the New Yorker,* p. 16.

Workbook, fall, 1998, Susan Dawson, review of *The Hard Work of Simple Living,* p. 117.

ONLINE

Levenger Press Web site, http://www.levenger.com/ (October 10, 2009), "Lewis Carroll's Newest Illustrator: The *New Yorker*'s Edward Koren."

Pippin Properties Web site, http://www.pippinproperties.com/ (October 10, 2009), "Edward Koren."*

*   *   *

KUSKIN, Karla 1932-2009
(Nicholas Charles, Nicholas J. Charles, Karla Seidman Kuskin, Karla Seidman)

OBITUARY NOTICE—

See index for *SATA* sketch: Born July 17, 1932, in New York, NY; died of cortical basal ganglionic degeneration, August 19, 2009, in Seattle, WA. Artist, illustrator, educator, poet, and author. Kuskin's award-winning career began when she was a graphic arts student at Yale University. Assigned to design and print a book, she added text as well, and the result was one of her most enduring titles, *Roar and More* (1956), in which she demonstrates the noises that animals make in the most vivid way possible without actually adding sound effects. Many of her other books brought animals together with the sounds they make, or invited the reader to muse on the impact of animals on their habitats, people on their world, and moving objects on their stationary surroundings. Kuskin published dozens of children's books, sometimes as author, more often as both author and illustrator. Her gift for impeccable rhyme and meter was irresistible to children and to the adults who read aloud to children; her ability to capture, absorb, and radiate the essence of childhood endeared her to critics as well. Most of her work reflected an unabashed celebration of the senses. Kuskin offered poetry and writing workshops to others, but it was her own talent that endured. She won many prizes from the American Institute of Graphic Arts, American Library Association, International Reading Association, Children's Book Council, and other organizations. She received a National Book Award nomination for *The Philharmonic Gets Dressed* (1982), in which she described what happens when an orchestra prepares for a performance before the curtain rises, in fact, before the musicians even leave their homes. Another popular book was *I Am Me* (2000), in which a little girl learns that different parts of her body resemble those of various relatives, but together the combination of features makes her unique. Collections of Kuskin's work include *Dogs & Dragons, Trees & Dreams: A Collection of Poems* (1980) and *Moon Have You Met My Mother? The Collected Poems of Karla Kuskin* (2002).

OBITUARIES AND OTHER SOURCES:

PERIODICALS

Los Angeles Times, August 24, 2009, p. A19.
New York Times, August 22, 2009, p. A13.
Washington Post, August 26, 2009, p. B5.

*   *   *

KUSKIN, Karla Seidman
See KUSKIN, Karla

L

LADD, London 1972(?)-

Personal

Born c. 1972; married; children: one daughter. *Education:* Syracuse University, B.A. (illustration), 2006.

Addresses

Home—Syracuse, NY. *E-mail*—london@londonladd. com.

Career

Illustrator, muralist, and educator. Syracuse University, Syracuse, NY, member of campus staff, 1999-2009, and instructor in art at Kuumba Project (after-school program), 2009. *Exhibitions:* Work exhibited at Everson Museum of Art and Syracuse, NY, Jazz Festival. Mural installations at Richmark Building, Syracuse.

Awards, Honors

Parents' Choice Award for historical fiction, 2008, and Andrew Carnegie Medal for Excellence in Children's Video, 2009, both for film adaptation of *March On!* by Christine King Farris.

Illustrator

Christine King Farris, *March On!: The Day My Brother Martin Changed the World,* Scholastic Press (New York, NY), 2008.
Carole Boston Weatherford, *The Little Speaker: Oprah Winfrey,* Marshall Cavendish (New York, NY), 2010.

Adaptations

March On! was adapted as a video recording with teacher's guide, Weston Woods, 2008.

Sidelights

London Ladd has loved drawing since his teen years. While working at Syracuse University in his late twenties, Ladd decided to return to school, and in 2006 he earned an illustration degree. Developing a painterly style, Ladd primarily uses acrylics, and his work has ranged from portraits and mural installations to artwork for book and album covers and magazine illustration. In addition, Ladd's paintings are a feature of the picture books *March On!: The Day My Brother Martin Changed the World,* by Christine King Farris, and *Oprah: The Little Speaker,* by award-winning writer Carole Boston Weatherford.

Winner of the 2009 Andrew Carnegie Medal in its video adaptation, *March On!* commemorates the 45th anniversary of Reverend Martin Luther King, Jr.'s famous "I Have a Dream" speech. Written by Dr. King's sister, the book follows the hours leading up to the speech, the action captured in Ladd's colorful images. In addition, Farris provides a backdrop to the speech, educating young readers about the civil-rights movement and the history of the historic March on Washington for Jobs and Freedom. Praising the artist's "use of color" and his ability to "create . . . visual energy," Lucinda Snyder Whitehurst described *March On!* as an "informative" resource for the early grades. A *Kirkus Reviews* writer cited Farris's "singular perspective," adding that Ladd's "fresh and affecting" images show him to be "a talented figure painter." In *Booklist* Hazel Rochman also had praise for *March On!,* describing the book as "a stirring, intimate view of a watershed moment."

Biographical and Critical Sources

PERIODICALS

Booklist, August 1, 2008, Hazel Rochman, review of *March On!: The Day My Brother Martin Changed the World,* p. 66.
Horn Book, August, 2008, review of *March On!,* p. 56.
Kirkus Reviews, August 15, 2008, review of *March On!*
Publishers Weekly, August 11, 2008, review of *March On!,* p. 47.

School Library Journal, October, 2008, Lucinda Snyder Whitehurst, review of *March On!,* p. 130; January, 2009, Teresa Bateman, review of *March On!* (video recording), p. 57.

Syracuse University Magazine, spring, 2009, Amy Speach, "Illustrating History" (profile), p. 16.

ONLINE

London Ladd Home Page, http://londonladd.com (October 30, 2009).

*   *   *

LANDSTRÖM, Lena 1943-

Personal

Born July 12, 1943, in Stockholm, Sweden; daughter of Bertil Löfquist (a doctor of engineering) and Ingrid Bern (a homemaker); married Olof Landström (an author and illustrator), June 11, 1971; children: Albin, Karl, Viktor. *Ethnicity:* "Swedish." *Education:* Attended Beckman's School of Design, 1966-69.

Addresses

Home—Sweden. *Office*—Umeå University, 901 87 Umeå, Sweden. *Agent*—Rabén & Sjögren, Tryckerigatan 4, Box 2052, 103 12 Stockholm, Sweden. *E-mail*—lena.landstrom@jus.umu.se.

Career

Children's book author, illustrator, and filmmaker. Freelance author and filmmaker creating projects for Swedish television, 1970—. Teaches at Umeå University.

Member

Föreningen Svenska Tecknare (Swedish Association of Illustrators and Graphic Designers), Sveriges Författarförbund (Swedish Writers' Union).

Awards, Honors

Parents Choice award for picture book, 1992, for *Will's New Cap;* Society for the Promotion of Literature award, for "Will" series of books; several international awards.

Writings

SELF-ILLUSTRATED

En flodhästsaga, Rabén & Sjögren (Stockholm, Sweden), 1993, translated by Joan Sandin as *A Hippo's Tale,* R&S Books (New York, NY), 2007.

De nya flodhästarna, Rabén & Sjögren (Stockholm, Sweden), 2002, translated by Joan Sandin as *The New Hippos,* R&S Books (New York, NY), 2003.

Småflodhästarnas äventyr, Rabén & Sjögren (Stockholm, Sweden), 2003, translated by Joan Sandin as *The Little Hippos' Adventure,* R&S Books (New York, NY), 2003.

"WILL" SERIES; WITH HUSBAND, OLOF LANDSTRÖM

Nisses nya mössa, Rabén & Sjögren (Stockholm, Sweden), 1990, translated by Richard E. Fisher as *Will's New Cap,* R&S Books (New York, NY), 1992.

Nisse hos frisören, Rabén & Sjögren (Stockholm, Sweden), 1991, translated by Elisabeth Dyssegaard as *Will Gets a Haircut,* R&S Books (New York, NY), 1993.

Nisse på stranden, Rabén & Sjögren (Stockholm, Sweden), 1992, translated by Carla Wiberg as *Will Goes to the Beach,* R&S Books (New York, NY), 1995.

Nisse gå till posten, Rabén & Sjögren (Stockholm, Sweden), 1993, translated by Elisabeth Dyssegaard as *Will Goes to the Post Office,* R&S Books (New York, NY), 1994.

"BOO AND BAA" SERIES; WITH OLOF LANDSTRÖM

Bu och Bä på kalashumör, Rabén & Sjögren (Stockholm, Sweden), 1995, translated by Joan Sandin as *Boo and Baa in a Party Mood,* R&S Books (New York, NY), 1996.

Bu och Bä i blåsväder, Rabén & Sjögren (Stockholm, Sweden), 1995, translated by Joan Sandin as *Boo and Baa in Windy Weather,* R&S Books (New York, NY), 1996.

Bu och Bä i städtagen, Rabén & Sjögren (Stockholm, Sweden), 1996, translated by Joan Sandin as *Boo and Baa on a Cleaning Spree,* R&S Books (New York, NY), 1997.

Bu och Bä på sjön, Rabén & Sjögren (Stockholm, Sweden), 1996, translated by Joan Sandin as *Boo and Baa at Sea,* R&S Books (New York, NY), 1997.

Bu och Bä i skogen, Rabén & Sjögren (Stockholm, Sweden), 1999, translated by Joan Sandin as *Boo and Baa in the Woods,* R&S Books (Stockholm, Sweden), 2000.

Bu och Bä blir blöta, Rabén & Sjögren (Stockholm, Sweden), 1999, translated by Joan Sandin as *Boo and Baa Get Wet,* R&S Books (London, England), 2000.

Bu och Bä får besök, Rabén & Sjögren (Stockholm, Sweden), 2006, translated by Joan Sandin as *Boo and Baa Have Company,* R&S Books (London, England), 2006.

OTHER

(Illustrator) Veronica Wägner, *Orpan tar täten,* Rabén & Sjögren (Stockholm, Sweden), 1996.

(Illustrator) Veronica Wägner, *Orpan försvinner,* Rabén & Sjögren (Stockholm, Sweden), 1997.

Fyra hönor och en tupp, illustrated by Olaf Landström, Rabén & Sjögren (Stockholm, Sweden), 2004, translated by Joan Sandin as *Four Hens and a Rooster,* R&S Books (New York, NY), 2005.

Landström's books have been translated into over a dozen languages, including French and Persian.

Adaptations

Sidelights

Together with her husband Olof Landström, author and illustrator Lena Landström has created several picture-book series that have captivated young readers both in Sweden and in the United States. Translated into over a dozen languages and published worldwide, the Landströms' engaging books include four volumes about a young boy named Will as well as the "Boo and Baa" series, which follows a pair of wide-eyed lambs through various humorous mishaps. *Will's New Cap* was the first Landström book to appear in English; since then the couple has produced three other "Will" books as well as seven books in the humorous "Boo and Baa" series. In praise of *Will Gets a Haircut*, *School Library Journal* reviewer Anna DeWind commented: "This Swedish import has a wonderfully kooky visual style and a positive, self-affirming, heartwarming message."

The Landströms' "Will" books feature the day-to-day activities of a young boy, all drawn in a cartoon style where characters are "brightly colored to stand out against the prevalent beiges and grays," explained a *Publishers Weekly* contributor. In *Will's New Cap*, the boy rushes out to show his friends his new baseball cap, but panic sets in when a sudden cloudburst wilts the brim and, unable to see, Will tumbles onto the sidewalk. With Mom to the rescue, all is made well in a book that *Five Owls* reviewer Barbara Knutson praised for its ability to focus on childhood concerns with "a satisfying simplicity." *Horn Book* critic Martha V. Parravano also offered warm words for the book, finding *Will's New Cap* "fresh and wonderfully child centered."

Will Gets a Haircut finds Will nervously awaiting the barber's shears, until he realizes that he can make his hair cut unique and one-of-a-kind, while a huge box sent by an uncle holds tantalizing mysteries for the young boy in *Will Goes to the Post Office*. Praising the latter book for its "brief text" and evocative yet simple illustrations, *Horn Book* contributor Parravano dubbed *Will Goes to the Post Office* a "slightly offbeat, very funny book," while in her *School Library Journal* review, Pamela K. Bomboy called it "a charmer." In another book in the series, *Will Goes to the Beach*, a rainy day at the seashore becomes an opportunity for Will to practice his swimming without distractions. Olof Landström's watercolor-and-ink drawings "deftly express nuances of action and feeling," according to Carolyn Phelan in a *Booklist* review.

In the Landströms' "Boo and Baa" series, two round-eyed sheep go about typical sheep business: practicing for dancing lessons, going to birthday parties, and playing croquet. Praised by many critics for their cheerful texts, these stories of two sheep that persevere despite a host of small-scale setbacks encourage young readers to take things in stride. Praising the creators of these "guileless sheep" in *Booklist*, Ilene Cooper commended the Landströms for creating stories with "a good balance of action and homey detail."

The "Boo and Baa" books have allowed Landström and her husband to indulge in their "talent for imbuing their bare-bones stories with funny narrative" asides, according to a *Publishers Weekly* reviewer. Continual mishaps confound the two sheep's efforts to get ready for a friend's birthday party in *Boo and Baa in a Party Mood*, while in *Boo and Baa in Windy Weather* the young sheep find that their trip home from the grocery store—uphill and during a snowstorm—is fraught with difficulty. Phelan praised the "simple texts" in the "Boo and Baa" titles, noting that they "underscore the humor and set the tone" for the series. Noting the "satisfying" nature of *Boo and Baa Get Wet*—where a sudden rain shower puts a damper on the sheeps' croquet plans—and *Boo and Baa in the Woods*—where a berry-picking trip find the pair hunted by ants—in her *School Library Journal* review of the two titles, Denise Reitsma stated that the illustrators' attention to Boo and Baa's facial expressions "add charm to the simple, pleasing stories."

In a slightly longer work, *Boo and Baa Have Company*, the two sheep interrupt their yard chores to rescue a cat that is stuck in a tree. After their attempts to lure kitty down with sardines and to entice it to cross a wooden plank both fail, Boo decides to climb up after the feline, only to find himself stranded in the branches when his ladder breaks. "The larger format means more space for the pictures and the comic possibilities thereof," reported *Horn Book* critic Martha V. Parravano. Critics especially noted the humor in the narrative. According to Amy Lilien-Harper, writing in *School Library Journal*, "the story is likely to tickle youngsters' funny bones," and a contributor in *Kirkus Reviews* remarked that young readers will "laugh out loud at the slapstick rescue attempts."

The Landströms have also combined their talents to produce *Four Hens and a Rooster*, a picture book with feminist overtones. When a quartet of chickens grows tired of sharing a cramped space at the feeding trough, they ask an arrogant rooster for more room. Instead of honoring their request, he tries to intimidate the hens by hiring a pair of tough "booster roosters." Undaunted, the hens enroll in a self-esteem course where they learn to stand up to the bully. A contributor in *Kirkus Reviews* applauded the "sunny, simple illustrations," noting that they "will draw at least as much laughter as the tongue-in-cheek plot."

In addition to her many collaborations with her husband, Landström has also created several self-illustrated books featuring a hippo family. In *The Little Hippos' Adventure*, she introduces the characters featured throughout the series. *The Little Hippos' Adventure* finds the trio of small hippos dissatisfied with the amenities at their family watering hole and wishing there was a higher diving board available. After repeated naggings by the young hippos, their fatigued parents relent and give their permission for the excited youngsters to clamber through the jungle to a new jumping-off spot high up on Tall Cliffs. Once granted, however, their wish brings worry, as the hippos realize that the dark, mysterious jungle with its hidden creatures is not such a fun place after all. Praising Landström's text and illustrations, a *Publishers Weekly* contributor cited in particular the "endearing images of the diminutive threesome . . . as they timidly make their way through the jungle." Reviewer Be Astengo echoed this praise in *School Library Journal,* noting that Landström's "cartoonlike" drawings create "a lovely, jungly effect" in a picture book that is "charming" over all.

In Landström's follow-up, *The New Hippos,* the arrival of a hippo mother and her baby at the riverbank upsets the residents of the hippo community, who initially prove to be most inhospitable neighbors. At first, the little hippos refuse to allow the new hippo youngster to use their diving board, but their reticence fades after he performs a stunning somersault into the water. Meanwhile, the adult hippos warily eye the newcomer as she constructs an unusual-looking but sturdy hut. After their new neighbors go missing, however, the hippos band together to search the jungle. Phelan called *The New Hippos* "a simple, yet satisfying, story that expresses the uneasiness groups and individuals sometimes experience" when they encounter significant change, and Bina Williams, writing in *School Library Journal,* noted that Landström's watercolor-and-ink illustrations "done in a shadowy palette of greens and browns effectively capture the emotions and charm of these creatures."

A third entry, *A Hippo's Tale,* focuses on Mrs. Hippopotamus, a private creature who prefers to live in solitude, apart from other hippos. When a monkey begins fishing just off her beach, she constructs a fancy bath house which unfortunately draws the attention of nosy, noisy neighbors. Mrs. Hippopotamus values her peace and quiet, though, and she ultimately devises a creative solution to her problem. "The fact that Landstrom allows her character to enjoy herself without becoming social is unique in picture books," remarked a critic in *Kirkus Reviews,* and Phelan noted that the "quiet picture book manages to convey a wide range of human emotions through its hippo heroine." In *School Library Journal,* Blair Christolon complimented Landström's artwork, noting that the "attractive ink-and-watercolor illustrations in a cool palette will entertain children."

Biographical and Critical Sources

PERIODICALS

Booklist, November 1, 1993, Carolyn Phelan, review of *Will Gets a Haircut,* p. 530; November 1, 1994, Carolyn Phelan, review of *Will Goes to the Post Office,* p. 507; September 1, 1995, Carolyn Phelan, review of *Will Goes to the Beach,* p. 87; November 1, 1996, Carolyn Phelan, reviews of *Boo and Baa in Windy Weather* and *Boo and Baa in a Party Mood,* p. 507; July, 1997, Ilene Cooper, reviews of *Boo and Baa at Sea* and *Boo and Baa on a Cleaning Spree,* p. 1822; November 15, 2000, Ilene Cooper, reviews of *Boo and Baa Get Wet* and *Boo and Baa in the Woods,* p. 648; April 15, 2003, Carolyn Phelan, review of *The New Hippos,* p. 1478; October 1, 2005, Hazel Rochman, review of *Four Hens and a Rooster,* p. 64; August 1, 2006, Carolyn Phelan, review of *Boo and Boa Have Company,* p. 75; May 1, 2007, Carolyn Phelan, review of *A Hippo's Tale,* p. 99.

Five Owls, November-December, 1992, Barbara Knutson, review of *Will's New Cap,* p. 32.

Horn Book, March-April, 1993, Martha V. Parravano, review of *Will's New Cap,* p. 199; March-April, 1994, Martha V. Parravano, review of *Will Gets a Haircut,* p. 224; March, 1995, Martha V. Parravano, review of *Will Goes to the Post Office,* p. 184; September-October, 2006, Martha V. Parravano, review of *Boo and Baa Have Company,* p. 568.

Kirkus Reviews, July 1, 1995, review of *Will Goes to the Beach,* p. 948; October 1, 2005, review of *Four Hens and a Rooster,* p. 1082; August 15, 2006, review of *Boo and Baa Have Company,* p. 846; March 15, 2007, review of *A Hippo's Tale.*

Publishers Weekly, October 26, 1992, review of *Will's New Cap,* p. 69; August 5, 1996, reviews of *Boo and Baa in Windy Weather* and *Boo and Baa in a Party Mood,* p. 440; April 7, 1997, review of *Boo and Baa on a Cleaning Spree,* p. 93; September 11, 2000, review of *Boo and Baa Get Wet,* p. 92; April 8, 2002, review of *The Little Hippos' Adventure,* p. 225; February 24, 2003, review of *The New Hippos,* p. 74; April 30, 2007, review of *A Hippo's Tale,* p. 163.

School Library Journal, February, 1994, Anna DeWind, review of *Will Gets a Haircut,* p. 88; December, 1994, Pamela K. Bomboy, review of *Will Goes to the Post Office,* p. 78; November, 1995, Ann Cook, review of *Will Goes to the Beach,* p. 74; November, 1996, Sharon R. Pearce, reviews of *Boo and Baa in Windy Weather* and *Boo and Baa in a Party Mood,* pp. 87-88; July, 1997, Darla Remple, reviews of *Boo and Baa on a Cleaning Spree* and *Boo and Baa at Sea,* p. 70; September, 2000, Denise Reitsma, reviews of *Boo and Baa in the Woods* and *Boo and Baa Get Wet,* p. 203; April, 2002, Be Astengo, review of *The Little Hippos' Adventure,* p. 114; April, 2003, Bina Williams, review of *The New Hippos,* p. 130; December, 2005, Kirsten Cutler, review of *Four Hens and a Rooster,* p. 118; September, 2006, Amy Lilien-Harper, review of *Boo and Baa Have Company,* p. 177; July, 2007, Blair Christolon, review of *A Hippo's Tale,* p. 80.

Tribune Books (Chicago, IL), October 10, 1993, Mary Harris Veeder, review of *Will Gets a Haircut,* p. 6.

Washington Post Book World, November 27, 2005, Elizabeth Ward, review of *Four Hens and a Rooster,* p. 1.

ONLINE

Rabén & Sjögren Web site, http://www.norstedtsforlags
grupp.se/ (April 1, 2008), "Lena Landström."*

*   *   *

LAUNDER, Sally

Personal
Born in England.

Addresses
Home—Ipswich, Suffolk, England. *E-mail*—sally@
sallylaunder.co.uk.

Career
Illustrator and animator.

Member
Association of Illustrators.

Illustrator
Mary Cockett, *Tower Raven,* Abelard-Schuman (London,
England), 1975.
Felicia Law, *The Ballet Class,* Octopus Books (London,
England), 1980.
D.K. Swan, *The Princess and the Pea,* Longman (Harlow,
England), 1986.
D.K. Swan, *The Four Musicians,* Longman (Harlow,
England), 1986.
D.K. Swan, *The Emperor's New Clothes,* Longman (Har-
low, England), 1986.
D.K. Swan, *Rapunzel,* Longman (Harlow, England), 1986.
D.K. Swan, *Puss in Boots,* Longman (Harlow, England),
1986.
H.C. Anderson, *The Ugly Duckling,* Longman (Harlow,
England), 1986.
Nicola Hall, *Ice Skating,* Hodder Children's (London,
England), 2000.
(With Michael Woods) George Grey, *America: The Mak-
ing of a Nation,* Little, Brown (New York, NY), 2008.

Contributor of illustrations to *Association of Illustrators
Annual.*

Biographical and Critical Sources

PERIODICALS

School Library Journal, February, 2009, Sarah Provence,
review of *America: The Making of a Nation,* p. 126.

ONLINE

Sally Launder Home Page, http://www.sallylaunder.co.uk
(October 28, 2009).*

LESTER, Mike 1955-

Personal
Born March 3, 1955, in Atlanta, GA; son of Bob (an
automobile dealer) and Helen (a homemaker) Lester;
married Cynthia Yancey (a teacher), November 20,
1982; children: Grady, Hope. *Education:* University of
Georgia, B.A. (graphic design), 1977. *Hobbies and
other interests:* Family, golf, cooking.

Addresses
Home—Rome, GA. *Office*—Mike Lester Studio, 301 E.
5th Ave., Rome, GA 30161; Rome News-Tribune, 305
E. 6th Ave., P.O. Box 1633, Rome, GA 30161. *E-mail*—
mlester101@comcast.net.

Career
Cartoonist and designer. Freelance artist, 1985—; *At-
lanta Journal-Constitution,* Atlanta, GA, illustrator and
section designer for five years; *Rome News-Tribune,*
Rome, GA, editorial cartoonist, 2002—; syndicated car-
toonist, 2008—. Creator of sports mascots for Georgia
Institute of Technology and Navy; artist for "Rivalry
Series" by Collegiate Collectibles.

Member
National Cartoonists Society.

Awards, Honors
Best Book Award, National Cartoonists Society, 2000,
for *A Is for Salad;* Designer of the Year, Georgia Press
Association, 2003; Best Advertising Illustration, 2004;
Sigma Delta Chi Award, Society of Professional Journalists, 2006, for editorial cartooning; Better Newspaper
Contest winner, National Newspaper Association, 2008,
for editorial cartooning; Reuben Award for book illustration, 2009, for *Cool Daddy Rat.*

Writings

(Self-illustrated) *A Is for Salad,* Putnam & Grosset (New
York, NY), 2000.

ILLUSTRATOR; FOR CHILDREN

Lisa Rojany-Buccieri, *Santa's New Suit!: A Dress-up and
Fold-out Santa,* Penguin (New York, NY), 1993.
Katy Hall, *Really, Really, Really Bad Jokes,* Candlewick
Press (Cambridge, MA), 1999.
Elizabeth Werley-Prieto, *Racing through Time on a Flying
Machine,* Raintree Steck-Vaughn (Austin, TX), 1999.
Rick Winter, *Dirty Birdy Feet,* Rising Moon (Flagstaff,
AZ), 2000.
Cynthia Rothman, *Funny Bugs,* William H. Sadlier (New
York, NY), 2000.

Natasha Wing, *The Night before the Night before Christmas,* Grosset & Dunlap (New York, NY), 2002.

Deanna Calvert, *Wings,* Children's Press (New York, NY), 2004.

Rhonda Gowler Greene, *This Is the Teacher,* Dutton (New York, NY), 2004.

Suzanne Collins, *When Charlie McButton Lost Power,* Putnam (New York, NY), 2005.

Alan Katz and Caissie St. Onge, *United Jokes of America,* Scholastic (New York, NY), 2005.

Erica S. Perl, *Ninety-three in My Family,* Abrams Books (New York, NY), 2006.

Kristyn Crow, *Cool Daddy Rat,* Putnam (New York, NY), 2007.

Kimberly Marcus, *Flit-flit Flapped the Flea,* Putnam (New York, NY), 2010.

Artie Bennett, *The Butt Book,* Bloomsbury (New York, NY), 2010.

Author and illustrator of *Mike Du Jour* (daily animated online cartoon).

ILLUSTRATOR; FOR ADULTS

Gary D. Christenson, *Fatherhood Is Not Pretty,* Peachtree Publishers (Atlanta, GA), 1986.

Lewis Grizzard, *Lewis Grizzard on Fear of Flying,* Longstreet Press (Atlanta, GA), 1989.

Lewis Grizzard, *Lewis Grizzard's Advice to the Newly Wed,* Longstreet Press (Atlanta, GA), 1989.

Rita Rudner, *Naked beneath My Clothes: Tales of a Revealing Nature,* Viking (New York, NY), 1992.

Jim Minter, *Some Things I Wish We Wouldn't Forget,* Midtown Publishing (Atlanta, GA), 1998.

Sidelights

Mike Lester is an award-winning editorial cartoonist for the *Rome News-Tribune.* He has also created images for advertising campaigns for major corporations and national magazines. Among his most recognizable creations is "Buzz," the yellow jacket logo used by the Georgia Institute of Technology. In addition, Lester has provided the artwork for a number of critically acclaimed children's books, including *A Is for Salad* and *Cool Daddy Rat.*

A Is for Salad was Lester's self-illustrated picture-book debut. Not your typical alphabet book, *A Is for Salad* presents each letter alongside humorous, mismatched text. The "A is for salad" text, for instance, is accompanied by an alligator munching on a bowl of mixed greens, painted in bright acrylic colors. "B is for Vi-

***Mike Lester crafts a quirky abecedarium in his self-illustrated picture book* A Is for Salad.** (Illustration © 2000 by Mike Lester. Reproduced by permission.)

Kristyn Crow's jazzy picture book Cool Daddy Rat *is given extra energy by Lester's scritch-scratchy art.* (Illustration copyright © 2008 by Mike Lester. Reproduced by permission.)

king" shows a beaver wearing a horned helmet, and so on it goes, until X and Y are deemed unimportant and hauled to a trash bin. While some critics noted that *A Is for Salad* might be confusing to young children unfamiliar with the alphabet, others focused on the book's humor. "More advanced readers will appreciate the book's tricky premise," wrote Peter D. Sieruta in *Horn Book,* while a *Publishers Weekly* contributor described *A Is for Salad* as a "fun cavort through the 26 letters." Likening the work to the break-the-mold picture books written by Jon Scieszka, *Booklist* reviewer Hazel Rochman wrote that Lester "makes parody into a hilarious farce that both mocks the original and creates its own wonderful silliness."

Lester also illustrates works by other authors. In Rhonda Gowler Greene's *This Is the Teacher,* a cumulative tale reminiscent of "This Is the House That Jack Built," a well-meaning educator finds herself overwhelmed by a rush of energetic students. Here "Lester's cartoons capture the manic milieu with a wonderful repertoire of ex-

aggerated expressions and visual slapstick," a *Publishers Weekly* critic stated. "The pictures are a riot of color and burst with motion and exaggerated details," Shelle Rosenfeld noted in her *Booklist* review of *This Is the Teacher,* and Laurie Edwards commented in *School Library Journal* that "the energetic lines of Lester's cartoons capture the vibrant action."

When Charlie McButton Lost Power, a work by Suzanne Collins, centers on a computer-loving youngster who suffers a meltdown after his personal computer crashes. When he tries to steal a battery for his handheld video game, Charlie is given a time out and angrily lashes out at his little sister, until her tears make him reconsider his actions. According to Barbara Auerbach in *School Library Journal,* Lester's "hilarious cartoon illustrations are bold and appealing and depict the siblings' many emotions with exaggerated clarity," and a critic in *Kirkus Reviews* remarked that young computer users "may take a break from their screens to enjoy the over-the-top art."

In Erica S. Perl's *Ninety-three in My Family*, a boy describes the outlandish variety of creatures that share his family's home, including owls, armadillos, goldfish, frogs, and a pygmy hippo named Bernice. Lester's pictures "make what might have been a mildly silly book into a comic masterpiece, with innocent characters that are impervious to the bizarre," Susan Weitz commented in *School Library Journal*. In Kristyn Crow's *Cool Daddy Rat*, winner of the Reuben Award for book illustration, a curious young rodent named Ace stows away in his stylish father's instrument case, and the pair spends the day exploring New York City's vibrant jazz scene. During an impromptu street performance, Ace discovers his own talent for scat singing. Here "Lester's . . . computer-assisted watercolor illustrations in a heady palette show characters seemingly in perpetual motion," as a *Publishers Weekly* contributor wrote in a review of *Cool Daddy Rat*. In *School Library Journal* Terri Markson observed that the illustrations "have a cartoon-like quality that adds energy and exuberance to the whole."

Biographical and Critical Sources

PERIODICALS

Booklist, June 1, 2000, Hazel Rochman, review of *A Is for Salad*, p. 1896; August, 2004, Shelle Rosenfeld, review of *This Is the Teacher*, p. 1948.

Editor and Publisher, October 31, 2008, "United Feature Syndicate Now Offering Conservative Mike Lester's Editorial Cartoons."

Horn Book, March, 2000, Peter D. Sieruta, review of *A Is for Salad*, p. 188.

Instructor, August, 2001, Judy Freeman, review of *A Is for Salad*, p. 20.

Kirkus Reviews, May 1, 2005, review of *When Charlie McButton Lost Power*, p. 536; August 1, 2006, review of *Ninety-three in My Family*, p. 794; March 1, 2008, review of *Cool Daddy Rat*.

Publishers Weekly, April 28, 1989, reviews of *Lewis Grizzard on Fear of Flying* and *Lewis Grizzard's Advice to the Newly Wed*, p. 71; May 11, 1992, review of *Naked beneath My Clothes: Tales of a Revealing Nature*, p. 60; April 3, 2000, review of *A Is for Salad*, p. 79; June 28, 2004, review of *This Is the Teacher*, p. 50; March 17, 2008, review of *Cool Daddy Rat*, p. 68.

School Library Journal, April, 2000, Grace Oliff, review of *A Is for Salad*, p. 108; October, 2002, Susan Patron, review of *The Night before the Night before Christmas*, p. 65; August, 2004, Laurie Edwards, review of *This Is the Teacher*, p. 87; July, 2005, Barbara Auerbach, review of *When Charlie McButton Lost Power*, p. 71; October, 2006, Susan Weitz, review of *Ninety-three in My Family*, p. 123; April, 2008, Teri Markson, review of *Cool Daddy Rat*, p. 104.

U.S. News & World Report, May 29, 2000, John Molinaro, review of *A Is for Salad*, p. 66.

ONLINE

Mike Lester Web site, http://www.mikelester.com (October 10, 2009).

Museum of Comic and Cartoon Art Web site, http://www.moccany.org/ (October 10, 2009), "Mike Lester."*

*   *   *

LOWE, Helen 1961-

Personal

Born 1961, in New Zealand. *Education:* B.A. (English literature); Postgraduate diploma in Social Science (urban and regional planning). *Hobbies and other interests:* Aikido, reading, history, hiking, cooking.

Addresses

Home—Christchurch, New Zealand. *Agent*—Robin Rue, Writers House Literary Agency, 21 W. 26th St., New York, NY 10010. *E-mail*—contact@helenlowe.info.

Career

Novelist, poet, and author of short fiction. Worked in environmental management until 2003. *Women on Air* (monthly poetry feature on New Zealand public radio 96.9FM), host. Member, Storylines Children's Literature Trust.

Member

New Zealand Society of Authors, New Zealand Poetry Society, Authors Guild.

Awards, Honors

Robbie Burns Poetry Competition winner, 2003, for "Rain Wild Magic"; New Zealand Society of Authors/Creative New Zealand Mentorship for Emerging Writers, 2005; Takahe National Poetry Competition finalist, 2006, for "The Wayfarer"; New Zealand Society of Authors Literary Competition runner-up, 2006, for "The Spit"; Alpha2Omega Poetry Competition winner, 2007, for "Argos"; Takahe National Poetry Competition finalist, 2008, for "Fey"; Sir Julius Vogel Award, 2009, for Best New Talent; Notable Books selection, Storylines Children's Literature Trust, and Sir Julius Vogel Award for Best Book: Young Adult, both 2009, both for *Thornspell*.

Writings

Thornspell (novel), Knopf (New York, NY), 2009.

Contributor to anthologies, including *Home: New Short Short Stories by New Zealand Writers*, edited by Graeme Lay and Stephen Stratford, Random House

New Zealand, 2005; *Tiny Gaps,* edited by Margaret Vos, New Zealand Poetry Society, 2006; *The Taste of Nashi,* edited by Nola Borrell and Karen P. Butterworth, Windrift, 2008; *Before the Sirocco,* New Zealand Poetry Society, edited by Joanna Preston, 2008; *Crest to Crest: Impressions of Canterbury, Prose and Poetry,* edited by Karen Zelas, Wily Publications, 2009; and *Moments in the Whirlwind,* edited by Barbara Strang, New Zealand Poetry Society, 2009. Contributor to periodicals, including *New Zealand Listener, Takahe, Bravado, JAAM, Yellow Moon, foam:e, Borderlands, Carve, Christchurch Press,* and *Waikato Times.*

Sidelights

Helen Lowe, a New Zealand author of poetry and short fiction, is also the author of the fantasy novel *Thornspell.* A retelling of *Sleeping Beauty,* Lowe's novel retells the well-known story from the prince's point of view. Lowe's inspiration came when she attended a performance of Tchaikovsky's *Sleeping Beauty* ballet. As the prince entered the stage, she realizes that his character remains unexplored in the traditional tale in favor of that of the bewitched princess.

Cover of Helen Lowe's middle-grade fantasy Thornspell, *featuring artwork by Antonio Javier Caparo.* (Illustration copyright © 2008 by Antonio Javier Caparo. Used by permission of Alfred A. Knopf, an imprint of Random House Children's Books, a division of Random House, Inc.)

Thornspell, which was described as a "nicely crafted blend of fairy tale and dreamscape" by a *Kirkus Reviews* contributor, focuses on Prince Sigismund, a quiet dreamer who lives in a remote castle while his father quells a rebellion in the kingdom. Although Sigismund longs to explore the thick woods that surround the castle, he is strictly prohibited from doing so. When a mysterious visitor bearing a mystical ring approaches the castle one day, the prince begins a fantastic adventure that takes him into the forbidden zone. Aided by a dragon, a girl bound in thorns, and his mentor and master-at-arms, Balisan, Sigismund must battle an evil fairy—the Margravine—that hopes to gain enormous powers. According to Krista Hutley in *Booklist,* Lowe's debut novel "fittingly has more swordplay and dangerous escapades than romance, but it still ends happily ever after," and in *School Library Journal* Beth L. Meister wrote that in *Thornspell* Lowe presents a "fun retelling" that features "both complexity and a believable hero."

Biographical and Critical Sources

PERIODICALS

Booklist, November 1, 2008, Krista Hutley, review of *Thornspell,* p. 41.
Bulletin of the Center for Children's Books, July-August, 2008, Cindy Welch, review of *Thornspell,* p. 482.
Kirkus Reviews, August 15, 2008, review of *Thornspell.*
Sacramento Book Reviews, December 14, 2008.
School Library Journal, April, 2009, Beth L. Meister, review of *Thornspell.*

ONLINE

Helen Lowe Home Page, http://www.helenlowe.info (October 10, 2009).
New Zealand Book Council Web site, http://www.bookcouncil.org.nz/ (November 10, 2009), "Helen Lowe."
Pulse Web site, http://www.thepulse.org.nz/ (September, 2008), Richard Liddicoat, "Christchurch Author Cracks U.S. Market."

*   *   *

LOWELL, Susan 1950-
(Susan L. Humphreys)

Personal

Born October 27, 1950, in Chihuahua, Mexico; daughter of J. David (a geologist) and Edith (a rancher) Lowell; married William Ross Humphreys (a management consultant), March 21, 1975; children: Anna, Mary. *Education:* Stanford University, A.B., 1972, A.M., 1974;

Princeton University, M.A., Ph.D., 1979. *Religion:* Episcopalian. *Hobbies and other interests:* Reading, cooking, hiking, horseback riding.

Addresses

Home—Tucson, AZ. *Office*—Treasure Chest Books/Rio Nuevo Publishers, 451 N. Bonita Ave., Tucson, AZ 85745. *E-mail*—susanlowell@rionuevo.com.

Career

Writer, publisher, and rancher. Freelance writer, 1980—. University of Texas at Dallas, visiting assistant professor of English, 1979-80; University of Arizona, Tucson, adjunct lecturer of creative writing, 1989. Also worked as a journalist, editor, and publisher. Treasure Chest Books/Rio Nuevo Publishers (distributor and publisher), Tucson, AZ, co-owner with husband, Ross Humphreys.

Member

Society of Children's Book Writers and Illustrators, Southern Arizona Society of Authors, Phi Beta Kappa.

Awards, Honors

Milkweed National Fiction Award, Milkweed Editions, 1988, for *Ganado Red;* children's regional book award, Mountains and Plains Booksellers' Association, and Distinguished Children's Book citation, *Hungry Mind Review,* both 1993, both for *I Am Lavina Cumming;* Arizona Young Readers' Award for picture books, 1994, both for *The Three Little Javelinas;* named Arizona Children's Author of the Year, Arizona Library Association, 1994.

Writings

FOR CHILDREN

The Three Little Javelinas, illustrated by Jim Harris, Northland (Flagstaff, AZ), 1992, with audiotape, Scholastic (New York, NY), 1993.

I Am Lavina Cumming (novel), Milkweed Editions (Minneapolis, MN), 1993.

The Tortoise and the Jackrabbit, illustrated by Jim Harris, Northland (Flagstaff, AZ), 1994, bilingual edition, Rising Moon (Flagstaff, AZ), 2004.

The Boy with Paper Wings, Milkweed Editions (Minneapolis, MN), 1995.

Little Red Cowboy Hat, illustrated by Randy Cecil, Holt (New York, NY), 1997.

The Bootmaker and the Elves, illustrated by Tom Curry, Orchard Books (New York, NY), 1997.

Cindy Ellen: A Wild Western Cinderella, illustrated by Jane Manning, HarperCollins (New York, NY), 2000.

Dusty Locks and the Three Bears, illustrated by Randy Cecil, Holt (New York, NY), 2001.

(With Anna Humphreys) *Saguaro: The Desert Giant,* Rio Nuevo Publishers (Tucson, AZ), 2002.

Cactus Flowers, Rio Nuevo Publishers (Tucson, AZ), 2005.

Josefina Javelina: A Hairy Tale, illustrated by Bruce MacPherson, Rising Moon (Flagstaff, AZ), 2005.

The Elephant Quilt: Stitch by Stitch to California!, illustrated by Stacey Dressen-McQueen, Farrar, Straus (New York, NY), 2008.

OTHER

Ganado Red: A Novella and Stories, Milkweed Editions (Minneapolis, MN), 1988.

Clouds for Dessert: Sweet Treats from the Wild West, photographs by Robin Stancliff, Rio Nuevo Publishers (Tucson, AZ), 2002.

Navajo Rug Designs, photographs by Robin Stancliff, Rio Nuevo Publishers (Tucson, AZ), 2005.

Contributor, under name Susan L. Humphreys, of scholarly articles to literature journals.

Sidelights

Susan Lowell is known for creating original stories for young readers as well as for her retellings of traditional tales from a Southwestern point of view. Her books *The Three Little Javelinas, Cindy Ellen: A Wild Western Cinderella,* and *Dusty Locks and the Three Bears* each take a story familiar to most young children and give it a southwestern flair, while the novel *I Am Lavinia Cumming* is based on a story from Lowell's own family. In addition to her writing, Lowell is also a rancher and publisher who specializes in books focusing on her beloved Southwest.

Lowell patterned her first picture book, *The Three Little Javelinas,* after the familiar story of "The Three Little Pigs," but she sets her version in a desert. The three javelinas, or peccaries, are pursued by Coyote, the traditional trickster of Southwestern lore. While the first little javelina builds his house out of tumbleweed, and the second builds his house out of the ribs of the saguaro tree, their sister is the one who provides an adequate shelter made of mud adobe bricks. The text is accompanied by explanatory notes. According to a critic for *Bloomsbury Review, The Three Little Javelinas* "is a funny and clever retelling of a familiar tale," and a *Publishers Weekly* reviewer called it "sprightly fun."

Readers who enjoy the antics of the desert pigs in *The Three Little Javelinas* will also root for the heroine in Lowell's *Josefina Javelina: A Hairy Tale.* Josefina is a frisky peccary with a dream of becoming a ballet dancer. Determined to make her dream a reality, she decides to travel to the big city, where she meets a tricky (and hungry) coyote that is posing as a talent agent named White E. Lamb. When the coyote forces the pig to take flight, she impresses all onlookers with her agility and ultimately lands a humorous role in a production of a classic holiday ballet. *Josefina Javelina* showcases Lowell's "originality and storytelling talents," asserted a *Children's Bookwatch* contributor, and in *School Library Journal* Polly L. Kotarba enjoyed the sophisticated text with its "swine and pig puns and tongue-in-cheek" humor.

Lowell again teams up with illustrator Jim Harris for a new take on the "Tortoise and the Hare" fable. Featuring a Southwestern theme, *The Tortoise and the Jackrabbit* finds a mature, white-gloved tortoise in a race against a flashy, bandana-topped jackrabbit. As the duo travels across the desert, Lowell introduces young readers to the unique and varied plant life there, identifying saguaro cacti and mesquite trees, as well as other vegetation that is native to the Southwest. Calling the book

"a merry blend of play, allegory, and environmentalism," a *Publishers Weekly* reviewer wrote that, "precise and punchy, Lowell's undated prose turns hip alongside Harris's comical characterizations." *School Library Journal* reviewer Donna L. Scanlon described *The Tortoise and the Jackrabbit* as a "sprightly, fresh approach," while *Booklist* reviewer Ellen Mandel believed that Lowell's tale is "fetchingly told."

Little Red Riding Hood is transformed by Lowell into Little Red Cowboy Hat in her book of the same name. Here, Little Red dons a sheriff's badge and keeps an eye out for rattlesnakes in her dusty Southwest town. One day, however, a bigger threat appears in the form of a wolf who blocks her path. Raised to be polite, Little Red feels obliged to talk to the wolf who asks

Susan Lowell's picture-book retelling of a traditional story is brought to life by Tom Curry's art in **The Bootmaker and the Elves.** (Illustration copyright © 1999 by Tom Curry. Reproduced by permission.)

Lowell recasts a well-known story with creatures native to the American Southwest in **The Three Little Javelinas,** *a book featuring artwork by Jim Harris.* (Illustration copyright © 1992 by Jim Harris. Reproduced by permission.)

many questions. She again encounters the wolf at her grandmother's house and worries that he has done something terrible to her granny. Instead of running off, Little Red tries to figure out what happened to Grandma who, as it turns out, was actually out chopping wood. When the missing relative finally rescues Little Red, the girl learns an important life lesson. Writing in *School Library Journal,* Ruth Semrau called *Little Red Cowboy Hat* "an amusing addition to the growing collection of fairy-tale spoofs."

Cinderella meets the Southwest in *Cindy Ellen.* Instead of keeping the house clean while her mean stepmother and stepsisters relax as in the traditional tale, Cindy Ellen must make repairs on the family's ranch, from fixing the fences to mucking out the corral. After she is forbidden to attend a neighbor's rodeo, Cindy Ellen receives a visit from her fairy godmother. Presenting her with a golden six-shooter, the fairy godmother insists that her magic is useless without a bit of Cindy Ellen's

spunk. With that advice, the young girl sets out to win both the rodeo and the heart of Joe Prince, her wealthy neighbor's son. "Lowell's savory slang adds punch to this tale," claimed a *Publishers Weekly* reviewer. Starr LaTronica, a contributor to *School Library Journal,* found that "an abundance of action combined with humor and high-spirited hyperbole make this a rip-roaring rendition" of the traditional Cinderella tale.

Goldilocks also receives the Wild West treatment whens Lowell sets the story about the young trespasser and three bears in the American West. In *Dusty Locks and the Three Bears* a cowboy-boot-wearing girl comes across an empty cabin in the woods. Hungry for a good meal, Dusty Locks walks inside and tests the biggest bear's beans, which are much too spicy for her taste. Although Lowell has the young heroine follow the traditional storyline, breaking the cub's stool, falling asleep in his bed, and being awoken by the bears, she adds a twist at the end when Dusty Locks's mother finally catches up with her. *School Library Journal* critic Adele Greenlee described *Dusty Locks and the Three Bears* as a "humorous and fresh retelling," while a *Publishers Weekly* reviewer predicted that "with its zippy lines and range of voices . . . this should be a read-aloud hit."

I Am Lavina Cumming was inspired by the life of Lowell's grandmother and is a novel infused with folktales. In the story, the widowed father of ten-year-old Lavina decides that his daughter should learn ladylike behavior from her aunt and sends the girl from the Arizona Territory to Santa Cruz, California. While Lavina misses her family and has trouble coping with a younger girl, she begins to appreciate her aunt and the lessons she learns in her home. A reviewer for *Publishers Weekly* wrote that "Lavina is both likable and believable, her credibility enhanced by the author's skillful use of period details."

Also set during the mid-1800s, *The Elephant Quilt: Stitch by Stitch to California!* is based on the real-life experiences of settlers traveling by wagon from Missouri to California. Featuring illustrations by Stacey Dressen-McQueen, the story focuses on Lily Rose, who sews her impressions of the trip—including the hardships of the Santa Fe Trail, the birth of a baby sister, and meetings with Native Americans, trappers, and gold miners—into the colorful quilt top that her mother and grandmother are making. In her *School Library Journal* review of *The Elephant Quilt*, Shawn Brommer praised Lowell's "conversational style" and Linda Perkins dubbed Lily Rose an "exuberant" young heroine in her *Booklist* review. A *Kirkus Reviews* critic also enjoyed the story's up-beat perspective, concluding that *The Elephant Quilt* "kicks the energy level up a notch above" similar picture-book accounts of wagon-train travel.

Lowell once told *SATA* about her life in the southwest: "I was born in Chihuahua, Mexico. I have lived on both sides of the border since then, and in many other places, too, but my real home, and my family's home for five generations, is southern Arizona. A giant saguaro cactus is my favorite kind of tree, and I love to see sand-colored coyotes sneak through the desert outside my kitchen window. Sometimes we also see hairy, pig-like javelinas snuffling along, hungry for cactus (which they eat thorns and all).

"My husband and daughters and I own a small ranch at the base of a high mountain called Baboquivari, a sacred peak to the Tohono O'odham Nation, our neighbors on the other side of the mountain. For them, Baboquivari is the center of the universe. For me this is also true. My books, which I write for adults as well as children, have all grown from my lifelong experience of the West. Family stories, some handed down to me from pioneer days, fascinate me, and I am also particularly interested in the rich mixture of Native American, Mexican, and Anglo cultures in my region. Flying coyotes, lost treasures, bandit ghosts, tiny rubies in the sand—there are many stories here to tell, and I hope to keep on writing them down. Yet they are not necessarily all Southwestern stories. A center is not a limit. It's a beginning, a heart. The wide world lies open all around it."

Biographical and Critical Sources

PERIODICALS

Bloomsbury Review, October, 1992, review of *The Three Little Javelinas,* p. 25.

Booklist, January 15, 1995, Ellen Mandel, review of *The Tortoise and the Jackrabbit,* p. 937; April 15, 1997, Ilene Cooper, review of *Little Red Cowboy Hat,* p. 1436; September 15, 1997, Julie Corsaro, review of *The Bootmaker and the Elves,* p. 242; July, 2001, Hazel Rochman, review of *Dusty Locks and the Three Bears,* p. 2014; April 15, 2008, Linda Perkins, review of *The Elephant Quilt: Stitch by Stitch to California!,* p. 57.

Children's Bookwatch, February, 2006, review of *Josefina Javelina: A Hairy Tale.*

Horn Book, July, 2001, review of *Dusty Locks and the Three Bears,* p. 464.

Kirkus Reviews, March 1, 2008, review of *The Elephant Quilt.*

Stacey Dressen-McQueen contributes colorful computer-enhanced art to Lowell's history-themed picture book **The Elephant Quilt.** (Illustration copyright © 2008 by Stacey Dressen-McQueen. Used by permission of Farrar, Straus & Giroux, LLC.)

Los Angeles Times Book Review, September 11, 1988, Georgia Jones-Davis, review of *Ganado Red: A Novella and Stories,* p. 3.

Publishers Weekly, September 14, 1992, review of *The Three Little Javelinas,* p. 123; July 5, 1993, review of *I Am Lavina Cumming,* p. 74; November 7, 1994, review of *The Tortoise and the Jackrabbit,* p. 77; November 20, 1995, review of *The Boy with Paper Wings,* p. 78; March 3, 1997, review of *Little Red Cowboy Hat,* p. 75; September 22, 1997, review of *The Bootmaker and the Elves,* p. 80; June 19, 2000, review of *Cindy Ellen: A Wild Western Cinderella,* p. 78; May 21, 2001, review of *Dusty Locks and the Three Bears,* p. 107.

School Library Journal, February, 1995, Donna L. Scanlon, review of *The Tortoise and the Jackrabbit,* p. 76; May, 1997, Ruth Semrau, review of *Little Red Cowboy Hat,* pp. 104-105; June, 2000, Starr LaTronica, review of *Cindy Ellen,* p. 134; July, 2001, Adele Greenlee, review of *Dusty Locks and the Three Bears,* p. 96; May 31, 2004, review of *Clouds for Dessert: Sweet Treats from the Wild West,* p. 96; February, 2006, Polly L. Kotarba, review of *Josefina Javelina,* p. 106; July, 2008, Shawn Brommer, review of *The Elephant Quilt,* p. 77.

ONLINE

Susan Lowell Home Page, http://www.susanlowell.com (October 30, 2009).*

M

MacEACHERN, Stephen

Personal

Born August 22, in Brampton, Ontario, Canada; married; wife's name Jeanette; children: Ethan, Kylie. *Education:* Attended Sheridan Institute of Technology and Advanced Learning. *Hobbies and other interests:* Hockey.

Addresses

Home—Erin, Ontario, Canada. *Office*—Quack Communications, Erin, Ontario, Canada. *E-mail*—info@ quackcom.ca.

Career

Graphic designer and illustrator. Worked at Nelvana (entertainment company), Toronto, Ontario, Canada; instructor at Sheridan Institute of Technology and Advanced Learning, Oakville, Ontario, Canada.

Awards, Honors

Storytelling World Award, Rocky Mountain Book Award finalist, and Red Cedar Book Award finalist, all for *Escapes!;* Silver Birch Award shortlist, 2005, and Hackmatack Children's Choice Award shortlist, 2006, both for *The Kid's Guide to Money Cent$;* Hackmatack Children's Choice Award shortlist, 2009, for *Gotcha!*

Illustrator

Lisa O'Brien, *Lights, Camera, Action!: Making Movies and TV from the Inside Out,* Greey de Pencier Books (Toronto, Ontario, Canada), 1998, second edition, Maple Tree Press (Toronto, Ontario, Canada), 2007.

Ann Douglas, *The Family Tree Detective: Cracking the Case of Your Family's Story,* Owl Books (Toronto, Ontario, Canada), 1999.

Dette Hunter, *Thirty-eight Ways to Entertain Your Babysitter,* Annick Press (Toronto, Ontario, Canada), 2003.

Laura Scandiffio, *Escapes!: True Stories from the Edge,* Annick Press (Toronto, Ontario, Canada), 2003.

Keltie Thomas, *The Kid's Guide to Money Cent$,* Annick Press (Toronto, Ontario, Canada), 2004.

Trudie Romanek, *Switched on, Flushed down, Tossed out: Investigating the Hidden Workings of Your Home,* Annick Press (Toronto, Ontario, Canada), 2005.

Nancy Hallas, *Here Comes the Parade,* Scholastic Canada (Markham, Ontario, Canada), 2005.

Alicia Martell, *Home Run!,* Scholastic Canada (Markham, Ontario, Canada), 2005.

Jill Bryant, *Backyard Circus,* Annick Press (Toronto, Ontario, Canada), 2006.

Keltie Thomas, *How Soccer Works,* Maple Tree Press (Toronto, Ontario, Canada), 2007.

David Acer, *Gotcha!: Eighteen Amazing Ways to Freak out Your Friends,* Kids Can Press (Toronto, Ontario, Canada), 2008.

Jeff Szpirglas, *Just a Minute!: A Crazy Adventure in Time,* Maple Tree Press (Toronto, Ontario, Canada), 2009.

Keltie Thomas, *How Figure Skating Works,* Maple Tree Press (Toronto, Ontario, Canada), 2009.

Sidelights

An accomplished graphic designer, Stephen MacEachern has contributed the illustrations to more than a dozen works for young readers, including *Thirty-eight Ways to Entertain Your Babysitter* and *Switched on, Flushed down, Tossed out: Investigating the Hidden Workings of Your Home.* A native of Ontario, Canada, who lives and works in a rural area northwest of Toronto, MacEachern concentrates primarily on nonfiction titles. *Lights, Camera, Action!: Making Movies and TV from the Inside Out,* a work by producer and screenwriter Lisa O'Brien, offers youngsters helpful advice about the television and film industry, from auditioning for a role to securing an agent to marketing a production. According to Etta Kaner in *Quill and Quire,* "MacEachern's offbeat colour illustrations" for this book "enhance the text but don't overwhelm it."

With a text by Dette Hunter, *Thirty-eight Ways to Entertain Your Babysitter* presents a variety of creative games, crafts, and recipes to help children pass the time while their parents are away. "The wonderful whimsical illustrations by . . . MacEachern perfectly complement the fun tone of the text while also providing enough detail to make the instructions easy to follow," Liz Greenaway observed in her review of the book for the *Canadian Review of Materials*. *The Kid's Guide to Money Cent$,* a work by Keltie Thomas, follows three classmates who are preparing a report on finances. According to Sarah Treleaven in *Quill and Quire,* "MacEachern's colourful, comic strip-style illustrations are well suited" to the text and appeal to young readers. Julie Chychota wrote in the *Canadian Review of Materials* that these "drawings minimize the potentially intimidating effect of the book's sophisticated subject matter."

MacEachern has also provided the illustrations for Trudie Romanek's *Switched on, Flushed down, Tossed out,* which explores the inner workings of a typical family house. "The art is eye-catching," Steven Engelfried commented in *School Library Journal,* and Hazel Rochman, writing in *Booklist,* stated that the book's pages "burst with bright cartoon images" of a curious boy investigating his home's electrical, heating, and plumbing systems. Jill Bryant's *Backyard Circus* offers suggestions for children interested in putting on their own show. "The text is accompanied by bright simple graphics, some of them illustrating step by step techniques for magic tricks," Barb Taylor wrote in the *Canadian Review of Materials,* and *Resource Links* contributor Linda Berezowski noted that McEachern's "bright graphics are used throughout the book as an aid to clarify directions as well as to add visual interest."

Biographical and Critical Sources

PERIODICALS

Booklist, June 1, 1998, Lauren Peterson, review of *Lights, Camera, Action!: Making Movies and TV from the Inside Out,* p. 1760; July, 2005, Hazel Rochman, review of *Switched on, Flushed down, Tossed out: Investigating the Hidden Workings of Your Home,* p. 1919.

Canadian Review of Materials, October 3, 2003, Liz Greenaway, review of *Thirty-eight Ways to Entertain Your Babysitter;* March 26, 2004, Julie Chychota, review of *The Kid's Guide to Money Cent$;* September 30, 2005, Linda Ludke, review of *Switched on, Flushed down, Tossed out;* November 24, 2006, Barb Taylor, *Backyard Circus;* May 25, 2007, Myra Junyk, review of *Lights, Camera, Action!*

Kirkus Reviews, July 1, 2005, review of *Switched on, Flushed down, Tossed out,* p. 742.

Quill and Quire, April, 1998, Etta Kaner, review of *Lights, Camera, Action!;* February, 2004, Sarah Treleaven, review of *The Kid's Guide to Money Cent$;* May, 2009, Paul Challen, review of *Just a Minute!: A Crazy Adventure in Time.*

Resource Links, October, 2005, Rosemary Anderson, review of *Switched on, Flushed down, Tossed out,* p. 27; December, 2006, Linda Berezowski, review of *Backyard Circus,* p. 25.

School Library Journal, January, 2004, Augusta R. Malvagno, review of *Thirty-eight Ways to Entertain Your Babysitter,* p. 118; December, 2005, Steven Engelfried, review of *Switched on, Flushed down, Tossed out,* p. 133.

ONLINE

Annick Press Web site, http://www.annickpress.com/ (October 10, 2009), "Stephen MacEachern."

Kids Can Press Web site, http://www.annickpress.com/ (October 10, 2009), "Stephen MacEachern."

Quack Communications Web site, http://www.quackcom.ca/ (October 10, 2009).*

*   *   *

MAGUIRE, Jesse
See SMITH, Sherwood

*   *   *

MALEY, Carleen
See HUTCHINS, Carleen Maley

*   *   *

McKENZIE, Riford
See WAITE, Michael P.

*   *   *

MELDRUM, Christina

Personal

Female. *Education:* University of Michigan, B.A. (religious studies and political science), 1990; Harvard Law School, J.D., 1994.

Addresses

Home—CA. *Agent*—Laura Rennert, Andrea Brown Literary Agency; laura@andreabrownlit.com. *E-mail*—christina@christinameldrum.com.

Career

Attorney and author. Worked for International Commission of Jurists, Geneva, Switzerland; Shearman & Sterling (law firm), litigator; also worked in grassroots development in Ghana. Women of the World Investments (micro-financing organization), member of advisory board.

Awards, Honors

Best Book for Young Adults selection, and William C. Morris Young-Adult Debut Award finalist, both American Library Association, both 2009, both for *Madapple.*

Christina Meldrum (Photograph by Victor Hong. Reproduced by permission.)

Writings

Madapple (novel), Knopf (New York, NY), 2008.

Author's work has been translated into several languages, including Italian and German.

Adaptations

Madapple was adapted as an audiobook, Listening Library, 2008.

Sidelights

A former litigator, Christina Meldrum is the author of the young-adult novel *Madapple,* "a fascinating look at belief and the interplay between the rational and the religious," observed *Kliatt* reviewer Janis Flint-Ferguson. "In *Madapple,* I wanted to explore how we humans, in our attempt to understand the world, at times simplify and thereby distort it," Meldrum stated in a *Slayground* online interview. "I wanted to think about how we create categories, based on what we want or have felt or believe is socially acceptable, and then divide the world into these categories. Specifically, I wanted to explore the dichotomy between science and religion."

After graduating from the University of Michigan with a bachelor's degree in religious studies and political science, Meldrum spent time in Ghana doing grassroots development before attending Harvard Law School. She worked for the International Commission of Jurists in Geneva, Switzerland, and as an attorney at Shearman & Sterling; her experiences there, combined with her background in comparative literature, spurred her writing of *Madapple.* "As a litigator, I spent my days formulating arguments for my clients, selecting and emphasizing those facts that best supported my position," the author explained to Ilene Cooper in a *Booklist* interview. "Opposing counsel did the same for their clients. In theory, the truth would somehow filter through: the judge or jury would sort through the extreme arguments and parse out what was fair and true. In actuality, each argument oversimplified reality, and the end result, while perhaps fair, often had little to do with truth. This experience made me think about how we humans try to simplify our very complex world in an attempt to understand it."

Madapple, which was described as "part literary mystery, part botanical thesis" by a *Teenreads.com* contributor, took Meldrum more than ten years to complete. The work centers on Aslaug Hellig, a sixteen year old who was raised in isolation by her fiercely intelligent and eccentric mother, Maren. Maren educates her daughter in the languages and sciences, especially herbology, the study of medicinal herbs. After Maren dies under mysterious circumstances, Aslaug makes her way through the Maine woods to a nearby town, where she locates her aunt Sara, a charismatic preacher, and her teenaged cousins Susanne and Rune. The contemporary world both frightens and fascinates Aslaug, who believes that she is the product of a virgin birth. When Sara and Susanne are killed in a church fire, Aslaug is arrested and charged with murder; Meldrum's narrative weaves the trial transcripts of the trial that follows with Aslaug's own account of her life with Maren. "Plot summary does little justice to this haunting book, which is as much mysticism as it is story," Cooper remarked.

Madapple garnered praise for its poetic language and mythical properties. The work was also recognized for Meldrum's ability to incorporate scientific concepts, including a wealth of botanical information. Writing in *Horn Book,* Jonathan Hunt described the novel as "a stellar debut . . . that explores the nexus between the natural world and the spiritual realm," and Patricia A. Kossmann noted in *America* that "philosophical questions abound; science and faith, reality and fantasy are in constant collision." According to a contributor in *Publishers Weekly,* "audiences will need some intellectual mettle for the densely seeded ideas, but they won't be able to stop reading." "With this spellbinding debut," concluded a critic in *Kirkus Reviews,* "Meldrum marks herself as an author to watch."

Biographical and Critical Sources

PERIODICALS

America, July 21, 2008, Patricia A. Kossman, review of *Madapple,* p. 42.

Booklist, April 1, 2008, Ilene Cooper, review of *Madapple,* p. 48; November 15, 2008, Ilene Cooper, interview with Meldrum, p. 56.

Horn Book, May-June, 2008, Jonathan Hunt, review of *Madapple,* p. 322.

Kirkus Reviews, May 1, 2008, review of *Madapple.*

Kliatt, May, 2008, Janis Flint-Ferguson, review of *Madapple,* p. 14.

Publishers Weekly, May 26, 2008, review of *Madapple,* p. 67.

School Library Journal, July, 2008, review of *Madapple,* p. 104.

ONLINE

Christina Meldrum Home Page, http://www.christina meldrum.com (October 10, 2009).

National Public Radio Web site, http://www.npr.org/ (July 20, 2008), Liane Hansen, interview with Meldrum (transcript).

Cover of Christina Meldrum's young-adult novel Madapple, *featuring artwork by Jonathan Barkat.* (Jacket art copyright © 2008 by Knopf Children. Used by permission of Alfred A. Knopf, an imprint of Random House Children's Books, a division of Random House, Inc.)

Slayground Web log, http://slayground.livejournal.com/ (May 14, 2008), interview with Meldrum.

Teenreads.com, http://www.teenreads.com/ (June, 2008), Author Talk: Christina Meldrum."

* * *

MORTIMER, Anne 1958-
(Anne Mortimer Young)

Personal

Born March 28, 1958, in England; married August 30, 1980; husband's name, Buscombe. *Education:* South Wales College of Art, Natural History diploma in illustration. *Religion:* Church of England (Anglican).

Addresses

Home—Parklands, Dulverton, Somerset, England. *E-mail*—anne@annemortimer.com.

Career

Children's book illustrator. Illustrator for greeting cards and stationary for clients Images & Editions, W.H. Smith, and Marks & Spencer (all in England); illustrations have been licensed to appear on woven tapestry pillows, tableware, coffee mugs, plates, tins, prints, puzzles, needlecraft kits, and fabrics.

Member

Royal Society of Miniature Painters, Society of Botanical Artists.

Awards, Honors

Honorable mention, Miniature Society awards, 1986.

Writings

SELF-ILLUSTRATED

(Under name Anne Mortimer Young) *Antique Medicine Chest; or, Glyster, Blister, and Purge,* Vernier Press (London, England), 1994.

Catopia: A Cat Compendium, HarperCollins (New York, NY), 2007.

ILLUSTRATOR

Margaret Wise Brown, *A Pussycat's Christmas,* Frances Lincoln (London, England), 1977, reprinted, Harper-Collins (New York, NY), 1994.

Matthew Sturgis, *Tosca's Christmas,* Dial (New York, NY), 1989.

Matthew Sturgis, *Tosca's Surprise,* Dial (New York, NY), 1991.

Eleanor Farjeon, *Cats Sleep Anywhere,* HarperCollins (New York, NY), 1996.

Carol Greene, *Cat and Bear,* Hyperion (New York, NY), 1998.

Nancy Raines Day, *A Kitten's Year,* HarperCollins (New York, NY), 2000.

Eileen Spinelli, *Kittycat Lullaby,* Hyperion (New York, NY), 2000.

Sue Stainton, *Santa's Snow Cat,* HarperCollins (New York, NY), 2001.

Sue Stainton, *Snow Cat, Santa's Littlest Cat,* Hyperion (New York, NY), 2001.

Margaret Wise Brown, *Sneakers: The Seaside Cat,* Harper-Collins (New York, NY), 2003.

Sue Stainton, *The Lighthouse Cat,* Katherine Tegan Books (New York, NY), 2004.

Edward Lear, *The Owl and the Pussycat,* Katherine Tegan Books (New York, NY), 2006.

Sue Stainton, *I Love Cats,* Katherine Tegan Books (New York, NY), 2007.

Sue Stainton, *The Chocolate Cat,* Katherine Tegan Books (New York, NY), 2007.

Sue Stainton, *Santa's Snow Kitten,* Katherine Tegan Books (New York, NY), 2008.

Sidelights

Anne Mortimer is an illustrator whose works have appeared on stationery, fabrics, china, collector plates, and other items. She is also known for illustrating picture books about cats in which, reviewers note, her realistic miniature paintings evoke the essence of a cat's rippling, soft fur. Among her titles are Margaret Wise Brown's *A Pussycat's Christmas* and Edward Lear's classic poem *The Owl and the Pussycat.*

One of Mortimer's first book illustration projects, *Tosca's Christmas,* written by Matthew Sturgis, tells the story of the holiday from a disgruntled, woebegone cat's perspective as Tosca is chased out of the kitchen, shooed away from the room where presents are being wrapped, and is finally deposited out of doors after accidentally pulling down the Christmas tree. "Both Sturgis and Mortimer have succeeded in capturing the warmth of the holidays from a delightfully different viewpoint," remarked Diane Roback in *Publishers Weekly.* A sequel, *Tosca's Surprise,* tells the story of Tosca's search for a quiet place to give birth to her litter of kittens. *School Library Journal* contributor Caroline Ward wrote that Mortimer's paintings of Tosca and her mate "are so precise and finely textured that the fur appears real enough to stroke."

In Eleanor Farjeon's poem *Cats Sleep Anywhere,* the feline propensity to climb into any small place and curl up for a nap is celebrated by both author and illustrator. *Booklist* reviewer Laura Tillotson remarked that Mortimer's painted cats "look so cozily realistic . . . that they almost purr." Mortimer's skill as a miniaturist was also remarked upon, including the detailed precision used in capturing small, homey scenes and the way

they complement Farjeon's verse. "The easy rhythm of the spare text and the attractive paintings will appeal to cat lovers of all ages," predicted Margaret Bush in the *School Library Journal.*

Mortimer's illustrations for Nancy Raines Day's *A Kitten's Year* include twelve paintings of a kitten month-by-month as it finally becomes a full-grown cat. "Children will appreciate the kitten's lifelike poses and its gradual progress toward cathood," observed a critic for *Publishers Weekly.* Carolyn Jenks, writing in *School Library Journal,* applauded the realism of Mortimer's illustrations, noting that young readers "may reach out to pat the fuzzy, appealing animal." Eileen Spinelli's *Kittycat Lullaby,* also illustrated by Mortimer, is a poem about a kitten's busy day. In *Booklist* Gillian Engberg praised the artist's "cozy, detailed paintings," and a *Publishers Weekly* critic stated that the "realistic water-color illustrations make Kittycat's fluffy softness palpable."

In Sue Stainton's *The Lighthouse Cat,* a lighthouse keeper takes in a stray feline and names it Mackerel. When the lighthouse lantern burns out during a storm, Mackerel gathers eleven cat friends. The cats climb to the top of the lighthouse and use their bright eyes to guide ships to safety. Terry Glover, writing in *Booklist,* found that Mortimer's "artwork is warm and full of wonderful detail," while a *Kirkus Reviews* critic praised the book's "amazingly realistic art." Writing in *School Library Journal,* Sheilah Kosco called *The Lighthouse Cat* a "beautifully illustrated tale."

In Mortimer's version of nineteenth-century British poet Edward Lear's *The Owl and the Pussycat* she brings to life the story of the two title characters as they fall in love and sailing away together. A *Kirkus Reviews* critic found much to like in Mortimer's artwork, noting especially that her "fascinating borders infused with flowers, ferns, insects and butterflies breathe life into the rhyme." "Lear's poem is beautifully illustrated," concluded Kirsten Cutler in her review of the book for *School Library Journal.*

I Love Cats, written by Stainton and illustrated by Mortimer, presents two dozen cats in a variety of typically feline poses. Mortimer uses an "almost photo-realistic technique" for her illustrations, Ilene Cooper state in *Booklist,* while Kara Schaff Dean concluded in *School Library Journal* that "Mortimer's cats are second to none."

Biographical and Critical Sources

PERIODICALS

Booklist, September 1, 1996, Laura Tillotson, review of *Cats Sleep Anywhere,* p. 133; August, 2001, Gillian Engberg, review of *Kittycat Lullaby,* p. 2133; August, 2004, Terry Glover, review of *The Lighthouse Cat,* p. 1945; March 15, 2007, Ilene Cooper, review of *I Love Cats,* p. 55.

Kirkus Reviews, July 1, 2004, review of *The Lighthouse Cat,* p. 637; June 1, 2006, review of *The Owl and the Pussycat,* p. 575.

Plain Dealer (Cleveland, OH), August 3, 2003, "Cat's Seaside Adventure Is a Welcome Return," p. J7.

Publishers Weekly, October 13, 1989, review of *Tosca's Christmas,* p. 53; September 16, 1996, review of *Cats Sleep Anywhere,* p. 81; January 17, 2000, review of *A Kitten's Year,* p. 56; June 25, 2001, review of *Kittycat Lullaby,* p. 71; July 20, 2007, review of *Catopia: A Cat Compendium,* p. 87.

School Library Journal, August, 1991, Caroline Ward, review of *Tosca's Surprise,* p. 156; December, 1996, Margaret Bush, review of *Cats Sleep Anywhere,* p. 112; April, 2000, Carolyn Jenks, review of *A Kitten's Year,* p. 97; October, 2001, Robin L. Gibson, review of *Kittycat Lullaby,* p. 132; July, 2003, Laura Scott, review of *Sneakers: The Seaside Cat,* p. 16; September, 2004, Sheilah Kosco, review of *The Lighthouse Cat,* p. 181; July, 2006, Kirsten Cutler, review of *The Owl and the Pussycat,* p. 91; March, 2007, Kara Schaff Dean, review of *I Love Cats,* p. 186.

ONLINE

Anne Mortimer Home Page, http://www.annemortimer. com (April 21, 2008).*

*   *   *

MOURNING, Tuesday

Personal

Born in CO; married; children: one son. *Education:* Brigham Young University, B.F.A.

Addresses

Home—Knoxville, TN. *Agent*—Shannon Associates, 630 9th Ave., New York, NY 10036. *E-mail*—tuesday@ tmourning.com.

Career

Illustrator and artist. Commercial work includes book-cover art.

Illustrator

Allan Wolf, *Immersed in Verse: An Informative, Slightly Irreverent, and Totally Tremendous Guide to Living the Poet's Life,* Lark Books, 2006.

Jake Maddox, *Full Court Dreams,* Stone Arch Books (Minneapolis, MN), 2008.

Jake Maddox, *Storm Surfer,* Stone Arch Books (Minneapolis, MN), 2008.

Jake Maddox, *Jump Serve,* Stone Arch Books (Minneapolis, MN), 2008.

Pam Calvert, *Princess Peepers,* Marshall Cavendish Children (New York, NY), 2008.

Jake Maddox, *Cheer Challenge,* Stone Arch Books (Minneapolis, MN), 2008.

Eve Feldman, *Billy and Milly, Short and Silly!,* G.P. Putnam's Sons (New York, NY), 2009.

Jake Maddox, *Back on the Team,* Stone Arch Books (Mankato, MN), 2009.

Jake Maddox, *Skater's Secret,* Stone Arch Books (Mankato, MN), 2009.

Jake Maddox, *Over the Net,* Stone Arch Books (Mankato, MN), 2009.

Jake Maddox, *Horseback Hopes,* Stone Arch Books (Mankato, MN), 2009.

Jake Maddox, *Soccer Spirit,* Stone Arch Books (Mankato, MN), 2009.

Jake Maddox, *Stolen Bases,* Stone Arch Books (Mankato, MN), 2009.

Jake Maddox, *Running Rivals,* Stone Arch Books (Mankato, MN), 2009.

Jake Maddox, *Tennis Trouble,* Stone Arch Books (Mankato, MN), 2009.

Jake Maddox, *Ballet Bullies,* Stone Arch Books (Mankato, MN), 2010.

Jake Maddox, *Half-Pipe Prize,* Stone Arch Books (Mankato, MN), 2010.

Jake Maddox, *Field Hockey Firsts,* Stone Arch Books (Mankato, MN), 2010.

Jake Maddox, *Hoop Doctor,* Stone Arch Books (Minneapolis, MN), 2010.

Biographical and Critical Sources

PERIODICALS

Booklist, May 15, 2006, Hazel Rochman, review of *Immersed in Verse: An Informative, Slightly Irreverent, and Totally Tremendous Guide to Living the Poet's Life,* p. 44; April 1, 2008, Ilene Cooper, review of *Full Court Dreams,* p. 46.

Kirkus Reviews, August 1, 2008, review of *Princess Peepers.*

School Library Journal, October, 2006, Allan Wolf, review of *Immersed in Verse*; October, 2008, Susan E. Murray, review of *Princess Peepers,* p. 102; March, 2009, Kate Kohlbeck, review of *Running Rivals* p. 150.

ONLINE

Tuesday Mourning Home Page, http://tmourning.com (October 25, 2009).

Tuesday Mourning Web log, http://tmourning@blogspot. com (October 25, 2009).*

*   *   *

MUSSI, Sarah

Personal

Born in Gloucestershire, England; married; children: two daughters, one son. *Education:* Royal College of Art, degree; attended university in Nigeria.

Addresses

Home—London, England.

Career

Author and educator. School teacher in Accra, Ghana, and in London, England.

Awards, Honors

Children's Book of the Year designation, Glen Dimplex New Writers' Awards/Irish Writer's Centre, 2007, for *The Door of No Return.*

Writings

The Door of No Return, Hodder (London, England), 2007, Margaret K. McElderry Books (New York, NY), 2008.
The Last of the Warrior Kings, Hodder (London, England), 2008.

Contributor to *Free? Stories Celebrating Human Rights,* Walker (London, England), 2009.

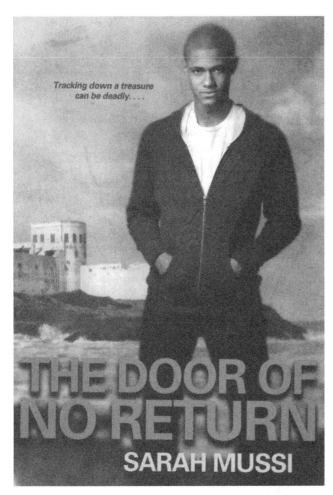

Cover of Sarah Mussi's young-adult novel The Door of No Return, *in which a young man explores his Ghanaian family history.* (Jacket photograph of boy copyright © 2008 by Michael Frost. Jacket photo illustration copyright © 2008 by Kamil Vojnar. Reproduced by permission.)

Sidelights

After attending London's Royal College of Art, Sarah Mussi continued her studies in Nigeria before settling in Ghana for an eighteen-year-long stay. Returning to England in 2001, Mussi began teaching as well as crafting her first young-adult novel, *The Door of No Return.* Published in 2007, *The Door of No Return* relates the story of Zac Baxter, an English boy growing up under the care of his grandfather. The older man enjoys sharing stories of his Ghanaian ancestors—including a kidnapped prince and a story involving a hidden treasure of gold—although Zac dismisses them as invented tales. However, when the young teen discovers that his grandfather has been murdered, he slowly begins to realize that much has been true in these family history. Now Zac must risk his own life to save his grandfather's books and maps from government officials.

Describing *The Door of No Return* as "a complex, masterful story for confident readers," *School Library Journal* critic Margaret Auguste also offered a favorable assessment of Mussi's characters, finding them "unique and fully developed." In her London *Times* review, Amanda Craig described *The Door of No Return* as "a really excellent and original thriller," calling the protagonist's "wry, streetwise voice . . . fresh, funny and compelling." Comparing *The Door of No Return* to other adventure stories, such as Robert Louis Stevenson's *Treasure Island* and H. Rider Haggard's *King Solomon's Mines,* a *Kirkus Reviews* contributor concluded that Mussi offers readers "suspense and important history in one fine novel."

Biographical and Critical Sources

PERIODICALS

Kirkus Reviews, July 15, 2008, review of *The Door of No Return.*
Kliatt, September, 2008, Claire Rosser, review of *The Door of No Return,* p. 18.
School Library Journal, November, 2008, Margaret Auguste, review of *The Door of No Return,* p. 132.
Times (London, England), June 9, 2007, Amanda Craig, review of *The Door of No Return,* p. 15.

ONLINE

Sarah Mussi Home Page, http://www.sarahmussi.co.uk (November 6, 2009).*

* * *

MUTH, Jon J. 1960-

Personal

Born July 28, 1960, in Cincinnati, OH; father an educator, mother an art teacher; married; children: four. *Education:* Studied stone sculpture and sho (brush calligraphy) in Japan; studied painting, printmaking, and drawing in England, Austria, and Germany; attended State University of New York, New Paltz. *Hobbies and other interests:* Playing guitar and piano.

Addresses

Home—Upstate NY.

Career

Author, illustrator, artist, and musician. *Exhibitions:* Solo show at Wilmington College, Wilmington, DE; group shows at Collector's Art Group, Cincinnati, OH, 2008.

Awards, Honors

Eisner Award for excellence in painting; Gold Medal, Society of Illustrators, 1999, for *Come on, Rain!;* Notable Children's Book selection, American Library Association (ALA), National Jewish Book Award finalist, Sydney Taylor Book Award, Association of Jewish Libraries, and National Parenting Book Award, all for *Gershon's Monster;* National Parenting Book Award, for *Stone Soup;* Notable Social Studies Trade Book for Young People designation, National Council for the Social Studies/Children's Book Council (CBC), for *The Three Questions;* Quill Award nominee, and Caldecott Honor Book, ALA, 2006, both for *Zen Shorts;* Frances and Wesley Bock Book Award for Children's Literature, Neumann University Library/Neumann Institute for Franciscan Studies, and Children's Choice Book Award for Illustrator of the Year, CBC/International Reading Association, both 2009, both for *Zen Ties.*

Writings

GRAPHIC NOVELS AND COMICS

Dracula: A Symphony in Moonlight and Nightmares (based on the story by Bram Stoker; originally published in comic-book format), Marvel Comics Group (New York, NY), 1986, second edition, Nantier, Beall, Minoustchine (New York, NY), 1992.

(Illustrator, with others) J.M. DeMatteis, *Moonshadow* (originally published in comic-book format), Epic Comics (New York, NY), 1989.

(Illustrator) Walter Simonson, *Havok and Wolverine: Meltdown* (originally published in comic-book format), Epic Comics (New York, NY), 1990.

The Mythology of an Abandoned City (originally published in comic-book format, 1983-91), Tundra Publishing (Northampton, MA), 1992.

(Illustrator) Grant Morrison, *The Mystery Play* (originally published in comic-book format), Vertigo (New York, NY), 1994.

(Illustrator) J.M. DeMatteis, *The Compleat Moonshadow* (originally published in comic-book format), DC Comics (New York, NY), 1998.

Swamp Thing: Roots (originally published in comic-book format), DC Comics (New York, NY), 1998.

M (based on Fritz Lang's film of the same name; originally published in comic-book format), Abrams (New York, NY), 2008.

Contributor of artwork to comic-book series, including "Moonshadow," by J.M. DeMatteis, 1985-87, "Sandman" by Neil Gaiman, and others.

FOR CHILDREN; SELF-ILLUSTRATED

The Three Questions (based on a story by Leo Tolstoy), Scholastic (New York, NY), 2002.
(Reteller) *Stone Soup,* Scholastic (New York, NY), 2003.
Zen Shorts, Scholastic (New York, NY), 2005.
Zen Ties, Scholastic (New York, NY), 2008.

ILLUSTRATOR

John Kuramoto, *Stonecutter,* Donald M. Grant (Hampton Falls, NH), 1995, Feiwel and Friends (New York, NY), 2009.
Kelley Puckett, *Batman's Dark Secret,* Scholastic (New York, NY), 1999.
Patrick Jennings, *Putnam and Pennyroyal,* Scholastic (New York, NY), 1999.
Karen Hesse, *Come on, Rain,* Scholastic (New York, NY), 1999.
Eric A. Kimmel, reteller, *Gershon's Monster: A Story for the Jewish New Year,* Scholastic (New York, NY), 2000.
Remy Charlip, *Why I Will Never Ever Ever Ever Have Enough Time to Read This Book,* Tricycle Press (Berkeley, CA), 2000.
Jacqueline Woodson, *Our Gracie Aunt,* Hyperion Books for Children (New York, NY), 2002.
Douglas Wood, *Old Turtle and the Broken Truth,* Scholastic (New York, NY), 2003.
Sonia Manzano, *No Dogs Allowed!,* Atheneum Books for Young Readers (New York, NY), 2004.
Amy Hest, *Mr. George Baker,* Candlewick Press (Cambridge, MA), 2004.
Caroline Kennedy, compiler, *A Family of Poems: My Favorite Poetry for Children,* Hyperion (New York, NY), 2005.
Linda Zuckerman, *I Will Hold You 'til You Sleep,* Arthur A. Levine Books (New York, NY), 2006.
Ann M. Martin, *On Christmas Eve,* Scholastic (New York, NY), 2006.
Lauren Thompson, *The Christmas Magic,* Scholastic (New York, NY), 2009.

Contributor to *Knock, Knock!,* Dial (New York, NY), 2007.

OTHER

Vanitas: Paintings, Drawings, and Ideas, Tundra Publishing (Northampton, MA), 1991.

Sidelights

Author and illustrator Jon J. Muth is the creator of a number of highly regarded picture books for young readers. *Zen Shorts,* his most well-known title, was named a Caldecott Honor Book, and its sequel, *Zen Ties,* garnered the Bock Book Award for Children's Literature. "I'm very interested in what words and pictures can do together that they can't do separately," Muth stated in an *Indiebound* online interview with Andrew Duncan. "There is a third thing which occurs. I'm drawn to what is suggested by both the images and the text but remains un-mentioned by either. It can be intellectual, or a logical story point, or emotional. This space seems to be as flexible as either words or pictures. It's a dance between the two."

Muth inherited his passion for the graphic arts while growing up as the son of an art teacher. Encouraging his growing talent, Muth's mother took her son to museums across the United States, exposing him to a wide variety of paintings, prints, drawings, and other art forms. "I don't remember ever not drawing," Muth recalled in a *Book Wholesalers* interview, reprinted on the *Allen Spiegel Fine Arts* Web site. "I don't remember ever having to choose to be an artist. Art was always just my way of being in the world." Muth debuted his paintings and drawings in a one-man invitational exhibit at age eighteen at Wilmington College. Determined to expand his influences, he then traveled throughout England, Austria, Germany, and Japan, studying not only drawing and painting, but also stone sculpture, sho—brush calligraphy—and printmaking in classes and as an apprentice.

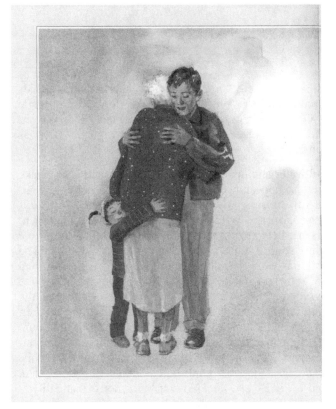

Jon J. Muth's sensitive, family-centered images celebrate the multigenerational bonds in Linda Zuckerman's I Will Hold You 'til You Sleep.
(Illustration copyright © 2006 by Jon J. Muth. Reproduced by permission of Scholastic, Inc.)

Muth began his professional career working as a comic-book illustrator, and he quickly established himself as a talent in that field. In addition to developing and illustrating the groundbreaking "Moonshadow" series written by J.M. DeMatteis and creating art for portions of Neil Gaiman's well-known "Sandman" comic-book epic, Muth also wrote and illustrated several original story arcs based on existing characters and published in their entirety as graphic novels, among them *Dracula: A Symphony in Moonlight and Nightmares* for Marvel Comics and *Swamp Thing: Roots* for DC Comics. As Muth was quoted as saying on the Candlewick Press Web site, comic-book illustration is "a natural forum for expressions of angst and questioning one's place in the universe."

Muth has earned accolades for his Asian-influenced art, a style he developed as a young artist. As he told a *Reading Rockets* interviewer, "I was making marks on a page, there were marks that when I got them right, they had a certain quality and I couldn't describe to you what that quality is, but I just knew it was authentic and it was right. The place that I encountered similar marks was in Asian art—in Japanese paintings, landscape painting and calligraphy—and Chinese painting." Muth added, "I wanted to know more about the culture that produced people who would make that kind of work. I kind of entered into an interest in Asian art sort of from the surface down and I became more interested in the people and the culture and the spiritual life of people in the East. It's interwoven now through all of my work and my life."

With the birth of his own children, Muth naturally began to turn toward children's literature, and he took account of a new potential audience with the need to hear other messages. "I believe it's important that kids read to 'become,' not to escape," he related in his *Book Wholesalers* interview. "They are becoming every moment and every culture has a rich wellspring of literature to draw from. By reading to your children you're giving them more of the world. And the world becomes more their own."

In addition to illustrating texts for a variety of children's-book authors, Muth has created original texts to pair with his highly praised watercolor art. In *The Three Questions,* based on a story by noted Russian writer Leo Tolstoy, he encouraged young readers to consider the needs of others as well as oneself when making decisions. When is the best time to do things? Who is the most important one?, and What is the right thing to do? are the questions raised in the author/ illustrator's gentle story about a boy named Nikolai who learns to find answers to his own questions by relying on the natural wisdom of animals, in this case a wise old turtle named Leo. Noting the Asian inspiration in Muth's art, *School Library Journal* critic Susan Hepler commented that the book's "languid watercolors,

***Muth draws on his personal interest in Buddhism in his self-illustrated poetry collection* Zen Shorts.** (Illustration copyright © 2005 by Jon J. Muth. Reproduced by permission of Scholastic, Inc.)

some sketchy and others fully developed, . . . become less dramatic and more ethereal as the story moves towards its thematic statement." In *Publishers Weekly* a reviewer praised Muth's "misty, evocative watercolors" as well as the text, which is "moral without being moralistic," while in *Kirkus Reviews* a critic dubbed *The Three Questions* "a soaring achievement."

Compared by several critics to *The Three Questions,* *Zen Shorts* contains another simple story that poses three thoughtful questions and imparts a resonant message based on Zen teachings. In this tale a giant panda named Stillwater appears at the home of three children. Over several days, Karl, Michael, and Addy each spend time alone with Stillwater as the bear shares both fun and Zen stories, while also posing a philosophical question to each child. Noting that the author includes a valuable commentary about Zen at the book's conclusion, *Booklist* contributor Gillian Engberg wrote that, for even young readers, "Stillwater's questions will linger . . . and the peaceful, uncluttered pictures . . . will encourage children to dream and fill in their own answers." Coop Renner noted the value of *Zen Shorts* as a teaching tool, commenting in his *School Library Journal* review that the "visually lovely" book draws on fa-

miliar images to "prod children to approach life and its circumstances in profoundly 'un-Western' ways," while a *Kirkus Reviews* contributor concluded: "Every word and image comes to make as perfect a picture book as can be."

Stillwater and his friends Karl, Michael, and Addy make a return appearance in *Zen Ties,* called "a rich and wonderful offering" by Marianne Saccardi in *School Library Journal.* After introducing the three children to his nephew, Koo, Stillwater proposes that they take some soup to an elderly neighbor, Miss Whitaker. The children view the old woman as crabby and mean and are reluctant to go, until Stillwater convinces them to overcome their fears. At Miss Whitaker's home, the children learn that she was once a marvelous teacher, and she offers to help Michael prepare for an important spelling bee. The narrative's "overt messages about compassionate action [is] knit smoothly into Buddhist teachings," *Booklist* contributor Gillian Engberg stated, and a *Publishers Weekly* contributor noted that Stillwater "continues to combine his slow-moving grace with genuine spiritual tranquility." Daniel Handler, writing in the *New York Times Book Review,* praised the lush illustrations, commenting that "Muth's artwork blends representation and abstraction in misty, elusive ways—much like the ancient Buddhist stories that inspire him." The critic added that the pictures "have the yearning gorgeousness displayed in the first volume. The cover alone is a keeper—Stillwater and Koo with their backs to us, sitting on a picnic table and staring out into Muth's melancholy space."

Muth contributes the artwork to *A Family of Poems: My Favorite Poetry for Children,* a volume compiled by Caroline Kennedy. Containing more than 100 selections, the book includes work by such well-known poets as Robert Frost, Walt Whitman, and Ogden Nash as well as by contemporary writers like Jack Prelutsky, Nikki Giovanni, and Sandra Cisneros. "Providing stunning backdrops for these timeless works are Muth's richly textured watercolor paintings, which capture with remarkable insight the spirit of each poem," according to a *Publishers Weekly* reviewer. "The wide variety of artistic styles—ethereal, realistic, comical, energetic, sweet, romantic—matches the mood of the poems," Susan Scheps commented in *School Library Journal,* and Cooper, writing in *Booklist,* also complimented Muth's illustrations, "which are as adept in catching the humor of some poems as they are in reflecting the power of others."

Linda Zuckerman's *I Will Hold You 'til You Sleep* celebrates the power of familial love by depicting moments in a boy's life from childhood to adulthood. "Muth graciously balances the weight of the scenes with an objective view," wrote a contributor in *Publishers Weekly,* and a critic in *Kirkus Reviews* offered praise for the combination of Zuckerman's lyrical narrative and Muth's pictures, stating, "This isn't cheap sentimentality but deep feeling and lovely art perfectly in

Muth teams with Douglas Wood, creating artwork for Wood's picture book **Old Turtle and the Broken Truth.** (Illustration copyright © 2003 by Jon J. Muth. Reproduced by permission of Scholastic, Inc.)

tune." In Ann M. Martin's *On Christmas Eve,* a tale set in 1958, third-grader Tess McAlister desperately wants some holiday magic to help her best friend Sarah, whose father has cancer. Sneaking downstairs late at night, Tess witnesses a miracle that helps her learn a valuable lesson about faith and hope. Muth introduces each chapter in Martin's book with "a full-page, decorative black-and-white watercolor painting," according to *School Library Journal* contributor Susan Patron.

Muth takes his responsibilities as a creator of children's book very seriously. "The people who are the guardians of the gateway to children's literature are very passionate about what they're doing, and that's magnificent," he stated in his *Book Wholesalers* interview. "The gates are high. It was an honor to be welcomed into that space. It wasn't really a challenge as much as a matter of saying, 'This is how I feel. Is this something that would be appropriate here?'"

Biographical and Critical Sources

PERIODICALS

Booklist, March 15, 2002, Hazel Rochman, review of *The Three Questions,* p. 1264; January 1, 2003, Stephanie Zvirin, review of *Stone Soup,* p. 900; March 1, 2005, Gillian Engberg, review of *Zen Shorts,* p. 1194; October 15, 2005, Ilene Cooper, review of *A Family of Poems: My Favorite Poetry for Children,* p. 48; September 1, 2006, Ilene Cooper, review of *On Christmas Eve,* p. 129; February 15, 2008, Gillian Engberg, review of *Zen Ties,* p. 86.

Bulletin of the Center for Children's Books, March, 2003, review of *Stone Soup,* p. 282.

Horn Book, July, 1999, Leo Landry, review of *Come on, Rain!,* p. 454; January, 2000, review of *Putnam and Pennyroyal,* p. 77; March-April, 2003, Margaret A. Chang, review of *Stone Soup,* p. 221.

Kirkus Reviews, March 15, 2002, review of *The Three Questions,* p. 420; February 1, 2005, review of *Zen Shorts,* p. 179; September 15, 2006, review of *I Will Hold You 'til You Sleep,* p. 971; November 1, 2006, review of *On Christmas Eve,* p. 1131.

Magazine of Fantasy and Science Fiction, April, 1995, Charles de Lint, review of *Stonecutter,* p. 37.

New York Times Book Review, November 14, 2004, Jenny Allen, "Just the Two of Us," review of *Mr. George Baker,* p. 35; July 10, 2005, Bruno Navasky, review of *Zen Shorts,* p. 20; May 11, 2008, Daniel Handler, "When We Last Saw Our Heroes . . .," review of *Zen Ties,* p. 18.

Publishers Weekly, August 28, 2000, review of *Gershon's Monster: A Story for the Jewish New Year,* p. 78; September 11, 2000, review of *Why I Will Never Ever Ever Ever Have Enough Time to Read This Book,* p. 90; February 11, 2002, review of *The Three Questions,* p. 187; January 13, 2003, review of *Stone Soup,* p. 60; October 27, 2003, review of *Old Turtle and the Broken Truth,* p. 68; February 28, 2005, review of *Zen Shorts,* p. 66; August 29, 2005, review of *A Family of Poems,* p. 58; September 25, 2006, review of *On Christmas Eve,* p. 72; October 2, 2006, review of *I Will Hold You 'til You Sleep,* p. 61; November 19, 2007, review of *Zen Ties,* p. 55.

School Library Journal, June, 2002, Susan Hepler, review of *The Three Questions,* p. 104; December, 2002, Anna DeWind, review of *Our Gracie Aunt,* p. 114; February, 2003, Lee Bock, review of *The Three Questions,* p. 96; March, 2003, Grace Oliff, review of *Stone Soup,* p. 222; August, 2003, Teresa Bateman, review of *Come on, Rain,* p. 63; October, 2003, review of *Our Gracie Aunt,* p. 28; February, 2005, Coop Renner, review of *Zen Shorts,* p. 108; December, 2005, Susan Scheps, review of *A Family of Poems,* p. 130; October, 2006, Susan Patron, review of *On Christmas Eve,* p. 98, and Judith Constantinides, review of *I Will Hold You 'til You Sleep,* p. 132; April, 2008, Marianne Saccardi, review of *Zen Ties,* p. 117.

ONLINE

Allen Spiegel Fine Arts Web site, http://www.allen spiegelfinearts.com/ (May 6, 2005), "Book Wholesalers Inc. Staff Interview with Jon J. Muth."

Candlewick Press Web site, http://www.candlewick.com/ (October 10, 2009), "John J. Muth."

IndieBound Web site, http://www.indiebound.org/ (October 10, 2009), Andrew Duncan, interview with Muth.

Reading Rockets Web site, http://www.readingrockets.org/ (October 10, 2009), interview with Muth.

Scholastic Web site, http://www2.scholastic.com/ (October 10, 2009), "John J. Muth."*

N

NEWTON, Vanessa
See NEWTON, Vanessa Brantley

*   *   *

NEWTON, Vanessa Brantley 1962(?)-
(Vanessa Newton)

Personal
Born c. 1962; married Ray Newton; children: Zoe. *Education:* Attended Fashion Institute of Technology; Attended School of Visual Arts. *Hobbies and other interests:* Cooking, crafts, collect vintage children's books.

Addresses
Home—East Orange, NJ. *Agent*—Lori Nowicki, infopainted-words.com. *E-mail*—oohlaladesignstudio@gmail.com.

Career
Illustrator and author.

Member
Society of Children's Book Writers and Illustrators.

Writings

SELF-ILLUSTRATED

(As Vanessa Newton) *Let Freedom Sing,* introduction by Ruby Bridges, Blue Apple Books (Maplewood, NJ), 2009.

ILLUSTRATOR

Derrick D. Barnes, *Brand New School, Brave New Ruby* ("Ruby and the Booker Boys" series), Scholastic (New York, NY), 2008.

Vanessa Brantley Newton (Photograph by Ray Newton. Reproduced by permission.)

Derrick D. Barnes, *Trivia Queen, Third-Grade Supreme* ("Ruby and the Booker Boys" series), Scholastic (New York, NY), 2008.

Derrick D. Barnes, *The Slumber Party Payback* ("Ruby and the Booker Boys" series), Scholastic (New York, NY), 2009.

(As Vanessa Newton) Thea Guidone, *Drum City,* Tricycle Press (Berkeley, CA), 2010.

Biographical and Critical Sources

PERIODICALS

Kirkus Reviews, June 15, 2008, review of *Brand New School, Brave New Ruby.*

ONLINE

Vanessa Brantley Newton Web log, http://oohlaladesign studio.blogspot.com (October 25, 2009).*

* * *

NICHOLS, Travis

Personal

Male. *Education:* Texas Tech University, degree, 2002. *Hobbies and other interests:* Art, comics, writing, gardening.

Addresses

Home—San Francisco, CA. *E-mail*—trav@ilikeapple juice.com.

Career

Painter, cartoonist, writer, and musician. I Like Applejuice Arts and Media, owner, 2004—; worked at The Art Pad, Austin, TX, 2005-07. Musician; performed with Omega Monster Patrol! and The Needies (musical groups). Has also taught elementary school. *Exhibitions:* Work included in group show in Austin, TX, 2007.

Awards, Honors

Best Book for Young Adults selection and Popular Paperbacks for Young Adults selection, both American Library Association, both 2009, both for *Punk Rock Etiquette.*

Writings

(Self-illustrated) *Punk Rock Etiquette: The Ultimate How-to Guide for Punk, Underground, DIY, and Indie Bands,* Roaring Brook Press (New York, NY), 2008.

Contributor to *The Best American Comics 2006,* edited by Anne Elizabeth Moore and Harvey Pekar, Houghton Mifflin, 2006. Contributor of cartoons to periodicals, including *Nickelodeon, Soundcheck,* and *Herbivore.*

Sidelights

Travis Nichols, a San Francisco-based artist and musician, is the author of *Punk Rock Etiquette: The Ultimate How-to Guide for Punk, Underground, DIY, and*

Travis Nichols (Reproduced by permission.)

Indie Bands, his award-winning self-illustrated debut. A former elementary-school teacher, Nichols is also a cartoonist whose work has appeared in such publications as *Nickelodeon* and *Herbivore.* As a musician, he performs in such independent bands as The Needies and Omega Monster Patrol!

In *Punk Rock Etiquette* Nichols presents a guidebook for aspiring musicians, complete with advice about forming a band, recording songs, promoting shows, selling merchandise, and touring. He also includes a tongue-in-cheek look at the personalities of various band-mate archetypes, such as the "tortured poet" and the "rock star." A contributor to *Kirkus Reviews* stated that Nichols "knows his turf" and praised the author's "breezy but firm tone" and "worthwhile advice." In *School Library Journal,* Alana Abbott noted that the "illustrations . . . are most successful" in depicting a band's road trip and Nichols's "advice is valuable and will appeal to a broad audience." Although Ian Chipman commented in *Booklist* that punk rock purists might prefer playing music to reading about it, the critic added that many teens "will find a lot to laugh about and maybe even a little to learn in this irreverent guide."

Biographical and Critical Sources

PERIODICALS

Booklist, September 1, 2008, Ian Chipman, review of *Punk Rock Etiquette: The Ultimate How-to Guide for Punk, Underground, DIY, and Indie Bands,* p. 86.

Herbivore, Issue 8, "Travis Nichols: Aw. Zing!," interview with Nichols.

Kirkus Reviews, August 15, 2008, review of *Punk Rock Etiquette.*

Onion, July 5, 2007, Sean O'Neal, "Cute Is What They Aim For," interview with Nichols.

School Library Journal, December, 2008, Alana Abbott, review of *Punk Rock Etiquette,* p. 152.

ONLINE

Austinist Web site, http://austinist.com/ (October 31, 2007), Clarisa Ramirez, "Austinist Interviews I Like Apple Juice."

Macmillan Web site, http://us.macmillan.com/ (October 10, 2009), "Travis Nichols."

Punk Rock Etiquette Web log, http://punkrocketiquette. blogspot.com/ (October 10, 2009).

Travis Nichols Home Page, http://ilikeapplejuice.com (October 10, 2009).

Travis Nichols Web log, http://megustoapplejuice.blogspot. com/ (October 10, 2009).*

*   *   *

NUMEROFF, Laura 1953-
(Laura Joffe Numeroff)

Laura Numeroff (Reproduced by permission.)

Personal

Born July 14, 1953, in Brooklyn, NY; daughter of William (an artist) and Florence (a teacher) Numeroff. *Education:* Pratt Institute, B.F.A. (with honors), 1975; attended Parsons College, 1975. *Religion:* Jewish. *Hobbies and other interests:* Reading memoirs, playing tennis, going to a lot of movies.

Addresses

Home—Los Angeles, CA. *E-mail*—email@laura numeroff.com.

Career

Author and illustrator of children's books. Lecturer at schools in California; worked variously running a merry-go-round and doing private investigation.

Awards, Honors

Alabama Young Reader Medal, 1986, California Young Reader Award, 1987, Colorado Children's Book Award, Nevada Young Reader Award, and Georgia Children's Picture Storybook award, all 1988, and Ohio Buckeye Medal, 1989, all for *If You Give a Mouse a Cookie;* Parents' Choice Award, 1991, for *If You Give a Moose a Muffin;* Quill Award, 2006, for *If You Give a Pig a Party;* Milner Award (Atlanta, GA), 2007.

Writings

(Under name Laura Joffe Numeroff) *If You Give a Mouse a Cookie,* illustrated by Felicia Bond, Harper (New York, NY), 1985.

(Under name Laura Joffe Numeroff) *If You Give a Moose a Muffin,* illustrated by Felicia Bond, HarperCollins (New York, NY), 1991.

Dogs Don't Wear Sneakers, illustrated by Joseph Mathieu, Simon & Schuster (New York, NY), 1993.

Why a Disguise?, illustrated by David McPhail, Simon & Schuster (New York, NY), 1994.

Chimps Don't Wear Glasses, illustrated by Joseph Mathieu, Simon & Schuster (New York, NY), 1995, new edition, Aladdin (New York, NY), 2006.

Mouse Cookies: Ten Easy-to-Make Cookie Recipes, illustrated by Felicia Bond, HarperCollins (New York, NY), 1995.

(With Barney Saltzberg) *Two for Stew,* illustrated by Sal Murdocca, Simon & Schuster (New York, NY), 1996.

The Chicken Sisters, illustrated by Sharleen Collicott, HarperCollins (New York, NY), 1997.

What Mommies Do Best/What Daddies Do Best, illustrated by Lynn Munsinger, Simon & Schuster (New York, NY), 1998, published separately as *What Daddies Do Best,* 2001, and *What Mommies Do Best,* Simon & Schuster (New York, NY), 2002.

Monster Munchies, illustrated by Nate Evans, Random House (New York, NY), 1998.

If You Give a Pig a Pancake, illustrated by Felicia Bond, Laura Geringer Books (New York, NY), 1998.

Sometimes I Wonder If Poodles Like Noodles, illustrated by Tim Bowers, Simon & Schuster (New York, NY), 1999.

The Best Mouse Cookie, illustrated by Felicia Bond, Laura Geringer Books (New York, NY), 1999.

(With Wendy S. Harpham) *The Hope Tree: Kids Talk about Breast Cancer,* illustrated by David McPhail, Simon & Schuster (New York, NY), 1999.

If You Take a Mouse to the Movies, illustrated by Felicia Bond, Laura Geringer Books (New York, NY), 2000.

What Grandmas Do Best/What Grandpas Do Best, illustrated by Lynn Munsinger, Simon & Schuster (New York, NY), 2000, published separately as *What Grandmas Do Best* and *What Grandpas Do Best,* 2001.

If You Take a Mouse to School, illustrated by Felicia Bond, Laura Geringer Books (New York, NY), 2002, miniature edition, 2003.

If You Give an Author a Pencil (autobiography), photographs by Sherry Shahan, Richard C. Owen Publishers (Katonah, NY), 2002.

Laura Numeroff's Ten-Step Guide to Living with Your Monster, illustrated by Nate Evans, Laura Geringer Books (New York, NY), 2002.

What Sisters Do Best/What Brothers Do Best, illustrated by Lynn Munsinger, Simon & Schuster (New York, NY), 2003.

(With Nate Evans) *Sherman Crunchley,* illustrated by Tim Bowers, Dutton (New York, NY), 2003.

What Aunts Do Best/What Uncles Do Best, illustrated by Lynn Munsinger, Simon & Schuster (New York, NY), 2004.

If You Give a Pig a Party, illustrated by Felicia Bond, Laura Geringer Books (New York, NY), 2005.

Mouse Cookies and More: A Treasury (with CD-ROM), Laura Geringer Books (New York, NY), 2006.

When Sheep Sleep, illustrated by David McPhail, Abrams Books for Young Readers (New York, NY), 2006.

A Mouse Cookie First Library, illustrated by Felicia Bond, Laura Geringer Books (New York, NY), 2007.

(With Nate Evans) *The Jellybeans and the Big Dance,* illustrated by Lynn Munsinger, Abrams Books for Young Readers (New York, NY), 2008.

Time for School, Mouse!, illustrated by Felicia Bond, Laura Geringer Books (New York, NY), 2008.

If You Give a Cat a Cupcake, illustrated by Felicia Bond, Laura Geringer Books (New York, NY), 2009.

Would I Trade My Parents?, illustrated by James Bernardin, Abrams Books for Young Readers (New York, NY), 2009.

What Puppies Do Best/What Kittens Do Best, illustrated by Lynn Munsinger, Chronicle Books (San Francisco, CA), 2010.

Many of Numeroff's works have been translated into other languages, including Spanish, Hebrew, French, Korean, Afrikaans, Italian, Japanese, Danish, Swedish, and German.

SELF-ILLUSTRATED

Amy for Short, Macmillan (New York, NY), 1976.

Phoebe Dexter Has Harriet Peterson's Sniffles, Greenwillow (New York, NY), 1977.

Walter, Macmillan (New York, NY), 1978.

(With Alice Richter) *Emily's Bunch,* Macmillan (New York, NY), 1978.

(With Alice Richter) *You Can't Put Braces on Spaces,* Greenwillow (New York, NY), 1979.

The Ugliest Sweater, F. Watts (New York, NY), 1980.

Doesn't Grandma Have an Elmo Elephant Jungle Kit?, Greenwillow (New York, NY), 1980.

Beatrice Doesn't Want To, F. Watts (New York, NY), 1981, revised edition, illustrated by Lynn Munsinger, Candlewick Press (Cambridge, MA), 2004.

Digger, Dutton (New York, NY), 1983.

Adaptations

You Can't Put Braces on Spaces and *The Ugliest Sweater* were adapted as educational filmstrips by Westport Communications Group; *If You Give a Mouse a Cookie* was adapted as an interactive CD-ROM, HarperCollins, 1995, and recorded on audiocassette, read by Carol Kane, 1997. Other adaptations include: *If You Give a Moose a Muffin,* read by Robbie Benson, HarperAudio, 1997; *If You Give a Pig a Pancake,* read by David Hyde Pierce, HarperAudio, 1999; *If You Take a Mouse to the Movies,* read by Jason Alexander; and *If You Take a Mouse to School,* read by Diane Lane, Laura Geringer Books, 2003. *If You Give a Mouse a Cookie* was adapted as a play by Joy Davidson, produced throughout the United States.

Sidelights

In her lighthearted picture books for children, author and illustrator Laura Numeroff plays with language, pairing her playful rhymes and syncopated rhythms with original bright and bold artwork as well as illustrations by artists such as Felicia Bond, Lynn Munsinger, and David McPhail. The phenomenal success of her 1985 children's story *If You Give a Mouse a Cookie*

Numeroff teams with artist Felicia Bond to create the popular picture book If You Give a Mouse a Cookie. (Illustration copyright © 1985 by Felicia Bond. Reproduced by permission of HarperCollins Publishers, Inc.)

transformed that book into a childhood classic. In the years since, Numeroff has become even more well known due to the popularity of related books such as *If You Give a Moose a Muffin, If You Take a Mouse to School, If You Give a Pig a Party,* and *Mouse Cookies and More: A Treasury,* as well as standalone stories such as *When Sheep Sleep* and *Sometimes I Wonder if Poodles Like Noodles.* Her stories continue to engage nonsense lovers of all ages.

The youngest of three daughters, Numeroff was encouraged in her reading and artwork by her father, a staff member of New York's *World Telegram & Sun,* as well as by her mother, a middle-school economics teacher. "I grew up in a world of books, music, and art," she once told *SATA.* "I was a voracious reader and read six books every week," among them stories by Beverly Cleary and Marguerite Henry, the "Dr. Doolittle" books by Hugh Lofting, *Eloise* by Kay Thompson, *Stuart Little* by E.B. White, and *The Cat in the Hat* by Dr. Seuss. "I've also been drawing pictures since I was old enough to hold a crayon, and writing came soon after. Doing children's books combines the two things I love the most."

Despite her love of writing and illustrating her own stories, at age fifteen Numeroff decided to follow in the footsteps of her older sister Emily, a fashion designer. She enrolled at New York City's Pratt Institute but disliked everything about the fashion department. "I couldn't sew to save my life," she lamented on her home page. Instead, she decided to take classes that appealed to her, one of which was "Writing and Illustrating for Children's Books" taught by author Barbara Bottner. Numeroff's first published book, *Amy for Short,* got its start as a homework assignment for this class.

With illustrations by the author, *Amy for Short* describes the friendship between Mark and Amy, who are brought together because they stand out from the rest of their classmates due to their height. As the tallest kid in the class, Amy is cast in the coveted role of a tree in her school play and acts the part of Abraham Lincoln in a summer-camp performance. When she suddenly shoots past Mark in stature, Amy worries that he will no longer be her pal, but Mark proves his friendship by bowing out of the most important Little League game of the year to attend her birthday party.

A brother and sister who butt heads are the focus of *Beatrice Doesn't Want To,* a story that was originally illustrated by Numeroff, and then reissued with artwork by Munsinger. In the story, Henry the dog has to take his stubborn little sister to the library while he does his homework. Young Beatrice makes studying impossible until Henry brings her to the children's room where a story hour is in progress. Resistant at first, Bea soon becomes caught up in the magic of reading, and ultimately the stubborn child has to be dragged out of the library through the same door she did not want to enter in the first place. Reviewing the new edition of the picture

Numeroff continues her humorous demanding-animal theme in **If You Give a Cat a Cupcake,** *featuring artwork by Felicia Bond.* (Illustration copyright © 2008 by Felicia Bond. Reproduced by permission.)

book, Jennifer Mattson wrote in *Booklist* that Munsinger's "endearing" characters "extend the humor of Numeroff's typically pitch-perfect text," and *School Library Journal* contributor Wanda Meyers-Hines dubbed *Beatrice Doesn't Want To* a "charming tale."

Numeroff produced several more self-illustrated picture books, including *Digger* and *The Ugliest Sweater,* before teaming up with Bond for what would be the first of many collaborations: *If You Give a Mouse a Cookie.* A "what if" story about an insistent young mouse and the increasingly bewildered young boy who tries to assist the rodent, Numeroff's tale lets readers follow a chain of activities that ultimately leaves the polite young protagonist tired and fast asleep. "The similarities between mouse and child won't be lost on observant youngsters," noted a *Booklist* reviewer. *If You Give a Moose a Muffin* serves as the first of several humorous sequels, as "the complexities that can follow a simple act of kindness are played out with the same rampant silliness," according to a reviewer in *Publishers Weekly.* From jam to go on top, to more muffins, to a trip to the store, the demands of a moose on the loose add an even greater element of absurdity to Numeroff's circular plot.

More silliness is served up in *If You Take a Mouse to the Movies* and *If You Take a Mouse to School,* both featuring artwork by Bond. In *If You Take a Mouse to the Movies* the little mouse from *If You Give a Mouse a Cookie* wants to go the movies along with the patient little boy from the first title. At the movies the popcorn reminds the mouse of stringing popped corn to put on the Christmas tree, and from there he ruminates about snowmen, caroling, and other aspects of the Christmas season. A critic writing in *Publishers Weekly* commended Numeroff's "playful what-if scenario," and in *Booklist* Gillian Engberg described *If You Take a Mouse to the Movies* as a "lively cause-and-effect romp." Janice M. Del Negro, reviewing the book for the *Bulletin of the Center for Children's Books,* cited Numeroff's "understated humor," which "is reinforced by the cumulative effect of the events." A reviewer for *School Library Journal* summed up the book by calling it a "wonderfully silly story."

Described as "a rollicking romp" by a contributor to *Publishers Weekly, If You Take a Mouse to School* finds the mouse asking for a lunchbox, a snack, a notebook, and pencils, all before it hops into the little boy's backpack and sets off for school. At school, the rodent runs from activity to activity, spelling out words on the blackboard, building a tiny house with building blocks, and making mouse-sized furniture from clay. The *Publishers Weekly* reviewer called *If You Take a Mouse to School* a "winner," and a critic for *Kirkus Reviews* dubbed the book "a giggle-fest." Maryann H. Owen, reviewing Numeroff's story for *School Library Journal,* called the tale "a lively experience for mouse and boy."

Numeroff continues her what-if formula in *If You Give a Pig a Pancake, If You Give a Pig a Party,* and *If You Give a Cat a Cupcake.* In the first title, a little girl's gift of a pancake requires syrup, which makes the piggy recipient sticky. A quick clean-up leads to a tap dance, the need to send photos to friends, the construction of a tree house, and . . . more pancakes. The same pig continues its demands in *If You Give a Pig a Party,* as a simple request mushrooms into balloons, a street fair, and a pajama party. A gray kitten desiring a cupcake creates a full circle of demands that move from some decorative sprinkles to a bathing suit and a trip to the beach, to rides at an amusement park and another cupcake, all of which readers can track in *If You Give a Cat a Cupcake.*

Critics responded warmly to *If You Give a Pig a Pancake,* a contributor for *Publishers Weekly* noting that "if you give a child this book, chances are, they'll devour it eagerly." Shirley Lewis, writing in *Teacher Librarian,* called the book a "charmer," and a critic for *Kirkus Reviews* lauded "the funny, clever formula [that] creates just the right amount of anticipation." Featuring Bond's "familiar madcap illustrations," *If You Give a Cat a Cupcake* also treats readers to a "wry" story with "zany childhood logic," according to *School Library Journal* contributor Rachael Vilmar. A portion of Numeroff's royalties for the "If You Give. . ." series is donated to First Book, a national nonprofit organization that promotes children's literacy.

In addition to her "If You Give. . ." series, Numeroff creates other picture-book series that showcase her wacky inventiveness. The titles of *Dogs Don't Wear Sneakers* and *Chimps Don't Wear Glasses* give readers a hint of what is to come: two full plates of nonsense rhymes along with animal-themed illustrations by Joseph Mathieu that show exactly the opposite. A *Kirkus Reviews* critic wrote that the "deliciously silly text" in *Dogs Don't Wear Sneakers* is presented in "a spirited, comical style."

Numeroff explores family roles in a series that includes *What Mommies Do Best/What Daddies Do Best, What Grandmas Do Best/What Grandpas Do Best, What Sisters Do Best/What Brothers Do Best,* and even *What Cats Do Best/What Dogs Do Best.* In *Booklist* Stephanie Zvirin called *What Mommies Do Best/What Daddies Do Best* a "sweet picture book" that works against stereotypes. An animal mother's activities—reading to the children or playing ball in the park—are told with the book right side up, while the father's activities are told with the book held upside down, and this double-sided format is repeated in other series titles. Writing in the *New York Times Book Review,* Scott Veale called *What Mommies Do Best/What Daddies Do Best* a "light-hearted catalogue" of activities, and Catherine T. Quattlebaum, reviewing *What Grandmas Do Best/What Grandpas Do Best* in *School Library Journal,* deemed it "wonderful for quiet lap-sit storytimes" and a "charming introduction to the special times shared with grandparents." Another series title, *What Aunts Do Best/What Uncles Do Best,* is "an upbeat offering [that] just might inspire a family reunion," according to Gay Lynn Van Vleck.

Numeroff and Nate Evans tell a tall tale about a small mouse in **Sherman Crunchley,** *a book featuring illustrations by Tim Bowers.* (Illustration copyright 2003 by Tim Bowers. All rights reserved. Reproduced by permission of Puffin Books, a division of Penguin Putnam Books for Young Readers.)

Evans and Numeroff continue their storytelling collaboration in **The Jellybeans and the Big Dance,** *featuring cartoon art by Lynn Munsinger.* (Illustration copyright © 2008 by Lynn Munsinger. All rights reserved. Reproduced by permission.)

In addition to series titles, Numeroff has channeled her whimsical humor into a number of solo picture books. In *Two for Stew* a matronly woman will not believe the waiter at Chez Nous when he claims that the restaurant is out of its special stew. Describing the story, which follows this conversation between the woman and the waiter, a critic in *Publishers Weekly* applauded the "lilting stanzas" created by Numeroff and coauthor Barney Saltzberg, calling the work a "giddy and sometimes campy salute to stew." In *The Chicken Sisters* Numeroff's "loony story gently pokes fun at three eccentric sisters," as a reviewer for *Publishers Weekly* remarked. In this case, sibling chickens have somewhat bothersome hobbies: One bakes terrible sweets, another sings off-tune, and the third knits everything with pom-poms. Although these hobbies annoy the neighbors, when a wolf moves nearby the sisters' talents are used to advantage. A *Publishers Weekly* contributor called *The Chicken Sisters* "off-the-wall fun," while in *Booklist* Ilene Cooper described it as "a snappy story in every way."

Numeroff continues her habit of casting humorous animal characters in *Sherman Crunchley,* a story coauthored by Nate Evans in which the canine police officer in Biscuit City tries to avoid a promotion that would make him chief when his dad retires from the top-cop spot. Sherman has a hard time saying "No, thanks," but when he musters up the courage to do so, his doggy dad's reaction is not what he expects. Praising Tim Bowers' colorful illustrations for *Sherman Crunchley,* Sheilah Kosco predicted in *School Library Journal* that "children will enjoy this funny tale, and . . . might

even learn a lesson about life in the process." Another collaboration with Evans, *The Jellybeans and the Big Dance,* finds a young pup named Emily dancing whenever she can, even though her dance-class friends Pig, Cat, and Rabbit are less enthusiastic. Through Emily's imaginative way to muster confidence among her fellow dancers, the story concludes with "a winning recital" in which the friends "work . . . out their problems and appreciat[e] . . . each other's uniqueness," according to *School Library Journal* contributor Julie R. Ranelli.

A traditional method of falling asleep is given a humorous twist in *When Sheep Sleep,* featuring artwork by David McPhail. In the picture book, a girl hopes to count sheep as a way to fall asleep, but the wooly creatures are snoozing at the foot of her bed and show no signs of waking up. From sheep, she turns to cows, then pigs, but all the creatures she can find are sleeping soundly. *When Sheep Sleep* was recommended as a "gentle, rhyming lullaby" by Linda Ludke, who predicted in *School Library Journal* that the book will "become a bedtime favorite." In *Kirkus Reviews* a writer wrote that Numeroff's "pleasant, satisfying" story features "warm and cozy pen-and-watercolor" art, and *Booklist* critic Shelle Rosenfeld described *When Sheep Sleep* as "a delight."

Featuring illustrations by Tim Bowers, *Sometimes I Wonder If Poodles Like Noodles* presents twenty-one simple rhyming poems that are told from a girl's point of view, while *Laura Numeroff's Ten-Step Guide to Living with Your Monster* is a tongue-in-cheek affirmation of the dos and don'ts of pet raising, albeit in the guise of training a monster. John Sigwald, writing in *School Library Journal,* described *Laura Numeroff's Ten-Step Guide to Living with Your Monster* as a "silly picture book," and a reviewer for *Publishers Weekly* deemed it a "comically outlandish outline to the parameters of monster (a.k.a. pet) ownership."

While most of her work features fun, Numeroff deals with a more serious topic in *The Hope Tree: Kids Talk about Breast Cancer.* Here she attempts to instruct and comfort children about what happens when a parent has cancer. Employing cuddly animal characters, the author uses a fictional support group of kids talking about their mothers' breast cancer to discuss issues many families face while fighting the illness. Mary R. Hoffman, writing in *School Library Journal,* called *The Hope Tree* "a comforting picture book," and a contributor for *Publishers Weekly* praised the work as "comforting and compassionate." All the proceeds received by Numeroff, her advisor, and illustrator David McPhail for sales of *The Hope Tree* are donated to the Susan Komen Foundation.

As well as possessing an offbeat sense of humor, Numeroff has always been an avid reader, and prefers to read biographies, and memoirs. She also collects children's books and can often be found in the library or bookstore. "My work is my life," she once commented to *SATA.* "I can draw no distinction between the words 'work' and 'spare time.' I love what I'm doing and the only time it becomes work is when there's re-writing. I hope to be writing until my last days."

Biographical and Critical Sources

BOOKS

Numeroff, Laura, *If You Give an Author a Pencil* (autobiography), photographs by Sherry Shahan, Richard C. Owen Publishers (Katonah, NY), 2002.

PERIODICALS

Booklist, June 1, 1985, review of *If You Give a Mouse a Cookie,* p. 1404; May 1, 1997, Ilene Cooper, review of *The Chicken Sisters,* p. 1497; April, 1998, Stephanie Zvirin, review of *What Mommies Do Best/What Daddies Do Best,* p. 1333; May 15, 1998, Carolyn Phelan, review of *If You Give a Pig a Pancake,* p. 1633; November 15, 2000, Hazel Rochman, review of *What Grandmas Do Best/What Grandpas Do Best,* p. 649; December 1, 2000, Gillian Engberg, review of *If You Take a Mouse to the Movies,* p. 722; December 1, 2004, Jennifer Mattson, review of *Beatrice Doesn't Want To,* p. 661; October 15, 2005, Karin Snelson, review of *If You Give a Pig a Party,* p. 581; September 1, 2006, Shelle Rosenfeld, review of *When Sheep Sleep,* p. 139; April 15, 2008, Gillian Engberg, review of *The Jellybeans and the Big Dance,* p. 49.

Bulletin of the Center for Children's Books, December, 2000, Janice M. Del Negro, review of *If You Take a Mouse to the Movies,* p. 157.

Kirkus Reviews, February 15, 1983, review of *Digger,* p. 182; July 1, 1993, review of *Dogs Don't Wear Sneakers,* p. 864; August 1, 1995, review of *Chimps Don't Wear Glasses,* p. 1115; May 1, 1998, review of *If You Give a Pig a Pancake,* p. 663; September 1, 2000, review of *What Grandmas Do Best/What Grandpas Do Best,* p. 1288; June 15, 2002, review of *If You Take a Mouse to School,* p. 886; October 15, 2004, review of *Beatrice Doesn't Want To,* p. 1012; September 1, 2006, review of *When Sheep Sleep,* p. 910; February 15, 2008, review of *The Jellybeans and the Big Dance.*

New York Times Book Review, May 17, 1998, Scott Veale, review of *What Mommies Do Best/What Daddies Do Best,* p. 31.

Publishers Weekly, June 28, 1991, review of *If You Give a Moose a Muffin,* p. 100; July 29, 1996, review of *Two for Stew,* p. 87; April 7, 1997, review of *The Chicken Sisters,* p. 90; March 16, 1998, review of *If You Give a Pig a Pancake,* p. 62; November 9, 1998, review of *Chimps Don't Wear Glasses,* p. 80; June 14, 1999, review of *Sometimes I Wonder If Poodles Like Noodles,* p. 69; August 21, 2000, review of *What Grandmas Do Best/What Grandpas Do Best,* p. 72; September 25, 2000, review of *If You Take a Mouse to the Movies,* p. 69; October 15, 2001, review of *What Grandmas Do Best/What Grandpas Do Best,* p. 73; December 10, 2001, review of *The Hope Tree: Kids Talk about Breast Cancer,* p. 73; February 25, 2002, review of *Laura Numeroff's Ten-Step Guide to Living with Your Monster,* p. 65; June 24, 2002, review of *If You Take a Mouse to School,* pp. 54-55; October 13, 2003, review of *Sherman Crunchley,* p. 77; August 15, 2005, review of *If You Give a Pig a Party,* p. 57; September 11, 2006, review of *When Sheep Sleep,* p. 53; February 11, 2008, review of *The Jellybeans and the Big Dance,* p. 69; September 22, 2008, review of *If You Give a Cat a Cupcake,* p. 57.

School Library Journal, December, 1996, Betty Teague, review of *Two for Stew,* pp. 102-103; May, 1997, Jane Marino, review of *The Chicken Sisters,* p. 109; April, 1998, Susan Hepler, review of *What Mommies Do Best/What Daddies Do Best,* p. 106; July, 1998, Diane Janoff, review of *If You Give a Pig a Pancake,* p. 81; May, 1999, Nina Lindsay, review of *Sometimes I Wonder If Poodles Like Noodles,* p. 111; October, 2000, review of *If You Take a Mouse to the Movies,* p. 62, and Catherine T. Quattlebaum, review of *What Grandmas Do Best/What Grandpas Do Best,* p. 132; October, 2001, Mary R. Hoffman, review of *The Hope Tree,* p. 127; June, 2002, John Sigwald, review of *Laura Numeroff's Ten-Step Guide to Living with Your Monster,* p. 106; September, 2002, Maryann H. Owen, review of *If You Take a Mouse to School,* p. 202; December, 2003, Sheilah Kosco, review of *Sherman Crunchley,* p. 122; October, 2004, Gay Lynn Van Vleck, review of *What Aunts Do Best/What Uncles Do Best,* p. 126; November, 2004, Wanda Meyers-Hines, review of *Beatrice Doesn't Want To,* p. 113; October, 2006, Linda Ludke, review of *When Sheep Sleep,* p. 120; June, 2008, Julie R. Ranelli, review of

The Jellybeans and the Big Dance, p. 112; December, 2008, Rachael Vilmar, review of *If You Give a Cat a Cupcake,* p. 98.

Teacher Librarian, September, 1998, Shirley Lewis, review of *If You Give a Pig a Pancake,* p. 47.

ONLINE

Laura Numeroff Home Page, http://www.lauranumeroff. com (September 17, 2009).

* * *

NUMEROFF, Laura Joffe
See NUMEROFF, Laura

* * *

NYEU, Tao

Personal

Born in Niskayuna, NY. *Education:* Cornell University, B.F.A.; School of Visual Arts, M.F.A. (illustration).

Addresses

Home—Los Angeles, CA. *Agent*—Pippin Properties, 155 E. 38th St., Ste. 2H, New York, NY 10016. *E-mail*—tao@tao-illustration.com.

Career

Illustrator and author.

Awards, Honors

Society of Illustrators Founders Award, 2008, and Marion Vannet Ridgway Honor Book designation, and Best Book of the Year, Bank Street School of Education, both 2010, all for *Wonder Bear.*

Writings

(Self-illustrated) *Wonder Bear,* Dial Books for Young Readers (New York, NY), 2008.
(Self-illustrated) *Bunny Days,* Dial Books for Young Readers (New York, NY), 2010.

Sidelights

Raised in upstate New York, Tao Nyeu studied graphic arts at Cornell University, then moved to New York City to earn her M.F.A. in illustration at the School of Visual Arts. Concentrating on etching and silkscreening, Nyeu has created a unique cartoon style that features heavy, textured lines and large blocks of color. In 2008 she achieved her longtime dream of becoming a chil-

dren's book author and illustrator when her book *Wonder Bear* was published. Acclaimed by critics, *Wonder Bear* also attracted the attention of Nyeu's peers: in 2008 she was awarded the Founders Award from the Society of Illustrators.

Nyeu created *Wonder Bear* during her second year of study at the School of Visual Arts. A whimsical, wordless fantasy, Nyeu's story starts as two children plant a special garden. Overnight one seed sprouts into a beautiful plant with a large bud yielding a white bear and a bright blue hat. From the hat, Wonder Bear pulls such wonders as a sea of orange monkeys, creating a fantasy world into which he carries the sleepy children. Noting the "bold palette" of blues and orange employed in the book's ilustrations, Kate McClelland added in *School Library Journal* that Nyeu's "assertive line, and handsome design are strikingly confident." A *Kirkus Reviews* writer cited influences from Wanda Gag to Japanese block prints, adding that the artist's "lush" images "pulse with stylized yet organic forms" and "teetering perspectives." Although a *Publishers Weekly* contributor questioned whether the illustrations coalesce into a successful story, "Nyeu's art makes a strong impression," and her use of curved lines, organic shapes, and "gem tones" creates "a sumptuous, Art Nouveau-meets psychedelic feel."

Tao Nyeu attracted critical acclaim for the restrained art in her self-illustrated picture book **Wonder Bear.** (Illustration copyright © 2008 by Tao Nyeu. Reproduced by permission.)

Nyeu's second self-illustrated book for children, *Bunny Days,* further expands her artistic approach to the picture-book genre. Again featuring graphic block-print art, the story finds six bunnies getting into a surprising series of mishaps before all is resolved in classic storybook fashion.

Biographical and Critical Sources

PERIODICALS

Booklist, September 15, 2008, Kristen McKulski, review of *Wonder Bear,* p. 58.

Kirkus Reviews, August 15, 2008, review of *Wonder Bear.*
New York Times Book Review, November 9, 2008, Ann Hodgman, review of *Wonder Bear,* p. 36.
Publishers Weekly, August 4, 2008, review of *Wonder Bear,* p. 60.
School Library Journal, September, 2008, Kate McClelland, review of *Wonder Bear,* p. 156.

ONLINE

Pippin Properties Web site, http://www.pippinproperties. com/ (October 30, 2009), "Tao Nyeu."
Tao Nyeu Home Page, http://www.tao-illustration.com (October 30, 2009).

O-P

ORR, Wendy 1953-
(Sally George)

Personal

Born November 19, 1953, in Edmonton, Alberta, Canada; daughter of Anthony M. (an air force pilot) and Elizabeth Ann (a teacher and homemaker) Burridge; married Thomas H. Orr (a farmer), January 11, 1975; children: James Anthony, Susan Elizabeth. *Education:* London School of Occupational Therapy, diploma, 1975; LaTrobe University, B.Sc., 1982. *Hobbies and other interests:* Animals, reading, gardening, people, travel, tai chi.

Addresses

Home—Mornington Peninsula, Victoria, Australia. *Agent*—Debbie Golvan, Golvan Arts Management, P.O. Box 766, Kew, Victoria 3101, Australia; golvan@ bigpond.net.au.

Career

Writer. Albury Community Health, Albury, Australia, occupational therapist, 1975-80; Language and Development Clinic, Shepparton, Australia, occupational therapist, 1982-91; author, 1986—. Also owner of a dairy farm in Victoria, Australia, for twenty years.

Member

Australian Society of Authors, Australian Children's Book Council, Red Hill Readers.

Awards, Honors

Shared first place award, Ashton Scholastic Picture Book Awards, 1987, for *Amanda's Dinosaur;* Book of the Year for Junior Readers shortlist, Children's Book Council of Australia (CBCA), 1993, for *Leaving It to You;* New South Wales Premier's Award shortlist, 1995, for *Yasou Nikki;* Book of the Year for Junior Readers,

Wendy Orr (Photograph by Albert Dodman. Reproduced by permission.)

CBCA, 1995, for *Ark in the Park;* Australian Family Therapy Association Recommended designation, 1995, for *Ark in the Park,* and high commendation, 1997, for *Peeling the Onion;* Honor Book designation, CBCA, 1997, Best Books for Young Adults inclusion, American Library Association (ALA), Books for the Teen Age designation, New York Public Library, both 1998, and Best of the Best listee, ALA, all for *Peeling the Onion;* West Australian Young Readers' Book Award shortlist, 1998, for *Paradise Palace;* Honor Book designation, CBCA, 1999, for *Arabella;* BILBY Award shortlist, CBCA, 2000, for *Dirtbikes;* West Australian Young Readers' Book Award shortlist, and One Hundred Titles for Reading and Sharing inclusion, New York Public Library, both 2001, both for *Nim's Island;* West Australian Young Readers' Book Award shortlist, and Young Australian Readers' Award shortlist, both 2004, both for *Spook's Shack;* Community Relations Award and New South Wales Premier's Award shortlist, both for *Across the Dark Sea.*

Writings

Amanda's Dinosaur, illustrated by Gillian Campbell, Ashton Scholastic (Australia), 1988.

The Tin Can Puppy (picture book), illustrated by Brian Kogler, HarperCollins Australia/Angus & Robertson (Sydney, New South Wales, Australia), 1990.

Bad Martha, illustrated by Carol McLean Carr, Angus & Robertson (Sydney, New South Wales, Australia), 1991.

Aa-Choo! (picture book), illustrated by Ruth Ohi, Annick Press (Toronto, Ontario, Canada), 1992.

Leaving It to You, Angus & Robertson (Sydney, New South Wales, Australia), 1992.

The Great Yackandandah Billy Cart Race, illustrated by Neil Curtis, HarperCollins Australia (Sydney, New South Wales, Australia), 1993.

Mindblowing! (middle-grade reader), illustrated by Ruth Ohi, Allen & Unwin Australia (St. Leonards, New South Wales, Australia), 1994, published as *A Light in Space,* Annick Press (Toronto, Ontario, Canada), 1994.

Ark in the Park, illustrated by Kerry Millard, Angus & Robertson (Sydney, New South Wales, Australia), 1994, Henry Holt (New York, NY), 1999.

The Laziest Boy in the World, illustrated by Farbio Nardo, HarperCollins Australia/Angus & Robertson (Sydney, New South Wales, Australia), 1994.

Yasou Nikki, illustrated by Kim Gamble, HarperCollins Australia (Sydney, New South Wales, Australia), 1995.

Dirtbikes, HarperCollins Australia (Sydney, New South Wales, Australia), 1995.

The Bully Biscuit Gang, HarperCollins Australia (Sydney, New South Wales, Australia), 1995.

Jessica Joan, illustrated by Ann James, Mammoth Australia (Port Melbourne, Victoria, Australia), 1995.

Grandfather Martin, illustrated by Kate Ellis, Houghton Mifflin (Boston, MA), 1996.

Alroy's Very Nearly Clean Bedroom, illustrated by Bettina Guthridge, Longman & Cheshire (Melbourne, Victoria, Australia), 1996, Sundance Publishing (Littleton, MA), 1997.

Peeling the Onion (young-adult novel), Allen & Unwin Australia (St. Leonards, New South Wales, Australia), 1996, Holiday House (New York, NY), 1997.

Paradise Palace, illustrated by David Mackintosh, HarperCollins Australia (Pymble, New South Wales, Australia), 1997.

Sally's Painting Room, illustrated by Janice Bowles, Koala Books (Redfern, New South Wales, Australia), 1997.

Arabella, illustrated by Kim Gamble, HarperCollins Australia (Pymble, New South Wales, Australia), 1998.

Paradise Gold, illustrated by David Mackintosh, HarperCollins Australia (Pymble, New South Wales, Australia), 1999.

Poppy's Path, illustrated by Ritva Voutila, Koala Books (Mascot, New South Wales, Australia), 2001.

The House at Evelyn's Pond (adult novel), Allen & Unwin Australia (St. Leonards, New South Wales, Australia), 2001.

Spook's Shack, illustrated by Kerry Millard, Allen & Unwin Australia (St. Leonards, New South Wales, Australia), 2003.

Across the Dark Sea, illustrated by Donna Rawlins, National Museum of Australia Press (Canberra, Australian Capital Territory, Australia), 2006.

Too Much Stuff, illustrated by Kerry Millard, Penguin Australia (Camberwell, Victoria, Australia), 2006.

Mokie and Bik, illustrated by Beth Norling, Allen & Unwin Australia (Crows Nest, New South Wales, Australia), 2006, illustrated by Jonathan Bean, Henry Holt (New York, NY), 2007.

Mokie and Bik Go to Sea, illustrated by Jonathan Bean, Henry Holt (New York, NY), 2008.

Orr's works have been translated into French, Japanese, Italian, German, Spanish, Basque, Korean, Thai, Dutch, and Denmark.

"NIM" SERIES

Nim's Island, illustrated by Kerry Millard, Allen & Unwin Australia (St. Leonards, New South Wales, Australia), 1999, Knopf (New York, NY), 2001.

Nim at Sea, illustrated by Kerry Millard, Knopf (New York, NY), 2007.

"MICKI AND DANIEL" PICTURE-BOOK SERIES

Pegasus and Ooloo Mooloo, illustrated by Ruth Ohi, Annick Press (Toronto, Ontario, Canada), 1993.

The Wedding, illustrated by Ruth Ohi, Annick Press (Toronto, Ontario, Canada), 1993.

The Train to the City, illustrated by Ruth Ohi, Annick Press (Toronto, Ontario, Canada), 1993.

Published in Australia as "Micki Moon and Daniel Day" series, illustrated by Mike Spoor, Allen & Unwin Australia (St. Leonards, New South Wales, Australia).

UNDER PSEUDONYM SALLY GEORGE

Bad Dog George, Thomas Nelson Australia (Melbourne, Victoria, Australia), 1994.

Breakfast in Bed, Thomas Nelson Australia (Melbourne, Victoria, Australia), 1994.

George at the Zoo, Thomas Nelson Australia (Melbourne, Victoria, Australia), 1994.

Adaptations

Nim's Island was adapted as a major motion picture, Fox-Walden, 2008, and as an audio book, Blackstone Audio, 2008; *Nim's Island Movie Storybook* was adapted by Sonia Sander from Orr's series, Scholastic (New York, NY), 2008; *Nim's Friends,* a book by Danielle Denega, is based on characters created by Orr, Scholastic (New York, NY), 2008.

Sidelights

Australian author Wendy Orr has written books for children and young adults that are noted for their elements of fantasy and humor. She is widely known for her award-winning novel *Nim's Island,* which was adapted as a feature film, as well as its sequel, *Nim at Sea.* The inspiration for Orr's many works come from a variety of sources, as she noted in an interview on her Web log. "Lots of ideas present themselves to you daily, and some stick around for a little while . . . but there are some that simply don't let you go. I presume those ones fulfill some psychic need, but I truly don't know. And sometimes I think there's enough magic in writing that it's best not to investigate too much and risk driving it away!"

Orr was fortunate to have a father who worked for the Royal Canadian Air Force. She spent her childhood in locations all across Canada, traveling to France and liv-

Orr's novel **A Light in Space** *features ink-and-watercolor art by Ruth Ohi.* (Illustration copyright © 1994 by Ruth Ohi. All rights reserved.)

ing for a time in Colorado. Her broad experiences were put to good use later, when she began her career as a writer. "My parents instilled a love of language early," Orr once commented, "with books at bedtime and my father's stories of our dog's Great Great Great Grandfather, in the car. My own first 'book' was written when I was eight. 'Glossy the Horse' was a full four pages long and bore a striking resemblance to *Black Beauty,* which my mother had just read to us. Dramatic poems followed; how delighted my grandmother must have been to receive a 'Poem on Death' for her sixtieth birthday!"

"On leaving high school," Orr continued, "I spent a year studying animal care in Kingston, Ontario, went to England for a holiday, and stayed for three years to complete a diploma at the London School of Occupational Therapy. In my final year, 1975, I met and married an Australian farmer holidaying in the United Kingdom and returned to New South Wales with him after graduation.

"The business of growing up, and starting a career and family took over and except for an article on 'Living in Wheelchairs' when I was a student, my writing was limited to patient records and weekly epistles to my parents. At the end of 1982, however, when I had completed a bachelor of applied science and another postgraduate certificate, I decided that it was time to do what I had always wanted. In December 1986 I entered the Ashton Scholastic competition for a picture book manuscript. *Amanda's Dinosaur,* which shared the first place, was published in 1988 and subsequently had rights sold to Canada, New Zealand, and the United States."

Written shortly after *Amanda's Dinosaur,* Orr's "Micki and Daniel" picture-book series centers on the friendship between two young children and their pets, Pegasus, a miniature horse, and Ooloo Mooloo, a parrot. Although some critics have found these stories to be somewhat constrained by the author's attempt to be "politically correct," others consider their adventures amusing and appealing to children. "It is refreshing to see stories of friendship featuring human children instead of the more usual animal quasi-adults," remarked Sarah Ellis in her *Quill & Quire* review of *The Wedding* and *The Train to the City.* In *Pegasus and Ooloo Mooloo,* Micki and Daniel find the animals that accompany them throughout the rest of the series. The four encounter evil circus-owners who want to steal Pegasus, the miniature horse, but Ooloo Mooloo the parrot saves the day when it makes a noise like a police siren and scares the bad guys away. *The Wedding,* the second book in the series, describes a wedding ceremony in which Micki and Daniel are invited to take part, although their pets are not. Ooloo Mooloo and Pegasus insist on joining in nonetheless, "and it all adds up to a satisfying slapstick climax," according to Ellis.

Orr's science-fiction adventure *Mindblowing!,* published outside Australia under the title *A Light in Space,* was widely praised as a fast-paced, compelling story of a boy who meets a being from outer space who, though friendly to him, intends to capture the earth's oxygen for her own planet. "This is top-quality science fiction," a reviewer for *Books in Canada* reported. Critics noted the skillful way in which the author contrasts the viewpoints of the human boy and the alien girl who intends to mine the earth's oxygen for her own planet, despite the deadly effect this would have on the earth's inhabitants. "The plot of this light book is entertaining and fast paced, while the characters are well drawn," remarked J.R. Wytenbroek in *Quill & Quire*. Anne Connor, reviewing *A Light in Space* for *School Library Journal*, praised Orr's character development and suspenseful plot, dubbing *A Light in Space* "unusual and fun."

Reflecting on *A Light in Space*, Orr once explained, she "realized that despite being science fiction, it had also been influenced by my own life and concerns at the time of writing. It was actually started the week before [a car accident in 1991 that dramatically curtailed my mobility], and was written in the two years following—I am sure that some of the issues of control versus independence in the story must have been influenced by my own disabilities and fight to regain independence."

Peeling the Onion, a novel for young adults, centers on a similar theme. In this work, seventeen year-old Anna is tragically disabled in a car accident. While learning to make physical adjustments in order to function independently, Anna must also cope with the reactions of her family and friends, recognizing the inevitable strains that are put upon these relationships. According to *Booklist* critic Frances Bradburn, the novel "is superbly crafted. The physical pain Anna feels is palpable, and the fear that the doctors aren't quite on target, insidious." Reviewing *Peeling the Onion* for *Australian Bookseller & Publisher*, Olivia Craze wrote that Orr "mixes the spicy ingredients of authentic characters and relationships with a compelling plot to produce a novel full of power and honesty, touched with humour." Anne Briggs, writing in *Magpies*, reported that *Peeling the Onion* Orr "displays yet again" the author's "precise observation of family relationships and her flair for creating original and richly individual characters of all ages."

Orr's books for preschoolers and young readers share a humorous approach to the common and uncommon dilemmas faced by her young characters. Often employing elements of fantasy or science fiction, she is noted for blending realistic human characters and their animal or alien counterparts in a way that illuminates the hearts and minds of both. While Orr is occasionally faulted for creating slim plots or both showing and telling readers about her characters, her most successful books have been cited by critics for their solid blend of character development, swift pacing, and humorous viewpoint.

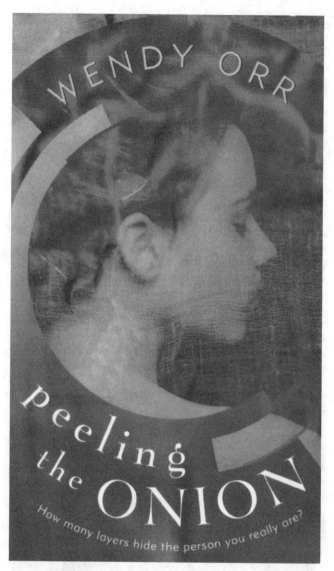

Cover of Orr's teen novel Peeling the Onion, *featuring a photograph by Jacqui Henshaw.* (Bantam Doubleday Dell Books for Young Readers, 1996. Cover photograph by Jacqui Henshaw. Reproduced by permission.)

In *The Tin Can Puppy*, readers meet a young boy named Dylan, who has been told he is too young to take care of the pet he so badly wants. Then he finds a puppy in a tin can in the dump while he is looking for wheels for his cart. Dylan takes the puppy home and hides it, and when his parents discover the creature Dylan is allowed to keep him. This is "a slight story," according to Joyce Banks in a review for *School Librarian*, "but told in an amusing, percipient and economical way." Like *The Tin Can Puppy*, *Aa-Choo!* presents a common problem critics felt would be appreciated by the preschool audience for whom the book is intended. In Orr's story, Megan wakes up one morning too sick to go to daycare. When no one can take the day off of work to stay home with her, Megan goes to work with her mother, camps out under Mom's desk during an important meeting, and has a few adventures while exploring the office looking for the bathroom. "The delicate dilemma of what to do when a young child is ill and parents have to work is treated gently and humorously," stated Theo Hersh in a review of the book for the *Canadian Review of Materials.* Although Phyllis Simon found Orr's story "rather contrived" in her review in *Quill & Quire,* Hersh called *Aa-Choo!* "a book working parents will want to share with their children."

Ark in the Park, a chapter book for young readers, focuses on Sophie, a sensitive and lonely girl who lives in a high-rise apartment building with her family. Sophie has but two wishes: she wants cousins to visit her (although she has no extended family nearby) and she wants a pet to call her own. On her seventh birthday, Sophie convinces her parents to join her on a trip to The Noahs' Ark, a wondrous pet shop with a seemingly endless variety of animals. Mr. and Mrs. Noah, the shop's owners wish for children of their own, and they take Sophie under their wing. The girl soon proves herself a responsible and capable helper, and by story's end, Catherine Abdronik noted in *Booklist,* "all the wishes have come true, if not literally, then where it counts—in the heart."

Orr introduces a pair of rambunctious siblings in *Mokie and Bik,* an easy reader. Fraternal twins Mokie and Bik live on a houseboat with their mother, an artist, and Ruby, their nanny, while their father is away at sea. The energetic duo shares a colorful and unusual vocabulary all their own. They find no shortage of adventures around the harbor and spend their days helping a fisherman unload his catch, learning to swim with a rope tied around their waists and doing battle with an enormous fish in the process. "Orr has created a memorable tale with vivid characters," Carole Phillips remarked in her *School Library Journal* review of the book, and a *Kirkus Reviews* contributor stated that the author's "rollicking, fancifully worded narrative" will appeal to "easy-reader graduates and read-aloud audiences in general." *Mokie and Bik Go to Sea* chronicles the further exploits of the two twins as they enjoy a clambake with their father, find themselves adrift in their houseboat, and rescue their dog, Waggles, when it falls overboard. A critic in *Kirkus Reviews* described the work as a "rollicking nautical slice of life," and Debbie Whitbeck, writing in *School Library Journal,* commented that *Mokie and Bik Go to Sea* "packs so much energy that readers will be panting when they finish."

Orr's popular story *Nim's Island,* illustrated by Kerry Millard, centers on Nim, an intelligent and resourceful girl who lives on a remote tropical island with her scientist father, Jack. When Jack sets off on a three-day trip to collect plankton, Nim stays behind with a marine iguana, a sea turtle, and a sea lion to keep her company. After her father's boat is disabled, Nim must fend for herself, and she soon faces a series of crises, including a violent storm and a volcanic eruption. Fortunately, the youngster receives sound advice from Alex Rover, a female novelist who had been corresponding via e-mail with Nim's father on his solar-panel-powered computer. Critics offered praise for the fantastical narrative of *Nim's Island.* "If readers can suspend belief long

enough to accept this plot, they will have a great time with this modern survival/adventure story," Whitbeck wrote, and a *Publishers Weekly* contributor similarly noted that "the tale portrays the improbable so cleverly that readers will want to believe everything about the likable Nim and her idyllic isle."

In *Nim at Sea,* a sequel, Nim stows away aboard a cruise ship to chase an evil poacher who has kidnapped her beloved sea lion, Selkie. Meanwhile, Alex, who had since moved to the island and is dating Nim's father, leaves abruptly after a misunderstanding, leaving Jack to set out on his raft to track down both his daughter and his girlfriend. Nim, Jack, and Alex eventually meet again in New York City, where they attempt to disrupt the poacher's plan to illegally sell exotic animals. According to Eva Mitnick in *School Library Journal* Nim's "upbeat, unflappable affability is convincing enough to carry her through all manner of far-fetched scenarios and coincidences," and a *Kirkus Reviews* critic remarked that the tale ends in a "comically tumultuous climax, rescue and loving reunion."

"I tend to carry an idea for a story in my head for a year or so before I start writing," Orr once commented. "the characters develop further as I redraft and the plot usually changes considerably from my first ideas. Although much of my work verges on fantasy, it has also been influenced by my own life. My childhood in a French village gave me the emotional background for *Ark in the Park*—like Sophie, I not only longed for the normalcy of nearby grandparents, but was lucky enough to find some. Similarly, *Yasou Nikki* was loosely based on my own first day of school, when a little girl named Jacqueline took me under her wing, taught me to speak

Orr teams with artist Ruth Ohi to tell a comforting story in her get-well picture-book **Aa-Choo!** (Illustration copyright © 1992 by Ruth Ohi. All rights reserved. Reproduced by permission.)

French, and remained a close friend ever after. And *Leaving It to You*, while not drawn on any particular situation, was influenced by my first job as a community-based occupational therapist in Albury—both by my memories of the people that I met, and of myself, as an idealistic young therapist coming to terms with life."

Biographical and Critical Sources

PERIODICALS

Australian Bookseller & Publisher, July, 1996, Olivia Craze, review of *Peeling the Onion,* p. 78.

Booklist, April 1, 1997, Frances Bradburn, review of *Peeling the Onion,* p. 1322; September 15, 2000, Catherine Abdronik, review of *Ark in the Park,* p. 243; June 1, 2001, Catherine Andronik, review of *Nim's Island,* p. 1883; June 1, 2007, Carolyn Phelan, review of *Mokie and Bik,* p. 82; March 1, 2008, Thom Barthelmess, review of *Nim at Sea,* p. 68; July 1, 2008, Carolyn Phelan, review of *Mokie and Bik Go to Sea,* p. 62.

Books in Canada, February, 1995, review of *A Light in Space,* p. 50.

Canadian Review of Materials, May, 1992, Theo Hersh, review of *Aa-Choo!,* p. 161.

Kirkus Reviews, May 1, 2007, review of *Mokie and Bik;* March 1, 2008, review of *Nim at Sea;* May 1, 2008, review of *Mokie and Bik Go to Sea.*

Magpies, September, 1996, Anne Briggs, review of *Peeling the Onion,* p. 38.

Publishers Weekly, March 10, 1997, review of *Peeling the Onion,* p. 67; February 19, 2001, review of *Nim's Island,* p. 91; June 18, 2007, review of *Mokie and Bik,* p. 54.

Quill & Quire, March, 1992, Phyllis Simon, review of *Aa-Choo!,* p. 66; July, 1993, Sarah Ellis, reviews of *The Wedding* and *The Train to the City,* pp. 55-56; December, 1994, J.R. Wytenbroek, review of *A Light in Space,* pp. 33-34.

School Librarian, November, 1993, Joyce Banks, review of *The Tin Can Puppy,* p. 156.

School Library Journal, February, 1995, Anne Connor, review of *A Light in Space,* p. 100; June, 2000, Kit Vaughan, review of *Ark in the Park,* p. 123; February, 2001, Debbie Whitbeck, review of *Nim's Island,* p. 104; July, 2007, Carole Phillips, review of *Mokie and Bik,* p. 82; May, 2008, Eva Mitnick, review of *Nim at Sea,* p. 105; July, 2008, Debbie Whitbeck, review of *Mokie and Bik Go to Sea,* p. 79.

ONLINE

Wendy Orr Home Page, http://www.wendyorr.com (October 10, 2009).

Wendy Orr Web log, http://wendyorrjournal.blogspot.com/ (October 10, 2009).*

PANG, YaWen Ariel

Personal

Female. *Education:* Academy of Art College (San Francisco, CA), degree.

Addresses

Home—Taiwan, China.

Career

Illustrator.

Illustrator

Tim Myers, *The Out-Foxed Fox,* Marshall Cavendish (New York, NY), 2007.

Kathy-jo Wargin, *P Is for Pumpkin,* Zonderkidz (Grand Rapids, MI), 2008.

Biographical and Critical Sources

PERIODICALS

Kirkus Reviews, July 15, 2008, review of *P Is for Pumpkin.*

School Library Journal, January, 2009, Lee Bock, review of *P Is for Pumpkin,* p. 87.

ONLINE

Zondervan Web site, http://www.zondervan.com/ (October 30, 2009), "YaWen Ariel Pang."*

* * *

PENDLETON, Thomas 1965-
(Dallas Reed, Lee Thomas)

Personal

Born 1965, in WA. *Education:* Graduated from University of Colorado. *Hobbies and other interests:* Movies and television, music, video games.

Addresses

Home—Austin, TX. *Agent*—(Literary) Howard Morhaim, Morhaim Literary Agency, howardmorhaim literary.com; (film and television) Sarah Self, Gersh New York, sselfgershny.com. *E-mail*—tlpendleton@aol.com; leethomas1@aol.com.

Career

Writer.

Awards, Honors

Bram Stoker Award nomination, for short stories "Turtle" and "An Apiary of White Bees"; Bram Stoker Award for Superior Achievement in First-Novel Cat-

Thomas Pendleton (Photograph by Michael J. Hall. Reproduced by permission.)

egory, 2004, for *Stained;* Lambda Literary Award for Science Fiction, Fantasy, and Horror, 2008, for *The Dust of Wonderland.*

Writings

Mason, HarperTeen (New York, NY), 2008.

"WICKED DEAD" SERIES

(With Stefan Petrucha) *Lurker,* HarperTeen (New York, NY), 2007.
(With Stefan Petrucha) *Torn,* HarperTeen (New York, NY), 2007.
(With Stefan Petrucha) *Skin,* HarperTeen (New York, NY), 2008.
(With Stefan Petrucha) *Snared,* HarperTeen (New York, NY), 2008.
(With Stefan Petrucha) *Crush,* HarperTeen (New York, NY), 2008.
(With Stefan Petrucha) *Prey,* HarperTeen (New York, NY), 2008.

AS DALLAS REED

Shimmer, HarperTeen (New York, NY), 2008.

AS LEE THOMAS

Stained, Wildside Press, 2004.
Parish Damned, Telos (Surry, England), 2005.
The Dust of Wonderland, Alyson Books (New York, NY), 2007.
In the Closet, under the Bed (stories), Dark Scribe Press (Long Island, NY), 2009.

Author of *Damage,* Sarob Press. Contributor to anthologies, including *A Walk on the Darkside,* ROC (New York, NY), 2004, and *Unspeakable Horror: From the Shadows of the Closet,* Dark Scribe Press (Long Island, NY), 2008. Contributor to periodicals, including *Doorways* and *Sybil's Garage,* and to Web sites, including Gothic.net and Horrorfind.com.

Sidelights

Under the pen name Thomas Pendleton, horror writer Lee Thomas has authored *Mason,* a paranormal thriller for young adults, and has also collaborated with Stefan Petrucha on the "Wicked Dead" series of horror novels. Writing as Dallas Reed, Thomas has also released several books, including *Shimmer,* a tale of suspense. "I've always dug dark storytelling—movies, books, comics— and writing has always been a hobby of mine," the author noted in a Fearnet.com interview with John Picacio.

In *Mason,* readers are introduced to Mason Avrett, a developmentally disabled youth with special, hidden powers. Older brother Gene has abused Mason for years, and as the pair enters their teens, the amoral Gene becomes the mastermind of a drug ring. When Mason's only friend, a kindhearted girl named Rene, is savagely beaten by Gene's cronies, the younger teen enacts revenge by employing a terrifying array of psychological weapons. According to Lorie Paldino in *Kliatt,* in *Mason* Pendleton "weaves a thrilling tale of suspense and mystery as he slowly reveals the pieces to the puzzle that is Mason Avrett." Caryl Soriano, writing in *School Library Journal,* stated that "readers can't help but feel the pain of this poignant young man whose birth places him in a dangerous environment," while a *Kirkus Reviews* critic stated that the author "holds nothing back with this thrilling tale told at a breakneck pace."

Discussing his interest in writing horror novels for teens, Thomas told *Cynsations* online interviewer Cynthia Leitich Smith: "The young adult audience is in this wonderful place between childhood when anything was possible and the world was full of mysteries, miracles and monsters, and adulthood where many of the mysteries have been solved, many of the miracles have a price, and the monsters wear human faces. They really get the themes in fantastic fiction, even if it's only subconsciously, because they are close enough to look behind them and see the magic or look ahead and see the reality."

Biographical and Critical Sources

PERIODICALS

Booklist, May 15, 2008, Jennifer Mattson, review of *Mason,* p. 38.
Kirkus Reviews, June 15, 2008, review of *Mason.*
Kliatt, July, 2008, Lorie Paldino, review of *Mason,* p. 28.
School Library Journal, November, 2007, Angela M. Boccuzzi-Reichert, review of *Lurker,* p. 134; October, 2008, Caryl Soriano, review of *Mason,* p. 158.
Voice of Youth Advocates, August, 2007, Lynn Evarts, review of *Lurker,* p. 262; June, 2008, Alissa Lauzon, review of *Snared,* p. 164; October, 2008, Alissa Lauzon and Ashley Brown, review of *Crush,* p. 355; February, 2009, Alissa Lauzon and Ashley Brown, review of *Prey,* p. 545.

ONLINE

Cynsations Web log, http://cynthialeitichsmith.blogspot.com/ (October 9, 2008), Cynthia Leitich Smith, interview with Pendleton.
Fearnet.com, http://www.fearnet.com/ (October 2, 2008), John Picacio, interview with Thomas.
Lee Thomas Home Page, http://www.leethomasauthor.com (October 15, 2009).
Lee Thomas Web Log, http://leethomas.livejournal.com/ (October 15, 2009).
Strange Machines Web site, http://www.dallasreed.com/ (October 15, 2009).

* * *

Brian Pinkney (Photograph by Dwight Carter. Reproduced by permission.)

PINKNEY, Brian 1961-
(J. Brian Pinkney)

Personal

Born August 28, 1961, in Boston, MA; son of Jerry (an illustrator) and Gloria Jean (a writer) Pinkney; married Andrea R. Davis (an editor and writer), October 12, 1991; children: Chloe, one other child. *Education:* Philadelphia College of Art (now University of the Arts), B.F.A., 1983; School of Visual Arts, M.F.A. (illustration), 1990. *Hobbies and other interests:* Tae kwon do, playing drums.

Addresses

Home—Brooklyn, NY. *Agent*—Rebecca Sherman, Writer's House, 21 W. 26th St., New York, NY 10010.

Career

Illustrator. Taught at Children's Art Carnival, Harlem, NY, and School of Visual Arts, New York, NY. *Exhibitions:* Works exhibited at School of Visual Arts Student Galleries, 1989; in group shows, including Original Art Show, New York, NY, 1990-96, Society of Illustrators Annual Exhibit, New York, NY, 1991, 1994; and at museums, including Montclair Art Museum, Montclair, NJ, Detroit Institute of Art, Detroit, MI, Birmington Art Museum, Birmingham, AL, Cleveland Museum of Art, Cleveland, OH, and Cedar Rapids Museum of Art, Cedar Rapids, ID.

Member

Society of Illustrators, Society of Children's Book Writers and Illustrators, Graphic Arts Guild.

Awards, Honors

National Arts Club Award of Distinction, 1990; Parents' Choice Honor Award for Illustration, 1990, for *The Boy and the Ghost;* Parents' Choice Honor Award for Story Books, 1990, for *The Ballad of Belle Dorcus;* Notable Children's Book in the Field of Social Studies designation, for *The Ballad of Belle Dorcus, Cut from the Same Cloth, Dear Benjamin Banneker, The Dark-Thirty,* and *Bill Pickett: Rodeo Ridin' Cowboy;* Parents' Choice Picture Book Award, 1991, for *Where Does the Trail Lead?* and *A Wave in Her Pocket;* Golden Kite Honor Award, Society of Children's Book Writers and Illustrators, 1991, for *Where Does the Trail Lead?;* Aesop Prize, 1993, for *Cut from the Same Cloth;* Coretta Scott King Honor Book Award for Illustration, American Library Association (ALA), and Notable Book selection, ALA, 1993, both for *Sukey and the Mermaid;* NAPPA Award, 1993, for *Alvin Ailey;* Randolph Caldecott Honor Book designation, ALA, and California Book Award for juvenile fiction, both 1996, both for *The Faithful Friend;* Sydney Taylor Book Award, Association of Jewish Libraries, 1996, and Joan G. Sugarman Children's Book Award, 1997, both for *When I Left My Village; Boston Globe/Horn Book* Award for Illustration, 1997, for *The Adventures of Sparrowboy;* Mountains and Plains Booksellers Association Award, 1997, for *Bill Pickett;* Randolph Caldecott Honor Book designation, 1998, and International Board on Books for Young People Honor List inclusion, 2000, both for *Duke Ellington;* Coretta Scott King Award for Illustration, ALA, 2000, for *In the Time of the Drums.*

Writings

SELF-ILLUSTRATED

Max Found Two Sticks, Simon & Schuster (New York, NY), 1994.

JoJo's Flying Side Kick, Simon & Schuster (New York, NY), 1995.

The Adventures of Sparrowboy, Simon & Schuster (New York, NY), 1997.

Cosmo and the Robot, Greenwillow Books (New York, NY), 2000.

(Reteller) Hans Christian Andersen, *Thumbelina,* Greenwillow (New York, NY), 2003.

(Adaptor) *Hush, Little Baby,* Greenwillow (New York, NY), 2006.

ILLUSTRATOR

(As J. Brian Pinkney) Roy Wandelmaier, *Shipwrecked on Mystery Island,* Troll (Mahwah, NJ), 1985.

(As J. Brian Pinkney) R. Rozanne Knudson, *Julie Brown: Racing with the World* (biography), Viking (New York, NY), 1988.

(As J. Brian Pinkney) Robert D. San Souci, *The Boy and the Ghost,* Simon & Schuster (New York, NY), 1989.

William H. Hooks, *The Ballad of Belle Dorcus,* Knopf (New York, NY), 1990.

Polly Carter, *Harriet Tubman and Black History Month,* Silver Press (Englewood Cliffs, NJ), 1990.

Burton Albert, *Where Does the Trail Lead?,* Simon & Schuster (New York, NY), 1991.

Lynn Joseph, *A Wave in Her Pocket: Stories from Trinidad,* Clarion (New York, NY), 1991.

Christopher Cat and Countee Cullin, *The Lost Zoo,* Silver Burdett (Englewood Cliff, NJ), 1992.

Virginia Hamilton, *Drylongso,* Harcourt (San Diego, CA), 1992.

Robert D. San Souci, *Sukey and the Mermaid,* Four Winds (New York, NY), 1992.

Patricia C. McKissack, *The Dark-Thirty: Southern Tales of the Supernatural,* Knopf (New York, NY), 1992.

Judy Sierra, *The Elephant's Wrestling Match,* Lodestar (New York, NY), 1992.

Robert D. San Souci, *Cut from the Same Cloth,* Philomel Books (New York, NY), 1993.

(As J. Brian Pinkney) Jean Marzollo, *Happy Birthday, Martin Luther King,* Scholastic (New York, NY), 1993.

Andrea Davis Pinkney, *Alvin Ailey,* Hyperion (New York, NY), 1993.

Andrea Davis Pinkney, *Seven Candles for Kwanzaa,* Dial (New York, NY), 1993.

Andrea Davis Pinkney, *Dear Benjamin Banneker,* Harcourt (San Diego, CA), 1994.

Maxine Rose Schur, *Day of Delight: A Jewish Sabbath in Ethiopia,* Dial (New York, NY), 1994.

Langston Hughes, *The Dream Keeper, and Other Poems,* Knopf (New York, NY), 1994.

Robert D. San Souci, *The Faithful Friend,* Simon & Schuster (New York, NY), 1995.

Maxine Rose Schur, *When I Left My Village,* Dial (New York, NY), 1996.

Judy Sierra, reteller, *Wiley and the Hairy Man,* Dutton (New York, NY), 1996.

Andrea Davis Pinkney, *Bill Pickett: Rodeo-Ridin' Cowboy,* Harcourt (San Diego, CA), 1996.

Andrea Davis Pinkney, *I Smell Honey,* Harcourt (San Diego, CA), 1997.

Andrea Davis Pinkney, *Pretty Brown Face,* Harcourt (San Diego, CA), 1997.

Andrea Davis Pinkney, *Shake Shake Shake,* Harcourt (San Diego, CA), 1997.

Andrea Davis Pinkney, *Duke Ellington: The Piano Prince and His Orchestra,* Hyperion (New York, NY), 1997.

Andrea Davis Pinkney, *Watch Me Dance,* Harcourt (San Diego, CA), 1997.

Robert D. San Souci, *Cendrillon: A Caribbean Cinderella,* Simon & Schuster (New York, NY), 1997.

Kim L. Siegelson, *In the Time of the Drums,* Hyperion (New York, NY), 1999.

(With father Jerry Pinkney and brother Myles C. Pinkney) Gloria Jean Pinkney, *In the Forest of Your Remembrance: Thirty-three Goodly News Tellings for the Whole Family,* Phyllis Fogelman (New York, NY), 2001.

Andrea Davis Pinkney, *Mim's Christmas Jam,* Harcourt (San Diego, CA), 2001.

Andrea Davis Pinkney, *Ella Fitzgerald: The Tale of a Vocal Virtuosa,* Hyperion (New York, NY), 2002.

Karen Hesse, *The Stone Lamp: Eight Stories of Hanukkah through History,* Hyperion (New York, NY), 2003.

(With Jerry and Myles Pinkney) Gloria Jean Pinkney, compiler, *Music from Our Lord's Holy Heaven,* HarperCollins (New York, NY), 2003.

Marybeth Lorbiecki, *Jackie's Bat,* Simon & Schuster (New York, NY), 2003.

Andrea Davis Pinkney, *Sleeping Cutie,* Gulliver Books (San Diego, CA), 2004.

Andrea Davis Pinkney, *Peggony-Po: A Whale of a Tale,* Hyperion (New York, NY), 2006.

Ysaye M. Barnwell, *We Are One,* Harcourt (New York, NY), 2008.

Andrea Davis Pinkney, *Boycott Blues: How Rosa Parks Inspired a Nation,* Greenwillow (New York, NY), 2008.

Andrea Davis Pinkney, *Sit-in,* Little, Brown (New York, NY), 2010.

Contributor to *Jump Back, Honey: The Poems of Paul Laurence Dunbar,* Hyperion (New York, NY), 1999. Contributor to periodicals, including *New York Times Magazine, Women's Day, Business Tokyo, Ebony Man,* and *Instructor.*

Adaptations

Duke Ellington: The Piano Prince and His Orchestra was adapted for audio cassette, read by Forest Whitaker, Disney, 2001, and adapted for video, also read by Forest Whitaker, Scholastic, 2000.

Sidelights

Brian Pinkney is an illustrator and author who works in a striking and unusual medium: oil painting over scratchboard. Pinkney's unique illustrations have graced the pages of numerous books for children since he began his career in the late 1980s. The son of note illustrator Jerry Pinkney, and married to children's book author Andrea Davis Pinkney, his work is notable for revealing the diverse experiences of African Americans, their ancestors, and blacks in other parts of the world. Among his many illustration projects, as well as his

Pinkney's unique scratchboard art is a feature of Lynn Joseph's illustrated story collection **A Wave in Her Pocket.** (Illustration copyright © 1991 by Brian Pinkney. Reprinted by permission of Clarion Books, an imprint of Houghton Mifflin Harcourt Publishing Company. All rights reserved.)

original, self-illustrated picture books, Pinkney has brought to life folklore from the American South, the Caribbean, and Africa, recreated the lives and contributions of important African Americans, and related experiences from his own life.

Born in Boston, Massachusetts, Pinkney was raised in an artistic household. "My two brothers and sister and I played musical instruments, and we were always drawing, painting, or building things," the illustrator once recalled of his childhood. While his mother, children's book author Gloria Jean Pinkney, inspired all her children with a love of reading, it was be his father, Jerry Pinkney, who served as a mentor to young Brian. "I did everything he did," Pinkney later admitted. "My desk was a miniature version of his desk. The paintbrushes and pencils I used were often the ones from his studio that were too old or too small for him to use. I had a paint set like his and a studio like his. Except my studio was a walk-in closet, which made it the perfect size for me."

Although Pinkney closely studied his father's working methods, he was never the elder Pinkney's student. After graduating from high school, he enrolled at the Philadelphia College of Art and earned his bachelor's degree in fine arts in 1983. While at college, he gained exposure to different artistic mediums, including pen and ink, watercolors, oils, and acrylics. Printmaking was one of Pinkney's favorite courses of study because he enjoyed the three-dimensional aspects of etching and lithography techniques.

Pinkney began experimenting in scratchboard techniques while pursuing a master's degree at the School of Visual Arts in New York City. Mastering scratchboard—a technique similar to engraving, wherein the artist uses small tools to scrape and scratch away the surface of a prepared board's black coating to reveal the white clay underneath—was pivotal in Pinkney's career, and he employs this method in most of his illustrations, overlaying the cut image with oils when color is desired. "I like working in scratchboard because it allows me to sculpt the image," he once explained. "When I etch the drawing out of the board, I get a rhythm going with my lines which feels like sculpture to me."

Before obtaining his master's degree, Pinkney began to do some illustration work on a freelance basis. Under the name J. Brian Pinkney, he provided illustrations for Roy Wandelmaier's *Shipwrecked on Mystery Island,* as well as noted author Robert D. San Souci's *The Boy and the Ghost.* He also illustrated San Souci's *Cendrillon: A Caribbean Cinderella,* which places the familiar Cinderella story in a tropical setting, as a washerwoman is given a magic wand and uses it to benefit her goddaughter. Joanna Rudge Long commented in *Horn Book* that in *Cendrillon,* "Pinkney's signature multimedia art . . . glows with the richly saturated colors of the Caribbean."

Pinkney's other illustration projects include creating artwork for Patricia C. McKissack's award-winning *The*

Pinkney teams with wife, Andrea Davis Pinkney, to create the picture-book bibliography Duke Ellington. (Illustration © 1998 by Brian Pinkney. In the U.S. reproduced by permission of Disney Publications. In the U.K. reproduced by permission of the illustrator.)

Dark-Thirty: Southern Tales of the Supernatural and Judy Sierra's retelling *Wiley and the Hairy Man.* His work for *Wiley and the Hairy Man* was praised by *Booklist* reviewer Janice Del Negro as "full of motion and feeling," and equally lauded by Maria B. Salvadore, who cited them in *Horn Book* as creating "a fresh and appropriately nefarious look for an ever-popular, appealing folktale." When Patricia J. Williams reviewed Kim L. Siegelson's *In the Time of the Drums* for the *New York Times Book Review,* she described Pinkney's contributions as "gentle and luminous scratchboard illustrations [that] provide subtly intelligent counterpoint to the text."

While Pinkney's early illustration projects featured scratchboard, his more-recent works also weave in watercolor and ink. In bringing to life Marybeth Lorbiecki's *Jackie's Bat,* which imagines baseball great Jackie Robinson's first season playing with the Brooklyn Dodgers, Pinkney opts for watercolor, and with "bright hues and expressive details" he "enliven[s] the characters with sinewy, curvacious lines," according to *School Library Journal* critic Marilyn Taniguchi. *We Are One,* Pinkney's collaboration with Ysaye M. Barnwell, a member of the a capella group Sweet Honey in the Rock, features watercolor illustrations that achieve what

a *Publishers Weekly* critic characterized as a "soft-focused style" while also capturing Pinkney's characteristic movement and energy.

When Pinkney looks for illustrating assignments, he chooses those with which he feels personally involved, such as Burton Albert's *Where Does the Trail Lead?,* which he illustrated by recalling his own boyhood memories of summer months spent on Cape Cod. "I like illustrating stories about African-American subject matter because I learn about my culture and heritage," he once noted. In addition to illustrating works that focus on American blacks, Pinkney has worked with author Maxine Rose Schur on *Day of Delight: A Jewish Sabbath in Ethiopia,* which portrays the traditions of a young boy and his family who live in an isolated settlement of African Jews, as well as *When I Left My Village,* a sequel that follows the family on their journey from their mountain home to Israel. "Pinkney's scratchboard illustrations are lovingly rendered and full of grace and dignity," commented Hannah B. Zeiger in a review of *Day of Delight* for *Horn Book.*

Pinkney's first self-illustrated work, *Max Found Two Sticks,* is based on the artist's experience playing the drums. In the story, a boy taps out the rhythms of his urban neighborhood—church bells, rain on the window sill, the rhythmic click-click of a train, pigeons taking flight—using two branches found at the base of a nearby tree. Praised by *Horn Book* critic Helen Fader as "a deceptively simple picture book that will appeal to children's sense of enjoyment in making noise," *Max Found Two Sticks* was lauded by Hazel Rochman for its high-quality balance between text and art. In her *Booklist* review, Rochman described Pinkney's text as "a spare, rhythmic accompaniment" to his oil-and-scratchboard illustrations, which "swirl and circle" through the pages, "filling them with energy and movement."

Other works both written and illustrated by Pinkney include *JoJo's Flying Side Kick,* which grew out of its author's interest in and practice of the martial arts. In this book a young girl awaits her test to receive her yellow belt in Tae Kwon Do. Eliminating her nervousness by channeling her fears into visions of a burglar standing in front of her, JoJo executes a perfect side kick and earns her belt. *The Adventures of Sparrowboy* is an exuberant fantasy that finds a paperboy suddenly gifted with the power of flight. With his newly acquired bird's-eye view of the city, the boy earns superhero status after he prevents a local bully from harassing the neighborhood and also finishes his newspaper deliveries on time. Pinkney tells Sparrowboy's story in both book and comic-book style, his scratchboard illustrations enhanced with "transparent dyes and gouaches in creamy colors never before seen in a comic book," according to a *Publishers Weekly* reviewer.

Another original self-illustrated picture book, *Cosmo and the Robot,* tells the story of a brother and sister living on Mars who have familiar squabbles over toys, except that the quarrels include the interference of Cosmo's malfunctioning robot, Rex. *Hush, Little Baby,* Pinkney's illustrated adaptation of a traditional Appalachian lullaby, updates the original by trading the horse and cart of the well-known song for a more-contemporary fire truck. A *Publishers Weekly* reviewer noted of *Cosmo and the Robot* that Pinkney's artwork achieves the "slightly kitschy tradition of '50s science fiction," although the author/illustrator still "lets ordinary family dynamics shine brightly." According to *Horn Book* critic Joanna Rudge Long, *Hush, Little Baby* features clayboard-and-ink images in which "exuberant . . . figures swirl across the pages," and in *Booklist* Jennifer Mattson cited Pinkney's characters as exuding "a dancing energy that seems to spin right off of a 1920s Harlem dance floor."

Pinkney's most frequent collaborator is his wife, Andrea Davis Pinkney. The couple met when their careers—he as an illustrator working for a magazine art department, and she as a magazine editor—brought them together, and they chose a biography of dancer Alvin Ailey as their first project. "Brian and I had wanted to work on a project together," Andrea Pinkney told Susan Stan in *Five Owls,* "and we have always gone to see the Alvin Ailey American Dance Theater. At one point I said to Brian, 'I just wish there was a subject we were both interested in working on, like Alvin Ailey.'" *Alvin Ailey* is the life story of the famed African-American choreographer whose pioneering, blues-and-gospel-inflected choreography popularized modern dance among black audiences. "When I illustrated the book *Alvin Ailey,* . . . I got to act out Alvin's

life as a dancer," Pinkney once confided. He and his wife took dance lessons with one of the original members of Ailey's famous dance company, "which was a lot of fun." With the understanding of Ailey's modern dance style gained through these lessons, Pinkney used himself as a model for the famous choreographer.

In *Seven Candles for Kwanzaa, Dear Benjamin Banneker, Bill Pickett: Rodeo-Ridin' Cowboy, Mim's Christmas Jam,* and *Boycott Blues: How Rosa Parks Inspired a Nation* the Pinkneys bring to life little-known facets of African-American history and culture for young readers. The "swirling strokes" of Pinkney's characteristic scratchboard illustrations bring to life *Bill Pickett,* the biography of a famous black rodeo rider, and were praised by *Horn Book* reviewer Lauren Adams for "captur[ing] . . . the young [Pickett's] enthusiasm and the excitement of the rodeo. Featuring an urban topic, *Mim's Christmas Jam* honors the workers who built the New York City subway system, performing difficult and dangerous work with little reward. Pinkney's illustrations for this book add "visual clarity to the stark differences between the settings," noted a *Kirkus Reviews* writer, the critic dubbing *Mim's Christmas Jam* as "a moving, sensitive story with which modern young readers can identify." In her text for *Boycott Blues,* Andrea Davis Pinkney focuses on the civil-rights movement of the mid-twentieth century, and the drama of her rhythmic text is "exuberantly captured by Brian Pinkney's agile brush," according to Long. "With thick, swirling ink lines on bright washes" of color, the illustrator "express[es] the . . . inspiring history," concluded Rochman.

Pinkney and Pinkney collaborate to share the life and times of another jazz great for young children in **Ella Fitzgerald.** (Illustration copyright © 2002 by Brian Pinkney. Reprinted by permission of Hyperion Books for Children.)

Biographical and Critical Sources

BOOKS

Cummings, Pat, editor, *Talking with Artists,* Bradbury Press (New York, NY), 1992.

Marcus, Leonard S., *Pass It Down: Five Picture Book Families Make Their Mark,* Walker & Co. (New York, NY), 2006.

St. James Guide to Children's Writers, fifth edition, St. James Press (Detroit, MI), 1999.

PERIODICALS

Black Issues Book Review, January, 2001, Kalilah Shambry, review of *Duke Ellington: The Piano Prince and His Orchestra,* p. 23; March-April, 2002, Kay Badalamenti, review of *Cendrillon: A Creole Cinderella,* p. 69; September-October, 2002, Lynda Jones, review of *Ella Fitzgerald: The Tale of a Vocal Virtuosa,* p. 58.

Booklist, April 1, 1994, Hazel Rochman, review of *Max Found Two Sticks,* p. 1441; March 1, 1996, Janice Del Negro, review of *Wiley and the Hairy Man,* p. 1186; April 1, 1997, Michael Cart, review of *The Adventures of Sparrowboy,* p. 1338; June 1, 1998, Bill Ott, review of *Duke Ellington,* p. 1757; October 15, 1998, Ilene Cooper, review of *Cendrillon,* p. 417; April 1, 1999, Hazel Rochman, review of *In the Time of the Drums,* p. 1428; July, 2000, Tim Arnold, review of *Cosmo and the Robot,* p. 2042; April 1, 2002, Gillian Engberg, review of *Ella Fitzgerald,* p. 1338; October 1, 2003, Jennifer Mattson, review of *Thumbelina,* p. 323, and Ilene Cooper, review of *The Stone Lamp: Eight Stories of Hanukkah through History,* p. 334; September 15, 2004, Carolyn Phelan, review of *Sleeping Cutie,* p. 254; February 1, 2006, Jennifer Mattson, review of *Hush, Little Baby,* p. 70; April 1, 2006, Carolyn Phelan, review of *Peggony-Po: A Whale of a Tale,* p. 49; October 15, 2008, Hazel Rochman, review of *Boycott Blues: How Rosa Parks Inspired a Nation,* p. 40.

Five Owls, September-October, 1995, Susan Stan, interview with Andrea Davis Pinkney, pp. 6-8.

Horn Book, May-June, 1994, Ellen Fader, review of *Max Found Two Sticks,* p. 319; November-December, 1994, Hannah B. Zeiger, review of *Day of Delight: A Jewish Sabbath in Ethiopia,* p. 747; May-June, 1996, Maria B. Salvadore, review of *Wiley and the Hairy Man,* pp. 333-344; November-December, 1996, Lauren Adams, review of *Bill Pickett: Rodeo-Ridin' Cowboy;* July-August, 1997, Roger Sutton, review of *The Adventures of Sparrowboy,* pp. 445-446; November, 1998, Joanna Rudge Long, review of *Cendrillon,* p. 747; May, 1999, review of *In the Time of the Drums,* p. 345; July, 2000, review of *Cosmo and the Robot,* p. 444; November-December, 2003, Susan P. Bloom, review of *The Stone Lamp,* p. 765; January-February, 2006, Joanna Rudge Long, review of *Hush, Little Baby,* p. 94; January-February, 2009, Joanna Rudge Long, review of *Boycott Blues,* p. 82.

Kirkus Reviews, September 15, 2001, review of *Mim's Christmas Jam,* p. 1365; September 1, 2004, review of *Sleeping Cutie,* p. 873; December 1, 2005, review of *Jackie's Bat,* p. 1277; February 15, 2008, review of *We Are One.*

New York Times Book Review, August 15, 1999, Patricia J. Williams, review of *In the Time of the Drums,* p. 24; December 16, 2001, review of *Mim's Christmas Jam,* p. 21.

Publishers Weekly, March 10, 1997, review of *The Adventures of Sparrowboy,* p. 66; March 2, 1998, review of *Duke Ellington,* p. 68; July 13, 1998, review of *Cendrillon,* p. 76; December 7, 1998, review of *JoJo's Flying Side Kick,* p. 62; April 26, 1999, review of *In the Time of the Drums,* p. 82; November 8, 1999, review of *Bill Pickett,* p. 71; May 1, 2000, review of *Cosmo and the Robot,* p. 70; September 24, 2001, review of *Mim's Christmas Jam,* p. 50; February 25, 2002, review of *In the Forest of Your Remembrance: Thirty-three Goodly News Tellings for the Whole Family,* p. 63; March 11, 2002, review of *Ella Fitzgerald,* p. 72; August 18, 2003, review of *Thumbelina,* p. 78; September 22, 2003, review of *The Stone Lamp,* p. 66; January 9, 2006, review of *Jackie's Bat,* p. 53; April 17, 2006, review of *Peggony-Po,* p. 187; March 3, 2008, review of *We Are One,* p. 44.

School Library Journal, April, 1997, John Peters, review of *The Adventures of Sparrowboy,* p. 115; May, 1998, Beth Tegart, review of *Duke Ellington,* p. 136; September, 1998, Judith Constantinides, review of *Cendrillon,* p. 198; May, 1999, Linda Greengrass, review of *In the Time of the Drums,* p. 96; June, 2000, Marie Orlando, review of *Cosmo and the Robot,* p. 124; September, 2000, Linda R. Skeele, review of *Duke Ellington,* p. 74; September, 2001, Kathryn Kosiorek, review of *In the Forest of Your Remembrance,* p. 252; May, 2002, Shauna Yusko, review of *Ella Fitzgerald,* p. 142; September, 2003, Cris Riedel and Ellis B. Hyde, review of *Thumbelina,* p. 166; July 25, 2005, review of *Music from Our Lord's Holy Heaven,* p. 80; January, 2006, Marilyn Taniguchi, review of *Jackie's Bat,* p. 106; June, 2006, Kirsten Cutler, review of *Peggony-Po,* p. 125; October, 2008, Barbara Elleman, review of *Boycott Blues,* p. 118.

ONLINE

Brian Pinkney Home Page, http://www.brianpinkney.net (October 30, 2009).*

*   *   *

PINKNEY, J. Brian
See PINKNEY, Brian

*   *   *

PURMELL, Ann 1953-

Personal

Born November 15, 1953, in Ann Arbor, MI; daughter of Burton G., II (a store owner) and Helen (a store

Ann Purmell (Photograph by Marcia Butterfield. Reproduced by permission.)

owner) McGarry; married Bruce Purmell (a dentist), July 6, 1974; children: Michael McGarry, Hilary Ann. *Education:* Eastern Michigan University, B.S. (cum laude), 1979; attended Spring Arbor University (elementary education), 1994-98. *Politics:* Republican. *Religion:* Episcopalian. *Hobbies and other interests:* Reading, gardening, "being outside on farms, at the ocean, and on Lake Michigan."

Addresses

Home—Jackson, MI.

Career

Writer and health-care worker. Worked in family-owned business, 1966-76, and as a psychiatric nurse, 1979-94.

Member

Society of Children's Book Writers and Illustrators, Sigma Theta Tau.

Awards, Honors

Premier Selection Award, Junior Library Guild, and Ohio Farm Bureau Federation Award for Children's Literature, 2007, both for *Christmas Tree Farm.*

Writings

Apple Cider Making Days, illustrated by Joanne Friar, Millbrook Press (Brookfield, CT), 2002.
Giraffes, illustrated by Jean Cassels, Random House (New York, NY), 2002.
Where Wild Babies Sleep, illustrated by Lorianne Siomades, Boyds Mills Press (Honesdale, PA), 2003.
Christmas Tree Farm, illustrated by Jill Weber, Holiday House (New York, NY), 2006.
Maple Syrup Season, illustrated by Jill Weber, Holiday House (New York, NY), 2008.

Contributor to periodicals, including *Jackson* magazine and *Jackson Citizen Patriot.*

Sidelights

"Ann Purmell churns out children's stories like a pioneer mother making butter," observed Pat Rombyer in Michigan's *Jackson Citizen Patriot.* Purmell, a Michigan resident, is the author of the picture books *Apple Cider Making Days* and *Christmas Tree Farm,* the latter which received the Ohio Farm Bureau Federation Award for Children's Literature. "Children's books are a lot like poetry," Purmell remarked to Rombyer. "I've considered myself a poet all through my life."

Children have always had a primary role in Purmell's life. "I have always loved children," the author wrote on her home page. "In high school, I was the busiest baby-sitter in the neighborhood." After studying nursing in college, Purmell became a psychiatric nurse in Michigan and for about eleven years she worked with children and teenagers in a mental-health-care setting. When she and her husband, Bruce, moved to Jackson, Michigan, she started working with senior citizens who had chemical dependency problems.

After a successful decade and a half in the nursing field, Purmell pursued a major change in her career. While her husband was busy with his successful dental practice, "I decided to become an elementary teacher and went back to college when I was forty-two years old," she explained on her home page. Then, in 1999, with her program almost finished and only her student-teaching experience left to complete, Purmell was diagnosed with sarcoidosis, an autoimmune system disease of the lungs that left her bedridden and unable to work. While recovering, she began writing regularly, keeping journals on yellow legal pads and writing at the computer. Writing helped her keep her mind off her physical symptoms, and it also instilled in her a discipline she had never had before, as Purmell explained in an interview for *Writer's Digest.* She began freelancing for local newspapers and publications, and eventually realized that her true calling was writing for children.

While accompanying her daughter on a field trip to a local cider mill, Purmell found the idea for her first published children's book. *Apple Cider Making Days,* illustrated by Jill Weber, tells the story of how cider is made, from the initial picking and sorting of the apples to the sales of bottled cider in local stores. In the book, young Alex and Abigail help the family with their cider-making activities on their grandfather's farm. They learn how apples are sorted for eating and for cider making (apples with imperfections become cider). The fruits are chopped up into apple mush and pressed into cider, which is bottled and sold with jams, pies, and other products at Grandpa's store. The book describes the cider-making process in detail and, in combination with the illustrations, allows children to see all the tools and machinery up-close, from the conveyor belts to the apple graters to the cider presses. A section on cider lore provides additional inside information on apples and cider. Helen Rosenberg, writing in *Booklist,* called *Apple Cider Making Days* "an excellent resource for autumn units or to use in preparation for a trip to the orchard." A *Kirkus Reviews* critic remarked that the book is "a great new addition to an overstuffed field."

In *Giraffes,* a shaped picture book, Purmell follows a family of giraffes during one day on the African plains. Also dealing with the natural world for younger readers, her book *Where Wild Babies Sleep* explores the many burrows, caves, nests, and other locations where young animals bed down in safety with their families. Writing in *School Library Journal,* Julie Roach wrote that *Where Wild Babies Sleep* "makes a nice bedtime story or conversation starter about different places to sleep."

Purmell again collaborates with Weber on *Christmas Tree Farm.* A young boy, who serves as the story's nar-

rator, accompanies his grandfather on a tractor ride through a forest of spruces, pines, and firs, where they measure and cut down the trees they will sell during the upcoming holiday season. On Christmas Eve, with their work done, the boy's family celebrates their good fortune by trimming their own trees. In her tale, Purmell also examines the growth cycles of trees; chronicles the year-round activities of a tree farm, which includes planting seedlings and pruning branches; and offers fun facts about Christmas-tree lore. "The text makes the book interesting; the art gives it charm," remarked *Booklist* critic Ilene Cooper.

Maple Syrup Season, a volume that "blends light fiction with nuts-and-bolts about an outdoorsy family business," according to *Booklist* reviewer Jennifer Mattson, marks another creative collaboration between Purmell and Weber. Three generations of the Brockwell family gather at the grandparents' home for the annual tradition of making syrup. Each member of the family has a

Purmell's picture book **Christmas Tree Farm** *features colorful art by Jill Weber.* (Illustration copyright © 2006 by Jill Weber. Reproduced by permission of Holiday House, Inc.)

Purmell and Weber count* Maple Tree Season *among their seasonal-themed picture books. (Illustration copyright © 2008 by Jill Weber. Reproduced by permission of Holiday, Inc.)

role in the process, which includes tapping the maple trees, collecting the sap, heating and processing it at the sugarhouse, and grading and bottling the batches. "The focus truly is on the family and their coming together in this special way each year," a contributor in *Kirkus Reviews* noted. Writing in *School Library Journal*, Mary Hazelton remarked that Purmell's "gentle story has a straightforward text and folksy, colorful gouache illustrations."

Purmell's writing career detoured her from her plans to enter the classroom, but her work keeps her in contact with teachers, children, and the education field through lectures and presentations that she gives at schools, conferences, and book-related events around the country. "Although I wanted to be a teacher, being invited to visit classrooms to talk to kids about writing is a great joy," she remarked on her home page. "I thank every teacher, librarian, and school who has allowed me to be a part of their students' lives, even if only for an hour."

Purmell's success continues to inspire her literary efforts. As she remarked to *Kids in Common* interviewer Carolyn Widman, "What I would like most is to somehow, someway develop [in children] a love of reading, of words, a love of all things that are the craft." "I tell aspiring writers that writing is a craft and not a hobby," Purmell once told *SATA*. "You spend years and thousands of pages of paper as you are first an apprentice, then a journeyman, and finally a master. I also recommend a mentor, someone who has published and is willing to share experiences and knowledge. A true mentor is more than a person to critique manuscripts."

Biographical and Critical Sources

PERIODICALS

Booklist, December 1, 2002, Helen Rosenberg, review of *Apple Cider Making Days*, p. 676; September 1, 2006,

Ilene Cooper, review of *Christmas Tree Farm,* p. 140; March 15, 2008, Jennifer Mattson, review of *Maple Syrup Season,* p. 56.

Childhood Education, fall, 2004, Isabel Killoran, review of *Where Wild Babies Sleep,* p. 47; spring, 2009, Audra Parker, review of *Maple Syrup Season,* p. 195.

Jackson Citizen Patriot (Jackson, MI), July 21, 2002, Monetta L. Harr, "The Write Way: Unexpected Turn in Life Led Woman to Become a Children's Book Author"; November 12, 2006, Pat Rombyer, "Ann-Thology: Jackson Author Ann Purmell Finds Niche in Children's Books."

Kids in Common, September, 2005, Carolyn Widman, "Born to Write Books," profile of Purmell.

Kirkus Reviews, October 15, 2002, review of *Apple Cider Making Days,* p. 1536; September 1, 2003, review of *Where Wild Babies Sleep,* p. 1129; November 1, 2006, review of *Christmas Tree Farm;* February 15, 2008, review of *Maple Syrup Season.*

New York Times Book Review, December 17, 2006, Julie Just, review of *Christmas Tree Farm.*

School Library Journal, January, 2004, Julie Roach, review of *Where Wild Babies Sleep,* p. 104; October, 2006, Susan Patron, review of *Christmas Tree Farm,* p. 100; March, 2008, Mary Hazelton, review of *Maple Syrup Season,* p. 174.

Writer's Digest, February, 2003, Jessica Yerega, "First Success," p. 52.

You Can Write for Children, June, 2003, Jessica Yerega, "Being Hit by Lightning," pp. 46-47.

ONLINE

Ann Purmell Home Page, http://www.annpurmell.com (October 10, 2009).*

R

RAWLINS, Donna 1956-

Personal
Born March 16, 1956, in Sunshine, Victoria, Australia.

Addresses
Home—Sydney, New South Wales, Australia.

Career
Illustrator, book designer, and educator. Has worked in print and publishing industries as a darkroom operator, graphic designer, silkscreen and offset printer, book designer, and editor; freelance illustrator, designer, and book packager, 1984—. Cofounder, with Wayne Harris, of Monkeyfish (design studio), Sydney, New South Wales, Australia; creator, with Harris, of course in children's book illustration at Sydney University. Chisholm Institute, lecturer in graphic design, 1983-84.

Awards, Honors
Picture Book of the Year shortlist, Children's Book Council of Australia (CBCA), 1988, and Notable Children's Book selection, American Library Association, both for *Tucking Mummy In;* Book of Year Award for Younger Readers, CBCA, and Eve Pownall Award for Information Books, both 1988, and Young Australians' Best Book Award, all for *My Place;* Eve Pownall Award for Information Books Honor designation, 1996, for *Ten Little-Known Facts about Hippopotamuses and More Little-Known Facts and a Few Fibs about Other Animals;* Lady Cutler Award, Children's Book Council of New South Wales, 2003, for outstanding contribution to the children's-book industry; Early Childhood Book of the Year Honor designation, CBCA, 2005, for *Seven More Sleeps.*

Writings

SELF-ILLUSTRATED

Digging to China, Orchard Books (New York, NY), 1988.

Big and Little, Random House Australia (Milsons Point, New South Wales, Australia), 2006.

ILLUSTRATOR

(With Randy Glusac) Gwen Morrish and Diane Snowball, *The Australian Writer's Wordbook,* Nelson (Melbourne, Victoria, Australia), 1984.

Morag Loh, *The Kinder Hat,* Hyland House (Melbourne, Victoria, Australia), 1985.

Judy Tuer and Cheryl Semple, *Joey's Bear,* Dove Communications (Melbourne, Victoria, Australia), 1986.

Faye Bolton and Diane Snowball, *Growing Radishes and Carrots,* Martin Educational (Gosford, New South Wales, Australia), 1986.

Five Little Monkeys: A Traditional Rhyme, Macmillan (South Melbourne, Victoria, Australia), 1987.

Nadia Wheatley, *My Place,* Collins Dove (Blackburn, Victoria, Australia), 1987, Kane/Miller (New York, NY), 1992, reprinted, Walker Books Australia (Newtown, New South Wales, Australia), 2008.

Morag Loh, *Tucking Mummy In,* Ashton Scholastic (Sydney, New South Wales, Australia), 1987, published as *Tucking Mommy In,* Orchard Books (New York, NY), 1988.

Kaylyn Taylor, *Dear Nana,* Collins Dove (Blackburn, Victoria, Australia), 1987.

David Hicks, *George Looks for God,* Collins Dove (Blackburn, Victoria, Australia), 1987.

Jenny Pausacker, *Fast Forward,* Angus & Robertson (North Ryde, New South Wales, Australia), 1989, Lothrop, Lee & Shepard (New York, NY), 1991.

Duncan Ball, *Jeremy's Tail,* Ashton Scholastic (Sydney, New South Wales, Australia), 1990, Orchard Books (New York, NY), 1991, reprinted, Scholastic Press (Lindfield, New South Wales, Australia), 2006.

Margaret Wild, *My Dearest Dinosaur,* Orchard Books (New York, NY), 1992.

Margaret Wild, *First Best Friends,* Roads and Traffic Authority of New South Wales (Sydney, New South Wales, Australia), 1992.

(With David Francis) Douglas Little, *Ten Little-Known Facts about Hippopotamuses and More Little-Known*

Facts and a Few Fibs about Other Animals, Ashton Scholastic (Sydney, New South Wales, Australia), 1994.

(With Randy Glusac and Nancy Keltner) Diane Snowball, *Writer's Word Book,* Mondo (Greenvale, NY), 1999.

Margaret Wild, *Robber Girl,* Random House Australia (Milsons Point, New South Wales, Australia), 2000.

Simon French, *Guess the Baby,* Clarion Books (New York, NY), 2002.

Margaret Wild, *Babs the Baby and Fog the Dog,* Working Title Press (Kingswood, South Australia, Australia), 2003.

James O'Laughlin, *Andy's Secret Weapon,* Hodder Headline Australia (Sydney, New South Wales, Australia), 2004.

Margaret Wild, *Seven More Sleeps,* Working Title Press (Kingswood, South Australia, Australia), 2004.

Wendy Orr, *Across the Dark Sea,* National Museum of Australia Press (Canberra, Australian Capital Territory, Australia), 2006.

Anthony Hill, *Riverboy,* National Museum of Australia Press (Canberra, Australian Capital Territory, Australia), 2006.

Donna Rawlins' picture-book projects includes creating the engaging artwork for Sue Whitings' **The Firefighters.** (Illustration copyright © 2008 by Donna Rawlins. Reproduced by permission of Candlewick Press, Inc., Somerville, MA, on behalf of Walker Books Ltd., London.)

Christopher Cheng, *Seams of Gold,* National Museum of Australia Press (Canberra, Australian Capital Territory, Australia), 2007.

Simon French, *What Will You Be?,* Allen & Unwin (Crows Nest, New South Wales, Australia), 2007.

Sue Whiting, *The Firefighters,* Candlewick Press (Cambridge, MA), 2008.

Sidelights

An Australian writer, illustrator, editor, designer, and teacher, Donna Rawlins has provided the artwork for more than two dozen children's books, including such critically praised titles as *Tucking Mummy In, My Place,* and *Seven More Sleeps.* Among her many awards, Rawlins is the recipient of the prestigious Lady Cutler Award, presented by the Children's Book Council of New South Wales, for her outstanding contributions to children's literature.

Rawlins collaborated with author Duncan Ball to produce *Jeremy's Tail.* This humorous picture book concerns a young boy who, during a game of Pin the Tail on the Donkey, walks out the front door of his home and wanders, blindfolded, through a series of madcap adventures. Jeremy finds himself climbing aboard a bus, an ocean liner, and a hot-air balloon in turn, and his travels take him to an African savanna, an Arab marketplace, and then to a lively carnival where he is shot out of a cannon and lands back at his party. "Rawlins's bright, colored-pencil illustrations . . . are cheerful, nicely detailed, and perfectly on target," Martha Topol remarked in her *School Library Journal* review of *Jeremy's Tail,* and a *Publishers Weekly* contributor stated that the "vivid, colorful illustrative style depicts the disparate cultures with panache."

Margaret Wild's *My Dearest Dinosaur* comprises a series of notes from a mother dinosaur to her partner, who is off searching for food for their children. "The mix of realism and fantasy in Rawlins's vibrant, dramatic artwork nicely matches the book's tone," a reviewer in *Publishers Weekly* noted of this work. Karen Jameyson, writing in *Horn Book,* expressed surprise at the tender nature of Wild's text and Rawlins' art, concluding that "this ingenuous string of letters combines with the engrossing colored pencil and acrylic illustrations" to "draw us in and prod at our emotions." The artist's nature-tinged palette, in shades of brown and green, "does a fine job of evoking setting from a variety of perspectives," Jameyson added, "and the scenes are set off effectively against white pages. The resulting combination with narrative is provocative, intriguing, and ultimately quite moving."

In *Guess the Baby,* a work by Simon French, an elementary-school student brings his infant brother to class for Show and Tell, spurring an intriguing game based on his classmates' baby pictures. Here "Rawlins' colorful, endearing illustrations . . . feature a smiling, multicultural classroom of kids," as Karin Snelson remarked in *Booklist.* A *Kirkus Reviews* critic observed of *Guess the Baby* that the artist's "colored pencil and acrylic gouache paintings are a medley of brilliant hues and genial faces." Also featuring Rawlins' art, Sue Whiting's *The Firefighters* follows a group of children who use their imaginations to transform a set of cardboard boxes into a fire engine, prompting their teacher to invite the workers at a nearby firehouse to visit the school. The book's "acrylic illustrations feature bright, primary colors that stand out against the clean, white backgrounds," Linda Ludke commented in *School Library Journal,* and a *Kirkus Reviews* critic wrote of *The Firefighters* that "Rawlins's preschoolers perfectly model the fun children can have when they use their imaginations."

Biographical and Critical Sources

PERIODICALS

Booklist, December 15, 2002, Karin Snelson, review of *Guess the Baby,* p. 766; September 1, 2008, Bina Williams, review of *The Firefighters,* p. 103.

Horn Book, March-April, 1993, Karen Jameyson, review of *My Dearest Dinosaur,* p. 241.

Kirkus Reviews, October 1, 2002, review of *Guess the Baby,* p. 1469; July 15, 2008, review of *The Firefighters.*

Publishers Weekly, July 12, 1991, review of *Jeremy's Tail,* p. 64; September 28, 1992, review of *My Dearest Dinosaur,* p. 78; October 21, 2002, review of *Guess the Baby,* p. 74.

School Library Journal, November, 1991, Martha Topol, review of *Jeremy's Tail,* p. 89; December, 2002, Leslie Barban, review of *Guess the Baby,* p. 95; December, 2008, Linda Ludke, review of *The Firefighters,* p. 106.

ONLINE

Lateral Learning Web site, http://www.laterallearning.com/ (October 15, 2009), "Donna Rawlins."

Walker Books Australia Web site, http://www.walkerbooks.com.au/ (October 15, 2009), "Donna Rawlins."*

*   *   *

REED, Dallas
See PENDLETON, Thomas

*   *   *

ROZEN, Anna 1960-

Personal

Born 1960, in Algiers.

Addresses

Home—Paris, France. *E-mail*—arozen@club-internet.fr.

Career

Novelist and author of children's books. Formerly worked in advertising; writer for television.

Writings

FOR CHILDREN

Le petit garçon qui n'existait pas, illustrated by Dupuy Berberian, Cornélius, 2000.
Chocolatine, Livre la Poche (Paris, France), 2002.
Le marchand de bruits, Nathan (Paris, France), 2002, illustrated by François Avril, translated by Carl W. Scarbrough as *The Merchant of Noises,* David R. Godine (Boston, MA), 2006.

FOR ADULTS

Plaisir d'offrir, joie de recevoir (short stories), Dilettante (Paris, France), 1999.
Méfiez-vous des fruits (novel), Dilettante (Paris, France), 2002.
Bonheur 230 (novel), Denoël (Paris, France), 2004.
Encore! (novella), Naïve, 2005.
(Translator) Andrew Kaufman, *Tous mes amis sont des super héros,* Naïve, 2007.
Vieilles peaux (short stories), Dilettante (Paris, France), 2007.

Translator of books into French, including *Sister Age* by M.K.F. Fisher. Contributor to French-language periodicals, including *Bordel.*

Biographical and Critical Sources

PERIODICALS

Kirkus Reviews, April 1, 2007, review of *The Merchant of Noises.*
Publishers Weekly, April 9, 2007, review of *The Merchant of Noises,* p. 53.
School Library Journal, June, 2007, Kirsten Cutler, review of *The Merchant of Noises,* p. 122.

ONLINE

Dilettante Web site, http://www.ledilettante.com/ (April 10, 2008), "Anna Rozen."*

*   *   *

RUGG, Jim

Personal

Male.

Addresses

Home—Pittsburgh, PA. *E-mail*—jimrugg@hotmail.com.

Career

Cartoonist and illustrator.

Illustrator

GRAPHIC NOVELS

Brian Maruca, *Street Angel, Volume 1: The Princess of Poverty* (originally published in five volumes in comic-book form), SLG Publishing, 2005.
Cecil Castellucci, *The P.L.A.I.N. Janes,* DC Comics (New York, NY), 2007.
Cecil Castellucci, *Janes in Love,* DC Comics (New York, NY), 2008.
Brian Maruca, *Afrodisiac,* Adhouse Books (Richmond, VA), 2009.
C. Allbritton Taylor, *One Model Nation,* Image Comics, 2009.

OTHER

Work collected in anthologies, including *24Seven,* 2006, and *Popgun, Volume 2,* 2008. Contributor to periodicals, including *New York* and *LA Weekly.*

Adaptations

Street Angel was published in a French-language edition by Le Lezard Noir.

Sidelights

The work of cartoonist Jim Rugg is familiar to teen fans of the "P.L.A.I.N. Janes" graphic-novel series, which features a storyline by writer Cecil Castellucci. Rugg's renown extends beyond a young-adult audience, however. In addition to his collaboration with Castellucci, he has also worked with writer Brian Maruca on the "Street Angel" comics and the graphic novel *Afrodisiac,* the latter featuring a story drawn from the blaxploitation films of the 1970s. In 2009 Rugg also teamed up with C. Allbritton Taylor to produce *One Model Nation,* the story of a 1970s-era West German industrial band that finds itself caught up in the terrorist activities of the radical Baader Meinhoff Group.

Introduced in 2007's *The P.L.A.I.N. Janes,* the series hinges on Jane Beckles, a teen living in Metro City whose life changes after she survives a terrorist bombing. Developing a kinship with a young artist who has been rendered unconscious by the explosion, Jane adopts a Goth look and an artist lifestyle that alienates her old friends and sparks the concern of her parents. Worried that a member of their family might not survive another attack, Jane's parents relocate the family to the Midwestern town of Kent Waters, where Jane is viewed as an outsider. However, Jane attracts three other girls in her new town who share her name and also her interest in art. The four Janes decide to become guerilla artists and form the gang known as People Loving Art In Neighborhoods, or P.L.A.I.N. While the girls enjoy waking up the residents of their sleepy suburban community by such clandestine art attacks as creating whimsical temporary structures out of building materials on construction sites or dressing up the town's fire hydrants, some in Kent Waters view the gang's actions as disruptive and want them to stop. In *Booklist* Jesse Karp dubbed Rugg's art for *The P.L.A.I.N. Janes* "absolutely engaging" and Castellucci's text "though-provoking stuff," while in *School Library Journal* contributor Lisa Goldstein compared the illustration style to the "spare, clean style of alternative comics creators such as Dan Clowes." Rugg's "clean-lined" drawings effectively communicate "not just detail and scope," wrote *Horn Book* reviewer Claire E. Gross, "but the drama, impact, and joy of [the Janes'] unfettered expression." Asserting that *The P.L.A.I.N. Janes* "perfectly captures the experiences of a teenage girl in a post-9/11 world," Jennifer Feigelman added in *Kliatt* that Rugg reveals "a mastery of teen life" in a graphic novel that ranks as "an absolute triumph."

Castellucci and Rugg team up for a P.L.A.I.N. Janes reunion in *Janes in Love*, which finds the four Janes scheduling their art attacks around school dances, dates, police harassment, an anthrax threat, and the odd grant application. "Rugg's clean, crisp" inked images have "a hip, indie look," wrote Goldstein, and in *Horn Book* Gross asserted of *Janes in Love* that "text and art complement each other with precision and wit."

Collected in graphic-novel format as *Street Angel, Volume 1: The Princess of Poverty*, the first five volumes of "Street Angel" comprise what a *Publishers Weekly* contributor described as "one of the oddest and most original works to surface in quite a while." In Maruca's storyline, twelve-year-old Jesse Sanchez has lived on the streets for a lifetime, and by honing her skills in martial arts and on the skateboard she has become a survivor. In Jesse's world, the streets yield up a host of bizarre dangers, from Satan worshipers to vicious gangs, to robots and maniacal scientists. The title character of

Afrodisiac also appears among the chaotic cast that is brought to life by Rugg's pen, making *Street Angel, Volume 1* "unapologetic fun," according to the *Publishers Weekly* critic. "The art is deceptively simple," noted *Booklist* reviewer Tina Coleman; Rugg's images for the comic range from "startlingly poignant" to "fabulously over-the-top."

Biographical and Critical Sources

PERIODICALS

Booklist, September 1, 2005, Tina Coleman, review of *Street Angel, Volume 1: The Princess of Poverty*, p. 113; March 15, 2007, Jesse Karp, review of *The P.L.A.I.N. Janes*, p. 56; October 1, 2008, Jesse Karp, review of *Janes in Love*, p. 38.

Horn Book, July-August, 2007, Claire E. Gross, review of *The P.L.A.I.N. Janes*, p. 390; November-December, 2008, Claire E. Gross, review of *Janes in Love*, p. 698.

Kliatt, May, 2007, Jennifer Feigelman, review of *The P.L.A.I.N. Janes*, p. 31.

Publishers Weekly, July 18, 2005, review of *Street Angel, Volume 1*, p. 191; April 9, 2007, review of *The P.L.A.I.N. Janes*, p. 56; September 1, 2008, review of *Janes in Love*, p. 41.

School Library Journal, September, 2007, Lisa Goldstein, review of *The P.L.A.I.N. Janes*, p. 222; November, 2008, Lisa Goldstein, review of *Janes in Love*, p. 151.

ONLINE

Comic Book Resources Online, http://www.comicbook resources.com/ (October 9, 2009), Josh Wigler, "C Al-lbritton Taylor and Jim Rugg Create a 'Nation.'"

Jim Rugg Home Page, http://www.jimrugg.com (October 30, 2009).

Jim Rugg Web log, http://jimrugg.blogspot.com (October 30, 2009).

Street Angel Web site, http://www.streetangelcomics.com/ (October 30, 2009).*

S

SASAKI, Ellen Joy

Personal
Female.

Addresses
Agent—Cornell & McCarthy, 2D Cross Hwy., Westport, CT 06880. *E-mail*—ejsasaki@comcast.net.

Career
Illustrator for books and advertising.

Illustrator
Neal Starkman, *Z's Gift,* Comprehensive Health Education Foundation (Seattle, WA), 1988.

Neal Starkman, *The Riddle,* Comprehensive Health Educational Foundation (Seattle, WA), 1990.

Fun Group, *Make Your Own Videos, Commercials, Radio Shows, Special Effects, and More,* Grosset & Dunlap/ Nickelodeon (New York, NY), 1992.

Christine Harder Tangvald, *Yea, Hooray! The Son Came Home Today, and Other Bible Stories about Wisdom,* Chariot Books (Elgin, IL), 1993.

Lois G. Grambling, *Mrs. Tittle's Turkey Farm,* Thomasson-Grant (Charlottesville, VA), 1994.

Patricia Griffith, *The Snow Game,* Open Court (Chicago, IL), 1995.

Anne O'Brien, *Wendell's Pets,* Open Court (Chicago, IL), 1995.

Jeffrey Kindley, *Choco-Louie,* Gareth Stevens (Milwaukee, WI), 1996.

Phyllis Jean Perry, *365 Science Projects and Activities,* Publications International (Lincolnwood, IL), 1996.

Kathy Barabas, *Let's Find out about Toothpaste,* Scholastic (New York, NY), 1997.

Jane Belk Moncure, *My Four Book,* Child's World (Chanhassen, MN), 2006.

Teresa Bateman, *Gus, the Pilgrim Turkey,* Albert Whitman (Morton Grove, IL), 2008.

Contributor to periodicals.

Biographical and Critical Sources

PERIODICALS

Booklist, September 15, 2008, Kay Weisman, review of *Gus, the Pilgrim Turkey,* p. 57.

Kirkus Reviews, August 1, 2008, review of *Gus, the Pilgrim Turkey.*

Publishers Weekly, September 19, 1994, review of *Mrs. Tittle's Turkey Farm,* p. 26.

School Library Journal, September, 2008, Lisa Egly Lehmuller, review of *Gus, the Pilgrim Turkey,* p. 137.

ONLINE

Ellen Joy Sasaki Home Page, http://www.ellensasaki.com (October 30, 2009).*

* * *

SEIDMAN, Karla
See KUSKIN, Karla

* * *

SMITH, Sherwood 1951-
(Nicholas Adams, Jesse Maguire, Robyn Tallis, a house pseudonym)

Personal
Born May 28, 1951, in Glendale, CA. *Education:* University of Southern California, B.A., 1973; University of California, Santa Barbara, M.A., 1977. *Hobbies and other interests:* Music, animals, children, nature, good tea, cozy firesides, stimulating conversation.

Addresses

Agent—Valerie Smith, 1746 Rte. 44-55, Modena, NY 12548. *E-mail*—Sherwood-Smith@worldnet.att.net.

Career

Writer. Taught elementary and high school for ten years. Has also tutored children with learning disabilities, run online workshops, and evaluated manuscripts for writers.

Member

Science Fiction Writers of America, Mythopoeic Society, RWA, NINC.

Awards, Honors

Best Books for Young-Adult Readers citation, New York Public Library, 1993, for *Wren's Quest*; New York Public Library Best Books for the Teen Age designation, and Mythopoeic Fantasy Award for Children's Literature finalist, all 1995, and Anne Lindbergh Honor Book designation, 1996, all for *Wren's War*; New York Public Library Best Books for the Teen Age designation, 1997, for *Crown Duel*, 1998, for *Court Duel*; Nebula Award finalist, 2001, for "Mom and Dad at the Home Front."

Writings

FANTASY; FOR YOUNG ADULTS

Wren to the Rescue, Harcourt (San Diego, CA), 1990.
Wren's Quest, Harcourt (San Diego, CA), 1993.
Wren's War, Harcourt (San Diego, CA), 1995.
Crown Duel (also see below), Harcourt (San Diego, CA), 1997.
(With Andre Norton) *Derelict for Trade,* Tor (New York, NY), 1997.
Court Duel (also see below) Harcourt (San Diego, CA), 1998.
(With Andre Norton) *A Mind for Trade,* Tor (New York, NY), 1999.
(With Andre Norton) *Echoes in Time,* Tor (New York, NY), 1999.
(With Andre Norton) *Atlantis Endgame,* Tor (New York, NY), 2000.
Journey to Otherwhere, Random House (New York, NY), 2000.
A Posse of Princesses, Norilana (Winnetka, CA), 2008.

"SARTORIAS-DELES" NOVEL SERIES

Crown Duel (revision of previously published novels *Crown Duel* and *Court Duel*), Firebird (New York, NY), 2002.
Inda (for adults), DAW (New York, NY), 2006.
Senrid, Norilana (Winnetka, CA), 2007.
The Fox (for adults), DAW (New York, NY), 2007.

Over the Sea: CJ's First Notebook, Norilana (Winnetka, CA), 2007.
The King's Shield (for adults), DAW (New York, NY), 2008.
The Trouble with Kings, Samhain (Macon, GA), 2008.
A Stranger to Command, Norilana (Winnetka, CA), 2008.
Mearsies Heili Bounces Back, Norilana (Winnetka, CA), 2008.
Once a Princess, Samhain (Macon, GA), 2009.
Twice a Prince, Samhain (Macon, GA), 2009.
Treason's Shore (for adults), DAW (New York, NY), 2009.

"EXORDIUM" NOVEL SERIES

(With Dave Trowbridge) *The Phoenix in Flight,* Tor (New York, NY), 1993.
(With Dave Trowbridge) *Ruler of Naught,* Tor (New York, NY), 1993.
(With Dave Trowbridge) *A Prison Unsought,* Tor (New York, NY), 1994.
(With Dave Trowbridge) *The Rifter's Covenant,* Tor (New York, NY), 1995.
(With Dave Trowbridge) *The Thrones of Kronos,* Tor (New York, NY), 1996.

"PLANET BUILDERS" YOUNG-ADULT NOVEL SERIES; UNDER PSEUDONYM ROBYN TALLIS

Rebel from Alphorion (book 3), Ivy Books (New York, NY), 1989.
Visions from the Sea (book 4), Ivy Books (New York, NY), 1989.
The Giants of Elenna (book 9), Ivy Books (New York, NY), 1989.
Fire in the Sky (book 10), Ivy Books (New York, NY), 1989.

"NOWHERE HIGH" SERIES; UNDER HOUSE PSEUDONYM JESSE MAGUIRE; YOUNG ADULT

The Beginning (book 1), Ivy Books (New York, NY), 1989.
Crossing Over (book 3), Ivy Books (New York, NY), 1990.
Getting It Right (book 5), Ivy Books (New York, NY), 1991.
Breaking the Rules (book 6), Ivy Books (New York, NY), 1992.

OTHER

(Under pseudonym Nicholas Adams) *Final Curtain: Horror High #8* (for young adults), Harper (New York, NY), 1991.
The Borrowers (novelization of the screenplay by Scott and John Kamps), Harcourt (San Diego, CA), 1997.
Gene Roddenberry's Earth: Final Conflict—Augur's Teacher, Tor (New York, NY), 2001.
Gene Roddenberry's Andromeda: Paradise Drift, Tor (New York, NY), 2005.
The Emerald Wand of Oz, HarperCollins (New York, NY), 2005.

Trouble under Oz, HarperCollins (New York, NY), 2006.

Author of short stories collected in anthologies, including "Ghost Dancers" in *Things That Go Bump in the Night,* "Beauty" in *Firebirds,* and "Curing the Bozos" in *Bruce Coville's Book of Aliens.*

Smith's works have been translated into Danish.

Sidelights

Fantasy writer Sherwood Smith became known in the mid-1990s for her strong heroines and girl-oriented adventures. Since then, she has published a number of novels for children, young adults, and adults that are set in her sweeping Sartorias-Deles world. Ranging from the adventures of girls from different cultures who work to secure a kingdom for a child queen, to the epic of a boy who becomes the greatest military strategist of all times, the "Sartorias-Deles" tales show "the depths of Smith's world-building," wrote a *Publishers Weekly* critic in a review of *The Fox. Voice of Youth Advocates* contributor Lesa M. Holstine, reviewing Smith's early novels, cited her as "a welcome addition to the fantasy field."

Smith's first novel introduces a young, adventure-craving heroine named Wren, who has a knack for magic. *Wren to the Rescue* introduces the title character, a twelve-year-old orphan whose best friend, Tess, is revealed to be a princess in hiding. Over the course of the book, Wren befriends two stalwart companions: Tyron, a magician's apprentice, and Prince Connor, Tess's cousin. The novel opens in an orphanage, where the two girls live until the day Tess's identity is revealed and she, accompanied by Wren, goes to live in the palace. Soon thereafter, however, Tess is kidnapped by her evil uncle, and Wren, eventually joined by Tyron and Prince Connor, goes in search of her friend. *School Library Journal* contributor Carol A. Edwards praised the fantasy world described in the girl's adventures as "solidly constructed and divertingly revealed." Edwards anticipated a sequel to *Wren to the Rescue* and expressed the hope that subsequent titles would bring further character development as well as answers to the questions raised in the first volume. "Young fantasy lovers will enjoy the spunky heroine, the suspenseful plot, and some inventive magic," concluded *Horn Book* critic Ann A. Flowers.

Smith's sequel, *Wren's Quest,* employs many of the same elements reviewers appreciated in *Wren to the Rescue,* including an action-packed plot set in a well-realized fantasy world populated by interesting characters. In this story, Wren seeks clues to the identity of her parents and begins learning more about her magical powers with the help of Tyron, while Princess Tess becomes involved in the mysterious troubles that have been plaguing the palace court. In the *Voice of Youth Advocates,* Lucinda Deatsman noted Smith's effective inclusion of magical elements, including commentary on the ethics of its use, and predicted that young readers will identify with Smith's "typical" teen characters. Deatsman concluded by suggesting that both *Wren to the Rescue* and *Wren's Quest* would "be popular with students and adults."

Wren's War, the third volume in the series, begins with the murder of Tess's royal parents. Now the princess must take on the role of the ruler of her nation, and she relies on Wren, Tyron, and Connor to keep her enemies at bay. "Readers will enjoy the fast-paced plot, but the novel's greatest strength is the subtle portrayal of its characters," wrote *Booklist* contributor Carolyn Phelan in a review of *Wren's War,* while in *Horn Book* Peter D. Sieruta complimented Smith's "richly worded descriptions."

Smith's novels *Crown Duel* and *Court Duel* originally shared the setting of the "Wren" books, but they were later rewritten to reflect their new setting of Sartorias-Deles. In 2002, the books were republished with added scenes in a single volume, *Crown Duel.* The heroine of *Crown Duel* is Meliara "Mel" Astair, the young and prickly countess of Tlanth, who is "one tough cookie in a land where women and girls fight, spy, run companies of military guards, and battle with short swords," according to a *Publishers Weekly* reviewer. The story begins with Mel and her brother Bran leading a revolution against an unjust ruler. When Mel is captured, she finds herself in the hands of Vidanric, Marquis of Shevraeth, a man she believes to be an enemy and the leader of the corrupt king's forces. There is more to Shevraeth than meets the eye, however, and more political maneuverings are in the works than Mel and Bran had realized. Phelan noted that the plot of *Crown Duel* relies "less on magical elements than in the 'Wren' trilogy." As the story continues, Mel navigates the dangers of the royal court, and finds them more treacherous than the battlefield. She is "constantly trying to tell friends from enemies as she endeavors to learn the subtle language of [her] courtiers," Phelan wrote in *Booklist.* Rich Horton reviewed the originally published pair for *SF Site,* writing: "Both these books are . . . great reads. . . . They are nice formal contrasts: the first almost all action and war, the second more magic and formal court life."

After a gap of several years, *Inda,* Smith's first adult novel to be in Sartorias-Deles, was published. The title character, who is the second son of a noble family in Marloven Hess, is summoned to military training, which had previously been reserved for the eldest sons, who are responsible for teaching their younger siblings. The heir prince has been unwilling to train his younger brother, however, so Inda and his peers become the first class of second sons to train in the royal capital. There the boy learns that the war games at which he has always excelled do not always follow the rules of honor, and he is betrayed, then forced to live away from his homeland.

The Fox picks up where *Inda* left off. Here Inda and his friends in exile have been captured by pirates and must now find a way to escape. Fortunately, the boy discovers two other Marlovens among the crew: Barend, the prince's cousin, and Fox, scion of an exiled noble house. The three plot together to overthrow the pirate who has captured them, and after taking his ship, they turn their attentions to hunting the pirates that still plague the coast. Their actions earn them the attention of some very powerful potential allies, including a mage who warns them of a great threat against Marloven Hess from the dark land of Norsunder. "*The Fox*, second in a brilliant, multi-layered series, is filled with thrilling action on land and at sea, captures and escapes, betrayals and treachery, and even some romance for its beleaguered leads," wrote Hilary Williamson in her *BookLoons* online review. Inda's story continues in *The King's Shield* and *Treason's Shore*.

The young-adult novel *Senrid* takes place in the same nation that serves as the setting of the "Inda" books, but it takes place many years later, when the boy-king Senrid of Marloven Hess seeks to conquer an adjoining kingdom in order to wrest control of his nation from his uncle. Bridging the story between *Sendrid* and *Crown Duel, A Stranger to Command* focuses on Vidanric of Shevraeth's training at the court of Marloven Hess. Sent away from home in secret, in order to avoid alerting the king to Shevraeth's true intentions, Shevraeth studies the art of war so that one day, he and his family can challenge the corrupt king. Marloven Hess is not itself at peace, however, and the young ruler Senrid knows that the land of Norsunder threatens his kingdom with powerful, dark magic. *BookLoons* critic Hilary Williamson called *A Stranger to Command* "an engaging prequel to Sherwood Smith's excellent and fast-paced *Crown Duel*."

While expanding her "Sartorias-Delos" books, Smith has also continued to write in Wren's world. *A Posse of Princesses* is the story of teenage Princess Rhis, who, along with the other young princes and princesses in her part of the world, is invited to the coming-of-age celebration for the Crown Prince Lios. When one of the other princesses is kidnapped, Rhis is determined to bring her back, and several of the other princesses join her. Along the way, Rhis discovers that she is attracted not to a prince, but to Lios's scribe. "Smith's humorous narrative, colorful descriptions of palace life, and fully realized characters will appeal to romance and fantasy buffs alike," predicted *School Library Journal* contributor Leah J. Sparks.

Along with her independent novels, Smith has also teamed up with other authors and contributed to expand ongoing novel series based on television shows. With André Norton, she wrote the "Solar Queen" and "Time Traders" novels, continuations of a series of books that stretch back to the 1950s. One entry, *A Mind for Trade,* was hailed by a *Publishers Weekly* reviewer as a worthy successor to the classic older tales in which the two au-

thors merge "their styles seamlessly." Smith also contributed two novels as tie-ins to television series created by Gene Roddenberry. In *Gene Roddenberry's Andromeda: Paradise Drift,* a *Kirkus Reviews* contributor felt, "one can practically hear Kevin Sorbo's voice when reading Hunt's dialogue." Smith has also written two novels continuing L. Frank Baum's "Oz" series. Elizabeth Bird of *School Library Journal,* in a review of *Trouble under Oz,* wrote, "The book's tone and content are faithful to L. Frank Baum's vision."

Biographical and Critical Sources

PERIODICALS

Analog Science Fiction & Fact, April, 2000, Tom Easton, review of *Echoes in Time,* p. 135.
Booklist, March 1, 1995, Carolyn Phelan, review of *Wren's War,* p. 1241; February 1, 1997, Roland Green, review of *Derelict for Trade,* p. 929; April 15, 1997, Carolyn Phelan, review of *Crown Duel,* p. 1430; October 1, 1997, Roland Green, review of *A Mind for Trade,* p. 312; March 1, 1998, Carolyn Phelan, review of *Court Duel,* p. 136; November 15, 1999, Roland Green, review of *Echoes in Time,* p. 609; September 15, 2001, Regina Schroeder, review of *Gene Roddenberry's Earth: Final Conflict—Augur's Teacher,* p. 201; December 15, 2002, Roland Green, review of *Atlantis Endgame,* p. 740; November 15, 2005, review of *Gene Roddenberry's Andromeda: Paradise Drift,* p. 34.
Horn Book, March-April, 1991, Ann A. Flowers, review of *Wren to the Rescue,* p. 202; September-October, 1995, review of *Wren's War,* p. 627.
Kirkus Reviews, November 15, 2002, review of *Atlantis Endgame,* p. 1664; September 15, 2005, review of *Gene Roddenberry's Andromeda: Paradise Drift,* p. 1006.
Library Journal, December, 1996, Susan Hamburger, review of *Derelict for Trade,* p. 152; October 15, 1997, Susan Hamburger, review of *A Mind for Trade,* p. 98; December, 1999, Jackie Cassada, review of *Echoes in Time,* p. 193; January, 2003, Jackie Cassada, review of *Atlantis Endgame,* p. 165.
New York Review of Science Fiction, February, 2002, review of *Gene Roddenberry's Earth: Final Conflict.*
Publishers Weekly, January 27, 1997, review of *Derelict for Trade,* p. 82; March 10, 1997, review of *Crown Duel,* p. 67; September 29, 1997, review of *A Mind for Trade,* p. 71; October 25, 1999, review of *Echoes in Time,* p. 56; October 8, 2001, review of *Gene Roddenberry's Earth,* p. 49; December 2, 2002, review of *Atlantis Endgame,* p. 38; July 16, 2007, review of *The Fox,* p. 151.
School Library Journal, November, 1990, Carol A. Edwards, review of *Wren to the Rescue,* p. 140; June, 1993, Patricia A. Dollisch, review of *Wren's Quest,* pp. 110, 112; August, 1997, Patricia Lothrop-Green, review of *Crown Duel,* p. 158; April, 1998, Eva Mitnick, review of *Court Duel,* p. 138; December, 2006, Elizabeth Bird, review of *Trouble under Oz,* p. 155; April, 2008, Leah J. Sparks, review of *A Posse of Princesses,* p. 148.

Voice of Youth Advocates, December, 1990, Lesa M. Holstine, review of *Wren to the Rescue,* p. 302; June, 1993, Lucinda Deatsman, review of *Wren's Quest,* p. 105; April, 1996, review of *Wren's War,* p. 23.

ONLINE

BookLoons Web site, http://www.bookloons.com/ (March 2, 2009), Hilary Williamson, reviews of *A Stranger to Command* and *The Fox.*

GoodReads.com, http://www.goodreads.com/ (March 2, 2009), profile of Smith.

Internet Speculative Fiction Database, http://www.isfdb.org/ (March 6, 2009), profile of Smith.

SF Site, http://www.sfsite.com/ (March 2, 2009), Rich Horton, reviews of *Crown Duel* and *Court Duel*; George T. Dodd, review of *A Posse of Princesses.*

Sherwood Smith Home Page, http://www.sherwoodsmith.net (March 6, 2009).

Autobiography Feature

Sherwood Smith

S herwood Smith contributed the following autobiographical essay to *SATA:*

Sometimes I wonder if being born in the middle of a population boom in a city that was already overcrowded shaped my cravings for adventure and individuality.

Or was it genetic?

My grandfather, Charles Smith, was a minor set designer in the film industry. On his brief visits to my father when he was a boy, he'd be driving a convertible and smoking a big cigar. My great-grandfather, John William Carlson, used to write and direct homemade plays on their farm near Red Wing, Minnesota, when work was done. He also painted pictures, and (this ability I didn't inherit) he had such a beautiful voice, he was in demand to sing at all the local weddings and funerals.

My grandmothers both had to make cross-country journeys, one just as the Great Depression of the 1930s began, the other in the middle. My father's mother was abandoned by her husband just after she got pregnant with my father. She was alone in Long Beach, California, but her in-laws refused to give my grandmother and her two daughters a home. She sat on a bus bench crying. A woman passing by took pity on her and offered her a place to stay; she eventually got work as an insurance adjuster and settled in a tiny house in Long Beach until the '32 quake brought the houses down on Signal Hill, after which she moved up to the valley.

My mother's mother had been kicked out of her house at age twelve because the man my widowed great-grandmother was going to marry in order to save her farm refused to have any girls cluttering it up. The two youngest stayed with relatives. My grandmother and her older sister, twelve and fourteen, had to go to work. After two years of being a housekeeper/cook/laundrymaid (no washing machines in those days) for a dollar a week, she and her sister hitch-hiked to Minneapolis and got jobs as waitresses. When my grandmother was seventeen, she married, thinking that good looks and attraction were love. He was so violent and abusive that she left him, and when he retaliated by putting my mom and her brother in an orphanage in Chicago (where they promptly escaped and made their way back to Minneapolis on a train, my seven-year-old mother getting them free rides from kind conductors), my grandmother

decided she had to get herself and the kids away. Some movie star had bought a luxury car for cheap in Detroit, but didn't want to drive it to California, so she and two friends who hoped to make it in Hollywood (they didn't, but they married men who did) crossed country in that fancy car, and arrived penniless. When the two friends started the rounds of casting offices, my grandmother got work as a waitress, and soon brought her kids out.

Both grandmothers thus came to California, in those days considered the land of adventure and dreams. Crossing the country without any money during those tumultuous days had a tremendous effect, and they told stories about it, which I grew up hearing.

The Fifties in West L.A.

I was born May 28, 1951, at the height of the Baby Boom. My parents settled in Westchester, a community on the west side of Los Angeles that would later be

Smith, dressed as a gypsy dancer, 1974 (Photo courtesy of Sherwood Smith.)

overshadowed by LAX. In those days there were no superstores. Milk was delivered by the milkman in glass bottles. There was a bread truck as well—the Helms Bakery. My mother felt that their bread and cakes were too expensive—a whole quarter for their chocolate-covered brownies, which were the best I have ever tasted—but we kids loved the wonderful smell of the baked goods, all kept in these long sliding drawers made of fine wood. Less pleasant was the garbage truck once a week, stinking for half a block away, the cans during the many months of summer usually crawling with maggots.

In the fifties, the smog over Los Angeles was profoundly bad. Cars emitted great belching clouds, and people burned their trash in backyard incinerators. My grandmother lived about five miles from the San Gabriel Mountains, but there was no sign of them from her house. One Christmas, when I was about eight, the infrequent rains came early enough that the air cleared, and suddenly there were these enormous mountains looming over us directly to the north. I was terrified, wondering how they'd leaped up so suddenly. On the smoggiest days we still ran and played, but it was difficult to breathe—the sensation was like having a tennis ball stuck in your chest right below your collarbones. Westport Heights, my school, had no grass, except a small patch in front of the office that we were not allowed to walk on. In those days, modern schools were covered with blacktop, and had no trees. When the weather was hottest, the blacktop stuck to the bottoms of your shoes. There was no air conditioning, so you got used to sweat running down into your socks during the autumn months, when the long Southern California summer is the fiercest.

My craving for greenery was profound, and my love of the rare cloudy or rainy days intense. How I loved rain! The smell of wet grass and trees, the puddles reflecting the sky and looking like mystery gates to the Upside Down World. The world was green and fresh after rain—though the price was sometimes lightning and thunder, which made me sick with terror. I still don't like strobing lights, or sudden loud noises: on my first birthday, a neighbor child popped a balloon in my face, something I can still remember, though only in brief flickers.

During the 1950s schools were overflowing. At mine there were close to forty in each class. More, at some schools, and those numbers would swell as my siblings reached the age of enrollment. Westport Heights, like many, had World War II bungalows set up as temporary classrooms, which took up some of the blacktop out by the cafeteria. Lunches at the cafeteria were thirty-five cents, so we ate there very rarely. On Fridays, sometimes, the duty teacher would make us sit in silence during lunch while an ancient, scratchy Victrola played patriotic marches.

We had bomb drills often. Why did they bother having us drop, duck, and cover in the event of an atomic bomb

Smith in first grade, with Mrs. Kelly and Mrs. Rees (Photo courtesy of Sherwood Smith.)

being dropped on us by the Russians? Every Friday the air-raid sirens went off, and we had a routine for those, too. There was a great deal of earnest talk about the dangers of communism and the importance of patriotism in those days. Our history books were full of facts about exports and imports, America's endless resources, and how we had never caused a war. The Founding Fathers were all in agreement, and Manifest Destiny was a laudable national goal. But along with that was the atmosphere of fear—that the "Commies" would send atom bombs at any time.

In 1957, when I was in first grade, the entire school was summoned out onto the blacktop, where we stood in rows while the principal, an elderly lady named Mrs. Kelly, told us in a low, serious voice that the Russians had just launched a Sputnik, which was a terrible danger to the United States. I didn't understand anything else she said. What I do remember is the sick terror of helplessness. I stooped forward a little, ready for the command to drop and cover right outside on the blacktop, in case this "Sputnik" was about to shoot bombs down on Los Angeles.

For several years the U.S. space program, science fiction, and horror were inextricably intertwined in my mind, fueled by the cheesy monster flicks of that time.

When our babysitter took us to the movies, as sometimes happened (you got a color movie, a black-and-white movie, and a half hour of cartoons between them for your fifty cents in those days), I believed the monsters were real, and those terrorized me as much as the bomb talk. I finally learned to leave and sit in the restroom for the remainder of the movie, or I'd walk along the lobby, where they had photos of all the Academy Award winners to date. I liked starting at the beginning, gazing at the peculiar clothes of the earliest winners, then progressing up to the color pictures in more modern times. I often paused at Shirley Temple, the only girl, and wondered what she was thinking.

My family was typical for the time: I was the eldest of three kids, which became four when I was twelve. When I was a teen, the existence of half-siblings was revealed to us (back then divorce, though very common and rapidly becoming more so, carried a stigma for women), and shortly thereafter step-siblings joined what became a very large extended family.

In those days, nobody was driven to school. We all walked, sometimes alone and in the dark after five p.m., when we were kept after school to write 500 sentences as a punishment for talking in class. In fact, at age seven and eight I took the bus alone (with a two-mile walk at either end) into a fairly dangerous part of L.A. to visit the orthodontist to have my overbite fixed. That's not to say there weren't dangers. The man two houses down attacked a little girl across the street, and my sister, age six, had to go to court to testify. But parents just weren't as protective as most urban parents are now.

My father had set a rule that we were not permitted to cross the street, but as my mother regularly sent me about a mile away to the grocery store with my Little Red Wagon to buy the family groceries for the week and haul it all home, we kids ignored this rule when he was safely gone. The grocery people knew me—I started doing this chore at age seven—and charged the food. They even tucked my parents' cigarette cartons into the grocery bags, although the law forbade selling cigarettes to anyone under sixteen.

From a very early age we were aware that there were two sets of rules for just about every situation: how you behaved at home and away from home, different rules for boys and for girls, rules for how the teenage girls would get boys to go steady and then to pin them, which was supposed to lead to a marriage proposal by Senior Prom in high school. (Basically, hide your brains and never let him see you without full makeup and perfect hair.) I resisted those double rules with all my strength. I hated the "you do what I say, not what I do" double-standard that seemed to prevail at every level of life. Though my sister and brother and I bathed together once a week, on Saturdays (which was also common for that time), I saw no meaningful difference between boys and girls, so why should boys get to play Little

League, and girls could only keep score, or sell hot dogs? Why should boys get to wear pants to school, and girls had to wear dresses, so when you fell, the blacktop scraped off the top layer of skin, mixing bits of black tar into the torn flesh? And in adventure stories, why, why, *why* did boys get to go away to adventure, but girls had to stay home cooking and sewing and waiting for marriage?

In my best friend's family, the girls were not permitted to wear pants or shorts, because proper ladies did not own such garments, with the result that the girls were climbing and jumping and running with their skirts flying up all the time. Not that anyone cared, once they'd screamed "I see London, I see France, I see someone's underpants!" after the first few dozen times, and the girls just shrugged. That mother despised my sister and me for not being ladylike because we wore shorts in summer and pedal pushers in winter, but her daughters were the wildest and most fearless on our block.

Kid Life on Our Block

The independence in getting around, and the double-standard and draconian punishments that were common then (but would be considered child abuse now), meant that we didn't tell adults anything if we could possibly help it. We had a different existence from the adults, especially as the moms (who were mostly housewives

"Here's my best pal before we moved, the one I played 'Spy vs. Spy' with, and the Princess Game, and did shows with . . ." (Photo courtesy of Sherwood Smith.)

back then) pretty much turned us loose all day when we were not in school. Even if we went on vacation for a week, as most middle-class (and working-class-trying-to-be-middle-class) families did in those days, kids and adults had separate activities.

When I wasn't reading, I was out of the house playing. In fact my mother used to lock us out when she wanted peace and quiet. There was this firm belief that sunshine was good for kids, the more the better. With those two sisters I mentioned above, my sister and I used to swing by our hands up on the six-to-eight-foot-high T-bars that held the laundry lines and drop onto the six-foot-high cement fences that ran between the houses. We would run on those narrow walls at top speed, and sometimes we'd leap onto garage roofs to hide during our long, complicated games.

My friends and I used to organize games that were different from the street baseball and hopscotch and relay tag common at the time. One game was Spy vs. Spy, the name coming from the comic in *Mad Magazine*. This was basically team hide and seek, complete with taking and guarding prisoners, secret hideouts, and the like. We played this when the boys joined us, which they sometimes did. We created a code and wrote secret messages to one another, leaving the papers in the bricks.

Then there was the Princess game. The four of us girls found cast-off cocktail dresses in one garage, with long filmy skirts that flared out most satisfyingly. We put these on over our clothes and played what now would be called RPGs—Role Playing Games—in which the walls and garage roofs and trees became castles, dungeons, and robber-infested roads. Our princesses were chased by bad guys and had to escape the direful commands of a wicked queen in order to find true love. We were hazy on the true love, except that it meant putting on a crown I'd made out of tin foil, and being the cynosure of all eyes at a wedding ceremony that was also a coronation.

Sometimes we put on shows for the local kids. Since none of us took lessons in anything, our singing and dancing was mostly copied from watching Saturday Morning shows, specifically *The Little Rascals*. Ballet was tough to emulate, but tap dancing seemed easy enough, and I experimented with crushing a tin can so that the top and bottom hugged the sides of my sneakers in order to make taps.

Role-playing, Lying, and Stories

There are things that I loved with passionate intensity at first encounter. Light filtering through forest green, long beautiful gowns, long hair, classical music. Though the prelude to the musical *Carousel*, when I first heard it, gave me that same bone-firing thrill that I got on my first hearing of Schubert's *Unfinished Symphony*, my

Smith, the year of the polio shot. "The photographer had popped some kind of loud noise on the practice picture, I guess to make us laugh, but I was so scared I kept putting my fingers in my ears, got yelled at, and so braced for more noise. (I vaguely remember him saying he wouldn't do it again, but who believed adults?) That's me, cringing up at the extreme top left." (Photo courtesy of Sherwood Smith.)

access to classical music was confined to brief, rare glimpses as my dad only listened to jazz, and no one was permitted to touch his home-built stereo. But cartoons sometimes had classical music, and at school the teachers occasionally played the more accessible classics, between the bouts of scratchy patriotic 78 rpm John Phillip Sousa marches.

I craved these things—music, beauty, cool greenery—with a hunger that no one else seemed to feel, or at least to express. I remember being taken to see Disney's *Peter Pan* when I was about five, and how I sobbed at the tragic ending! My mother scolded me, of course—I shouldn't act like a baby, what was wrong with me? I couldn't explain how horrible it was that Wendy, John, and Michael were forced back to a mundane life, when they could have stayed with Peter and had fun forever! I looked around the cinema, which in those days had velvet curtains and upholstered seats, where hundreds of kids were yelling, hopping, throwing popcorn boxes, poking one another, or racing up and down the aisles, just like they did at school. Like the movie was forgotten. Didn't anyone wish with all their being to be back in Neverland?

When I was five, another thing happened that had a profound effect on me. I had learned to read at a very early age. I can remember pestering my mother to tell me what this or that word was long before I went to school, and being told to sound it out. What did that mean? I'd spell it as fast as I could, and when that didn't work, I'd puzzle it out from context.

So when our teacher, Mrs. Darling (yes, that really was her name), sent us home with a yellow paper that must go to the parents, I was suspicious. The bigger kids acted strange about that yellow paper, which made me worry, so I did my best to read it. I couldn't quite understand what it was about, but the tone of what I did get made me anxious.

The next day, when Mrs. Darling lined us up and walked us down to the bungalows beside the cafeteria, my anxiety ramped steadily, spiking into terror when I saw some of the big kids—second and third graders—crying. The kids were lined up before the steps up to the doors of the two bungalow classrooms. Just inside each doorway was a little table full of hypodermic needles. Nurses in white starched uniforms swiped alcohol onto kids' arms, then jabbed in the needles! Then the kids had to go get back into line! When I saw a boy with blood on his arm, I slipped away from my class and escaped.

My father had been raised a Christian Scientist, so we kids had never had any shots. In those days, you didn't have to have them to go to school, like now. This was the height of the great polio epidemic, however, and people all over Southern California were emptying swimming pools. (Since no one I knew had a pool, this did not affect us.) I didn't know any of that at the time—adults seldom told kids the why of anything; we mostly heard, "Do what I tell you, and stop whining, or I'll give you something to whine about," and out would come the belt.

I ran back toward the classroom, but realized that Mrs. Darling would come looking for me there. So I swerved and hid in the auditorium, cowering in the area adjacent to the stage. Before too long I heard my name being called, but I did not respond until I recognized the voice of the principal. Oh no! We all believed that Mrs. Kelly had X-ray vision and superpowers, so I had to surrender. I crept out, crying so hard I couldn't breathe. She scolded me, but I didn't get the shots—and what's more, I didn't get into trouble at home. (I suspect my mother had signed the permission form without my father knowing.) In those days, kids who got in trouble at school would very often get punished again at home a second time.

From then on I was convinced that adults could not be trusted.

In first grade, since I was already reading, the teacher, Mrs. Fitzgerald, let me draw while the rest of the kids learned the alphabet and worked through phonics, then words. I joined the reading groups when we finally be-

One of Smith's drawings, 1964. (Photo courtesy of Sherwood Smith.)

gan on a book, though I was frequently so bored (having already read ahead) that I often missed my sentence, as I'd daydream while kids struggled painfully word by word. Once I counted sentences ahead, memorized mine, and recited it, but Mrs. Fitzgerald (who was a wonderful, patient woman—but rules were rules) scolded me for not *reading* it.

Anyway, I loved those times when I was left to myself to draw and imagine stories. I can still recall my favorite picture. I'd draw a swing set next to a tree with great reaching branches. Then I'd draw children flying back and forth from the swings to the tree. The teachers never liked this drawing—they always threw those away, and saved only the *proper* pictures of children playing ball and jumping rope and doing normal things—conformist things. But I wanted to fly, I wanted to experience adventure, and above all, I wanted to be someone more interesting than I was. A princess would be fine, if that meant wearing a crown, getting to have long hair and pretty gowns, and to live in a beautiful castle, preferably with a forest nearby. The handsome prince was only interesting insofar as he came equipped with crowns, castles, and courtiers.

School social dynamics began early. In first grade there was a girl leader named Susan. The chief thing I remember about Susan that year was that she not only picked the games (if we got to choose, mostly we were assigned), but she also bossed her followers at drawing time. Susan liked the girls at our table—the class was divided into three long tables—to pick up their crayon when she did, including the same color, and draw the exact same thing she did, stroke for stroke. She too had a favorite picture. Hers was a girl standing next to tulips, with a lollipop tree nearby. I loathed lollipop trees. I wanted branches. A few times I tried to gain Susan's approval by copying this boring picture along with the others, but her faint approval for my conformity never lasted long, and I'd go right back to my flying children.

The next year, Susan was once again the leader, and most definitely teacher's pet. But she had to leave mid-semester. Mrs. Lassen not only gave Susan a big going-away party, she required us to write letters to tell Susan how much we missed her. I got a visceral lesson in hypocrisy through that experience, when I designed and made a decorative card full of smarmy "We miss you!" messages that was generally admired, though in my heart I was so glad to be rid of Miss Perfect Susan. When Mrs. Lassen later brought her back to visit us, I fawned on her like the rest of the girls, in an effort to fit in, but Susan ignored me as thoroughly as she had when she'd been among us. This would characterize my occasional attempts to follow the crowd and fit in, which never quite worked—most of the time I was that annoying girl who talked too much, who was too full of wild stories.

In those days I mixed story-telling with role playing and outright lies in an effort to make myself and my world more interesting. Sometimes I'd try Hayley Mills's accent. (She was a British kid actor who showed up in a lot of Disney flicks.) But I soon learned that people questioned you, and you had to make up more lies to support the first ones. And more lies after that. And sometimes, if I tried to change my expression to what I imagined was heroine-like, people asked me if I was sick. My classmates thought I was definitely weird.

Lies got me into big trouble twice in first grade.

The first one was at semester break. The teacher sent home our first report card. I opened and read it on the way home, and though my marks were fairly good—plenty of checks in the A column, there were too many in the B column, and I thought I deserved far more A's. So when I got home I didn't give it to my mother. I sneaked it to the room I shared with my sister, got out the white crayon, and scribbled out the teacher's marks. Then I searched through my mother's stuff drawer in the alcove where the phone was kept, between the kitchen and the living room. When I found a ballpoint

pen whose ink matched the teacher's, I redid my report card. I gave myself a couple of A minuses (a check mark near the dividing line between the A and B column) for verisimilitude, then gave that to my mom.

In the middle of class the next day, I was summoned to the principal's office! I walked alone to the office as to an execution, for the fourth graders had assured us that Mrs. Kelly kept a spanking machine in her office closet. Now, in those days, spanking was common and not just with hands, but hairbrushes, or (like in our house) wire hangers and belts. Some families used paddles. So this was a fear-raising threat.

Well, Mrs. Kelly sat me down in her office and asked what happened to my report card, and I lied like a rug. I didn't know—my mom did it—my five-year-old brother did it—finally I broke down and confessed, but by then I was sick with terror, and when she rather crossly told me to get control of myself, I howled, "Are you going to put me on the spanking machine?" She said, "The *what?*" When I gasped and gobbled out what the big kids had told us, she yanked open her closet, and there was an umbrella on a hook, rubber galoshes below, and a coat on a hanger. Nothing else.

I still have most of my report cards, and in huge letters on the back of that one someone printed in huge letters DUPLICATE COPY.

One of Smith's report cards, marked DUPLICATE. (Photo courtesy of Sherwood Smith.)

You'd think I'd learned my lesson about lying—and about being lied to. No, not me! Along comes May. Each week, a kid got to be line leader. My time had already gone, and when the teacher told us how many more weeks of school we had until summer, I realized that though the kids whose last names began at the front of the alphabet were going to get a second chance, I wouldn't. I couldn't stand that! Being line leader not only meant going first, but you didn't have to wait forever for the line in front to shuffle along, and no one could pinch or kick or shove you. Best of all, no bigger or more popular kid could ram you back behind them as they cut in front of you.

Another thing about May was that we'd had an entire school year in which all those kids had had birthdays. That meant getting to stand up and talk about what you did at home for your birthday. There were no parties for kids at school. Well, early in May, a girl stood up and talked about her birthday the day before, and the presents she got. Her celebration and gifts weren't anything special, but I was so jealous—and I think still angry about not being line leader—that I jumped up from my chair and announced, "It was my birthday, too!"

Mrs. Fitzgerald was middle-aged, long-experienced, patient, and mild. How I respect her, looking back! At the time, the entire class stared at me, and she just said, "It was? Tell us about it!" So I did—and hoo boy, the presents I gave myself! The only two I remember now were a color television (something I'd heard about, but no one I knew had one, and our family would not get one until 1969) and a radio! Wow, were those kids impressed! I sat down again, and it felt great to get all that attention!

"*Here's that birthday party I got when I turned seven, after my big lie. The only such party I ever got! I don't think they got all the girls in, but there's me in the sailor dress I thoroughly loathed, but that was my one party/holiday dress until I finally outgrew it a year or so later.*"
(Photo courtesy of Sherwood Smith.)

Nobody said anything to me. But two weeks later, just before my real birthday, my mother sent me to school with party invitations for all the girls. This was how it was done then—if everybody was invited, you could hand out invitations at school. And now I was the party girl, handing out twenty-eight invitations! The girls were to follow me home after school that Friday.

I remember running at the head of the pack, screaming as loud as I could for sheer joy. Then one girl ran alongside me, and asked, "Why didn't you have this party when you had your birthday?"

"Oh, it was because my mother burned her hands pouring coffee," I said, inventing on the spot. The girl shrugged and accepted it. No one said anything more, including the adults. The kids didn't really care, and I guess the adults thought I'd learned my lesson about lying. The ironic thing is, this was the only time I ever had a party with that many guests, and all to myself. Before, and after, my sister's and my parties were celebrated together, as our birthdays were two days apart, and we would each be permitted to have one, maybe two girls at most.

What I learned about lying was not the lesson that I was expected to learn. Adults lied all the time, but no one would punish them, so in part the lesson was about control, not about telling the truth. More than that, the anxious moments convinced me that just because I wished for something didn't mean I could make it real. The only way I could make things real was by stories, first drawing them out in cartoon form, and then, at last, by writing them.

Role-playing was safer than lying, and gave me the chance to pretend to be something, yet get real reactions from people. There were three places I could take on roles and be someone else: YMCA summer camp, the municipal park, where mom would drop us off and pick us up at five, and on the weekends my dad took us to Topanga Canyon.

Topanga Canyon is located up in the hills behind Malibu, and you got there on a twisty, turny road that made me horribly car sick, though it was worth it when the ride was over. At the time we thought we made these visits every other weekend or so because the fathers were friends. That was partly true, but we discovered when we were teens that the oldest daughter was actually our half-sister. In those days, no one talked about divorce, though as the years went by, it became more and more common in every family we knew. Including ours.

Topanga Canyon fired my craving for forest greenery. Huge spreading California black oaks filtered the sunlight, creating cool, greeny shadows. Tall, whispering eucalyptus scented the air that was already heady with the fragrances of grass and wildflowers and berry bushes. The kids our age in the other family ran free and unsupervised. Over the several years we visited there, they built an underground house (it collapsed, luckily when the kids weren't in it), a tree house up over a stream (a boy fell off and broke his leg), and they made trails all up and down the hillside, often through poison oak and ivy (I got it once, and my siblings a couple of times apiece). We played all kinds of games, sometimes story games when I could get my ideas in. With their friends, I could play roles, take on accents, and be as weird as I wanted, as there was so little communication between the kid and adult worlds, unless someone got into trouble with other adults.

At the municipal park, my sister and I often pretended we were rich girls slumming—aliens—telepathic—from a foreign country (we talked gibberish, making gestures as if we understood one another)—blind and deaf, and other kids either accepted it or went along with it. It never occurred to me that faking a handicap was reprehensible, though I didn't do it for pity, I did it to be interesting, or to experience the world in a different way. My "blindness" experiment only happened once, when I smeared some candy on my eyelashes to keep me from inadvertently opening my eyes. I don't remember anything about the kids I fooled that day. What I do remember is how horrible my eyes felt—and how very difficult it was to negotiate the restroom. My appreciation for how the blind navigate a seeing world lingered, so that, years later, I volunteered to drive kids from Junior Blind to events that they couldn't get to otherwise. Experiencing how they did their Christmas shopping was a lesson in paying attention to the other senses.

During this time—when I was ten and eleven—I began two long stories. One was meant to please the adults who did their best to discourage fantasy and imagination. It was called "Twins' Triumph." When I say that it was a baseball novel and that the twins were a boy and a girl, the plot will be obvious. But before the girl could masquerade as her brother and pitch the winning game (which would be the climax), I got wound up in writing about classroom politics. I was some eighty pages into it, and still caught in a morass of clashing girl groups and their interactions with the boys, with baseball games appearing with increasing rarity. Then my mother went on one of her cleaning rampages. She found the blue plastic notebook containing this story stuffed in the piano bench with a lot of other drawings and paper, and into the trash it all went. So much for writing what "They" wanted to read!

The other novel I began was a story about CJ and Clair in the land of the Mearsies, but the thought of anyone finding that one was so horrible that I threw it away myself, and resorted to drawing the stories in cartoon form, then ripping them up as soon as I'd reached the end. I didn't start writing stories to keep until I began junior high and had a locker to hide them in.

As classes moved toward sixth grade and graduation, I often stayed for the after-school playground. The district hired a young college student to be our coach, and sometimes there were other high school or college students who offered clubs and classes. The clubs I loved most were art and drama. In the latter, I got to play roles! That club was run by a young female college student who I suspect now knew little about drama. She did not teach us anything about moving on stage, and we made up our own plays. But I loved that aspect—and here, at last, I wasn't too weird or too wild. The others loved my imaginative additions to our plays, and I got to act.

The only problem was when we developed a play around Cinderella. I thought of plenty of business for all the other characters, but I really wanted to be chosen to act the part of Cinderella. I was even a good prince, as I'd picked up waltzing (sort of) from old movies, and that was pretty much all he had to do. Since we were all girls in that club, nobody particularly cared much about the prince—he was just there to bring Cinderella to her triumphant ending. Everyone thought I was a fabulous wicked stepmother, and great as either of the nasty sisters, but oh, I so wanted to be Cinderella—my image being Disney's cartoon, of course.

So I guess I must have whined and moaned about it enough that one afternoon our club leader said I could play Cinderella. Oh, how thrilled I was! I swanned about with my eyes half closed, talking in what I thought was a sweet, soft voice. In truth I must have looked like I'd been hit over the head with a mallet, and I suspect no one could hear my "sweet" voice, because the play was flat—I could feel it falling apart around me before we even got to the invitations to the ball. The girl playing the stepmother was boring: she couldn't come up with commands for Cinderella, or cues for the step-sisters to react to. All of us, including me, knew it wasn't any good. About halfway through I said something, I don't remember what, but I do remember everyone clapped, and we went right back to our usual roles. This time I took on the wicked stepmother with verve and conviction, and ever afterward, I embraced character roles rather than wanting to be the star.

That brings me to 1963. Several things happened that had an enormous effect on me.

That summer, when I graduated from sixth grade, our parents announced that a new baby was coming along, so we'd have to move. We girls would still be stuck sharing a room, as our dad felt that girls did not need separate bedrooms, but we'd have a larger house with a room for the baby. This house would have a den—a converted garage. It was on the other side of Westchester, directly adjacent to the flight path of LAX, so we got used to the roar of planes every few minutes. (In later years, when the 747s began flying, the roar every three minutes or so during peak hours was so loud that

Smith at camp, the year of the Beatles talent show. Smith is in the center; one of her fellow Beatles is seated to her right. (Photo courtesy of Sherwood Smith.)

one got used to watching the mouths of characters on TV and having the windows rattle and dishes clatter in the cupboards.)

That summer, when my sister and I were sent to YMCA summer camp for a week, the parents would be organizing the move to the new house. At that point I had never actually heard the Beatles. Music was not nearly as ubiquitous then as it is now. Only the wealthiest teenagers had transistor radios, which emitted a tinny sound that did not reach far. Radios had to be plugged in. And my dad had absolutely forbidden us to touch the radio, stereo, or TV. We watched what he wanted to watch on our black-and-white TV, the radio was reserved for ball games or the races, and that was that. But I longed to be cool, of course, and knowing the words to Beatles' songs gave kids tremendous cool points.

Toward the end of our week at camp there was to be a talent show. Of course I had to be in it. The question was, what role to play, since I didn't get to study dance or gymnastics or baton twirling? I got the great idea of getting together three other girls, combing our hair in front of our faces (because everybody commented on the Fab Four's incredibly long hair, which now looks conservative), borrow guitars from the counselors (many of whom were budding Joan Baezes) and I would write new and funny words to Beatles' tunes, since nobody among my fellow eleven-and twelve-year-olds knew much more than the first verse or so of any song. So *She was just seventeen, you know what I mean* became *She was just ninety-four, and shaped like a door, and before too long I barfed over he-er.* A counselor taught us how to strum the Beatles' signature chord, and we

rehearsed away from everyone else, in secret. I could hardly wait until the other kids heard my incredibly clever lyrics!

So the talent show goes on like talent shows do—lots of gym tricks and baton twirls and some tap dancing—all of which gets polite clapping. Then it's our turn. We quickly push our hair in front of our faces, take our guitars up, and we strum that chord—and the entire summer camp erupted *screaming*. When we began belting out our song, they heard just enough of the familiar melody to scream even louder.

They shouted and shrieked as we sang all the way to the end. My fellow Beatles are now hazy faces in my mind, and I just remember them staring in wide-eyed amazement. We'd sung as loud as we could, but our voices were utterly lost in that astounding roar of sound, and we were both exhilarated and a little frightened, because the screaming was so loud. It took a long time for the head counselor to get control, and for the rest of that night and until we left, girls I had never spoken to before came up and said, "Weren't you one of the Beatles?" I was famous. For one day I was famous, and it felt . . . *unreal.*

The last event of that time that affected me was the assassination of President Kennedy in November of 1963. The school's loudspeaker announced that he'd been shot, but was in surgery, and our classroom sat there, stunned. Our teacher—a man—was crying! Kids started whispering that the Russians would attack next, and back came that sick terror that I got when contemplating a world that made little sense, in which I was helpless to do anything. I think that drove me deeper into the story world, where kids could have agency.

Where *girls* could have agency.

Reading

By then I was a voracious reader, and the move to the new house meant I no longer had to rely on the tiny school library. My mom had hated driving to the main library, so I got to go rarely. Now there was a branch library in walking distance, next to the park where my sister and I used to play and assume our roles.

For the first two years, when I was twelve and thirteen, I worked through the entire kids' section, skipping stuff I knew I'd hate, like Talking Animal stories. I couldn't stand inconsistency in stories, I think because I was so visual. What I "saw" in the text had to make sense. My mother bought me *Alice in Wonderland* when I was ten, which I hated. It reminded me of the way I felt during high fevers. At the big birthday party I mentioned above, I was given three books: *Black Beauty, Andersen's Fairy Tales,* and the *Arabian Nights.* I had just turned seven when I worked through these, and I loved *Black Beauty,* though Ginger's fate made me sob my heart out. As I read Andersen's tales, I dreaded each new one, but kept hoping I'd find one I liked. Girls suffered so in them, no happy endings ever. There were some ridiculous stories, with relatively funny endings, but never for girls! The *Arabian Nights* fed my craving for magic, but the characters were incomprehensible— the romance in them completely escaped me.

I tried *Wind in the Willows* in fourth grade, because some girls had a secret *Wind in the Willows* society. I wanted to join. I always wanted to be accepted in any group, and these girls were the nicest in class. But I just could not get past a toad driving a car. I disliked whimsy, especially when it didn't make sense, and animals wearing clothes and making tea Did Not Make Sense. In *Black Beauty,* the horses had talked, but they didn't wear clothes or drive cars, and who was to say that neighing was not secret horse language? So as I prowled the library shelves, I skipped over a book called *The Hobbit* because of course it had to be about dressed up rabbits. I wouldn't read that until I was fourteen (and only because my friend who recommended *Lord of the Rings* insisted I read it first).

A Wrinkle in Time was the first book I read in junior high under cover of my desk. I'd done that a lot in elementary school, especially when Debbie, the rich girl, kindly brought all her Nancy Drews to school for me to read, one a day. I'd promised myself I'd pay attention in junior high, because the work would be hard at last— but it never was, except for algebra, which I flunked twice. I loved Meg in *A Wrinkle in Time* because she was nearsighted like me, and also a moody, impatient social reject like me.

Other books I loved? *Loretta Mason Potts,* by Mary Chase. I had not discovered Narnia then, and the idea of a secret door at the back of a closet was utterly

thrilling. And again, there was a bratty social reject girl to identify with. Sally Watson's *Witch of the Glens* and Eloise Jarvis McGraw's *Mara, Daughter of the Nile* gave me a craving for history. I also read every Rosemary Sutcliff the library had, but I was ambivalent about them: found them interesting but not as compelling as the above because there wasn't any humor, any panache. As books got grittier and more realistic in grim detail, I became more choosy. After I read *To Kill a Mockingbird* in seventh grade, I craved emotional verity, but I didn't want stories about horrible real life stuff that the characters couldn't fix, especially horrible stuff that I couldn't quite understand, such as what the trial was really about. And of course I dared not ask.

That incomprehensible horribleness spiked sharply when I discovered my dad's copy of *The Carpetbaggers* on the shelf. I'm sure if he'd known I was reading it I would have been forbidden, and I wished I had been! That book hurt so deeply, especially as I couldn't understand the motivation behind the mutilation/suicide of one character, but in those days, girls were supposed to be ladylike, which meant innocent, which meant ignorant, so asking certain kinds of questions would get you punished horribly—and you wouldn't even know why.

My encounter with *The Carpetbaggers* made me realize that adult books could be as little trusted as adults, and I became more wary in my reading. But I could be fooled by kids' books. This was before the grim Problem Novels of the seventies, but there could be heart-wrenchers like *Old Yeller,* and *Lad, a Dog.* There was another, and like the fairy tales, had what I thought an abysmally inapt title, *The Happy Answer.* In that, a girl orphan is sent to live with a difficult middle-aged spinster. The woman was prickly, the girl was unhappy but just as they were beginning to understand each other and to change for the better, the girl meets a young couple about to have a baby, and ends up with them. I cried buckets for that poor spinster, though I could tell that the author meant for this other ending to be considered a happy one. But it wasn't earned—it came out of the blue, leaving the most difficult but interesting character alone and friendless.

I learned to avoid dog stories, because the dog always gets killed in the end. Then there were misleading descriptions. Like Easter, 1964, just before I turned thirteen, I checked out *Lord of the Flies,* because the back said something about "boys all alone on an island." I expected a Peter Pan story. By the time I realized it wasn't, I was sucked in. I still remember that day, the voices of the grownups in the far room as they drank cocktails before dinner, and on the radio a popular song was playing, Dusty Springfield's "Wishin' and Hopin'"—which I guess is a silly love song, but to this day, nearly half a century later, that song sounds sinister and creepy because the images it calls up are all from *Lord of the Flies.*

Another discovery that year was the long version of *The Count of Monte Cristo.* After that I loved panache, hated tragedy, and would never be afraid of long books. For a book review later that year, in seventh grade, I read *The Exodus,* and I suspected that the teacher didn't believe I read it because she let me yammer on the entire period when I was supposed to give a five-minute book report. Or maybe she let me talk on and on because the class was enthralled, because I remember they were (unlike most of the time when I blabbered on too much).

My taste for history was confirmed for life when I discovered the historical novels of Geoffrey Trease. (Not Treece, whose stories were good, but grimmer.) And in these, like Sally Watson's and Eloise Jarvis McGraw's, the girls actually got to be interesting, not just plot points. For fantasy, I reread Margot Benary-Isbert's *The Wicked Enchantment,* but my absolute favorite (until I discovered *Lord of the Rings*) divided between Lloyd Alexander's "Prydain" series, and Andre Norton's books. Until then I'd avoided science fiction as I associated it with horror, but that changed after I discovered Norton.

Another story that was formative was Elizabeth Marie Pope's *The Sherwood Ring,* with its dash, humor, hidden cabinets and codes. All along I would read any book that had the name "Sherwood" in either title or author. (Which led to my trying to make sense of Christopher Isherwood's dense writings at far too young an age!) I was writing my stories about CJ and the girls in secret all this time, and part of the secret was adopting myself among them, which meant I was really Sherwood, which was their last name. This never had anything to do with Robin Hood, but with images of a magical forest that somewhat resembled Topanga Canyon, mixed with magic, called *Sheer,* or *Share,* later *Shaer Wood.* I can't explain where that came from any more than I can explain where "Mearsies" came from, it was just there. But I liked the spelling of Sherwood from Sherwood Forest, so I adopted it, and didn't mind the reminder of Robin Hood at all—until later, when people would tease me about it.

Which brings me to . . .

Writing

Age now thirteen. Craving adventure and the ability to act and make a difference, which seemed denied to girls in general, especially to me; a passionate reader; still mostly drawing out stories and characters, which I kept in my locker, and in a box hidden up in my closet on the shelf under the blankets, during vacations.

All I needed was an audience. I had one before we moved, a girl my sister's age. She didn't want to read stories (she was eight to my eleven), she wanted to be told them aloud, so we sat on the roof of their play-

house out in her backyard, while ancient tortoises walked slowly over the bricks, and I told her stories. But we both moved, and though we exchanged a few letters, that correspondence dwindled.

In junior high I met another friend who loved the same sorts of stories I did, and there was my audience. Now I had a reason to keep them instead of throwing them away. We'd sit up in her attic talking and trading stories; in May of 1966, when I was busy writing my ninth notebook full of stories about the adventuring girls, and struggling with the concept of time zones and a world map, she was reading the "Lord of the Rings" trilogy.

I devoured Tolkien's work over a weekend. What I took away from that (besides a love of Middle-Earth) was a conviction that fantasy was not scribbling after all, because an adult had written this book for adults. But I wasn't an adult, I was a kid. I wanted to write about kids, and children's literature seemed still bound by firm rules: kids who went to fantasy worlds couldn't stay, they had to come back and grow up. Or far worse, they had to wake up and discover it was all a dream, an ending I loathed with atomic-level passion. Kids didn't live by themselves, or get an option never to grow up; and stories were rarely longer than a couple hundred pages.

Besides those issues, there was the deeper issue: that the stories about CJ and the girls felt like the truth. I couldn't change them to suit an imagined editorial need, any more than I could make my sister like fantasy instead of romance, or wish my family into riches. After I read *Lord of the Rings*—and Tolkien's essay "On Fairy Stories," which came out a year or so later—I no longer worried that my feeling that other worlds were possible, including mine, was crazy, or wrong. There simply were different kinds of truth, and the only truth I could define was that the stories were themselves, and I had to try to tell them as well as possible. Including rewriting scenes if I'd gotten it wrong the first time, but that was like finding corroborative artifacts in order to correct the faults of memory. I wouldn't—couldn't—arbitrarily change things.

But at the same time, we teens were being pushed to think about future careers. For us girls there were supposedly four choices: marriage, secretary, teacher, or nurse. I didn't want any of those. I wanted to be a writer. But in order to be a writer, I knew I had to write what They would publish, and so I wrote my own stories in secret, and I also wrote stories intended for Them. You can imagine which got the most passion and attention.

My audience for my stories had grown to include a couple of school friends, and a cousin in Wisconsin, after she came out for a summer visit. I sent her all my notebooks, which she loved—she kept asking for more. Having someone love my stories felt better than I had imagined, better even than acting roles. But the fear of being forced to change the CJ stories—the threat that someone wouldn't take them seriously, as real—and above all the fear of being made fun of, the way my flying children had been in first grade, made me reluctant to break the secret.

I began typing the "for Them" stories on my mother's manual typewriter at age thirteen, and as soon as I'd saved enough babysitting money for postage, off they went. They always came back after six months or so, sometimes with nice, encouraging notes of rejection. During high school, the local women's group held a creative writing contest. I turned in the first half of *Wren to the Rescue* (in those days called "Tess's Mess") which was my first attempt to bridge between what I liked in stories, and what I knew They wanted. The handwritten manuscript won the contest, which netted me twenty-five dollars to spend at the local bookstore. I bought Narnia, Oz books, and Lloyd Alexander books with that money, for in those days hardcovers were three dollars.

While it felt good to win, I soon learned that winning a contest judged by local women was not going to get me any attention from publishers. After I finished *Wren,* typed it up, and sent it out a few times, I decided it was time to stop, and just write my own stories, until I could read a favorite, then one of mine, and not barf at the comparison.

In other words, I had yet to learn about rewriting.

Writer to Author

The first rule of learning to rewrite, for me, was to let go of the images—the internal movie—and to see what was actually on the page. I'd thought myself such a marvelous hand at description, but when I actually examined my own text, it turned out that about ninety percent of the imagery was still in my head, not on the page. And most of the rest was cliché, or to be more kind, placeholder. No matter how fraught a scene is—how vivid a character—at the moment of highest conflict, if you write, "Her eyes flashed fire," the reader knows what it means, but does that really make the character distinct from the other 564,785,897 heroines whose eyes have flashed fire during the past 200 years of printed novels? So I had to figure out how *that character* looked when she was mad. That meant observing how real people express anger—and I discovered that there are numerous ways. "Eyes flashing fire" was easy, but kind of boring.

I had to go back to the very first baby steps and learn how to write words that would transfer my images to others' minds. And much as I loved writing, I didn't begin that process in earnest until I was in my mid-thirties.

Before then, I had a lot to learn about life.

The summer of 1969, I left California for the first time, on a road trip with my mother and siblings to Minnesota to visit the relatives my mother had left when she was a child. The scenery across country was spectacular. There are no rivers in Southern California, so encountering a real river was an astonishing experience.

Seeing buildings older than a hundred years was even more interesting to me. Architecture designed to ward off winter—the chewed up roads—the way the land is shaped in effect showed me the shadow of harsh winters, though the weather was hot and humid. My first (and only) experience of snow had to wait a couple of years; that summer, when I'd just turned eighteen, we piled all our luggage on the roof of our enormous country squire station wagon, and my mother drove us to the DMV, where I took the driving test. I actually flunked by one point, but the instructor gave me leeway because of all that luggage on the roof, and said as we got out of the car, "You need to be able to help your mother with that drive. By the time you get back from your trip you will be an expert driver." And he was right. (Because of the way I learned to drive, I love cross-country road trips. Seven hundred miles in a day is a comfortable drive for me even now.)

Seeing how people lived "Back East" (Minnesota being back east for Californians) was fascinating to me. I craved travel with an intensity that led to my applying for the Junior Year Abroad program at the University of

"Me during my Hollywood days, late '70s." (Photo courtesy of Sherwood Smith.)

Southern California, which was the college my dad selected for me. In those days the student unrest, the demonstrations, the hippie movement and all its fallout made my father declare that I would attend a conservative college, and so I only applied to the one. I was accepted, too, as I had enough credits (except for math) for four majors—history, English, German, and dance production. But because of my terrible math grades, I had to promise to finish my high school math at a night school.

But that was after the road trip, which was a varied experience in some ways. I had never seen the powerful thunderstorms of the Midwest; one night some cousins took us to see the depressing movie *Once upon a Time in the West,* at a drive-in. Halfway through the film a thunderstorm roared overhead, bleaching the screen. Right above were astonishing purple lightning twists. My oldest cousin, recently returned from Vietnam after being horribly wounded, kept flinching and jumping, because the thunder reminded him of artillery.

More fun were my other cousins in a small town called Eau Claire in Wisconsin, where I got to spend time with my cousin who had read all my stories. She took me all over Eau Claire. That town was so beautiful, full of old houses and cemeteries, and surrounded by forest. It was like all the wonderful family stories I'd read so eagerly as a child!

But finally it was time to return to California. I did most of the driving, reaching L.A. the day Neil Armstrong set foot on the moon.

College started a few weeks later. Two years after that my dad determined that a year abroad would cost no more than a year home if I was very careful, and I promised to be very careful. And I was. When I reached Vienna, Austria, I walked everywhere possible—and did a lot of hitchhiking, which almost got me killed once. I ate once a day only, most days, a meal of rice soaked with gravy. At first, Europe was a shock. I'd confidently expected it to be a huge Disneyland, full of charming ancient villages, old castles, cool museums, and people just thrilled to show me their rich pasts and lore. Well, the museums were there—and the castles—but people weren't always that forthcoming, especially to Americans. I met up with anti-American prejudice in a lot of places. Once, in Paris, a fellow took one look at my skinny blonde self in California clothes, spat out some sort of anti-American curses, and shoved me into the street in the path of an oncoming car. Luckily the car swerved. Then there was that hitchhiking disaster I mentioned, during which I had to wave the switchblade I'd bought for myself in Spain, where I'd discovered that a female traveling alone invited the kind of attention I emphatically did not want. In those Mediterranean cultures, "nice" girls did not travel alone. And blondes stuck out.

I survived it all, and learned a great deal. And in later years, when I gained a better historical perspective,

many of the attitudes I'd seen around me made more sense. In 1971, World War II was still in living memory for most, and what a terrible memory that was! Some of the stories I heard were horrific indeed.

When I returned home, I made two decisions: I'd get back to Europe somehow, and I'd continue studying history. I kept both promises, and meanwhile, I kept writing. I'd stopped sending things out—my focus was all on my own world, now.

Graduate school was a tough time writing-wise, as I now was living on my own, and the only jobs I could find were barmaid, and finally waitress, six days a week and double shifts on all holidays. I left school after I got my master's, because at the time we were told that there were far too many of us Baby Boomers (something I've heard my entire life) and that jobs in universities would not open up until the 1990s. I did not want to be a waitress until 1990! So I left Santa Barbara and moved back to L.A. Jobs varied for a few years: I was a housekeeper/governess for a year, then worked in an electrical supply house, then landed in a film industry job. That was by accident—my roommate at that time, recently divorced and a single mother, worked as a receptionist at CBS Studio Center, while she was trying to break into the animation world as an artist. Mean-

Smith's wedding photo, 1980. "I designed and made all the clothes."
(Photo courtesy of Sherwood Smith.)

while, a screenwriter named Harry Kleiner saw her looking sad one day, and offered to take her out to lunch.

This is the kind of man he was: he refused to lock his car if he'd picked up groceries for his wife, as he felt that anyone who stole groceries needed them. He was always interested in people. But my roommate had heard about "those film industry men" and asked him if she could bring her roommate. He said sure, and so I went along with her. The lunch turned out to be enormous fun, with Mr. Kleiner and me chatting about history and literature, ending with us capping each other with lines from T.S. Eliot's "Lovesong of J. Alfred Prufrock." I didn't think anything of it, but he remembered me, because a couple months later, out of the blue, I got a call from him offering me a job as his secretary—he was tired of girls who couldn't put together a grammatically correct sentence and didn't read anything but diet books.

So for a time I worked in the film industry. From Mr. Kleiner I got a crash course in screenplay writing. We listened to Puccini while working and talked history and literature. What fun that job was! But the problem with that industry is, nothing is permanent—your job only lasts as long as a show or a film in production. Though I did secretarial work for him off and on for years afterward, those projects were not reliable as a steady income, and so I ended up working for Lorimar Productions, which then had several of the top TV shows in production. In those days, it was still difficult for women to get past the secretarial glass ceiling, though I did try. Within a year I was running the entire Xerox department, which enabled me to read everything that came through. I learned a lot about the industry and even wrote a six-hour miniseries with my writing partner, Dave Trowbridge. We got an agent, and the miniseries was shaping up for a bid war between NBC and HBO (very new in those days), but then came the big strike of 1980, which lasted so long that pretty much all miniseries development stopped.

By then I was about to get married. Another crossroads: I left the industry after my wedding, and for a time my husband and I were houseparents for emotionally disturbed children. Some of them were quite violent, and I was about to have a baby, so we decided to leave that program.

I went back to writing, intending to try once more, when my daughter got old enough for school. This is

Smith, with "Bea Kolar (the one who crossed the country with two other friends), in 1980, at my bridal shower." (Photo courtesy of Sherwood Smith.)

when I began in earnest to learn to rewrite. I finally sold something! But hard on that came my first dose of reality about publishing: selling a novel for most writers does not come with megabucks. So even though I had an agent, and was now publishing, I still had to get a job, which ended up being teaching—though I'd never studied for it, all my role playing, and my various studies, enabled me to figure out how to make lessons fun. Writing and teaching meant getting up by four every day, seven days a week, but I did it.

My part-time teaching job ended up lasting nineteen years. I taught French, German, second grade, fourth grade, junior high, and high school in these subjects: literature, drama, history, creative writing. I wrote plays ("Pride and Prejudice," "Peter Pan") and rewrote musicals to fit my students' abilities and our stages. Since I'm pretty good at painting, I designed and made my own sets, and because I have a huge collection of costumes I'd made over the years for various character masquerades at conventions, I used those.

Meanwhile I've been writing, and rewriting, and slowly some of the books appear in print. My measure of success has changed since that day in 1963 when I borrowed someone else's name and fame just long enough to feel a glimpse of their glory. Money and world renown would be nice, but those are not my measure of success. For me, the glow of success comes each time I get a fan letter from someone I will never meet, who took my story images into her life, and tucked them among her own precious memories.

SPANYOL, Jessica 1965-

Personal

Born March 29, 1965, in Weymouth, Dorset, England; daughter of John (a naval captain) and Jill (an artist) Spanyol; partner of Richard Woods (an artist); children: Milo, Lorcan and Augusta (twins). *Education:* Attended Bath Academy of Art, 1983-84; Brighton Polytechnic, B.A., 1987; Royal College of Art, M.A. (with distinction), 1993.

Addresses

Home—London, England.

Career

Artist, illustrator, designer, and writer. Royal College of Art, London, England, research fellow, 1993-94; set designer, 1996-97; Royal Shakespeare Company, artist-in-residence, c. 2001. Lectures on art topics at schools, including University of Central England, Birmingham, England; Chelsea College of Art; and Buckingham and Chilterns College. *Exhibitions:* Work exhibited at Photographers Gallery, London, England, 1994; Whitechapel Art Gallery, London, 1994; South Bank Centre, London, 1994; 6X4 Gallery, London, 1998; and (solo exhibit) Contact Gallery, Norwich, England, 1998.

Awards, Honors

Folio Society Illustration Award; Basil Alkazzi traveling scholarship; Painter Stainers illustration bursary; Chris Garnham Memorial Prize; Random House Publishing Competition awards for best book jacket and poster design.

Writings

Go Bugs Go!, Candlewick Press (Cambridge, MA), 2006.
Little Neighbours of Sunnyside Street, Walker (London, England), 2007, published as *Little Neighbors of Sunnyside Street,* Candlewick Press (Cambridge, MA), 2007.

Spanyol's books have been published in France, Germany, Sweden, Denmark, and Spain.

"CARLO" SERIES

Carlo Likes Reading, Candlewick Press (Cambridge, MA), 2001.
Carlo Likes Counting, Candlewick Press (Cambridge, MA), 2002.
Carlo Likes Learning (with flash cards), Walker Books (London, England), 2002.
Carlo Likes Colors, Candlewick Press (Cambridge, MA), 2003.

Carlo and the Really Nice Librarian, Candlewick Press (Cambridge, MA), 2004.

"MINIBUG" SERIES

Bob and His No. One Van, Candlewick Press (Cambridge, MA), 2008.
Giorgio and His Star Crane Train, Candlewick Press (Cambridge, MA), 2008.
Keith and His Super-stunt Rally Racer, Candlewick Press (Cambridge, MA), 2008.
Clemence and His Noisy Little Fire Engine, Candlewick Press (Cambridge, MA), 2008.
Jo-Jo and Her Flower Roadboat, Walker Books (London, England), 2009.
Pauline and the Girls and Their Playtime Truck, Walker Books (London, England), 2009.
Stacie and Her Luxury Lady Helicopter, Walker Books (London, England), 2009.
The Triplets and Their Little Animal Cars, Walker Books (London, England), 2009.

Sidelights

A native of England, Jessica Spanyol is the author and illustrator of more than a dozen picture books for young readers, among them her "Minibugs" and "Carlo" series. *Carlo Likes Reading,* the debut of Spanyol's series featuring a friendly giraffe named Carlo, was dubbed "bright, well-conceived, and infectiously enthusiastic" by a *Kirkus Reviews* contributor. In addition to her literary efforts, Spanyol has worked as a set designer, a fine art photographer, and a university lecturer. "Making picture books for children is by far the best fun," she related in an essay on her home page. "I really like waking up each day knowing I can spend time making drawings."

The "Carlo" books are based on a character Spanyol wove into a story when she was only six years old. As the author/illustrator once told *SATA:* "Originally it was called 'Carlo the Giraffe Who Could Not Read.' The content, as the title suggests, tackled my lack of confidence in my reading ability. The main character was named after my brother's best friend and the idea for the giraffe came from a favorite blow-up toy." Other characters, such as Carlo's cat Crackers, also had their source in the author's juvenile stories. "My mum helped me write the stories to give me confidence with schoolwork," Spanyol explained, adding that because her mother is no longer alive, the writing process brings back happy memories. "Thirty years after the first version, I was delighted to see *Carlo Likes Reading* in print."

In *Carlo Likes Reading,* the bright-eyed giraffe lives in a world where every object bears a label spelling out what it is, from the bunny slippers Carlo tucks under his bed at night to the iron wrench in the garage. Comparing Spanyol's debut title to the works of Richard Scarry, *School Library Journal* critic Susan Lissim ob-

Jessica Spanyol's self-illustrated picture books include Clemence and His Noisy Little Fire Engine. (Copyright © 2008 by Jessica Spanyol. Reproduced by permission of Candlewick Press, Inc., Somerville, MA, on behalf of Walker Books Ltd., London.)

served that the pictured items "are realistically drawn in bright colors and very much a part of a child's world." With what a *Publishers Weekly* reviewer called a "bright-eyed, plush-toy cuteness," Carlo encourages readers in developing a variety of skills as they follow him through the brightly colored two-page spreads that characterize each book in the continuing series.

After her first book was published, Spanyol returned to teaching illustration and working on art projects, which, she explained, "included installations for galleries, a short film for a contemporary composer, set designs, and working as an artist-in-residence at the Royal Shakespeare Company." Feeling the need to adjust her busy schedule to accommodate her newborn son, she decided to pull out some more of her childhood storybooks and continue the saga of Carlo the giraffe. Like its predecessor, *Carlo Likes Counting* finds the curious

young giraffe exploring his environment; at each venue, including a café and a farm, he discovers a variety of figures and objects to count. *Booklist* contributor Julie Cummins stated that the author's second "Carlo" title "will encourage kids to count things in their daily activities and surroundings."

In *Carlo Likes Colors,* the title character spots a host of picturesque items, including bright yellow chicks and gorgeous red roses, as he visits different locales with his pet cat, Crackers. "Children will have fun looking at the labeled items and naming more things on their own," Diane Foote remarked in *Booklist,* and a *Kirkus Reviews* critic similarly noted that youngsters "will delight in the simple, but detailed cartoon drawings." In *Carlo and the Really Nice Librarian,* the protagonist must overcome his fear of Mrs. Chinca, the alligator who runs the new library in his neighborhood. The clever librarian soon wins over the reluctant young giraffe by reading to him, issuing him a library card, and teaching him how to shelve books. "Spanyol's illustrations, a combination of watercolor, acrylic, ink, and collage, have a sweet, childlike quality," Lauren Peterson commented in *Booklist.* The "rousing rhythms and the imagery" of *Carlo and the Really Nice Librarian* "are amplified by" the brightly colored art," concluded Gay Lynn Van Vleck in her *School Library Journal* review.

A close-knit, lively neighborhood is the setting for *Go Bugs Go!* and *Little Neighbors of Sunnyside Street,* a pair of self-illustrated works by Spanyol. In the former, readers are introduced to a group of insects that love to travel, be it by train, plane, or car. The Bugs return in *Little Neighbors of Sunnyside Street,* which also features Ian, a music-loving dog; Kelly, an exuberant pig; and Philip, an imaginative cow. Spanyol's work incorporates "simple shapes, flat dimension, and busy pages with plenty of preschool child appeal," Cummins wrote, and a *Kirkus Reviews* contributor described *Little Neighbors of Sunnyside Street* as "an irresistible invitation for younger readers to ruminate over how we are all the same in some ways, different in others."

In creating her illustrations, Spanyol first makes "roughs" by scanning sketches into the computer, and then coloring them. Her finished artwork is created using paint and collage. "I hope that my books can tackle

Spanyol introduces young children to a variety of interesting characters in her self-illustrated picture book Little Neighbors on Sunnyside Street. (Copyright © 2007 Jessica Spanyol. Reproduced by permission of Candlewick Press, Inc., Somerville, MA on behalf of Walker Books Ltd., London.)

learning in a light and enjoyable manner," she noted. "I have always found it useful to work from memories and to think about how I learned things like reading and counting. I hope that my books will help children learn and have a giggle at the same time. When I make the books I really don't think about children as a mass, anonymous audience; instead, I draw things that make my friends and family laugh."

Biographical and Critical Sources

PERIODICALS

Booklist, November 1, 2001, Annie Ayres, review of *Carlo Likes Reading,* p. 485; October 1, 2002, Julie Cummins, review of *Carlo Likes Counting,* p. 338; April 1, 2003, Diane Foote, review of *Carlo Likes Colors,* p. 1404; September 1, 2004, Lauren Peterson, review of *Carlo and the Really Nice Librarian,* p. 137; July 1, 2007, Julie Cummins, review of *Little Neighbors on Sunnyside Street,* p. 65.

Guardian (London, England), October 31, 2001, review of *Carlo Likes Reading.*

Kirkus Reviews, August 1, 2001, review of *Carlo Likes Reading,* p. 1132; March 1, 2003, review of *Carlo Likes Colors,* p. 398; July 1, 2004, review of *Carlo and the Really Nice Librarian,* p. 637; May 15, 2007, review of *Little Neighbors on Sunnyside Street.*

Orlando Sentinel, September 9, 2001, "Lively Books Take Learning outside School Walls."

Publishers Weekly, September 3, 2001, review of *Carlo Likes Reading,* p. 86.

School Library Journal, October, 2001, Susan Lissim, review of *Carlo Likes Reading;* October, 2004, Gay Lynn Van Vleck, review of *Carlo and the Really Nice Librarian,* p. 135.

ONLINE

Walker Books Web site, http://www.walker.co.uk/ (October 15, 2009), "Jessica Spanyol."*

*   *   *

SPENCER, Britt

Personal

Born in Lexington, KY; married; children: three. *Education:* Savannah College of Art and Design, B.F.A., 2005.

Addresses

Home—Los Angeles, CA. *Agent*—Illustration Ltd., 2 Brooks Ct., Cringle St., London SW8 5BX, England. *E-mail*—britt@brittspencer.com.

Career

Illustrator. *Exhibitions:* Work exhibited at Savannah College of Art and Design, Savannah, GA, 2006.

Member

Society of Illustrators.

Awards, Honors

Best in Show designation, Savannah, GA, Sidewalk Arts Festival, 2004; Teatrio "Circus" children's book competition finalist, 2004; second place award, Merriwell Children's Book Competition, 2004; Gray's Reef Fantastic Fishes Award, Savannah Sidewalk Arts Festival, 2005.

Illustrator

Judith St. George, *Make Your Mark, Franklin Roosevelt* ("Turning Point" series), Philomel Books (New York, NY), 2007.

Jeanne Steig, *Fleas!,* Philomel Books (New York, NY), 2008.

Judith St. George, *Zarafa: The Giraffe Who Walked to the King,* Philomel Books (New York, NY), 2009.

Contributor to periodicals, including *Saturday Evening Post* and *Gentleman's Quarterly.*

Sidelights

A commercial artist whose work is noted for its fanciful imagery and dry wit, Britt Spencer has illustrated such children's books as *Make Your Mark, Franklin Roosevelt* by Judith St. George and *Fleas!* by Jeanne Steig. Discussing the whimsical worlds he creates, Spencer commented in an *Altpick.com* interview, "It's my attempt, albeit a feeble one, to merge the asinine and the reasonable. I usually just refer to it as nonsensical sanity."

In *Make Your Mark, Franklin Roosevelt,* which is part of the "Turning Point" picture-book biography series, St. George looks at the childhood of the thirty-second president of the United States. Raised in a wealthy household by doting parents, young Franklin was greatly influenced to enter politics by his cousin, Theodore Roosevelt, and the headmaster of his boarding school, Reverend Endicott Peabody. According to John Peters in *Booklist,* Spencer portrays "Franklin's intense personality by portraying him throughout with wide open eyes and mouth," and a contributor in *Kirkus Reviews* noted that the artist employs "the conventions of political cartooning, oversized heads and exaggerated perspectives adding humor and movement to the narrative." Lee Bock, writing in *School Library Journal,* also praised Spencer's contributions, observing that his "spirited watercolor, gouache, and ink illustrations bring to life the culture and background of this American icon."

A farmer makes a series of outlandish trades in *Fleas!* When Quantz finds himself itching after a run-in with a shaggy dog, he unloads the insects on a young woman in exchange for her overly talkative uncle and later deals the uncle for some Limburger cheese, which is

Britt Spencer focuses on an unusual topic in his picture book Fleas!, *featuring artwork by Jeanne Steig.* (Illustration copyright © 2008 by Britt Spencer. Reproduced by permission.)

swapped for an old banjo. When the bartering concludes, Quantz finds himself face-to-face with the canine, which is guarding the opening to a tent that contains a huge surprise. Steig's narrative "is ably extended by Spencer's garishly hued, exaggerated portraits of dopey-faced Quantz and a cast of tall-tale characters," Gillian Engberg commented in *Booklist,* and a *Kirkus Reviews* contributor remarked that Spencer's pictures, "filled with humor and exaggeration, are just the right complement to the text's amiable foolishness."

Biographical and Critical Sources

PERIODICALS

Booklist, November 15, 2006, John Peters, review of *Make Your Mark, Franklin Roosevelt,* p. 47; May 15, 2008, Gillian Engberg, review of *Fleas!,* p. 47.

Kirkus Reviews, December 15, 2006, review of *Make Your Mark, Franklin Roosevelt,* p. 1273; April 15, 2008, review of *Fleas!*

Publishers Weekly, April 21, 2008, review of *Fleas!,* p. 56.

School Library Journal, February, 2007, Lee Bock, review of *Make Your Mark, Franklin Roosevelt,* p. 112; May, 2008, Joan Kindig, review of *Fleas!,* p. 110.

ONLINE

Altpick.com, http://altpick.com/ (May 19, 2009), "Britt Spencer."

Britt Spencer Home Page, http://www.brittspencer.com (October 15, 2009).

Illustration Ltd. Web site, http://www.illustrationweb.com/ (October 15, 2009), "Britt Spencer."*

*   *   *

STANLEY, Elizabeth 1947-

Personal

Born 1947, in Australia; married; husband's name Gordon; children: Rebecca. *Education:* University of Melbourne, B.A., Dip.Ed. *Hobbies and other interests:* Drawing and painting, writing poetry, swimming, gardening, traveling.

Addresses

Home—Fairlight, Sydney, New South Wales, Australia. *E-mail*—libby_stanley@hotmail.com.

Career

Author and illustrator. Worked as an English teacher and educational psychologist; Dromkeen Children's Literature Centre, former director.

Awards, Honors

Picture Book of the Year Honor Book selection, Children's Book Council of Australia, 1995, and Henry Bergh Children's Book Award, American Society for the Prevention of Cruelty to Animals, 2003, both for *The Deliverance of Dancing Bears.*

Writings

SELF-ILLUSTRATED

China's Plum Tree, Sandcastle/Freemantle Arts Centre Press (South Fremantle, Western Australia, Australia), 1992.
The Deliverance of Dancing Bears, Cygnet Books/ University of Western Australia Press (Nedlands, Western Australia, Australia), 1994, Kane/Miller (La Jolla, CA), 2003.
Night without Darkness, Penguin Australia (Ringwood, Victoria, Australia), 2001.
Tyger, Tyger, Enchanted Lion Books (New York, NY), 2007.

ILLUSTRATOR

Libby Hathorn, *The Wishing Cupboard,* Lothian Books (South Melbourne, Victoria, Australia), 2002.
Rosanne Hawke, *Yardil,* Benchmark Publications (Montrose, Victoria, Australia), 2004.

Sidelights

A former teacher of English and then an educational psychologist, Australian author and illustrator Elizabeth Stanley began publishing children's books in the early 1990s. Several of her books have also made it to the United States, earning her attention from reviewers who praise her timely stories about the mistreatment of animals.

Winner of a Henry Bergh Children's Book Award from the American Society for the Prevention of Cruelty to Animals, Stanley's *The Deliverance of Dancing Bears* shares the experiences of a female bear that is made to

Elizabeth Stanley combines her detailed artwork with a compelling story in **The Deliverance of Dancing Bears.** (Copyright © 1994 by Elizabeth Stanley. Reproduced by permission.)

perform on the streets of a small Turkish town. Owned by a cruel man named Haluk, the bear dreams of roaming free in the forests and interacting with members of its own kind. Tired of witnessing the abuse of the bear, a respected man in the village offers Haluk a large sum of money for the bear and returns the creature to the wilderness near his home. Unfortunately, Haluk replaces his ursine entertainer with a new cub he has captured; this time, however, the townspeople join the old man in winning the cub's freedom. When the elderly man releases the cub, it is united with the older female bear. The creatures then live in freedom as mother and child, mirroring the dreams the older bear cherished while living in chains.

Writing in *Kirkus Reviews,* a critic noted that *The Deliverance of Dancing Bears* offers young readers "a richly satisfying message," while *Booklist* contributor Karen Hutt described Stanley's narrative as "mostly simple and well paced." A *Publishers Weekly* critic wrote that in *The Deliverance of Dancing Bears* Stanley "delicately and accessibly addresses" complex moral issues, including the protection of animals, sacrificial giving, and "how one person can move a crowd from 'dumb curiosity' to moral outrage."

Stanley turns a true story about an actual animal sanctuary in Thailand into a fanciful fairy tale in *Tyger, Tyger.* Saddened by poachers that are killing tigers in the nearby jungle, a young Buddhist monk believes that he hears a divine voice compelling him to care for a pair of abandoned tigers. Taking the cubs into his temple, the monk expands his mission, providing a refuge for other orphaned animals and offering protection against extinction for the endangered felines. Reviewing *Tyger, Tyger* for *Kirkus Reviews,* a critic cited the book's "message" as "strong and supported by haunting images" created by the author. A *Publishers Weekly* contributor wrote that Stanley's decision to set her novel in a Thai monastery "adds a spiritual dimension to the story." In addition, the author/illustrator's "skillfully drafted, jewel-colored" pictures are well suited to an older readership, the critic added.

Biographical and Critical Sources

PERIODICALS

Booklist, May 1, 2003, Karen Hutt, review of *The Deliverance of Dancing Bears,* p. 1606.

Kirkus Reviews, February 1, 2003, review of *The Deliverance of Dancing Bears,* p. 240; May 15, 2007, review of *Tyger, Tyger.*

Publishers Weekly, February 17, 2003, review of *The Deliverance of Dancing Bears,* p. 74; May 28, 2007, review of *Tyger, Tyger,* p. 61.

School Library Journal, July, 2007, Heidi Estrin, review of *Tyger, Tyger,* p. 85.

ONLINE

Elizabeth Stanley Home Page, http://www.elizabethstanley. com.au (October 27, 2009).

*   *   *

STOCKDALE, Susan 1954-

Personal

Born October 3, 1954, in Miami, FL; daughter of Grant Stockdale (a former ambassador to Ireland) and Alice Boyd Magruder Proudfoot (an author and poet); married Todd S. Mann (president of a health care company); children: Chelsea, Justin. *Education:* Studied with illustrator Luis de Horna, Instituto de Cultura, Spain, 1974-75; studied with printmaker Ansai Uchima, Sarah Lawrence College, 1975; Occidental College, B.A. (art; cum laude), 1976.

Addresses

Home—Chevy Chase, MD. *E-mail*—susan1797@aol. com.

Career

Artist and textile designer. Worked variously as an art gallery manager, special-events coordinator, and public relations director. Speaker at schools and libraries; presenter at conferences. *Exhibitions:* Works have been exhibited in Atlanta, GA; Alexandria, VA; and Washington, DC.

Member

Society of Children's Book Writers and Illustrators.

Awards, Honors

Outstanding Science Trade Book for Children designation, National Science Teachers Association, 1999, for *Nature's Paintbrush,* 2008, for *Fabulous Fishes;* Parents' Choice Approved designation, and Best Children's Book designation, Bank Street College of Education, both 2005, both for *Carry Me!;* numerous awards from juried exhibitions.

Writings

SELF-ILLUSTRATED

(And illustrator) *Some Sleep Standing Up,* Simon & Schuster (New York, NY), 1997.

Nature's Paintbrush: The Patterns and Colors around You, Simon & Schuster (New York, NY), 1999.

Carry Me!: Animal Babies on the Move, Peachtree Publishers (Atlanta, GA), 2005.

Fabulous Fishes, Peachtree Publishers (Atlanta, GA), 2008.

Sidelights

Seeing a napping flamingo during a trip to the zoo with her children inspired Susan Stockdale to write and illustrate her first picture book, *Some Sleep Standing Up,* which *Booklist* contributor Ilene Cooper described as a winning combination of a "brief text and . . . charming pictures." "We saw a flamingo that was sound asleep while standing on one leg," the author once told *SATA.* "We all thought that was just amazing, and started talking about the different ways animals sleep." When a trip to the library produced no whimsical books on the subject, Stockdale decided to write her own. "My art work has always included images of animals in fanciful settings, so the subject matter was perfect for me," she recalled.

Stockdale's appreciation for nature comes through in her second children's book, *Nature's Paintbrush: The Patterns and Colors around You.* Featuring what John Peters described in *Booklist* as "sharply defined forms and opaque, brightly contrasting colors," the author/illustrator travels from coral reef to tundra, to rainforest and beyond, looking both up close and from a distance at each ecosystem. "Sometimes I think about creating a fictional book, but then I find another topic in nature that really interests me and I'm off researching again . . . ," she noted on her home page. "I continue to find tremendous joy and satisfaction in celebrating the natural world in my picture books."

Susan Stockdale showcases her intricate and colorful collage art in her picture book **Fabulous Fishes.** (Illustration copyright © 2008 by Susan Stockdale. Reproduced by permission.)

Stockdale continues her focus on nature in *Carry Me!: Animal Babies on the Move* and *Fabulous Fishes.* The comforting relationship between a mother and child is reflected in *Carry Me!,* wherein children can discover the whereabouts of fourteen tiny animal babies as they are safely transported, be it in a pouch, on a shoulder, or even settled on a foot. In *Booklist* Hazel Rochman praised Stockdale's book for making "the facts of zoology . . . both exciting and cuddly," while Blair Christolon commented in *School Library Journal* on the artist's ability to depict movement through the use of "slight gradiations in color." Suggesting the book as a "soothing" choice for bedtime, a *Kirkus Reviews* deemed *Carry Me!* as "a beautifully sweet look at how babies are carried."

A rhyming text is paired with colorful collage-and-acrylic art to transport young children under the sea in *Fabulous Fishes.* Here Stockdale introduces twenty dramatically different fish, from tiny sardines to giant sharks, including interesting facts about each. In *Kirkus Reviews* a critic remarked that the factual information Stockdale includes will make *Fabulous Fishes* "an excellent teaching tool," and cited the author/illustrator's use of "likeable, resonant rhyme." Rochman recommended *Fabulous Fishes* as "an exciting way to prepare kids for a visit to the aquarium," and in *School Library Journal* Kathy Piehl praised Stockdale's trademark acrylic paintings for their "bright hues, and . . . variety of details and textures."

Biographical and Critical Sources

PERIODICALS

Booklist, September 1, 1996, Ilene Cooper, review of *Some Sleep Standing Up,* p. 140; July, 1999, John Peters, review of *Nature's Paintbrush: The Patterns and Colors around You,* p. 1949; May 1, 2005, Hazel Rochman, review of *Carry Me!: Animal Babies on the Move,* p. 1588; April 1, 2008, Hazel Rochman, review of *Fabulous Fishes,* p. 52.

Kirkus Reviews, April 15, 1996, review of *Some Sleep Standing Up,* p. 610; February 15, 2005, review of *Carry Me!,* p. 236; February 1, 2008, review of *Fabulous Fishes.*

School Library Journal, April, 1996, review of *Some Sleep Standing Up,* p. 131; April, 2005, Blair Christolon, review of *Carry Me!,* p. 113; April, 2008, Kathy Piehl, review of *Fabulous Fishes,* p. 138.

Washington Post, Raymond M. Lane, March 5, 2008, review of *Fabulous Fishes.*

ONLINE

Susan Stockdale Home Page, http://www.susanstockdale. com (October 30, 2009).*

SULLIVAN, Edward T. 1966-

Personal

Born 1966; married; wife's name, Judy. *Education:* Glassboro State College, B.A., 1991; Memphis State University, M.A., 1993; University of Tennessee, M.S., 1995.

Addresses

Home—Oakridge, TN. *E-mail*—sully@sully-writer.com.

Career

Librarian, writer, editor, educator, and speaker. Mt. Pleasant Christian Academy, Mt. Pleasant, MS, English teacher, 1993-94; Lamar Memorial Library, Maryville, TN, reference librarian, 1995; New York Public Library, Staten Island, NY, young adult librarian, 1996-97, senior project librarian, 1997-99; supervising young adult specialist, 2000; Langston Hughes Library, Clinton, TN, director, 2000-01; Jefferson County Schools, White Pine, TN, library information specialist, 2001-03; Hardin Valley Elementary School, Knoxville, TN, library information specialist, 2003—. Memphis State University, Memphis, TN, adjunct professor, 1993-94; St. John's University, Staten Island, adjunct professor, 1999-2000; University of Tennessee, Knoxville, adjunct instructor, 2001-02. University of Tennessee Center for Children's and Young Adult Literature, member of board of directors.

Member

International Reading Association, American Library Association, Young Adult Library Services Association, Assembly on Literature for Adolescents (member of board of directors), Association for Library Service for Children, Authors Guild, Author's League of America, Children's Literature Assembly, Organization of American Historians, Society of Children's Book Writers and Illustrators, United States Board on Books for Young People, Tennessee Association of School Librarians, Tennessee Library Association, Tennessee Reading Association, Tennessee Writers Alliance, Smoky Mountain Reading Council, East Tennessee Library Association, Knoxville Writers Guild.

Awards, Honors

Ezra Jack Keats Foundation grant, 2000; Ezra Jack Keats/de Grummond Collection research fellowship, University of Southern Mississippi, 2003; Teaching Tolerance grant, Southern Poverty Law Center, 2003; Parents' Choice Silver Honor, 2007, Notable Social Studies Trade Books for Young People designation, National Council for the Social Studies/Children's Book Council (CBC), 2008, and Outstanding Science Trade Book for Students K-12 designation, National Science Teachers Association/CBC, 2008, all for *The Ultimate Weapon.*

Writings

NONFICTION

The Holocaust in Literature for Youth: A Guide and Resource Book, Scarecrow Press (Lanham, MD), 1999.
Reaching Reluctant Young Adult Readers: A Handbook for Librarians and Teachers, Scarecrow Press (Lanham, MD), 2002.
The Ultimate Weapon: The Race to Develop the Atomic Bomb, Holiday House (New York, NY), 2007.

Series editor, Scarecrow Press "Guides to Children's and Young Adult Literature." Serves on editorial advisory boards of several professional journals. Contributor of articles to periodicals, including *ALAN Review, Book Links, Booklist, School Library Journal,* and *Voice of Youth Advocates.*

Sidelights

Edward T. Sullivan is a man of many talents, including writer, teacher, librarian, editor, and public speaker. As a trained librarian, Sullivan is well acquainted with literature for young readers. His first two books use this knowledge to gather resources for Holocaust studies and to reach reluctant readers. His *The Holocaust in Literature for Youth: A Guide and Resource Book* is an "authoritative bibliography and discussion," according to *Booklist* contributor Hazel Rochman. In compiling his book, Sullivan collected a wide assortment of literature and resources, including drama, fiction, nonfiction, picture books, biography, autobiography, poetry, electronic sites, and museums, that spans reading abilities from elementary school through high school. "Sullivan is passionate about the need to teach the Holocaust," Rochman went on to observe.

In *Reaching Reluctant Young Adult Readers: A Handbook for Librarians and Teachers* Sullivan addresses another youth audience: those who can read but choose not to do so. For him, a "young adult" reader can be an adolescent from age ten to age fifteen. Sullivan places responsibility for getting these young people to read on the shoulders of librarians, teachers, and, of course, parents. To that end, he lists a wide assortment of materials that might interest this audience. These resources include short stories, comic books and graphic novels, magazines, and picture books. Writing in *Booklist,* Rochelle Glantz found *Reaching Reluctant Young Adult Readers* to be a "valuable tool to combat the nonreader."

Sullivan's award-winning *The Ultimate Weapon: The Race to Develop the Atomic Bomb,* is a "a valuable account of a critical event in the world's history," according to *School Library Journal* reviewer Jeffrey A. French. Sullivan was inspired to write this overview after moving to Oak Ridge, Tennessee, one of the secret centers of the U.S. Atom Bomb project, and discovered that there were no histories of the development of the atomic bomb available for young readers. He spent the next six years researching and writing *The Ultimate Weapon,* detailing "how scientists in universities around the country, and hundreds of thousands of civilian and military personnel living and working in secret cities in Los Alamos, New Mexico, Oak Ridge, Tennessee, and Hanford, Washington, worked together to build the first atomic bomb," as Sullivan noted on his author home page. His book not only looks at what was known as the Manhattan Project, but also reveals the competing Nazi program to develop the bomb. He presents a full cast of characters involved in the project, including physicist Albert Einstein, nuclear scientist J. Robert Oppenheimer, and U.S. President Franklin D. Roosevelt. He also goes into a discussion regarding the decision to use the bomb on the Japanese cities of Nagasaki and Hiroshima and the aftermath of the bombing, as well as the role of spies in this most secret of projects. Over a hundred black and white photographs complement the text.

French went on to call *The Ultimate Weapon* a "well-done review of the creation of the atomic bomb" and the decision-making process behind the weapon. Similar praise came from a *Kirkus Reviews* critic who termed the book "completely compelling, a straightforward narrative told with a light touch." Likewise, *Booklist* reviewer Bill Ott wrote that Sullivan's book "turns the human story behind the project into compelling drama."

Biographical and Critical Sources

PERIODICALS

Booklist, July, 1999, Hazel Rochman, review of *The Holocaust in Literature for Youth: A Guide and Resource Book,* p. 1957; March 1, 2003, Rochelle Glantz, review of *Reaching Reluctant Young Adult Readers: A Handbook for Librarians and Teachers,* p. 1245; July 1, 2007, Bill Ott, review of *The Ultimate Weapon: The Race to Develop the Atomic Bomb,* p. 47.
Bulletin of the Center for Children's Books, September, 1999, review of *The Holocaust in Literature for Youth,* p. 37; September, 2007, Elizabeth Bush, review of *The Ultimate Weapon,* p. 58.
Kirkus Reviews, June 1, 2007, review of *The Ultimate Weapon.*
School Library Journal, November, 1999, review of *The Holocaust in Literature for Youth,* p. 186; August, 2007, Jeffrey A. French, review of *The Ultimate Weapon,* p. 140.
Voice of Youth Advocates, June, 2007, Melissa Moore, review of *The Ultimate Weapon,* p. 176.

ONLINE

Balkin Buddies Web site, http://www.balkinbuddies.com/ (April 9, 2008), "Edward T. Sullivan."
Edward T. Sullivan Home Page, http://www.sully-writer. com (April 9, 2008).*

T-U

TALLIS, Robyn
See SMITH, Sherwood

*   *   *

TAYLOR, Eleanor 1969-

Personal
Born 1969, in England; married; children: one son.

Addresses
Home—London, England.

Career
Author and illustrator.

Writings

SELF-ILLUSTRATED

Beep, Beep, Let's Go!, Bloomsbury (New York, NY), 2005.
My Friend the Monster, Bloomsbury Children's Books (New York, NY), 2008.

ILLUSTRATOR

Michael Catchpool, *Sleepy Sam,* Little Tiger (London, England), 2001.
Sally Grindley, *No Trouble at All,* Bloomsbury Children's Books (New York, NY), 2002.
Nicola Moon, *Tick-Tock, Drip-Drop!: A Bedtime Story,* Gullane Children's (London, England), 2003, Bloomsbury Children's Books (New York, NY), 2004.
Sally Grindley, *A Little Bit of Trouble,* Bloomsbury Children's Books (New York, NY), 2004.
Tony Johnston, *Chicken in the Kitchen,* Simon & Schuster (New York, NY), 2005.

Julia Durango, *Cha-Cha Chimps,* Simon & Schuster Books for Young Readers (New York, NY), 2006.
Julia Durango, *Go-Go Gorillas,* Simon & Schuster Books for Young Readers (New York, NY), 2009.

Sidelights
Eleanor Taylor is an English artist and illustrator whose picture-book collaborations include stories by Sally Grindley, Tony Johnston, Nicola Moon, and Julia Durango. Working in pencil and water color, Taylor

Eleanor Taylor creates engaging watercolor-and-ink art for Sally Grindley's **No Trouble at All.** (Bloomsbury Children's Books, 2002. Reproduced by permission.)

Whimsy rather than horror is at the heart of Taylor's self-illustrated picture book **My Friend the Monster.** (Copyright © 2008 by Eleanor Taylor. Reprinted by permission of Bloomsbury Publishing Inc. All rights reserved.)

creates art that "lend[s] . . . an extra vibe of excitement" to the whimsical story in Durango's *Cha-Cha Chimps,* according to a *Publishers Weekly* reviewer, while in *Booklist* Gillian Engberg praised the "glorious, cheerful chaos" that the artist captures in her illustrations for Johnston's *Chicken in the Kitchen.* Taylor's "pencil and watercolor illustrations brim with humor, action and kid-pleasing detail," a *Publishers Weekly* critic wrote in a second review of Johnston's work, and in *School Library Journal* Judith Constantinides described Grindley's *No Trouble at All* as "spiced with gentle humor" on the strength of Taylor's "cozy watercolors."

Taylor's original self-illustrated picture books include *Beep, Beep, Let's Go!* and *My Friend the Monster.* In *Beep, Beep, Let's Go!* she pairs a variety of animals with unique modes of travel: a duck pilots a small airplane, the dog family crowds into a red convertible, a hippo drives an ice-cream truck, and two pigs peddle a two-seater bicycle. Although the means of transportation varies, the animals' goal is the same, and they all wind up at a sunny beach and hit the water with glee. According to *Booklist* contributor Hazel Rochman, *Beep, Beep, Let's Go!* is "just right for the lap-sit crowd," and Joy Fleishhacker deemed Taylor's soft-toned "cartoon artwork" for the book to be "energetic and inviting." The story is fueled by "a heady dose of

onomatopoeia," observed a *Kirkus Reviews* writer, and "youngsters will . . . enjoy the ride."

A little fox moves into a new house and discovers that he is sharing his new room with a fluffy, green, one-eyed, creature in *My Friend the Monster.* The creature, although large, is more timid than the fox, and by reassuring his new roommate how to overcome its fear and make new friends at a nearby park, the newcomer fox winds up with new friends as well. Taylor pairs her text with "quaintly drawn" characters, wrote *School Library Journal* critic Jayne Damron, and in *Kirkus Reviews* a contributor cited *My Friend the Monster* for its "deadpan narrative" and "adorable" monster character.

Biographical and Critical Sources

PERIODICALS

Booklist, August, 2002, GraceAnne DeCandido, review of *No Trouble at All,* p. 1971; May 15, 2004, Gillian Engberg, review of *Tick-Tock, Drip-Drop!: A Bedtime Story,* p. 1626; January 1, 2005, review of *Chicken in the Kitchen,* p. 870; May 1, 2005, Hazel Rochman, review of *Beep, Beep, Let's Go!,* p. 1594; January 1, 2006, Julie Cummins, review of *Cha-Cha Chimps,* p. 110; September 1, 2008, Hazel Rochman, review of *My Friend the Monster,* p. 106.

Kirkus Reviews, June 15, 2002, review of *No Trouble at All,* p. 882; March 15, 2004, review of *Tick-Tock, Drip-Drop!,* p. 274; August 15, 2004, review of *A Little Bit of Trouble,* p. 806; January 1, 2005, review of *Chicken in the Kitchen,* p. 53; June 1, 2005, *Beep, Beep, Let's Go!,* p. 644 December 15, 2005, review of *Cha-Cha Chimps,* p. 1321; July 1, 2008, review of *My Friend the Monster.*

Publishers Weekly, May 13, 2002, review of *No Trouble at All,* p. 69; February 28, 2005, review of *Chicken in the Kitchen,* p. 66; February 6, 2006, review of *Cha-Cha Chimps,* p. 68.

School Library Journal, July, 2002, Judith Constantinides, review of *No Trouble at All,* p. 92; November, 2004, Wendy Woodfill, review of *Tick-Tock, Drip-Drop!,* p. 113; December, 2004, Julie Roach, review of *A Little Bit of Trouble,* p. 110; May, 2005, Corrina Austin, review of *Chicken in the Kitchen,* p. 86; July, 2005, Joy Fleishhacker, review of *Beep, Beep, Let's Go!,* p. 83; February, 2006, Susan E. Murray, review of *Cha-Cha Chimps,* p. 96; September, 2008, Jayne Damron, review of *My Friend the Monster,* p. 160.*

*   *   *

THOMAS, Lee
See PENDLETON, Thomas

*   *   *

TORRECILLA, Pablo 1967-

Personal

Born 1967, in Madrid, Spain.

Addresses

Home—CA. *E-mail*—ilustrador@pablotorrecilla.com.

Career

Writer and illustrator. Worked variously as a storyboard artist, artistic director for the Spanish National Classical Ballet, and in animated film. Laredo Publishing, Los Angeles, CA, art director, 1991-92; Renaissance House, Los Angeles, art director, 2000-01; full-time freelance illustrator, beginning 2001. Also worked for Spanish-language publishers. *Exhibitions:* Work exhibited in Spain and United States. Mural installation at Santander Palace of Festivals.

Writings

SELF-ILLUSTRATED

El libro de las hojas muertas (homage to Gabriel García Márquez), Editiones Valnera (Spain), 2007.

ILLUSTRATOR

Clarita Kohen, *Pajaritos,* Laredo (Torrance, CA), 1993.

Alma Flor Ada, *Pregones,* Laredo (Torrance, CA), 1993.

Aïda E. Marcuse, *Caperucita Roja y la luna de papel,* Laredo (Torrance, CA), 1993.

Alma Flor Ada, *Barquitos de papel,* Laredo (Beverly Hills, CA), 1995.

Alma Flor Ada, *Barriletes,* Laredo (Beverly Hills, CA), 1995.

Alma Flor Ada, *Dias de circo,* Laredo (Beverly Hills, CA), 1995.

Alma Flor Ada, *Pin, Pin, Sarabin,* Laredo (Beverly Hills, CA), 1995.

Evangelina Vigil-Piñon, *Marina's Muumuu,* Piñata Books (Houston, TX), 2001.

Larry Dane Brimner, *Here Comes Trouble,* Children's Press (New York, NY), 2001.

Pat Mora, *The Bakery Lady,* Piñata Books (Houston, TX), 2001.

Pablo Torrecilla contributes his unique, stylized cartoon art to Kathy Whitehead's **Looking for Uncle Louie on the Fourth of July.** (Illustration copyright © 2005 by Pablo Torrecilla. Reproduced by permission.)

Torrecilla's artwork is a feature of Samuel Caraballo's large-format picture book Estrellita in the Big City. (Illustration copyright © 2008 by Pablo Torrecilla. Reprinted with permission from the publisher.)

Samuel Caraballo, *Estrellita Says Good-bye to Her Island,* Piñata Books (Houston, TX), 2002.

Raquel Benatar and Patricia Peterson, *Gabriel García Márquez and His Magical Universe,* Piñata Books (Houston, TX), 2002.

Raquel Benatar, *Isabel Allende: Recuerdos para un cuento,* Piñata Books (Houston, TX), 2002.

Cesar Vidal, *Gray Feather and the Big Dog: A Legend of the Plains Indians,* Peter Bedrick Books (Columbus, OH), 2002.

Joseph Bruchac, *Gluskabe and Old Man Winter,* Hampton Brown, 2002.

D.H. Figueredo, *The Road to Santiago,* Lee & Low Books (New York, NY), 2003.

Laura Dower, *Scribbles and Secrets,* Scholastic (New York, NY), 2003.

Gary Miller, *Runaway Ring,* Sundance, 2004.

Kathy Whitehead, *Looking for Uncle Louie on the Fourth of July,* Boyds Mills Press (Honesdale, PA), 2005.

Vicente Muñoz Puelles, *El vuelo de la razon: Goya, pintor de la libertad,* Anaya (Madrid, Spain), 2007.

Samuel Caraballo, *Estrellita en la ciudad grande/Estrellita in the Big City,* Piñata Books (Houston, TX), 2008.

Biographical and Critical Sources

PERIODICALS

Booklist, June 1, 1994, Isabel Schon, review of *Caperucita Roja y la luna de papel,* p. 1849; January 1, 2002, GraceAnne A. DeCandido, review of *Marina's Muumuu,* p. 860; May 1, 2002, John Peters, review of *Estrellita Says Goodbye to Her Island,* p. 1525; October 15, 2003, John Peters, review of *The Road to Santiago,* p. 410.

Kirkus Reviews, September 1, 2008, review of *Estrellita in the Big City.*

Publishers Weekly, September 22, 2003, review of *The Road to Santiago,* p. 71.

School Library Journal, January, 2002, Ann Welton, review of *The Bakery Lady,* p. 130; May, 2005, Linda

Staskus, review of *Looking for Uncle Louie on the Fourth of July,* p. 103; February, 2009, Mary Landrum, review of *Estrellita en la ciudad,* p. 73.

ONLINE

Crónica de Cantabria Online, http://www.cronicalde cantabria.com/ (April 18, 2007), "El pintor Pablo Torrecilla realiza un homenaje a 'Cien años de soledad' en un libro de la editorial cántabra Valnera."
Pablo Torrecilla Home Page, http://www.pablotorrecilla. com (October 30, 2009).*

*   *   *

ULRICH, Maureen 1958-

Personal

Born 1958, in Saskatoon, Saskatchewan, Canada; married Randy (a consultant to the oil industry); children: two daughters. *Education:* University of Saskatchewan, degrees (arts and education). *Hobbies and other interests:* Reading, skiing, riding her motorcycle, golf, curling.

Addresses

Home—Lampman, Saskatchewan, Canada. *E-mail*—maureen.ulrich@sasktel.net.

Career

Educator, author, and playwright. Middle-school teacher in Lampman, Milestone, and Estevan, Saskatchewan, Canada, beginning 1980. Active in writing, directing, and producing community theatre.

Awards, Honors

Moonbeam Award for Young-Adult Fiction, and Saskatchewan Book Award finalists for Reader's Choice, Young-adult Fiction, and First Book, all 2008, and Saskatchewan Snow Willow Award nomination, and British Columbia Stellar Award nomination, both 2010, all for *Power Plays.*

Writings

Power Plays, Coteau Books for Teens (Regina, Saskatchewan, Canada), 2007.
Sam Spud: Private Eye, Baker's Plays (Los Angeles, CA), 2009.

Author of dozens of plays for both children and adults.

Sidelights

Canadian author and teacher Maureen Ulrich began writing for fun in elementary school, when she was a self-confessed horse nut. "Nearly all my novels featured

feisty teenage girls, wild stallions and the foothills of Wyoming," she explained on the Coteau Books Web site. Although "the distractions of university, career, and family" prompted her to leave writing for a while, her interest was rekindled when she both wrote and directed a play at the middle school where she was then teaching. "I had so much fun [writing and directing] . . . that I began penning one or two student productions a year. I just kept on writing scripts and eventually stepped into the realm of adult community theatre in my home town of Lampman," Ulrich explained.

In Ulrich's first novel, the award-winning *Power Plays,* focuses on Jessie McIntyre, a fourteen year old who has to deal with the worries over making new friends in a new school following a family move. Attracting the attention of a school bully makes things go from bad to worse, and a fight with some local roughs ends with Jessie spending a night in jail. Fortunately, the teen's skill on ice skates provides her with a way to stop the downward spiral: as a member of the girls' ice hockey team at her new school, she gains the friends and confidence she needs to deal effectively with local bullies. In *Resource Links* Emily Springer wrote that in *Power Plays* Ulrich depicts "teen life and female bullying in a realistic and believable way," while Lori A. Guenthner wrote that the plot "moves quickly because of all the action on the ice." Observing that *Power Plays* will primarily attract readers with an interest in ice hockey, a *Kirkus Reviews* contributor recommended the story's on-ice action as "exciting reading," adding that Ulrich's "passion for hockey shines through."

Biographical and Critical Sources

PERIODICALS

Kirkus Reviews, July 15, 2008, review of *Power Plays.*
Resource Links, December, 2007, Emily Springer, review of *Power Plays,* p. 43.
School Library Journal, December, 2008, Lori A. Guenthner, review of *Power Plays,* p. 140.

ONLINE

Couteau Books Web site, http://www.coteaubooks.com/ (October 30, 2009), "Maureen Ulrich."
Maureen Ulrich Home Page, http://www.maureenulrich. com (October 30, 2009).
Maureen Ulrich Web Log, http://www.maureenulrich.net (October 30, 2009).

*   *   *

UNDERWOOD, Deborah 1962-

Personal

Born 1962, in WA; father a math professor, mother a teacher. *Education:* Pomona College, B.A. (philosophy).

Addresses

E-mail—mail@deborahunderwoodbooks.com.

Career

Writer and singer. Worked variously as a street musician and secretary.

Writings

The Northern Lights, KidHaven Press (San Diego, CA), 2004.

Librarian, KidHaven Press (Detroit, MI), 2005.

The Easter Island Statues, KidHaven Press (Detroit, MI), 2005.

Pirate Mom, illustrated by Stephen Gilpin, Random House (New York, NY), 2006.

Watching Giraffes in Africa, Heinemann Library (Chicago, IL), 2006.

Watching Orangutans in Africa, Heinmann Library (Chicago, IL), 2006.

Where Are Your Manners?, Raintree (Chicago, IL), 2006.

Colorful Peacocks, Lerner Publications (Minneapolis, MN), 2007.

Has a Cow Saved Your Life?, Raintree (Chicago, IL), 2007.

Africa, Heinemann Library (Chicago, IL), 2007.

Nat Love (biography), Lerner Publications (Minneapolis, MN), 2008.

Animal Secrets, Raintree (Chicago, IL), 2008.

Mexico or Bust, Raintree (Chicago, IL), 2008.

Safari Adventure, Raintree (Chicago, IL), 2008.

Australia, Hawaii, and the Pacific, Heinemann Library (Chicago, IL), 2008.

Graphing the Universe, Heinemann Library (Chicago, IL), 2009.

Graphing Transportation, Heinemann Library (Chicago, IL), 2009.

Staging a Play, Raintree (Chicago, IL), 2010.

Granny Gomez and Jigsaw, Disney/Hyperion (New York, NY), 2010.

Ballroom Dancing, raintree (Chicago, IL), 2010.

The Quiet Book, Houghton Mifflin (Boston, MA), 2010.

A Balloon for Isabel, Greenwood Books (New York, NY), 2010.

Contributor to periodicals, including *Highlights for Children, Ladybug, Spider, Children's Playmate,* and *National Geographic Kids.* Author for educational publishers.

"SUGAR PLUM BALLERINAS" SERIES; WITH WHOOPI GOLDBERG

Plum Fantastic, illustrated by Maryn Roos, Disney/Jump at the Sun (New York, NY), 2008.

Toeshoe Trouble, illustrated by Maryn Roos, Disney/Jump at the Sun (New York, NY), 2009.

Perfectly Prima, illustrated by Maryn Roos, Disney/Jump at the Sun (New York, NY), 2010.

Sidelights

Although she wanted to be an astronomer while growing up, Deborah Underwood now writes both fiction and nonfiction for children. A long-time vegan, she loves animals and is delighted that her job gives her the opportunity to learn and write about them. This curiosity has resulted in a range of fact-based books, such as *Colorful Peacocks, Ballroom Dancing, The Easter Island Statues,* and *Staging a Play.* "When a publisher asks me to write a nonfiction book, I usually don't know much about the topic," Underwood explained on her home page. "That means I have to learn fast. Now I know about lots of cool things, like smallpox and orangutans and Easter Island and whether or not it's okay to slurp your noodles in Japan (it is)."

Reviewing *The Easter Island Statues,* part of KidHaven's "Wonders of the World" series, *School Library Journal* contributor Christine E. Carr made special note of Underwood's "nicely prepared text," and praised the book as an "attractive, readable" volume for

*Deborah Underwood's engaging story for **Pirate Mom** is brought to life in Stephen Gillpin's cartoon art.* (Illustration copyright © 2006 by Stephen Gillpin. Used by permission of Random House Children's Books, a division of Random House, Inc.)

young researchers. *Colorful Peacocks* pairs the author's "charming" text with photographs that depict a fascinating bird species, according to *School Library Journal* writer Cynde Suite, and in *Booklist* John Peters wrote that Underwood's "properly enticing, wide-angled look" at a respected profession in *Librarian* is also "carefully nonsexist."

Turning to fiction, Underwood has also collaborated with actress Whoopie Goldberg on the "Sugar Plum Ballerinas" books, which include *Plum Fantastic, Toe-shoe Trouble,* and *Perfectly Prima.* The series focuses on a group of seven friends who attend a ballet school in Harlem. Each book focuses on a different character. In *Plum Fantastic,* for example, readers meet Alexandrea Johnson, whose move from a small southern town to Harlem throws her life into upheaval. Her mom, a costumer, wants to devote her life to the theatre, and it is decided that Al should do the same by trading in her speed skates for a pair of ballet shoes. In *Booklist* Bina Williams wrote that *Plum Fantastic* "earnestly addresses" a preteen's efforts at "making friends, and settling into a new routine."

Pirate Mom, with its easy-reading text, presents an "amusing take on the ever-popular pirate theme," noted *Booklist* contributor Carolyn Phelan. In Underwood's humorous story, a boy and his mother are watching a magic show by the Amazing Marco when Mom is chosen to be hypnotized. Marco successfully convinces the woman that she is a pirate, but he is called away on an emergency before his spell can be lifted. When the two return home the boy has to baby-sit his mother and keep her piratical behavior from causing chaos. A *Kirkus Reviews* critic made note of the "funny treatment" Underwood gives to a common tale, adding that Stephen Gilpin's "appealingly cartoony illustrations suit the silly fun" of the picture book.

In the picture book *Granny Gomez and Jigsaw* an elderly woman adopts a pet pig and soon realizes that there are problems involved with having a pig in the house. This book was inspired by Underwood's visit to a pig at Farm Sanctuary in Orland, California. Another story, *The Quiet Book,* finds the author discussing the different kinds of quiet in a child's life, while *A Balloon for Isabel* finds a determined porcupine named Isabel searching for a way to get around her school's no-balloons-for-porcupines rule.

Biographical and Critical Sources

PERIODICALS

Booklist, April 1, 2005, John Peters, review of *Librarian,* p. 1384; May 1, 2006, Carolyn Phelan, review of *Pirate Mom,* p. 94; January 1, 2009, Bina Williams, review of *Plum Fantastic,* p. 84.
Kirkus Reviews, April 15, 2006, review of *Pirate Mom,* p. 418.
School Library Journal, June, 2005, Christian E. Carr, review of *The Easter Island Statues,* p. 138; September, 2006, Cynde Suite, review of *Colorful Peacocks,* p. 197; March, 2008, Mary Elam, review of *Australia, Hawaii, and the Pacific,* p. 215.

ONLINE

Deborah Underwood Home Page, http://www.deborah underwoodbooks.com (October 30, 2009).

WAITE, Michael
See WAITE, Michael P.

* * *

WAITE, Michael P. 1960-
(Riford McKenzie, Michael Waite)

Personal
Born 1960, in VT; married; children: one son, one daughter. *Education:* University of Vermont, degree, 1982; University of Oregon, M.F.A., 1993.

Addresses
Home—Redmond, WA. *E-mail*—rifordmckenzie@ gmail.com.

Career
Video-game creator and author. Adelphi Productions, Los Angeles, CA, co-owner and producer, 1983-86; Dynamix/Sierra, Eugene, OR, game designer 1993-98; Electronic Arts, Seattle, WA, senior producer, 1998-2003; Adrenium Games, Kirkland, WA, studio head and executive producer, 2003-06; Amaze Entertainment, Kirkland, studio head and executive producer, 2006—. Has also taught at universities in Oregon.

Awards, Honors
Edgar Allen Poe Award finalist for best juvenile mystery, Mystery Writers of America, 2009, for *The Witches of Dredmoore Hollow.*

Writings

Lady Bug Island: My First Helping Book, illustrated by Sheila Lucas, Chariot Books (Elgin, IL), 1995.

Michael P. Waite (Reproduced by permission.)

(As Michael Waite) *Butterflies for Two: My First Sharing Book,* illustrated by Sheila Lucas, Chariot Books (Elgin, IL), 1995.
Jojofu, illustrated by Yoriko Ito, Lothrop, Lee & Shepard (New York, NY), 1996.

(As Michael Waite) *The Rhyme-time Book of Christian Virtues,* Chariot Victor Publishing (Colorado Springs, CO), 1997.

(As Michael Waite) *Helpful Hal's Treasury of Christian Virtues,* Chariot Victor Publishing (Colorado Springs, CO), 1997.

(As Riford McKenzie) *The Witches of Dredmoore Hollow,* illustrated by Peter Ferguson, Marshall Cavendish Children (New York, NY), 2008.

"BUILDING CHRISTIAN CHARACTER" SERIES

Buzzle Billy: A Book about Sharing, illustrated by Jill Colbert Trousdale, Chariot Books (Elgin, IL), 1987.

Miggy and Tiggy: A Book about Overcoming Jealousy, illustrated by Tony DeRosa, Chariot Books (Elgin, IL), 1987.

Handy-dandy Helpful Hal: A Book about Helpfulness, illustrated by Gary Trousdale, Chariot Books (Elgin, IL), 1987.

Suzy Swoof: A Book about Kindness, illustrated by Barbara DeRosa, Chariot Books (Elgin, IL), 1987.

Boggin, Blizzy, and Sleeter the Cheater: A Book about Fairness, illustrated by Barbara DeRosa, Chariot Books (Elgin, IL), 1988.

Casey the Greedy Young Cowboy: A Book about Being Thankful, illustrated by Anthony DeRosa, Chariot Books (Elgin, IL), 1988.

Max and the Big Fat Lie: A Book about Telling the Truth, illustrated by Gary Trousdale, Chariot Books (Elgin, IL), 1988.

Sir Maggie the Mighty: A Book about Obedience, illustrated by Jill Colbert Trousdale, Chariot Books (Elgin, IL), 1988.

Sylvester the Jester: A Book about Accepting Others, illustrated by Anthony DeRosa, Chariot Books (Elgin, IL), 1992.

Gilly Greenweed's Gift for Granny: A Book about Showing Love, illustrated by Barbara DeRosa, Chariot Books (Elgin, IL), 1992.

Sammy's Gadget Galaxy: A Book about Patience, illustrated by Gary Trousdale, Chariot Books (Elgin, IL), 1992.

The Hollyhonk Gardens of Gneedle and Gnibb: A Book about Forgiving, illustrated by Jill Colbert Trousdale, Chariot Books (Elgin, IL), 1993.

"CHRISTIAN ADVENTURE" SERIES

Hoomania: A Journey into Proverbs, Chariot Books (Elgin, IL), 1987.

Eddy and His Amazing Pet, Chariot Books (Elgin, IL), 1988.

Emma Wimble, Accidental Astronaut, Chariot Books (Elgin, IL), 1988.

"CAMP WINDY WOODS" SERIES; AS MICHAEL WAITE

The Parable of Bartholomew Beaver and the Stupendous Splash: In Which the Windy Woods Campers Learn the Biblical Value of Encouragement, illustrated by Sheila Lucas, Chariot Family Publishing (Colorado Springs, CO), 1996.

The Parable of Daisy Doddlepaws and the Windy Woods Treasure: In Which the Windy Woods Campers Learn the Biblical Value of Friendship, illustrated by Sheila Lucas, Chariot Family Publishing (Colorado Springs, CO), 1996.

The Parable of Shelby the Magnificent: In Which the Windy Woods Campers Learn the Biblical Value of Humility, illustrated by Sheila Lucas, Chariot Family Publishing (Colorado Springs, CO), 1996.

The Parable of Digger's Marvelous Moleberry Patch: In Which the Windy Woods Campers Learn the Biblical Value of Humility, illustrated by Sheila Lucas, Chariot Family Publishing (Colorado Springs, CO), 1996.

Sidelights

Michael P. Waite, a designer and executive in the computer-games industry, has written more than twenty books for young readers, including the works in the "Building Christian Character" and "Camp Windy Woods" series. Writing under the pseudonym Riford McKenzie, Waite has also released *The Witches of Dredmoore Hollow,* a middle-grade novel that "contains all the trappings of a good dark-and-stormy-night ghost story," according to a critic in *Kirkus Reviews.* Waite maintains that his literary efforts have provided him with different rewards than have his experiences in the gaming industry. As part of a team creating a video game, he remarked to *Vermont Quarterly* interviewer Amanda Waite, "You need to try to do things as a team member and test your ideas against everybody else's, absorb everybody else's. Writing a book is kind of an answer to that. It's very meditative for me. It gives me an opportunity to be selfish."

The Witches of Dredmoore Hollow was inspired in part by Waite's childhood. "I grew up in Vermont, which is the most wonderful place on the planet to spend one's childhood," he stated on his home page. "Home remedies and superstition were commonplace. My grandfather was a 'water witch'; he could find springs buried deep beneath the ground by use of a dowsing rod. He could also graft trees to grow whatever fruit he wanted (or so it seemed). Many of my ancestors had spurious backgrounds—moonshiners, horse thieves, and the like."

Set in rural Vermont in 1927, *The Witches of Dredmoore Hollow* follows the adventures of Elijah, an intelligent but timid eleven year old who lives with his parents on their old family farm in Dredmoore Hollow. After his estranged Aunt Serena and Aunt Agnes abduct the youngster and take him to their squalid home in Moaning Marsh, Elijah is shocked to learn that his plain-spoken mother is, in fact, a witch. Her sisters have kidnaped Elijah to help them reverse a spell that began fifteen years earlier; they need his first whisker to create the potion that will undo the curse. With the help of his friend, Dez, Elijah uses his recently discovered

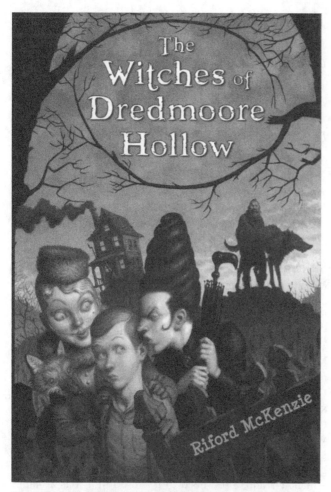

Waite's novel The Witches of Dredmoore Hollow, *published under his pen name Riford McKenzie, features cover art by Peter Ferguson.* (Art copyright © 2008 by Marshall Cavendish. Reproduced by permission.)

magical powers to defeat the aunts' nefarious plans. According to Lillian Hecker in *School Library Journal*, *The Witches of Dredmoore Hollow* "has continuous action and piles of demonic atmosphere." Betty Carter, reviewing the novel in *Horn Book*, called Elijah "a reluctant hero who . . . finds within himself the power to right dynastic wrongs."

Biographical and Critical Sources

PERIODICALS

Horn Book, January-February, 2009, Betty Carter, review of *The Witches of Dredmoore Hollow*, p. 96.
Kirkus Reviews, July 15, 2008, review of *The Witches of Dredmoore Hollow*.
School Library Journal, November, 2008, Lillian Hecker, review of *The Witches of Dredmoore Hollow*, p. 128.

ONLINE

Riford McKenzie Home Page, https://www.riordmckenzie.com (October 10, 2009).

Vermont Quarterly Online, http://alumni.uvm.edu/vq/ (spring, 2009), Amanda Waite, "Alternate Worlds: Gaming Expert Alum Pens Fantasy Novel for Young Adults."*

*   *   *

WARD, Helen 1962-

Personal

Born November 9, 1962, in Gloucestershire, England; daughter of Gordon (an artist) and Maureen (an artist) Ward. *Education:* Attended Gloucestershire College of Art, 1981-82; Brighton Polytechnic, B.A., 1985.

Addresses

Home and office—Gloucestershire, England.

Career

Author and illustrator.

Awards, Honors

Walker Prize for Children's Illustration, 1985; Second Prize (for books), National Art Library Illustration Award, Victoria & Albert Museum, 1999, for *The Hare and the Tortoise*, and 2001, for *The Wind in the Willows;* English Association Fiction Key Stage One Award, 2002, and Kate Greenway Medal shortlist, both for *Cockerel and the Fox;* Children's Book Award, United Kingdom Literary Association, 2004, for *The Boat;* Stockport Schools Book Award shortlist, for *Little Moon Dog;* English Association Fiction Key Stage One Award, for *Wonderful Life;* Design and Production Award of the Year shortlist, British Book Industry Awards, for *Spyology;* British Book Design and Production Award shortlist in Children's Trade Category, and English Association Fiction Key Stage-Two Award, both 2008, and Kate Greenaway Medal shortlist, 2009, all for *Varmints*.

Writings

The Tin Forest, illustrated by Wayne Anderson, Templar Publishing (Dorking, England), 2001.
The Dragon Machine, illustrated by Wayne Anderson, Dutton (New York, NY), 2003.
Twenty-five December Lane, illustrated by Wayne Anderson, Templar Publishing (Dorking, England), 2004.
Finding Christmas, illustrated by Wayne Anderson, Dutton (New York, NY), 2004.
The Boat, illustrated by Ian Andrew, Templar Publishing (Dorking, England), 2004.
Little Moon Dog, illustrated by Wayne Anderson, Templar Publishing (Dorking, England), 2005, Dutton (New York, NY), 2007.

Varmints, illustrated by Marc Craste, Templar Publishing (Dorking, England), 2007, Dutton (New York, NY), 2008.

SELF-ILLUSTRATED

The Moonrat and the White Turtle, Ideals Children's Books (Nashville, TN), 1990.
The Golden Pear, Ideals Children's Books (Nashville, TN), 1991.
The King of the Birds, Millbrook Press (Brookfield, CT), 1997.
(Reteller) *The Hare and the Tortoise,* Templar (Dorking, England), 1998, Millbrook Press (Brookfield, CT), 1999.
(With others) *The Animals' Christmas Carol,* Templar (Dorking, England), 2001.
Old Shell, New Shell: A Coral Reef Tale, Templar Publishing (Dorking, England), 2001, Millbrook Press (Brookfield, CT), 2002.
(Adapter) *Cockerel and the Fox,* Templar Publishing (Dorking, England), 2002, published as *The Rooster and the Fox: A Tale from Chaucer,* Millbrook Press (Brookfield, CT), 2003.
Unwitting Wisdom: An Anthology of Aesop's Fables, Chronicle Books (San Francisco, CA), 2004.
Wonderful Life: Snutt the Ift; or, A Small but Significant Chapter in the Life of the Universe, Templar Publishing (Dorking, England), 2007.

ILLUSTRATOR

Andrew Lang, adapter, *Sinbad the Sailor and Other Stories,* Longman Press (Harlow, England), 1986.
Geraldine McCaughrean, reteller, *The Story of Christmas,* Ideals Children's Books (Nashville, TN), 1989.
Geraldine McCaughrean, reteller, *The Story of Noah and the Ark,* Ideals Children's Books (Nashville, TN), 1989.
A.J. Wood, *Helen Ward's Amazing Animals,* Bell Books (Honesdale, PA), 1991.
A.J. Wood, *Helen Ward's Beautiful Birds,* Bell Books (Honesdale, PA), 1991.
(With Ann Savage) Theresa Greenaway, *Fur and Feathers* ("Head to Tail" series), Raintree Steck-Vaughn (Austin, TX), 1995.
Cecilia Fitzsimons, *Water Life* ("Nature's Hidden Worlds" series), Raintree Steck-Vaughn (Austin, TX), 1996.
Richard Balkwill and A.J. Wood, *Milton's Mystery,* Templar Publishing (Dorking, England), 1996.
Kenneth Grahame, *The Wind in the Willows,* Templar Publishing (Dorking, England), 2000.
Rudyard Kipling, *Just So Stories,* Templar Publishing (Dorking, England), 2001.
(With others) Dugald A. Steer, editor, *Dr. Ernest Drake's Dragonology: The Complete Book of Dragons,* Templar Publishing (Dorking, England), 2003.
(With others) Dugald A. Steer, editor, *Egyptology: Search for the Tomb of Osiris: Being the Journal of Miss Emily Sands, November 1926,* Candlewick Press (Cambridge, MA), 2004.
(With others) Dugald A. Steer, editor, *Piratology,* Candlewick Press (Cambridge, MA), 2006.
(With others) Dugald A. Steer, editor, *Spyology: The Complete Book of Spycraft,* Templar Publishing (Dorking, England), 2008.

ILLUSTRATOR; "JUNGLE HIDEAWAY" SERIES

A.J. Wood, *Animal Colours,* Macmillan (Basingstoke, England), 1987, published as *Animal Colors,* Price, Stern, Sloan (Los Angeles, CA), 1987.
A.J. Wood, *Animal Counting,* Price, Stern, Sloan (Los Angeles, CA), 1987.
A.J. Wood, *Animal Sounds,* Price, Stern, Sloan (Los Angeles, CA), 1987.
A.J. Wood, *Animal Opposites,* Price, Stern, Sloan (Los Angeles, CA), 1987.
A.J. Wood, *Animal Families,* Price, Stern, Sloan (Los Angeles, CA), 1989.
A.J. Wood, *Animal Food,* Price, Stern, Sloan (Los Angeles, CA), 1989.
A.J. Wood, *Animal Friends,* Price, Stern, Sloan (Los Angeles, CA), 1989.
A.J. Wood, *Animal Homes,* Price, Stern, Sloan (Los Angeles, CA), 1989.

ILLUSTRATOR; "CURIOUS CREATURES" SERIES

(With Stella Stilwell) Joyce Pope, *Living Fossils,* Steck-Vaughn (Austin, TX), 1991.
(With Stella Stilwell) Joyce Pope, *Two Lives,* Heinemann (Oxford, England), 1991, Steck-Vaughn (Austin, TX), 1992.
(With Stella Stilwell) Joyce Pope, *On the Move,* Steck-Vaughn (Austin, TX), 1991.
(With Stella Stilwell) Joyce Pope, *Mistaken Identity,* Steck-Vaughn (Austin, TX), 1992.
(With Adam Hook) Joyce Pope, *Making Contact,* Steck-Vaughn (Austin, TX), 1992.
(With Adam Hook) Joyce Pope, *Strange Nature,* Steck-Vaughn (Austin, TX), 1992.
(With Stella Stilwell) Joyce Pope, *Deadly Venom,* Steck-Vaughn (Austin, TX), 1992.
(With Stella Stilwell) Joyce Pope, *Life in the Dark,* Steck-Vaughn (Austin, TX), 1992.

Adaptations

Varmints was adapted as a short animated film by Marc Craste, Studio AKA, 2008.

Sidelights

Words and pictures are equally important in the work of Helen Ward, a British illustrator and author with more than forty children's books to her credit. Both her words and her detailed illustrations tell stories about animal life or retell classic fables through animal characters, and her artwork has also graced the pages of such famous works of English literature as Rudyard Kipling's *Just So Stories* and Kenneth Grahame's *The Wind in the*

Willows. According to Joanna Carey in the London *Guardian,* Ward "approaches the natural world with vision and integrity in a way that's neither dutifully pedantic nor patronisingly simplistic." Additionally, Ward is the author of original stories, some accompanied by her own illustrations. As she once told *SATA,* "To me as an illustrator and author, the pictures in my books are at least as important as the text. The plots and pictures develop together, usually from one or two images—real or imagined."

Ward has approached illustration and writing together since she was a child, and she enjoys the challenges of both. She once explained to *SATA,* "I determined to be an illustrator as soon as I became aware there was such a profession; this would have been about the age of nine. I soon added writing to this ambition. Most of my writing however has been for my own pleasure; in consequence, I find writing for publication difficult. The biggest challenge seems to be knowing when to stop reworking the text. With illustration this stage is obvious."

After attending the Gloucestershire College of Art, Ward trained as an illustrator at Brighton Polytechnic's school of art. Her first published works were illustrations of other writer's books, and from the beginning of her career, Ward's art was focused on her love for animals and the natural world. Her illustrations were included in the "Jungle Hideaway" series of animal picture books

Helen Ward's picture book The Dragon Machine *comes to life in detailed artwork by Wayne Andersen.* (Illustration © 2003 by Wayne Anderson. In the U.S. reproduced by permission of Penguin Young Readers Group. In the U.K. used by permission of Templar Publishing, Ltd., The Granary, North St., Dorking, Surrey RH4 1DN, UK. All rights reserved.)

written by A.J. Wood. Ward is also the illustrator of the "Curious Creatures" series by Joyce Pope, a series of science and nature books that has appeared in both England and the United States.

In 1990, Ward published her first original self-illustrated book. *The Moonrat and the White Turtle* is set in an invented landscape inspired by her studies of geology. Like many of her more-recent books, Ward's first story is an intricately illustrated fairy tale told through animal characters. Moonrat, a pirate who has amassed a fortune in treasures, wants more—the moon itself, to be exact. When he finds a map showing the location of Moonrise, he and his crew set out on a dangerous journey to find it, only to capture a giant white turtle instead. "Especially in her descriptions, Ward employs vivid vocabulary to set the scenes and create suspense," wrote *School Library Journal* reviewer Kathy Piehl.

The Golden Pear was also inspired by Ward's love for nature. "*The Golden Pear* was written some years after I watched a crow take a small pear from a tree," the author/illustrator once related to *SATA.* "The near silhouette of the bird's wings and the pear held delicately by the stalk in its beak was an impressive image." From that memory, Ward spun a fairy tale about a lonely wizard who has watched a golden pear grow on the top of his tree, only to see the fruit carried away by a crow. He sets off to find the pear, discovering during his journey that friendship and community are worth far more than the golden treasure. Barbara Chatton, writing in *School Library Journal,* described Ward's illustrations as "luminous" and called *The Golden Pear* "a useful addition to collections of modern tales and to help children understand the true meaning of wealth."

Ward's next self-illustrated book, *The King of the Birds,* centers on some old birds who decided they should have a king. Ward uses detailed, naturalistic illustrations in watercolor and ink to offset her "tightly composed, austerely written folktale," wrote Janice M. Del Negro in the *Bulletin of the Center for Children's Books.* According to *School Library Journal* contributor Jeanne Clancy Watkins, "Ward's brief and lyrical retelling works hand in hand with her glowing artwork to charm readers." In the book, Ward includes a key to the bird illustrations with facts about each species shown.

In her retelling of the classic Aesop's fable about the tortoise and the hare, Ward adds to her reputation for providing detailed, realistic animal illustrations that are "minimally anthropomorphized" and "the antithesis of cuteness, resembling zoological illustrations," according to Del Negro. Describing *The Hare and the Tortoise* as "a very commendable work," *Magpies*'s contributor Cynthia Anthony predicted that "any child . . . will delight in poring over this animal medley." Again, Ward provides an informative key to the animal illustrations, a feature well appreciated by critics.

The Tin Forest marked a couple of firsts for Ward: it was the first book she wrote but did not illustrate, and it

Ward casts her space-aged picture book Varmints *with unusual animal creatures that are brought to life in Marc Craste's art.* (Illustration copyright © 2007 by Marc Craste. Reproduced by permission of Candlewick Press, Inc., Somerville, MA.)

was the first of her books with a clearly ecological message. Illustrated with stark artwork by Wayne Anderson, the story tells of an old man who lives in a junk-filled, barren wasteland but dreams of past times, when beautiful forests were inhabited by exotic animals. Consequently, the man faithfully tries to make his land a bit cleaner, refusing to surrender to the mountains of trash that nearly engulf him. *The Tin Forest* ends on a note of hope, as birds drop seeds that sprout and bloom, bringing insects and other small creatures to the land once again. As Barbara Buckley wrote in *School Library Journal,* "With true eloquence, Ward has created a morality tale of environmental devastation."

Since the publication of *The Tin Forest* Ward and Anderson have enjoyed a successful collaboration on a number of other titles. In *The Dragon Machine,* a sensitive and overlooked youngster named George is the only one who can see the dragons that are all about, peeking from purses and scurrying into storm drains. Once George begins feeding the impish creatures, they prove themselves to be a great nuisance, so he ventures to the library for a solution to his problem. After consulting *The Encyclopedia of Dragons,* George constructs an elaborate flying machine to take them back to their homeland. "Both art and narrative . . . seesaw between

whimsical and somber tones," a *Publishers Weekly* critic noted, and Susan Oliver, writing in *School Library Journal,* remarked that young readers "will enjoy the dragons, the humor, and the upbeat twist at the end."

In *Finding Christmas,* Ward and Anderson offer a touching holiday tale. One snowy night, while searching for the perfect gift for a special person, a young girl comes upon an enticing shop on December Lane. As she gazes at the fantastic assortment of toys, another customer—who appears to be wearing a red suit beneath his too-tight overcoat—enters and purchases everything in the store, leaving the girl empty handed. Her disappointment is short-lived, however, as she is treated to a surprise on her walk home. "Ward's simple sentences have a pleasing, read-aloud rhythm," remarked Gillian Engberg in *Booklist,* and a reviewer for *Publishers Weekly* commented that Anderson's pictures for *Finding Christmas* give the "lovely fantasy some memorable depth."

With *Little Moon Dog,* Ward and Anderson offer "another otherworldly tale with a magical bent and a moral," in the words of a *Publishers Weekly* critic. When the Man in the Moon goes into hiding to avoid throngs of fairylike tourists, his companion, Little Moon Dog, follows the vacationers to their home. Although the fickle fairies soon tire of the canine and abandon him, the Man in the Moon hears Little Moon Dog's howling and comes looking for the furry creature. "Ward's lyrical, often alliterative writing . . . will likely appeal to most readers," the *Publishers Weekly* contributor noted, and Lynne Mattern, reviewing the tale in *School Library Journal,* remarked that Ward's "lessons of caring for our environment, false/true friendship, and that adventure is not as important as long-term love and understanding" would prove valuable to children.

Old Shell, New Shell: A Coral Reef Tale features Ward's story of a hermit crab finding a new home. In the crab's search, the author/illustrator shares with children the riches of a coral reef, illustrating with words and pictures the creatures that inhabit this unique ecosystem. Ward's book was praised for its "superb and scientifically accurate" pictures, as *School Librarian* critic John Feltwell remarked, while John Peters wrote in *Booklist* that Ward's "art imparts a clear sense of the astonishing density and range of reef life." In the self-illustrated collection *Unwitting Wisdom: An Anthology of Aesop's Fables,* Ward offers her take on a dozen familiar tales, including "Steady and Slow," a version of "The Tortoise and the Hare." "The retellings are elegant, and the grandiose language is part of the fun," Hazel Rochman observed in *Booklist.* "Beautifully rendered in pen and watercolor, the illustrations [for *Unwitting Wisdom*] incorporate cunning details and offer viewers a nice anticipation of characters and outcomes," wrote Margaret Bush in *School Library Journal.*

Ward teams up with illustrator Ian Andrew on *The Boat,* which recalls the story of Noah and the flood. The work concerns an elderly man who lives alone on a hill with his menagerie of abused and abandoned animals. The residents of a nearby village shun him, except for one young boy who is fascinated by the outcast. When torrential rains hit the area, the boy discovers a boat that appears from nowhere and he rows himself to the old man's home. The youngster's courage spurs the other villagers to mount a rescue effort, in what a *Kirkus Reviews* contributor deemed "a quiet story." In *School Library Journal* Teresa Pfeifer observed that *The Boat* "reminds readers that an individual, no matter how small or seemingly insignificant, can make a difference."

Varmints, an environmental tale illustrated by Marc Craste, follows a rabbit-like creature that lives on an idyllic, light-filled planet. After the mysterious "others" arrive and construct mammoth towers that cloud the sky, the tiny creature releases one remaining seedpod that once again transforms its world. A *Kirkus Reviews* contributor described *Varmints* as a "lament for the loss of nature's peace and quiet to rampant urbanization," while in *School Library Journal* Kate McClelland called the book an "abstract, transcendental story."

Biographical and Critical Sources

PERIODICALS

Booklist, January 1, 2002, John Peters, review of *Old Shell, New Shell: A Coral Reef Tale,* p. 868; March 15, 2003, John Peters, review of *The Dragon Machine,* p. 1334; September 15, 2004, Hazel Rochman, review of *Unwitting Wisdom: An Anthology of Aesop's Fables,* p. 242; October 1, 2004, Gillian Engberg, review of *Finding Christmas,* p. 338.
Bulletin of the Center for Children's Books, November, 1997, Janice M. Del Negro, review of *The King of the Birds,* p. 105; June, 1999, Janice M. Del Negro, review of *The Hare and the Tortoise,* p. 369.
Guardian (London, England), March 29, 2008, Joanna Carey, "Animal Magic" (interview with Ward), p. 20.
Kirkus Reviews, August 1, 2001, review of *The Animals' Christmas Carol,* p. 1134; September 15, 2004, review of *Unwitting Wisdom,* p. 922; April 1, 2005, review of *The Boat,* p. 428; November 1, 2005, review of *Egyptology: Search for the Tomb of Osiris: Being the Journal of Miss Emily Sands, November 1926,* p. 1188; February 1, 2007, review of *Little Moon Dog,* p. 130; February 15, 2008, review of *Varmints.*
Magpies, July, 1999, Cynthia Anthony, review of *The Hare and the Tortoise,* p. 28.
Publishers Weekly, September, 24, 2001, review of *The Animals' Christmas Carol,* p. 49; April 7, 2003, review of *The Dragon Machine,* p. 65; September 27, 2004, review of *Finding Christmas,* p. 61; February 19, 2007, review of *Little Moon Dog,* p. 168; October 27, 2008, review of *Spyology: The Complete Book of Spycraft,* p. 54.
Resource Links, December, 2005, Linda Berezowski, review of *The Boat,* p. 10.
School Librarian, spring, 2002, John Feltwell, review of *Old Shell, New Shell,* p. 39.
School Library Journal, March, 1991, Kathy Piehl, review of *The Moonrat and the White Turtle,* p. 180; January, 1992, Barbara Chatton, review of *The Golden Pear,* p. 100; January, 1998, Jeanne Clancy Watkins, review of *The King of the Birds,* p. 106; October, 2001, Barbara Buckley, review of *The Tin Forest,* pp. 133-134; July, 2003, Susan Oliver, review of *The Dragon Machine,* p. 108; October, 2004, Margaret Bush, review of *Unwitting Wisdom,* p. 152; November, 2004, Carol Whichman, review of *Egyptology,* p. 174; August, 2005, Teresa Pfeifer, review of *The Boat,* p. 108; April, 2007, Lynne Mattern, review of *Little Moon Dog,* p. 118; July, 2008, Kate McClelland, review of *Varmints,* p. 109.

ONLINE

Templar Publishing Web site, http://www.templarco.co.uk/ (October 15, 2009), "Helen Ward."*

*   *   *

WELCH, Holly

Personal

Married Shawn Olson (an architect), c. 2003; children: Mason, Summit (sons). *Education:* St. Olaf College, B.A. (English and art), 1991; University of Minnesota, M.A. (journalism), 1993. *Politics:* Lutheran. *Hobbies and other interests:* Nature, the arts.

Addresses

Home—South Minneapolis, MN. *E-mail*—holly@hollywelchdesign.com.

Career

Freelance artist and graphic designer. Guthrie Theatre, Minneapolis, MN, graphic designer for seven years.

Awards, Honors

First prize for book design, Midwest Independent Publishers Association, 2006, for *The Guthrie Theatre: Images, History, and Inside Stories;* Mom's Choice Silver Award, 2009, for *Inside All.*

Illustrator

Margaret H. Mason, *Inside All,* Dawn (Nevada City, CA), 2008.

Sidelights

Although Holly Welch trained as a journalist, she tapped into her talent in the visual arts while working as the graphic designer at Minneapolis's prestigious Guthrie Theatre. She stumbled upon a second outlet for her creative talents just before the birth of her first son: illustrating children's picture books. In 2008 Welch's first illustration project, creating artwork for Margaret H. Mason's poetic picture book *Inside All,* was released.

***Holly Welch's loosely drawn, evocative scenes bring to life Margaret H. Mason's story in* Inside All.** (Illustration copyright © 2008 by Holly Welch. Reproduced by permission.)

In *Inside All* Mason tackles a daunting subject: explaining the universe in a way that a young child will understand, while also making the concept of infinite space non-threatening. The book starts at the far-off edge of the universe and moves inward, from planets to landscape to town to neighborhood to home to the cozy room of a sleeping child. Noting the "metaphysical turn" the story takes when it turns from the physical world to concepts of love and feeling, Ilene Cooper added in *Booklist* that Welch's "impressionistic artwork" helps reflect the "idea of interconnectedness" behind Mason's tale. In pictures that "tend toward the abstract," according to a *Kirkus Reviews* writer, Welch uses "swirling colors and abstract spirals." Deeming *Inside All* primarily an "artistic" work, Judith Constantinides noted in *School Library Journal* that Mason and Welch "giv[e] . . . children a sense of belonging to the universe."

Biographical and Critical Sources

PERIODICALS

Booklist, October 1, 2008, Ilene Cooper, review of *Inside All,* p. 51.

Kirkus Reviews, August 1, 2008, review of *Inside All.*

School Library Journal, November, 2008, Judith Constantinides, review of *All Inside,* p. 96.

ONLINE

Dawn Publications Web site, http://www.dawnpub.com/ (October 30, 2009), "Holly Welch."

Holly Welch Home Page, http://www.hollywelchdesign. com (October 30, 2009).

Y-Z

YAMASAKI, Katie

Personal

Female. *Education:* Earlham College, B.A.; School of Visual Arts, M.F.A., 2003.

Addresses

Home—Brooklyn, NY. *Office*—Shy Studio, 225 W. 36th St., 5th Fl., New York, NY 10018. *E-mail*—mail@katieyamasaki.com.

Career

Illustrator, fine artist, educator, and muralist. Teacher of Spanish at public schools in Detroit, MI, and New York, NY; New York City Public School for Dance, art teacher. Groundswell Community Mural Project, participant in Voices Her'd program. *Exhibitions:* Work exhibited in Santiago de Cuba and Brooklyn College Library, Brooklyn, NY. Mural installations located in Earlham IN, Detroit, MI, Crossville, TN, and New York, NY.

Awards, Honors

Lee & Low New Voices Award Honor designation, 2008, for manuscript *Edward's Lucky Thirteen: The Story of Edwin Moses.*

Illustrator

Mark Weston, *Honda: The Boy Who Dreamed of Cars,* Lee & Low (New York, NY), 2008.

Sidelights

Katie Yamasaki is a teacher and artist whose dedication to children and community is reflected in her work. When she is not teaching art in a New York City public school, Yamasaki serves as an arts mentor in the Voices Her'd community mural project. Her colorful, stylized art, which includes large-scale paintings created for sites around the country, is also enjoyed by readers of Mark Weston's inspirational picture-book biography *Honda: The Boy Who Dreamed of Cars.*

In *Honda* readers meet Soichiro Honda, a boy who grew up as the son of a Japanese blacksmith and became an automobile mechanic, inventor, and car manufacturer. In her illustrations for Weston's text, Yamasaki "keep[s] the tone light with fanciful painted illustrations" that play with perspective and reality, according to *Booklist* critic John Peters. Honda, who revolutionized the piston ring and eventually designed the Honda Civic, is brought to life in a "clear and accessible" text, according to *School Library Journal* contributor Donna Cardon, and *Honda* provides American readers with their first view of a successful and innovative individual. "Yamasaki's creative composition makes the pictures interesting and dynamic," added Cardon, while in *Kirkus Reviews* a contributor wrote that *Honda* stands as "a worthwhile introduction to a neglected subject" on the strength of Yamasaki's "detailed and whimsical acrylics."

Biographical and Critical Sources

PERIODICALS

Booklist, October 15, 2008, John Peters, review of *Honda: The Boy Who Dreamed of Cars,* p. 38.
Horn Book, January-February, 2009, Susan Dove Lempke, review of *Honda,* p. 122.

Katie Yamasaki captures the life of a famous Japanese engineer in her art for Mark Weston's picture-book biography **Honda: The Boy Who Dreamed of Cars.** (Illustration copyright © 2008 by Katie Yamasaki. Reproduced by permission.)

Kirkus Reviews, August 1, 2009, review of *Honda.*
School Library Journal, September, 2008, Donna Cardon, review of *Honda,* p. 170.

ONLINE

Katie Yamasaki Home Page, http://www.katieyamasaki. com (October 30, 2009).*

*   *   *

YEE, Tammy

Personal

Married; children: two sons. *Education:* R.N. degree.

Addresses

Home—Oahu, HI. *E-mail*—yeeart@hawaiiantel.net.

Career

Author and illustrator. Formerly worked as a pediatric nurse.

Member

Society of Children's Book Writers and Illustrators.

Writings

SELF-ILLUSTRATED

The Hawaiian Wildlife Coloring and Activity Book, Bess Press (Honolulu, HI), 1997.

Baby Honu's Incredible Journey, Island Heritage (Waipahu, HI), 1997.

The Ugly 'Elepaio, Island Heritage (Waipahu, HI), 1998.

Iki, the Littlest 'Opihi, Island Heritage (Waipahu, HI), 1998.

Baby Honu Saves the Day, Island Heritage (Waipahu, HI), 1999.

Island Style Alphabet Coloring and Activity Book, Island Heritage (Waipahu, HI), 1999.

Island Style Alphabet, Island Heritage (Waipahu, HI), 2000.

Keiki Counting, Island Heritage (Waipahu, HI), 2001.

The Castle That Kai Built, Island Heritage (Waipahu, HI), 2001.

Peekaboo Shapes, Island Heritage (Waipahu, HI), 2001.

Leilani's Hula, Island Heritage (Waipahu, HI), 2001.

Island Opposites, Island Heritage (Waipahu, HI), 2001.

Mo'o's Colors, Island Heritage (Waipahu, HI), 2002.

From Hawai'i with Aloha, Grandma and Grandpa, Island Heritage (Waipahu, HI), 2008.

ILLUSTRATOR

Debra Ryll, *Goldie and the Three Geckos,* Island Heritage (Waipahu, HI), 2000.

Elaine Masters, *Lullaby Moon,* Island Heritage (Waipahu, HI), 2002.

Ellie Crowe, *The Boy Who Tricked the Ghosts,* Island Heritage (Waipahu, HI), 2003.

Ron Hirschi, *Swimming with Humuhumu: A Young Snorkeler's First Guide to Hawaiian Sea Life,* Island Heritage (Waipahu, HI), 2004.

U'ilani Goldsberry, *A Is for Aloha: A Hawaiian Alphabet,* Sleeping Bear Press (Chelsea, MI), 2005.

Connie J. Weber, *The Hawaiian Goodbye Book,* Island Heritage (Waipahu, HI), 2006.

Anthony D. Fredericks, *The Tsunami Quilt: Grandfather's Story,* Sleeping Bear Press (Chelsea, MI), 2007.

Also illustrator of *Journey of My Heart,* written by Sherry Gervacio, M & S Creative, and of "Hawaiian Way" quilting books by Elizabeth Root, including *Menehune Quilts, Pillows to Patch Quilt, Quilting Days,* and *Keeping in Touch.*

Sidelights

Through her work as an author and artist, Tammy Yee shares information about the unique qualities of her home state of Hawai'i. Using knowledge gained while growing up in the Hawaiian islands, Yee has written about wildlife on the island chain and also crafts stories about the original inhabitants of the volcanic lands. In 2007, she teamed up with writer Anthony D. Fredericks to cover another part of Hawai'i's history in *The Tsunami Quilt: Grandfather's Story.*

In *The Tsunami Quilt* Yee and Fredericks explain how a young boy named Kimo joins his grandfather each spring to visit a special memorial. This is a tradition

Kimo appreciates but does not understand. After his beloved grandfather dies, the boy finally learns the significance of his grandfather's actions: the elderly man was continued to remember his brother and the twenty-three others who died in a 1946 tsunami. In a *Booklist* review of *The Tsunami Quilt,* Carolyn Phelan commented favorably on Yee's artwork and Fredericks' text, deciding that "many readers will respond to [Yee's] . . . soft watercolors" and to Fredericks' "understated . . . and moving story."

Biographical and Critical Sources

PERIODICALS

Booklist, June 1, 2007, Carolyn Phelan, review of *The Tsunami Quilt: Grandfather's Story,* p. 91.

School Library Journal, November, 2007, Kathy Piehl, review of *The Tsunami Quilt,* p. 91.

ONLINE

Tammy Yee Home Page, http://www.tammyyee.com (October 23, 2009).

Tammy Yee Web Log, http://tammyyee.blogspot.com (October 23, 2009).

*   *   *

YOUNG, Anne Mortimer
See MORTIMER, Anne

*   *   *

ZEPEDA, Gwendolyn 1971-

Personal

Born December 27, 1971, in Houston, TX; daughter of Enrique Zepeda and Janis Fiedler; married; children: three sons. *Education:* Attended University of Texas at Austin. *Hobbies and other interests:* Knitting, singing, beading, cartooning.

Addresses

Home—Houston, TX. *E-mail*—gwendolyn.zepeda@gmail.com.

Career

Writer and blogger. Presenter at conferences and writing workshops.

Awards, Honors

Two Houston Art Alliance literary fellowships; Charlotte Zolotow Award Highly Commended designation, Tejas Star Award nomination, and *ForeWord* magazine Book of the Year finalist, all 2008, all for *Growing up with Tamales*.

Writings

FOR CHILDREN

Growing up with Tamales/Los tamales de Ana, illustrated by April Ward, Piñata Books (Houston, TX), 2008.
Sunflowers/Girasoles, illustrated by Alisha Ann Guadalupe Gambino, Piñata Books (Houston, TX), 2009.

FOR ADULTS

To the Last Man I Slept with and All the Jerks Just like Him (short stories), Arte Público Press (Houston, TX), 2004.

Houston, We Have a Problema, Grand Central (New York, NY), 2009.
Lone Star Legend, Grand Central (Houston, TX), 2010.

Author of *My Pattern Book* and *How to Be a Secretary* (chapbooks), privately printed. Author of blogs *Gwen's Trailer Trash Page* and *Gwen's Petty, Judgmental, Evil Thoughts.*

Adaptations

Growing up with Tamales was adapted as an audiobook, Lorito Books, 2009.

Sidelights

Born and raised in Texas, Gwendolyn Zepeda began writing when she realized that the medium of the Internet allowed her to share her thoughts, ideas, and quirky sense of humor with a wide audience. Zepeda's natural talent and her wry take on life quickly earned her an online following, and her site *Gwen's Trailer Trash*

Gwendolyn Zepeda's bilingual picture book **Sunflowers/Girasoles** *features pastel artwork by Ann Guadalupe Gambino.* (Illustration copyright © 2009 by Ann Guadalupe Gambino. Reprinted with permission from the publisher, Piñata Books/Arte Público Press.)

Page became one of the first popular blogs. Her first book, the short-story collection *To the Last Man I Slept with and All the Jerks Just like Him,* was published in 2004, and she has followed this with several novels with a Latina flair. In addition, Zepeda has produced the bilingual picture books *Growing up with Tamales/Los tamales de Ana* and *Sunflowers/Girasoles.*

In *Growing up with Tamales* six-year-old Ana joins her older sister in preparing for the family's holiday feast, and also imagines how her role will change as she grows older. Noting the book's bilingual text, *School Library Journal* Kirsten Cutler called *Growing up with Tamales/Los tamales de Ana* "an upbeat multicultural family story," and a *Kirkus Reviews* critic praised Zepeda's "blithe bilingual tale" for "celebrat[ing] . . . the satisfaction found in accomplishing a goal." From the Christmas holiday, the author turns to the family garden and young Marisol's love of working alongside her grandfather in *Sunflowers/Girasoles.* "A pleasing and effective multicultural offering," according to a *Kirkus Reviews* writer, the story follows the girl's efforts to share her grandfather's favorite plant with others by planting seeds for bright yellow sunflowers throughout her neighborhood.

Biographical and Critical Sources

PERIODICALS

Booklist, December 1, 2008, Aleksandra Walker, review of *Houston, We Have a Problema,* p. 22.

Houston Chronicle, July 22, 2003, Molly Glentzer, "August 28, 2009, Daphne Rozen, "Self-taught Author Becomes an Official 'Writer,'" p. 2.

Kirkus Reviews, May 1, 2008, review of *Growing up with Tamales/Los tamales de Ana*; April 1, 2009, review of *Sunflowers/Girasoles.*

Publishers Weekly, September 22, 2008, review of *Houston, We Have a Problema,* p. 36.

School Library Journal, July, 2008, Kirsten Cutler, review of *Growing up with Tamales,* p. 84.

ONLINE

Gwendolyn Zepeda Home Page, http://www.gwendolyn zepeda.com (October 30, 2009).

Gwendolyn Zepeda Web log, http://www.gwenworld.com (October 30, 2009).